Sofiya An, Tatiana Chubarova, Bob Deacon and Paul Stubbs (Eds.)

Social Policy, Poverty, and Inequality in Central and Eastern Europe and the Former Soviet Union

Agency and Institutions in Flux

About CROP

CROP, the Comparative Research Programme on Poverty, is a response from the academic community to the problems of poverty. The programme was initiated by the International Social Science Council (ISSC) in 1992, and the CROP Secretariat hosted by the University of Bergen (UiB) was officially opened in June 1993 by the Director General of UNESCO, Dr Frederico Mayor. In 2018, the ISSC merged with the International Council for Science (ICSU) to become the International Science Council (ISC).

In recent years, poverty-related issues have moved up on the international agenda, with poverty eradication now defined as the greatest global challenge facing the world today. In co-operation with the ISC and the UiB, CROP works with knowledge networks, institutions and scholars to establish independent and critical poverty research in order to help shape policies for long-term poverty prevention and eradication.

The CROP network comprises scholars engaged in poverty-related research across a variety of academic disciplines. Researchers from more than a hundred different countries are represented in the network, which is coordinated by the CROP Secretariat at the University of Bergen, Norway.

The CROP series on *International Studies in Poverty Research* presents expert research and essential analyses of different aspects of poverty worldwide. By promoting a fuller understanding of the nature, extent, depth, distribution, trends, causes and effects of poverty and poverty-related issues, this series will contribute to knowledge concerning the prevention and eradication of poverty at global, regional, national and local levels.

CROP Secretariat, University of Bergen

P.O Box 7800, 5020 Bergen, NORWAY

Email: crop@uib.no

Website: www.crop.org

Sofiya An, Tatiana Chubarova, Bob Deacon
and Paul Stubbs (Eds.)

SOCIAL POLICY, POVERTY, AND INEQUALITY IN CENTRAL AND EASTERN EUROPE AND THE FORMER SOVIET UNION

Agency and Institutions in Flux

Bibliografische Information der Deutschen Nationalbibliothek
Die Deutsche Nationalbibliothek verzeichnet diese Publikation in der Deutschen Nationalbibliografie; detaillierte bibliografische Daten sind im Internet über http://dnb.d-nb.de abrufbar.

Bibliographic information published by the Deutsche Nationalbibliothek
Die Deutsche Nationalbibliothek lists this publication in the Deutsche Nationalbibliografie; detailed bibliographic data are available in the Internet at http://dnb.d-nb.de.

ISBN-13: 978-3-8382-1308-8
ibidem-Verlag, Stuttgart 2019
copyright © CROP, 2019
Alle Rechte vorbehalten

Das Werk einschließlich aller seiner Teile ist urheberrechtlich geschützt. Jede Verwertung außerhalb der engen Grenzen des Urheberrechtsgesetzes ist ohne Zustimmung des Verlages unzulässig und strafbar. Dies gilt insbesondere für Vervielfältigungen, Übersetzungen, Mikroverfilmungen und elektronische Speicherformen sowie die Einspeicherung und Verarbeitung in elektronischen Systemen.

All rights reserved. No part of this publication may be reproduced, stored in or introduced into a retrieval system, or transmitted, in any form, or by any means (electronical, mechanical, photocopying, recording or otherwise) without the prior written permission of the publisher. Any person who does any unauthorized act in relation to this publication may be liable to criminal prosecution and civil claims for damages.

Printed in the EU

Contents

Sofiya An, Tatiana Chubarova, Bob Deacon and Paul Stubbs
Preface 7

PART ONE: INTRODUCTION 9

Paul Stubbs, Sofiya An and Tatiana Chubarova
Chapter 1:   Poverty, Inequality and Well-Being in the Global
East: Bringing the 'Social' Back in 11

**PART TWO: POVERTY AND INEQUALITY: FROM THEORY
                TO EVERYDAY LIFE** 45

Esuna Dugarova
Chapter 2:   Poverty Reduction through Social Protection and
Labor Policies in the Former Soviet Union 47

Natalia Grigorieva
Chapter 3:   Equality and Inequality in Social Scientific Studies
in Russia, 2000 – 2015 67

Tatiana Chubarova
Chapter 4:   Inequality of Access to the Health System in
Russia: The Case of Out-of-Pocket Payments 87

Natalija Atas
Chapter 5:   The Hidden Reality of Day-to-Day Struggles of
the Working Poor in Lithuania 105

PART THREE: POLICY ACTORS AND INSTITUTIONAL CHANGE 123

Maja Gerovska Mitev
Chapter 6:   IGOs' Strategic Frameworks and Poverty
Alleviation in Macedonia 125

Igor Guardiancich
Chapter 7:   Between Modern Design and Old Political Habits:
The Kosovar Pension System under Threat 147

Sofiya An
Chapter 8:   The Transformation of Child Welfare Institutions
             in Kazakhstan: Layering, Hybridization and
             Multiple Institutional Logics 169

Ann-Mari Sätre
Chapter 9:   The Impact of Women's Agency against Poverty
             in Russia 189

PART FOUR: WELFARE TRAJECTORIES AND ASSEMBLAGES 207

Elena Maltseva and Saltanat Janenova
Chapter 10: The Politics of Pension Reforms in Kazakhstan:
             Pressures for Change and Reform Strategies 209

Gulnaz Isabekova
Chapter 11: Diverse Health Care Developments in the Post-
             Soviet Space: The Role of National and
             International Actors 237

Noémi Lendvai-Bainton
Chapter 12: Diversified Convergence: Uneven Welfare
             Trajectories in Central and Eastern Europe 263

Paul Stubbs and Siniša Zrinščak
Chapter 13: Reforming Welfare Assemblages in Semi-Peripheral
             Spaces: Understanding 'Drivers of Inertia' in
             Bosnia-Herzegovina, Croatia and Serbia 285

Contributor Biographies 307

SOCIAL POLICY, POVERTY, AND INEQUALITY IN CENTRAL AND EASTERN EUROPE AND THE FORMER SOVIET UNION

Sofiya An, Tatiana Chubarova, Bob Deacon and Paul Stubbs (editors)

PREFACE

This book derives from a workshop of the same title organized by the Comparative Research Programme on Poverty (CROP) at the Norwegian University Center in St Petersburg, Russian Federation, in June 2017. The workshop provided an opportunity for a systematic stock-taking of recent and historical post-socialist social policy developments in an increasingly diverse world region. Authors from different disciplines address key aspects of social protection including health care, poverty reduction measures, active labor market policies, pension systems, and child welfare systems. Contributions range in focus from comparative studies of welfare arrangements in a number of countries, to micro-level studies of the lived experiences of welfare users and their everyday lives. Throughout, the importance of policies to combat growing poverty, inequality and social exclusion is a major theme, with a number of texts addressing the complex policy nexus emerging from the interactions between international and domestic actors.

The original idea for the workshop came from Bob Deacon, a distinguished social policy scholar whose work on social policy in Eastern Europe, from the 1980s to today, continues to inspire researchers around the world and from the region. Following a long battle with cancer, Bob sadly passed away on 1 October 2017, aged 73. He will be missed by all who are committed to social justice across the world. Bob's commitment to the workshop and to this book was inspirational. It was a privilege, as co-editors, to work with him on this project. We are sorry that he was not able to see the book published, but we hope that it represents another important part of the legacy that he leaves behind.

We also wish to thank all those at CROP who worked hard to ensure the success of the workshop and to see this book to publication, in particular Alberto Daniel Cimadamore, Charlotte Lillefjære-Tertnæs, and Maria Sollohub. Thanks to Stein Kuhnle for his hard work during the workshop. We thank all participants in the workshop and, particularly, all contributors, for their commitment to the project. From the publisher's side, Jakob Horstmann provided patient guidance throughout the process, for which we are extremely grateful. Comments at the proposal stage by Thomas Pogge and, at the full review stage, by an anonymous reviewer, were extremely helpful in preparing the volume for final publication. We dedicate the book to the memory of Bob Deacon.

Sofiya An, Tatiana Chubarova, and Paul Stubbs
Astana, Moscow and Zagreb
September 2018

PART ONE: INTRODUCTION

CHAPTER 1
POVERTY, INEQUALITY AND WELL-BEING IN THE GLOBAL EAST: BRINGING THE 'SOCIAL' BACK IN

Paul Stubbs, Sofiya An and Tatiana Chubarova

INTRODUCTION

More than a quarter of a century after the fall of the Berlin Wall, the collapse of the Soviet Union, and the beginning of the wars of the Yugoslav succession, this book takes stock of the diverse and divergent welfare trajectories of post-socialist countries across Central, Eastern and South Eastern Europe and the former Soviet Union. It traces the impacts, in terms of poverty, well-being and inequality, of over two decades of transformation, addressing both the legacy effects of socialist welfare systems and the installation of new social, political and economic structures and, in many cases, new independent nation-states. It addresses different phases both of reform and of approaches to welfare, paying particular attention to the economic and financial crisis of the late 2000s. The book examines the rescaling of welfare arrangements, the privileging of 'economic' over 'social' policies, and the financial, institutional and capacity constraints which, at times, have resulted in reforms being both ineffective and inequitable.

THE 'GLOBAL EAST'

Thinking about social welfare policies in terms of a rich and powerful 'Global North' and a poorer and less powerful 'Global South' leaves out vast swathes of the world; a 'Global East' has, in many ways, 'fallen between the cracks' (Müller, 2017; 3). The end of communism in the Soviet Union and in Central and Eastern Europe, a result of a series of momentous events between 1989 and 1991, neither confirmed nor corresponded to Fukuyama's (1992) idea of 'the end of history.' The countries which make up the zone of concern in this volume have been doubly marginalized, not rich or powerful enough to be part of the Global North, not poor or powerless enough to be part of the Global South. Their 'in-between' status has fed a rather uninspiring 'transitology' literature that, in seeking to grasp the enormity of the 'simultaneous transition to democracy and to market economy' (Dobry, 2000; 51), has constantly charted and re-charted the supposed 'dilemmas', 'problems' and 'challenges' in the way, creating a stereotypical image of a region 'stuck in eternal transition towards an elusive modernity' (Müller, 2017; 4).

Of course, the countries of the former Eastern bloc, the former Soviet Union, and the former Yugoslavia, are only one part of the 'Global East', a term often applied to include East Asia (cf. for example Shin et al., 2016). Apart from experiencing decades of varieties of communist or socialist rule, and sharing, in time if not always in terms of its characteristics, a dramatic transformation, countries which make up this part of the Global East may seem to have very little in common. In a sense, of course, all regions are 'politically constructed and subject to diverse and contested meanings' (Solioz and Stubbs, 2012; 17). Moreover, the Global East as a whole is less 'legible' than the Global South, more 'slippery' and 'hard to categorize' (Müller, 2017; 3). It seems not to 'fit the frame' in which mainstream commentators 'think the global' (ibid, 8), brought into academic scholarship only when hyphenated as 'the ex-', 'the post-', or 'the former-' (ibid, 9). It now contains countries as different from each other as the Central European countries who have been EU member states since 2004 (with Slovenia in 25th place and the Czech Republic in 28th place in terms of UNDP's Human Development Index) and countries in Central Asia, including Kyrgyzstan and Tajikistan (respectively in 120th and 129th place on the same index)[1].

At the same time, Müller makes a persuasive case for utilizing the concept of a Global East as a form of 'strategic essentialism' (Spivak, 1988). It can serve as a kind of mobilization, a plea for 'voice', recognition, even emancipation, of very diverse entities united only in terms of their, greater or lesser, exclusion from dominant hegemonic practices. This seems to return 'the Global East' to where it properly belongs, deeply entangled in global social relations, neither 'out of time and space' nor exoticizable as a not quite fully developed 'Other' (Müller, 2017; 9). This volume, and the chapters within it, contribute, then, to new knowledge production about and, in many cases, from, the Global East. Insofar as the book is comparative, it seeks to be so without 'a hidden referent' (Sušova-Salminen, no date; 17), usually that of 'Western Europe', seeking to avoid

---

1   http://hdr.undp.org/en/composite/HDI accessed 22 March 2018.

a 'hidden Eurocentrism' essentializing supposedly binary oppositions between 'modern – traditional, industrial – agricultural, nation-state – empire-state, developed – backward, individualist – collectivist, or new – old' (ibid.; 11). This book is, then, best seen as a work of translation allowing for 'multiple sites and forms of knowledge production and academic practices that are more able to elaborate the widely diverse social and epistemic practices that comparative research witnesses' (Lendvai and Bainton, 2013; 115).

To be clear, our use of the concept of 'the Global East' is meant to be provocative in the best sense of the word, provoking a different way of thinking about the countries gathered together in this volume. Of course, not unlike the notion of 'core' and 'periphery', the concept reflects a kind of 'developmentalist' approach over and above mere geography. At the same time, it may be that it covers too many, and too diverse, countries to be of analytical value beyond challenging a focus only on the North-South divide in social policy.

THE FORGOTTEN SOCIAL

Equally important as the marginalization of the Global East has been the marginalization of the 'social'. Here, the marginalization refers not so much to the 'social' life of the 'everyday', a topic of growing interest to anthropologists in and of the region (cf. Verdery, 1996; Hann (ed.), 2002; Brković, 2017). Rather, for our purposes, it is the marginalization of 'social policies' not only in the extant literature but, also, in terms of its significance as a discursive field of policy making, which matters. Although many of the chapters that follow focus on one or more 'traditional' aspects of social policy making, whether pensions, unemployment benefits and employment services, social assistance and social services, here we use a looser definition of social policies as 'fluid, complex, multi-actor assemblages' (Lendvai and Stubbs, 2009; 674), sets of welfare arrangements and trajectories, ways of meeting social need and responding to social risks, and sets of welfare outcomes in terms of human well-being, which are 'constructed, contested and contradictory' (Clarke, 2004; 5).

In terms of what Hegel termed the *Zeitgeist* or 'the spirit of the age,' the Hungarian social policy scholar Julia Szalai points to how different the transformations might have been across the region had they occurred in 1968 and not 1989. The confluence of the end of communism across the

Global East with the dominance, ideologically and practically, of a particular kind of free market neo-liberalism served, in Polanyian terms, to 'delink' the 'social' from the economic and the political. The very idea of a 'welfare state' or a 'social state' in Baumann's terms, already closer to the term used in many Slavic languages, was judged as, at best, 'premature' and at worst, a legacy of socialism which had to be shrunk, residualized, and responsibilized so as not to be an obstacle to economic reform. What followed was, of course, a kind of 'mass moral engineering' (Thrift, 2005; 10), initially in terms of 'shock therapy' with its origins in the mid-1980s in parts of Latin America which was, to all intents and purposes, 'a political strategy for implementing radical economic measures', promoting rapid economic reforms advocated by supposed 'technocrats' shielded from day-to-day political processes and pressures and, indeed, 'normal democratic procedures' (Orenstein, 2011).

The attempt to 'bring the social back in' throughout this volume and in the introductory text takes stock of and maps the very diverse welfare arrangements and welfare outcomes across the region in the last thirty years. Inevitably, although the breadth of the volume is considerable, it is far from exhaustive. Not all countries, sub-regions or themes could possibly be covered in such a volume. The book reflects the interests of those whose abstracts were selected for the conference in St. Petersburg held in June 2017 who were then willing to transform their initial paper into a chapter for the book. We offer the volume, then, as a snapshot or overview of some trends both in social policy across the region and social policy scholarship. It is best viewed as an invitation to discussion and dialogue, raising more questions than it can possibly provide answers to.

The main focus of the book can still be discerned, however, addressing:

- the drivers and determinants of social welfare across space and time in a very diverse region;
- the development of diverse 'welfare mixes' based on variegated, and changing, roles of state, sub-state, supranational, market, household and 'civil society' actors;
- possible welfare futures in the context of profound economic, demographic and geo-political changes; and
- future priorities for research on social policy and advocacy for more inclusive and socially responsible societies across the region.

SOCIAL POLICIES IN THE GLOBAL EAST: THE LEGACIES

Socialist social policies across the Global East date back to the Bolshevik revolution in Russia in 1917 and the formation of the Union of Soviet Socialist Republics (USSR) in 1922. Many of the other countries in the region came under the influence of Soviet-style socialism after the end of the Second World War. Socialist Yugoslavia, after Tito's rejection of Stalinism in 1948, developed a quite specific self-managed socialism and, alone in the region, introduced organized state social work from the early 1960s (Stubbs and Maglajlić, 2012). Albania and, to some extent, Romania, followed more isolationist socialist policies with the latter becoming infamous for its inhumane treatment of abandoned children, and children and adults with disabilities, in 'total institutions'. The extent to which different socialist societies overcame class antagonisms, or merely replaced the old capitalist ruling class with new political elites is, of course, beyond the scope of this text (for socialist Yugoslavia see Archer et al. (eds.), 2016). What is clear is that most continued to adhere to a logic of 'productivism', with a dominant mode of production still based on commodity production and exchange (Deacon, 1983; 47). They pursued policies designed to 'catch-up' with the Global North even as, in the crisis years of the 1970s and 1980s, the technological gap with the richer capitalist nations grew ever wider. Soviet social policy clearly aspired to become universalistic in its scope with Ramesh Mishra describing the socialist welfare system as the structural model of the welfare state (Mishra, 1981).

Socialist social policies, notwithstanding differences across time and space, had a number of features in common. Crucially, unlike the capitalist world, socialist societies sought to guarantee full employment allowing for social security to be, primarily, enterprise-based, alongside subsidized prices for many essential goods and services and the provision of social housing. Social protection was deemed a necessary part of the industrialization process, although in many countries this led to a kind of three-tier system: enhanced rights for managers, civil servants and members of the political *nomenclature*; basic rights for industrial workers; and limited or no rights for those working in agriculture or otherwise marginal to the industrializing economy. Ironically, the strong work-welfare link meant that, as the economies of the region faltered in the 1980s and, even more so, as 'shock therapy' took hold in the 1990s, under-employment and, later, unemployment, threatened the livelihoods of entire families and communities (Estrin, 1994).

Socialist societies tended to guarantee access for all to education, including pre-school education, and health care. Processes of industrialization in much of the region were also associated with mass literacy drives and much improved health outcomes. At the same time, failures of centralized planning meant that the quality of services was uneven and cuts in response to poor economic performance in the 1970s and 1980s increased inequalities in access to health and education and led to increasing informal marketization of services. Improvements in health outcomes for many groups of the population that had taken decades to achieve were, often, rapidly eroded in the context of economic recession and, later, post-socialist transition.

As some authors reflect upon in this volume, although poverty was a taboo topic for researchers in socialist societies, this does not mean it did not exist, sometimes alongside significant levels of inequality. Regional variations in development and, hence, in well-being were quite pronounced and rural poverty tended not to be a focus of policy interest. In addition, large families, some oppressed minorities, older people and anyone living outside the rigid work-eligibility of the system were particularly vulnerable. During the 1980s' economic crisis, as Branko Milanović showed in his pioneering studies of poverty and inequality, new urban poverty emerged for the first time since the end of the Second World War (Milanović, 1990). Socialist societies, albeit with uneven intensity, promoted gender equality, at least formally, although this tended to translate into a triple burden for women, encouraged to enter the formal labor market but expected to continue to perform caring and domestic labor within the household. It was the case that family allowances and cash and in-kind child care benefits did cushion, to an extent, the shocks associated with having children but, again, benefits for agricultural workers and those outside the formal economy were neither adequate in amount nor universal in their coverage (Sipos, 1994).

Although Romania, as noted above, was particularly problematic, across the region state care for abandoned children, orphans and persons with disabilities, both physical and mental, meant, in reality, abandonment for life in total institutions, often in remote areas. Despite undergoing many changes over the socialist period, what was termed 'special education' in the United States and the UK continued to be termed 'defectology' (*defektologiia*) in the Soviet Union and in much of the post-Soviet space later (cf. Byford, 2017). This indicates a continued insistence on individualized 'pathology' models of disability and deviance, resisting trends towards more 'social' approaches, and, often, resulting in punishment and restraint at the expense of care and reintegration within highly bureaucratized and stigmatizing services.

TRANSITION, SHOCK THERAPY AND SOCIAL LIBERALISM

Social scientific research was unable to keep pace with the rapid changes in the social conditions across the region in the early 1990s and probably could not have done so even if 'social policy' had been higher up the policy agenda. One important attempt to monitor the developments across the region was the UNICEF TransMonEE (Transformative Monitoring for Enhanced Equity) project, launched under the leadership of the economist Giovanni Andrea Cornia as Director of the Economic and Social Policy Research Programme of the International Child Development Centre (ICDC), to all intents and purposes UNICEF's global research center, based in Florence, Italy. Ironically, the database and the analytical reports deriving, in part, from it, are much less influential today even though the database now covers 28 countries (Kosovo is not included) and over 500 social and economic indicators[2]. In the early 1990s, the alarm bells sounded by Cornia and his colleagues, on the basis of statistics from only a few countries in the region, pointed to a significant decline in welfare and well-being across the board, not only of children. Those parts of the region where statistics were not readily available, the conflict-ridden post-Yugoslav space in the early 1990s, for example, suggest that available statistics may, if anything, have underplayed the extent of the crisis.

Returning to the early reports is instructive, however, not least in terms of understanding what, even amongst progressive social policy researchers, quickly became accepted as a kind of alternative common sense, the prevailing wisdom of 'global social reformists' (Deacon et al. 1997, 84), not only regarding the extent of the crisis but on its underlying causes and potential remedies. The first ICDC report, published in June

---

2   http://transmonee.org/about/ Accessed 9 April 2018.

1991, made the point that 'it is not always easy to distinguish between problems inherited from the socialist regimes and the current reform programmes' (Cornia and Sipos, 1991; 23). Indeed, it seemed to suggest that 'economic and political reforms' are both 'desirable and essential' if the region is to escape from 'the economic, social and political decline which began about twenty years ago' (ibid, 33).

It was the nature of some of these reforms, however, that needed to be questioned, reflections of what the authors termed 'the spread of neo-liberal views which assign a greater role to market forces and charities in the field of health, education and social insurance' (ibid.; 12 – 13), going hand-in-hand with 'substantial cuts in public spending' (ibid.; 19). The clear message was that the high social costs of reforms could 'endanger the entire transition process, rip apart the social fabric and undermine the popular consensus on which these new, and still weak, democracies are based' (ibid.; 33). There is little or no reference, of course, to synchronous attacks on the welfare state, linked precisely to the 'spread of neo-liberal views', in the Global North. However, for supposedly 'objective' reasons echoing Kornai's idea that these were 'premature welfare states' (Kornai, 1997)—notably the lower average per capita GDP and significantly higher proportion of the population working in agriculture—none of Esping-Anderson's types of Western 'welfare regimes' are seen as appropriate for the region (Esping-Anderson, 1990). Instead, what is needed, the report suggests, is a greater awareness of the (unintended) social impacts of reforms and the reconstruction of 'social safety nets' to protect the most vulnerable, no more and no less than the 'social liberalism' or 'liberalism with a human face' traced by Deacon et al. (1997; 69) as the dominant approach globally within the World Bank at the time.

The next study, published in 1994, taking stock of 'four years of transition' is memorable, primarily, for Cornia's dramatic introductory Overview where he stated:

> The mortality and health crisis burdening most Eastern European countries since 1989 is without precedent in the European peacetime history of this century. It signals a societal crisis of unexpected proportions, unknown implications and uncertain solutions. In most of the region, the crisis has caused, and continues to cause, large numbers of avoidable deaths and threatens to erode social stability and indeed the entire transition process. (Cornia, 1994; v)

Whilst noting lots of missing data for many of the countries of the region, the message was that many of the same alarming trends can found across 'practically the entire region' (ibid.) The crisis was constructed as having spread from 'the traditionally most vulnerable groups' with 'male adults in the 25 – 59 age group' the greatest concern, with higher than expected levels of premature death in the face of 'widespread impoverishment, erosion of … services, and social stress' (ibid.). Again, 'market reforms' are described as 'highly necessary and inescapable', echoing UK Prime Minister Margaret Thatcher's TINA ('there is no alternative') maxim, but now balanced with a need to preserve 'the positive achievements of the past in education, child care, and social security' (ibid.). Across the region, then, an 'unprecedented 'social adaptation crisis'', if not addressed urgently, represented 'a clear threat to the political viability of the entire reform process' (ibid.; 6).

The first indications of a much more variegated picture comes in the third monitoring report, published in 1995. Cornia's introduction still refers to 'a severe welfare crisis affecting children and adolescents, an upsurge in mortality, equally shocking falls in births and increases in poverty, and faltering social protection and child development programmes' (Cornia, 1995; v). However, the five countries of Central Europe (Czech Republic, Hungary, Poland, Slovenia and Slovakia) are said to have halted, if not reversed, earlier deterioration in welfare and well-being. There is even a tentative attempt at a typology in terms of four distinct patterns of welfare across the region, with praise for the 'reform-minded' Central European countries but concern about 'late' or 'reluctant' reformers in South Eastern Europe, the Western CIS and the Baltics states and the Caucuses. For the first time, explicitly, policies for 'transition with a human face' are outlined, based on new partnerships between states and their 'civil societies', more equitable forms of economic transition and a raft of rather conventional labor market, family support, health, education and, interestingly, housing policies.

The impact of conflicts and the crisis of forced migration are not given particular prominence until the two reports, from 1999 and 2001, both taking stock, in slightly different ways, of 'a decade of transition' (UNICEF, 1999; 2001). 'Transition with a human face' is, now, presented as being held back by two, competing, sets of views, one which promotes radical reform in which economic performance is the key and sees social policies as an 'optional extra' which can be dealt with 'when economic conditions allow' (UNICEF, 1999; 1), and the other which opposes any reforms based on 'authoritarian, anti-democratic mindsets' (ibid.) that are a legacy of the old socialist regimes.

In retrospect, the reports offer a complex, even contradictory, set of policy ideas, inscribed as more 'technical' than 'political', and supposedly driven by the 'evidence' in the form of 'real social facts' deriving from the monitoring of transition. They remain both economistic and reformist, in the sense that stable macro-economic balances and 'market building', including privatization policies, are seen as the *sine qua non* of more progressive and equitable social policies. Many of these echo the poverty alleviation and safety net ideas of the World Bank, albeit allied with a commitment to maintaining essential education, health and social services. Harsh rhetoric criticizing ill-considered, badly sequenced, and anti-social reform experiments tend to be downplayed as part of a 'battle of ideas', rather than as discursive assemblages for the integration of the Global East as a new periphery of an increasingly globalized capitalist world.

A POLITICAL ECONOMY OF VARIEGATED POST-SOCIALIST WELFARE ASSEMBLAGES

Amongst analysts of welfare assemblages in the Global East, there are those who seek to 'bring institutions and political agency back in' (cf. Cerami and Stubbs, 2011), engaging in a tentative and radically unfinished categorization of sub-regional welfare ideal types. Advocating a kind of 'political economy of social policy' (ibid.; 9), understanding both 'drivers' and 'impediments to change' (cf. Stubbs and Zrinščak, this volume), the uneven impact of processes of 'neo-liberalization', 'inter-scalar tensions' between state and state-like actors, and the heterogeneity of 'regulatory and institutional landscapes' (Lendvai and Stubbs, 2015; 449; Brenner et al., 2010; 208 – 9), suggests a marked hybridity and fluidity, as well as continuing crisis-proneness, in welfare assemblages across the region. The extent of the 'transition' from state planned to marketized economies, as well as the specific form of capitalist social relations developed, varies considerably, of course.

Across the region, then, volatility rather than settled welfare 'regimes' is the norm not the exception, re-animating the transnational space and leading to variegated welfare retrenchment and growing poverty and inequality, on the one side, and clientelistic capture, cuts in public spending and a growing 'layering' of welfare between 'protected insiders' and 'disciplined' or 'abandoned outsiders' (Jensen, 2014) on the other. Across the region as a whole, different international actors scramble for influence, provide variegated policy advice but are by no means all-powerful. Crucially, across the region, again in variegated ways, remittances from diaspora populations and foreign direct investment are as important in shaping welfare trajectories. Political agency, including but not limited to the state, also matters, albeit in very different ways across different parts of the region, whether in terms of pluralist democratic competition or the, more or less gradualist, institutionalization of autocratic regimes. Without lapsing into crude economic determinism, the nature of different countries' and regions' enrolment in global capitalism, whether as export- or import-driven economies, oil-producing or oil-dependent, and so on, also matters, not least in terms of framing the welfare choices available. Bringing social policy in the region back into the domain of political economy, not unlike Esping-Andersen did in his study of welfare regimes in Western Europe, is crucial.

Taking stock of over a quarter of a century of transition, winners and losers have emerged, but who they are varies greatly from sub-region to sub-region. The study of social policy is, still, the study of struggles between elites and vested interests, on one side, and more or less dispossessed populations on the other, and political struggles over institutions, resources, rights and regulations. Although the region's welfare assemblages are marked definitively by temporal, spatial and, crucially, policy domain heterogeneity, in the following sections we explore what might be some of the more pronounced sets of characteristics, drivers and challenges, across sub-regions covered in the book, necessarily only in the sketchiest of terms.

Post-Soviet Central Asian states: indeterminable welfare trajectories

After the disintegration of the Soviet Union in 1991, newly independent Central Asian states, including Kazakhstan, Kyrgyzstan, Tajikistan, Turkmenistan, and Uzbekistan, have been undergoing major social transformations including the drastic restructuring of their economies, polities, and welfare systems. Having departed from Soviet planning, one-party political systems and universal welfare systems, these close neighbors followed divergent pathways that have led to different outcomes (Pomfret, 2010). During the first decade, similarly to other former Soviet republics, Central Asian states experienced severe and protracted economic depression, or 'transformation crisis' (Myant and Drahokoupil, 2010). Soviet supply chains were disrupted, and consumer markets broken up, severely damaging industrial manufacturing. In addition, Central Asian states, arguably, suffered the most from the disintegration of Soviet economic ties, as compared to other former Soviet republics, and experienced a drastic reduction in GDP in the 1990s (Myant and Drahokoupil, 2008; Pomfret, 2010).

While the five states took different approaches to creating market economies and joining the global market, from drastic liberal reforms in Kyrgyzstan and Kazakhstan through state-controlled reforms in Uzbekistan to little reform in Turkmenistan, they have seen different degrees of success (Pomfret, 2010). The key factor that impacted on the success of economic reforms has arguably been the availability of resources more than economic policies (Pomfret, 2010). As Myant and Drahokoupil (2008) have convincingly argued, the oil-driven growth of Central Asian economies and exports and the 'downgrading' of export structures indicate that these countries have become integrated into the world economy but only as peripheral members, located outside of major industrial networks.

The UN Human Development Report (1999) described the socio-economic situation in the entire post-Soviet and post-socialist region as 'a human crisis of monumental proportions'. While the scope of poverty increased, poverty struck different social groups unequally. Regional inequality became the primary predictor of poverty (World Bank, 2004). In addition to 'old' categories of the poor, the 'new poor' emerged, such as low-paid and low-skilled workers (in rural areas and in the public sector), the unemployed, especially young people, and families with many children / large households; moreover, there was an increase in female poverty (Ruminska-Zimny, 1997). During the first decade of independence, Central Asian states responded to the economic crisis by drastic reductions in public expenditures on welfare, health care, and education. In line with the global neoliberal turn and an attack on the welfare state, newly independent states and major international actors, such as the World Bank, IMF, OECD, and USAID that guided post-Soviet reforms viewed social policy as subservient to economic and political reforms in the region (Boenker, Muller and Pickel, 2002). Following the contraction of GDP and state revenues, government expenditures on social welfare in 1997 plummeted to 25 – 30 percent of state expenditures before 1990 (Falkingham, 1999).

Dramatic cuts in Soviet-era welfare benefits across the Central Asia region in the 1990s faced little public resistance, with few exceptions. While the Soviet paternalist welfare state provided benefits in exchange for compliance, it was also the source of the lack of political organization and advocacy groups that made post-Soviet reforms too easy to implement. Essentially, post-Soviet social policy was an effort to redraft the social contract between the state and citizens (Cook, 1993). For instance, in Kazakhstan, a major theme in the policy discourse in the 1990s was family responsibility for providing care for family members and the need to end Soviet-type dependency on the state, thus effectively erasing the Soviet value system and re-instating Asian / traditional ethics (Maltseva, 2014). Public conformity can also be linked to oil-driven development in 'resource-cursed' or 'rentier' states, in which a small elite has access to the 'rent' paid by foreign actors, while the majority of the population depend on this elite (Luong and Weinthal, 2010; Franke, Gawrich and Alakbarov, 2008).

Social policy has been integral to nation-building projects with reforms evolving from early democratic reforms to so-called 'super-presidencies' with varying degrees of authoritarianism (Pomfret, 2010; Schatz, 2006). The return of social policy to the nation-states' agenda in the 2000s and 2010s was partly preconditioned by the economic revival, supporting the classical argument that links the expansion of Western welfare states to economic growth (Myles and Quadagno, 2002; Wilensky, 1975). More importantly, however, social policy has been an important tool of social control and redistribution of resources that non-democratic post-Soviet governments use to ensure political consent in conditions of uncertain market economies (Cook and Dimitrov, 2017; Forrat, 2012). Moreover, social policy has intertwined with the post-Soviet shift away from the state monopoly on welfare, as new non-governmental organizations (NGOs) have become welfare providers and policy actors

(Cook, 2015). NGOs in post-Soviet social policy have multiple identities and play contradictory roles, from an embodiment of civil society, to social advocates, to providers of social support, to project implementers, to a tool of social control employed by the state (Aksartova, 2009; Bindman, 2017; Stubbs, 2006). Yet, the shift from the centralized welfare system run by the Soviet state to the provision of welfare in multiple sites, including the state, the emerging market, and NGOs, has been, arguably, the key characteristic of post-Soviet welfare transformation (An, 2017).

All the Central Asian states continue to face many challenges that are affecting the majority of people living in the region. Poverty is a persistent problem in all Central Asian states: although the rate of absolute poverty has fallen, the proportion of people living below the threshold of $4.30 Purchasing Power Parity (PPP) per day remains high, ranging from 29 percent in Kazakhstan through 62 percent in Kyrgyzstan to 87 percent in Tajikistan in 2008 (UNDP, 2014). Along with poverty, there is a problem of rising inequality. Rural residents, people with disabilities, the unemployed, large families and single-parent families are at higher risk of income poverty (UNDP, 2014). Regional disparities, as a result of unequal distribution of natural resources and unequal economic growth, continue to be an issue in Kazakhstan (ADB, 2016). Finally, over the past two and half decades, a vast gap has emerged between the Central Asian post-Soviet states: Gross National Income (GNI) per capita in Kazakhstan of $11,550 makes it an upper-middle income country, while GNI in Kyrgyzstan is $1,210 in Kyrgyzstan and $990 in Tajikistan (World Bank, 2015, cited in O'Brien, 2015).

Social policy in Central Asia has received far less scholarly attention than welfare transformations in other former Soviet states. This feature is linked to the shifting global and regional geopolitics, as new regional categories have emerged to replace the USSR, such as the EU category of post-Soviet states, Russia as its own category, or the Central Asia category of states casually called 'stans', which includes five post-Soviet states along with Afghanistan and Pakistan. There is also a tendency to fall into one-sided and overly simplistic assessments of the success and failure of social policy reforms as a function of weak institutions, corruption, authoritarianism, poor governance, 'failing states', and a threat to regional security, while neglecting the complexity and multiplicity of factors that play a role in social policy development, including post-colonial legacies and unequal power relationships between the emerging states and their Western and non-Western counterparts.

The Russian Federation: rising inequality in a shifting welfare landscape

Transition brought dramatic societal changes that are well described in both Russian and international research and elaborated upon in this volume. These changes affected social policy formation and implementation, in many different, although inter-related, ways. First, ideologically, in terms of changing social values, shifting understandings of notions such as equality and equity, attitudes to private property, the promotion of the principle of individual responsibility, and the construction of a consumer society and changing behavior and patterns of consumption. Second, financially, as in much of the region, economic restructuring was accompanied by a significant decrease in public social expenditures. Health care is a good example with the share of GDP allocated by the state to health care having stabilized at levels much below those of the Northern and the Western countries, at around 3.4 percent. Third, institutional arrangements changed, with the development of a mixed economy of welfare, the emergence of a private sector, both for-profit and not-for-profit agencies, alongside tendencies to decentralization and a shifting of social responsibilities from national to regional and local levels.

As noted above, the results of the first wave of reforms in the Russian Federation were extremely disappointing; instead of improving individual capacities to secure personal well-being, the transition caused a substantial increase in the number of people in need of social protection, particularly rising numbers of those unemployed and the working poor. Nevertheless, later reforms, although not always consistent, have led to a particular welfare 'settlement' that, at least for the moment, seems to be more or less stable. There is an increased role for the private sector in satisfying social needs; state paternalism and centralized distribution and provision of passive social services has been replaced by a more active approach; and a degree of correction of the negative consequences of market functioning has been secured through creating basic safety nets for disadvantaged groups through targeted policies.

The issue of inequality has been of particular concern throughout the last two decades. Russia was a relatively egalitarian society in Soviet times with rather low Gini coefficients, a widely used measure of statistical dispersion of income in a country, and, hence, of inequality. However, rapidly after the start of transition, Russia was sharply transformed into one of the most unequal states in the world. There is a clear tension between the role of a welfare state in fighting poverty via supporting living standards and a wider commitment to fighting inequality. Poverty in Russia is high on the political agenda while little or nothing is said, much less done, at the political level to deal with inequality. To give some recent examples: the State Duma failed to adopt a law on wealth and progressive personal income taxation; and inequality was not mentioned in the annual Presidential address to the Federal Assembly. A continued faith in market mechanisms makes it politically risky, as well as administratively difficult, to introduce a significantly higher degree of redistribution into the system.

Research studies, mainly but not exclusively sociological, have paid particular attention to attitudes towards inequalities, with significant numbers of Russians considering some inequalities as unfair. The theme of inequality is inexorably tied to the outcomes of large scale privatization that still remains a very problematic and debatable issue. Two aspects of inequality are particularly persistent: income inequality and regional inequality. In the future, unless there are significant changes to the direction of social policies, the situation appears unlikely to improve and other aspects of inequality, including gender inequality, are likely to become more and more in focus.

Inequalities in healthcare is also a complex and contentious issue. At the most basic level, at least in principle, all citizens are still able to access healthcare and medical services that are free at the point of delivery, with state owned health services financed through compulsory health insurance (CHI) and taxes. However, government policies to promote 'fees for services' in publicly owned health services, in the face of the principle of 'free health for all', seems likely to increase inequality of access to healthcare and thus negatively affect the health of some strata of the population.

Questions of the welfare mix, of the extent to which NGOs should supplement or substitute for government programs, what mechanisms they should use to influence government policies, and how to combine top-down and bottom-up initiatives are, of course, not exclusive to the Russian Federation but they do take particular forms in this context. The fact that 'socially-oriented NGOs' have been officially recognized, underscores their importance in social policy whilst, perhaps, serving to draw a distinction between service providers and more advocacy- and rights-based initiatives. NGOs have become seen as a complement to governmental policies and state welfare institutions. A more empowering and transformative role for NGOs, over and above a broadly charitable or humanitarian frame is, however, still to be developed. Social policy is still financed mainly by the state in the Russian Federation but new ways of organizing social welfare open up opportunities for empowerment. The gender dimension of Russian social policy, although again not unique, is also important. Women dominate among both services users and service providers, although managers of services are, often, male. Women's activities in various spheres of NGO work, especially in the poorer regions, using both formal and informal networks to increase resources available for social welfare, are extremely important.

South East Europe: captured policies and crowded playgrounds

Here, South East Europe includes the EU Member States of Bulgaria and Romania (who joined on 1 January 2007), Croatia (who joined on 1 July 2013), and the countries and territories of the so-called Western Balkans who all aspire to join the European Union one day (Albania, Bosnia-Herzegovina, Kosovo, Macedonia[3], Montenegro, and Serbia). Throughout the 1990s and, indeed, beyond, parts of the region were embroiled in violent conflicts resulting in deaths, destruction of property and forced migration on a massive scale. The wars of the Yugoslav succession resulted in a large-scale international presence with a complex array of international humanitarian, security and 'state-building' actors all having direct and indirect impacts not only on people's well-being but, also, on welfare systems themselves (Deacon and Stubbs, 2007; 11). Although not facing violent conflicts, Romania and, to an extent, Bulgaria also faced a 'crowded playground' (Arandarenko and Golicin, 2007) of international actors responding to the crisis of children and people with disabilities in institutional care that was in breach of their human rights and dignity.

Although Bosnia-Herzegovina and Kosovo, at times resembling international protectorates, offer the most dramatic examples, all of the region remains impacted by a range of international actors moving from humanitarian relief efforts, via a large number of experimental 'pilot' projects, to a supposedly more structured and tailored support for

---

3   Throughout the book, the official name 'Macedonia' is used. Just prior to publication, this was changed to 'North Macedonia'.

'strategy development' (cf. Maglajlić Holiček and Rašidagić, 2007). The conflicts meant that early transition was, either, delayed, or the introduction of supposed free markets, through dominant models of privatization, allowed autocratic and, not unusually, kleptocratic political elites to capture resources (cf. Mujanović, 2018). Studies in Croatia regarding the extent of political clientelism and its impacts on social welfare at the national level (Stubbs and Zrinščak, 2015) and, indeed, local level (Hoffman et al., 2017) may well be generalizable across the region, pointing to the difficulties of universal and / or needs-based social policies. Certainly, the distortion caused by welfare rights for war veterans, their families, and survivors, in parts of Bosnia-Herzegovina (cf. Obradović, 2016), Croatia and Kosovo is, perhaps, the most dramatic example of this, with potentially long-term impacts.

Although it is possible to trace a positive role of the European Union in general governance issues, with some spill-over into social policy, in the period leading up to accession, for Bulgaria, Romania and Croatia, all three countries face renewed economic, political and social challenges. Not unlike Poland and Hungary in Central Europe, an authoritarian backlash has seen a return to nationalism, corruption and a radical reassertion of Christian values in terms of support of so-called 'normal' families. In their different ways, all three countries have seen retrenchment after joining the European Union and with cuts in welfare as the economic and financial crisis of 2008 – 10 hit large sections of the population particularly hard.

Across the rest of the region, similar issues suggest that European accession, notwithstanding 'enlargement fatigue' amongst the Member States, is likely to be a slow and extremely difficult process. A recent working paper, setting out alternative futures for welfare states in the Western Balkans, addresses some of the most important common challenges, including relatively low levels of development and a failure to 'catch up' with peers; demographic crises of various kinds marked, often, by low fertility, and sometimes by population decline and significant out-migration; population ageing; and widespread poverty, high unemployment and low participation rates in changing labor markets (Matković, 2017). High demand for support combines with a lack of investment or, at best, a clientelistic and rather passive approach to welfare. Although sometimes over-stated, the danger of the deep institutionalization of an 'ethnicized' welfare system, sometimes going beyond the borders of the nation state to offer support to diaspora populations living nearby (cf. Stubbs and Zrinščak, 2009), is also worrying.

Just as the European Union's social model for its Member States has moved from a broad social framework, via a prime focus on 'employability' and 'workfare', towards 'modernization', fiscal sustainability and austerity (cf. Stubbs and Lendvai, 2016), so too has the pre-accession process become far less 'social' and far more 'economic', framing accession in terms of political governance and fiscal frugality. Hence, of the options Matković presents for the future, the most likely, pushed by the World Bank, IMF and the European Union's Directorate General for Economics and Finance (DG ECFIN), is that of a 'small' or, as we would term it, 'residual' welfare state, with continued low levels of social protection expenditure but more efficiently targeted towards the poor or, indeed, 'the poorest of the poor' (Matković, 2017; 49 – 50). However, as Matković herself recognizes, the largest part of welfare spending in many of the countries of the region is 'locked-in' to insurance-based pension systems, the radical reform of which would be politically difficult and grossly unfair to those who have contributed across their working lives.

Croatia is one of the few countries in the region where a radical pension reform was implemented in the late 1990s, in large part because of the success of a powerful coalition of forces including the pension funds themselves, neo-liberal economists, and the World Bank. Other reforms have been slower to develop and implement although, ironically, the rather slow progress made by Croatia towards eventual membership of the European Union allowed for DG Employment to have some influence, at least discursively and technically, over Croatia's welfare reform agenda, through the Joint Inclusion Memorandum on Social Inclusion (JIM) and the Joint Assessment of Employment Policy Priorities (JAP) processes. The chapter by Stubbs and Zrinščak concludes that political elites' survival rests less on being reform-minded than on maintaining nationalist ideas, clientelistic networks and a kind of 'capture' of governance and resources, including social benefits.

Captured welfare arrangements leave too few funds to meet wider needs. Throughout the region, there is much more attention paid to cash benefits than to social services, particularly community-based services. In addition, although most pronounced in Bulgaria and Romania, the legacy of large-scale institutionalization of children and adults deemed to be 'at-risk' or 'threatening' to the wider population, often in inhumane residential facilities remote from centers of population, and often for long periods of time, still leaves its mark on the system (cf. Pop, 2013; Ivanova and Bogdanov, 2013). The development of responsive community-based services to address old and new risks, including what is likely to be soaring demand for long-term care in the future, is, perhaps the key challenge for welfare across South East Europe. Above all, a reform agenda that is responsive to the case for more extensive social welfare systems in the future, will need to replace the fragmented, inconsistent and *ad hoc* approach to social welfare in the current conjuncture.

The Baltic States: diverse paths within a European future

The transition experience of the Baltic States that were formerly part of the Soviet Union – Estonia, Latvia and Lithuania – seems to differ substantially from the Russian case as evidenced, in part, by the fact that these countries joined the EU in 2004. They appear to have made substantial economic, political and social progress since the early 1990s and have, to an extent, reformed their social policy arrangements. The OECD considers pension reforms in this region to be more advanced than those adopted in most OECD countries (OECD, 2003). However, the Baltic States still lag behind many European countries in terms of lower social spending, high unemployment, modest incomes and more unequal income distribution, as well as having experienced significant depopulation.

However, there are dangers attached to analyzing the social policy of the Baltic States solely from the point of view of 'catching up' with the developed EU countries. They still differ insofar as this cluster of countries pays most attention to coping with 'old' or 'traditional' social risks rather than increasing their capacity to address 'new' social risks (Toots Bachmann, 2010). The Baltic States share certain common features, above and beyond the simple fact that they all inherited the legacy of a common socialist social welfare system. In general, all three states have abandoned that system and have turned away from any kind of universal and comprehensive approach to welfare, preferring supposedly 'competition-friendly' low tax, and low welfare, arrangements. As researchers have pointed out, this is least pronounced in Estonia, which appears to have maintained more solidaristic arrangements and more universal social benefits compared to the residual models of Latvia and Lithuania (Aidukaite 2009, 2013). Lithuania's social security system is relatively well-financed but is targeted and means-tested with strict qualifying requirements while in Estonia and Latvia social benefits are income-tested.

Not unlike South East Europe, although there the picture was complicated by war-related humanitarianism, across the Baltic states the strong role of the International Financial Institutions, particularly the IMF and the World Bank, in framing social policy choices, was at first countered, to an extent, by the role of the European Union. Later, however, in the face of the economic and financial crisis, social policy choices were set within an EU governance apparatus framed almost exclusively in terms of debt reduction and austerity. In a sense, difficult political adjustment was followed by structural economic adjustment. In the future, it is very much an open question as to the role the Baltic States will play in debates about a 'new European social model.'

Central Europe: welfare contradictions in the new European 'core'

Although they are rather diverse, one can take the Czech Republic, Hungary, Poland, Slovakia and, to an extent, Slovenia together as constituting a cluster of welfare systems marked by a sense of 'returning to the core of Europe.' The first phase of socialist transition differed rather markedly in each country with, in large part, both the former Czechoslovakia and Slovenia as part of former Yugoslavia, initially pre-occupied with securing independence. Linkages between international actors and new elites, seeking to implement rapid neo-liberal reforms in the form of 'shock therapy', were often interrupted by elections lost by political forces most identified with the reforms resulting in, at the very least, a re-packaging and 'humanizing' of some reforms to make their impacts less severe (Cook and Orenstein, 1999). In any case, the so-called 'first wave' of reforms, attempting stabilization through liberalization and privatization (Guardiancich, 2004; 41), had mainly indirect impacts on social welfare, with social welfare reforms themselves being a direct focus only of later, 'second-wave', reforms (ibid.).

Deacon and Standing captured something of the diverse possibilities in the early years of transition, ranging from Poland's rapid withdrawal of the state and development of a 'residual' social policy, to Slovenia's move towards a more traditional European 'conservative corporatist' settlement (Deacon and Standing, 1993; 159). Interestingly, they also went beyond narrow 'national-cultural' explanations to suggest that 'the split of Czechoslovakia was in part a split reflecting the political choice for different paths of social policy reform, as well as for a different pace of economic reform' (ibid.; 159 – 160), placing the Czech Republic closer to a residual future and suggesting that Slovakia would attempt to hold on to social guarantees, albeit in the face of pressure from international organizations. Only three years later, Standing at least, was rather more pessimistic, suggesting the logic of privatization combined with cuts in many social benefits, a tightening of eligibility criteria, and ushering in a 'means-tested future', had become the new hegemony across the region (Standing, 1996; cf. also Cerami, 2005).

Throughout the 1990s, pension reforms and labor market reforms were, perhaps, the key arenas of contestation. The decade saw significant demographic ageing across Central and Eastern Europe (CEE), through declining fertility rates. At the same time, shocks of transition and increased life expectancy produced an increase in the ratio of pensioners to workers (Freyka and Sobotka, 2008). There were even suggestions that CEE countries tended to spend more on pensions than countries with similar demographic profiles, with the 'overshoot' on pensions spending creating a kind of 'inter-generational injustice' (Vanhuysse, 2014). Müller suggested the pensions debate was about whether technical changes to public pay-as-you-go systems, through changing benefit formulae, retirement ages and eligibility criteria would be enough or whether more radical, private pension schemes should be introduced, based on the Latin American or, more specifically, Chilean model (Müller, 1999). Differing structural conditions, constellations of actors, international and domestic, and technical choices were seen to interact in complex ways. In both Poland and Hungary, it often seemed as if the World Bank and the Ministry of Finance were pitted against the ILO and the Ministry of Welfare with a compromise reached in terms of a mixed system of Pay-As-You-Go (PAYG) and a mandatory private pension scheme, resembling the more 'democratic-tolerant' Argentinian model (cf. Deacon et al., 1997).

In both the Czech Republic and Slovenia, the 'new orthodoxy' (Müller, 2002; 135) of mandatory private schemes was resisted despite strong efforts from the World Bank. Slovakia was a late, but rather radical, reformer (Lesay, 2006) diverting a significant amount of pension contributions to the private pillar. Hungary was an earlier reformer, launching a partial privatization in 1998, introducing a mandatory private scheme as well as a so-called 'zero' or means-tested pillar for those without sufficient contributions (Augusztinovics, 2002). Famously, however, the experiment ended between 2010 and 2012 when the Orbán Government effectively re-nationalized private pension assets and abolished the private pillar, combined with significant parametric changes in the context of the economic and financial crisis that significantly reduced incomes in retirement, as well as abolishing disability pensions (Szikra, 2018). The Hungarian *volte face* shows the potentially contradictory nature of welfare arrangements, with 'financialization' originally used as the reason for reform and 'fear of financialization' for the re-nationalization. Crucially, 'the strong anti-market sentiment attached to the renationalization of pensions ... occurred at a time when strongly neo-liberal policies were being introduced such as a flat tax system, punitive workfare and radical cuts to social benefits' (Lendvai and Stubbs, 2015; 454).

It is not without significance that the European Union played almost no role in the pensions debate in the Central European countries that joined in the enlargement of 1 May 2004. This, broadly, coincided with what the EU itself would term a focus on 'modernizing' social protection, very much framed in terms of activation, responsibilization and a strong employment dimension. Generally, across the EU, there was a renewed focus on labor market reforms, nominally a translation of the Danish model of 'flexicurity' but, often, with a much greater emphasis on 'flexibility' in terms of shifting the balance of power towards capital and away from labor, whether organized or not. The Open Method of Co-ordination, of course, left the details of policy choices to Member States, so that the kind of 'workfare' that the new Member States opted for ranged from a 'punitive interventionist-neoliberal' policy to more 'inclusive, high-quality training-based activation' (Lendvai, 2007; 35). A new wave of labor market reforms followed in the wake of the economic and financial crisis of 2008 – 9. The picture regarding CEE is mixed with Poland and

Slovenia, along with Spain and Portugal, EU record holders in terms of the share of temporary contracts among new employment contracts at over 80 percent (Eichhorst et al., 2017; 5). At the same time, Poland and Slovakia, along with the South East European Member States, are among those countries that have the lowest coverage of unemployment benefits for the short-term unemployed (ibid.; 12).

Currently, in a sense, there are two contradictory tendencies structuring welfare across Central Europe. States of Central Europe have become more a part of the 'core' rather than the periphery of Europe. In terms of Human Development Index rankings, they form part of cluster of highly developed countries ranked between 25th (Slovenia) and 43rd (Hungary) and with GNI per capita around $25,000. The other tendency is the combination of neoliberal austerity policies with strong national and populist discourses and practices. The 'authoritarian neoliberal' turn in welfare is most pronounced in Hungary and in Poland. A universalist 'welfare for all' discourse is replaced by exclusionary discourses and a kind of divisive or 'layered' welfare, still redistributory in scope but taking highly ethnicized and moralizing forms. The seeming inability of an equally contradictory European Union, whose technicization of the integration process combined with a focus within the European Semester, the EU's six monthly economic governance cycle, only on debt reduction (cf. Stubbs and Lendvai, 2016), to challenge these tendencies is, itself, a kind of indictment of 'social Europe' precisely in part of Europe's new core.

THE STRUCTURE OF THE BOOK

Although the conference from which the book derives, and this opening chapter, addresses social policy developments within sub-regional structures, we have adopted a more thematic structure for the rest of the book. Following our own introductory chapter, the next four chapters focus on poverty and inequality. Esuna Dugarova's chapter analyses the unsatisfactory outcomes of poverty reduction policies in Russia, Belarus, Kazakhstan, Kyrgyzstan, and Uzbekistan, and points to the challenges of balancing multiple and contradictory goals of social protection and labor market policies in fledgling post-Soviet states. Natalia Grigorieva's overview of research on inequality in Russia suggests that there has been some renewed interest in inequality in scientific studies in the last fifteen years but little real attention to how various dimensions of inequality—access to social services, health care, and education, gender inequalities, regional inequalities, and so on—reinforce each other. Tatiana Chubarova's chapter explores how income inequality is translated into inequality in access to health care in contemporary Russia, focusing on out-of-pocket payments and their role as a barrier to access. Natalija Atas' chapter confronts gaps in knowledge of in-work poverty through a qualitative exploration of the constant struggle of the working poor in Lithuania and the coping strategies they employ.

Part Three contains four chapters that explore the role of diverse policy actors in institutional change. Maja Gerovska Mitev's chapter focuses on the role of key inter-governmental actors, including the World Bank, the EU and the UN agencies, in social policy and poverty reduction in Macedonia. Igor Guardiancich addresses the role of clientelistic social relations in the functioning of Kosovo's pension system, *de facto* and *de jure* redesigned completely, largely by external actors, in the aftermath of the war and NATO intervention in 1999. Sofiya An's chapter on post-Soviet child welfare reforms in Kazakhstan looks into the post-Soviet child welfare transformation as an interplay of Soviet institutional legacies and transported policy ideas that lead to incremental institutional change and to the shifts in institutional logics. Ann-Mari Sätre shows how women's work and engagement can complement state policies to combat poverty, exploring the effects of the continuing responsibility of women for social welfare.

Part Four contains four chapters that address wider issues of systemic change in terms of welfare trajectories and assemblages. The chapter by Elena Maltseva and Saltanat Janenova, a case study of the evolution of pension reforms in Kazakhstan, examines the role of endogenous and exogenous factors, such as the shifting global old age social security paradigm as well as the national policy makers' attempts to respond to multiple social, economic, demographic and financial pressures and to meet government development objectives. In her analysis of healthcare reforms in former Soviet states, Gulnaz Isabekova focuses on the interaction between nation-states and international actors, arguing that multiple trajectories of healthcare reforms result from different patterns of relations among transnational policy actors. The chapter by Noémi Lendvai-Bainton addresses the rise of authoritarian neoliberalism in parts of Central Europe as prefiguring a new welfare paradigm, that of 'social disinvestment' and 'layered' welfare, at the same time as a punitive and disciplinary state plays an ever-greater role in the surveillance of citizens and, crucially, unwelcome others. The chapter by Paul Stubbs and Siniša Zrinščak shows how 'domestic' and 'international' structures and actors co-produce a set of welfare paradoxes or contradictions in Bosnia-Herzegovina, Croatia and Serbia. Large-scale experimentation goes hand in hand with very limited real reform, and formally extensive social rights lead, in practice, to both welfare retrenchment and the 'layering' of rights in favor of some groups and not others.

As ever with any edited collection of this nature, it has been impossible to cover all possible topics relating to poverty, inequality and social welfare across the entire region in an encyclopedic manner. We have attempted, however, to include work that points to the diversity of approaches to different themes, from empirical studies of poverty, through ethnographic studies of coping strategies, to studies of institutional and policy change. We worked with the chapters that were proposed to us without seeking, in any sense, to get a balance of works that focused on different aspects of social policy across the region as a whole. Hence, the fact that more texts on the post-Soviet space focus on poverty and inequality and more texts on Central, Eastern and South Eastern Europe address the policy process should not be read as a reflection of a divergence in focus amongst scholars across the region. It is a strength of this book, we believe, that it indeed brings together, in one volume, analyses of the experiences of post-Soviet welfare states and the welfare trajectories of Central, Eastern and South Eastern Europe.

AN AGENDA FOR THE FUTURE

Although it would be wrong to make sweeping generalizations, the countries of what we have termed, with considerable reservations and caveats, as the 'Global East' have not achieved the kind of forward-looking liberal democratic social market economies that were dreamed of. All are, more or less, struggling in a space between a socialist past and a more or less authoritarian neoliberal present. Levels of wealth and economic development offer only partial explanations for the welfare arrangements that are in place. In addition, we have to look at legacy effects, at political and economic struggles, including but not limited to class relations, differential institutional arrangements and capacities, and to the role of diverse sets of international actors. The differential exposure to 'shock therapy', war and conflict, and the economic and financial crisis have also been important in terms of the differential welfare assemblages across such a broad region. All of this makes searching for one or more solidified 'welfare regimes' across the region a rather fruitless task.

In terms of research agendas, this book suggests that these are many and varied. There is clearly a need to consider inequality in a much longer-term historical context, as well as going beyond an over-reliance on traditional measures of income inequality, as exemplified in Filip Novokmet's recent doctoral thesis under the supervision of Thomas Piketty (Novokmet, 2017). Along with studies of agencies, institutions, structures and discourses, there is also a need to explore the workings of welfare at the micro-level, addressing day-to-day encounters between users and potential users of services and front-line bureaucrats. Studies of demographics, and of changing household structures as well as patterns of migration, both internal and external, need to be much more central to social policy research in the future. Above all, aggregate data provides only one form of evidence on social development and must be supplemented by studies of the impacts of social welfare arrangements on diverse populations.

Ultimately, we need to recognize that issues of poverty, inequality, and exclusion both horizontal and vertical, are challenges across the region, so that the Sustainable Development Goals agenda of 'leaving no one behind' is highly relevant. At the same time, although mainly intended for less developed regions, the UN's Global Social Protection Floor initiative—focusing on income support, for those capable of work, supporting children, persons with disabilities, and older people, together with essential services, such as health education and social care—also represents a broad framework that could 'bring the social back in' to reform agendas. Above all, this book has shown that there are significant gaps in our knowledge and understanding of key processes in terms of social welfare, across the region, mirroring similar concerns across the globe, expressed in the 2016 World Social Science Report (ISSC, IDS and UNESCO, 2016). More robust research, and closer connections between research, policy and advocacy, are clearly needed now and in the future.

REFERENCES

Aidukaite, Jolanta (2013) 'Social policy changes in the three Baltic states over the last decade (2000 – 2012)'. *EKONOMIKA*. 92(3); 89 – 104.

Aidukaite, Jolanta (2009) 'Transformation of welfare systems in the Baltic States: Estonia, Latvia and Lithuania.' In: Alfio Cerami, Peter Vanhuysse (eds.) Postcommunist Welfare Pathways: Theorizing Social Policy Transformations in CEE. Basingstoke, Palgrave Macmillan.

Aksartova, Sada (2009) *Promoting civil society or diffusing NGOs?* In Hemmack, David C. & Heydemann, Steven (Eds.), *Globalization, philanthropy, and civil society: projecting institutional logics abroad* (pp. 160 – 91). Bloomington, Indiana: Indiana University Press.

An, Sofiya (2017) 'Social work of boundaries': emerging multiple social work fields in post-Soviet Eurasia, *European Journal of Social Work*, 20:6, 894 – 906.

Arandarenko, Mihail and Pavle Golicin (2007) 'Serbia', in Bob Deacon and Paul Stubbs (eds.) *Transnationalism and the making of social policy in South East Europe*, Cheltenham: Edward Elgar; 167 – 186.

Archer, Rory, Igor Duda and Paul Stubbs (eds.) (2016) *Social Inequalities and Discontent in Yugoslav Socialism*, Abingdon: Routledge.

Augusztinovics, Maria (2002) 'The Hungarian Pension System Before and After the 1998 Reform', in Elaine Flutz (ed.) *Pension Reform in Central and Eastern Europe Volume 1*, Budapest: ILO.

Bindman, Eleanor (2015) The state, civil society and social rights in contemporary Russia, *East European Politics*, 31:3, 342 – 360.

Boenker, F. Müller, K. & Pickel, A. (Eds) (2002) *Postcommunist transformation and the social sciences: Cross-disciplinary approaches*. Lanham: Rowman & Littlefield.

Brenner, Neil, Jamie Peck and Nick Theodore (2010) 'Variegated Neoliberalization: geographies, mobilities, pathways', *Global Networks* 10(2); 182 – 222.

Brković, Čarna (2017) *Managing Ambiguity: how clientelism, citizenship and power shape personhood in Bosnia and Herzegovina*, New York: Bergahn.

Byford, Andy (2017) 'The Imperfect Child in Early Twentieth Century Russia', *History of Education* 46(5); 595 – 617.

Cerami, Alfio (2005) 'Social Policy in Central and Eastern Europe: the emergence of a new European model of solidarity?' Thesis, University of Erfurt, web: https://d-nb.info/974405647/34 (accessed 14 May 2018).

Cerami, Alfio and Paul Stubbs (2011) 'Post-Communist Welfare Capitalisms: bringing institutions and political agency back in', *EIZ Working Papers* EIZ-WP-1103, Zagreb: Institute of Economics, web: https://hrcak.srce.hr/index.php?show =clanak&id_clanak_jezik=111821 (accessed 10 April 2018).

Clarke, John (2004) *Changing Welfare, Changing States: new directions in social policy*, London: Sage.

Cocozzelli, Fred (2007) 'Kosovo', in Bob Deacon and Paul Stubbs (eds.) *Transnationalism and the making of social policy in South East Europe*, Cheltenham: Edward Elgar; 203 – 220.

Cook, Linda J. (1993) *The Soviet social contract and why it failed: Welfare policy and workers' politics from Brezhnev to Yeltsin*. Harvard University Press.

Cook, Linda J. & Martin K. Dimitrov (2017) The social contract revisited: evidence from communist and state capitalist economies. *Europe-Asia Studies*, 69:1, 8 – 26.

Cook, Linda and Mitchell Orenstein (1999) 'The Return of the Left and its Impact on the Welfare State in Russia, Poland and Hungary', in L. Cook, M. Orenstein and M. Rueschemeyer (eds.) *Left Parties and Social Policy in Postcommunist Europe*, Boulder: Westview; 47 – 108.

Cornia, Giovanni and Sandor Sipos (1991) *Children and the Transition to the Market Economy: safety nets and social policies in Central and Eastern Europe*, Florence: UNICEF, ICDC.

Cornia, Giovanni (1994) 'Overview' in UNICEF ICDC *Crisis in Mortality, Health and Nutrition*, Florence: UNICEF, ICDC Economies in Transition Studies, Regional Monitoring Report 2, web: https://www.unicef-irc.org/publications/pdf/monee2_eng.pdf (accessed 10 April 2018).

Cornia, Giovanni (1995) 'Overview' in UNICEF ICDC *Poverty, Children and Policy: responses for a brighter future*, Florence: UNICEF, ICDC Economies in Transition Studies, Regional Monitoring Report 3, web: https://www.unicef-irc.org/publications/pdf/monee3_eng.pdf (accessed 10 April 2018).

Deacon, Bob (1993) *Social Policy and Socialism: the struggle for socialist relations of welfare*, London: Pluto Press.

Deacon, Bob and Guy Standing (1993) 'Editorial Foreword: Social Policy in Central and Eastern Europe', *Journal of European Social Policy* 3(3); 159 – 161.

Deacon, Bob with Michelle Hulse and Paul Stubbs (1997) *Global Social Policy: international organizations and the future of welfare*, London: Sage.

Deacon, Bob and Paul Stubbs (2007) 'Transnationalism and the making of social policy in South East Europe', in Bob Deacon and Paul Stubbs (eds.) *Transnationalism and the making of social policy in South East Europe*, Cheltenham: Edward Elgar; 1 – 21.

Dobry, Michel (2000) 'Paths, Choices, Outcomes, and Uncertainty', in Michel Dobry (ed.) *Democratic and Capitalist Transitions in Eastern Europe: lessons for the social sciences*. Dordrecht: Kluwer; 49 – 70.

Eichhorst, Werner, Paul Marx and Caroline Wehner (2017) 'Labor Market Reforms in Europe: towards more flexicure labor markets?' *Journal for Labour Market Research* 51(3); 1 – 17, web: https://link.springer.com/content/pdf/10.1186%2Fs12651-017-0231-7.pdf (accessed 15 May 2018).

Esping-Andersen, Gosta (1990) *The Three Worlds of Welfare Capitalism*, Princeton: University Press.

Estrin, Saul (1994) 'The Inheritance', in Nicholas Barr (ed.) *Labor Markets and Social Policy in Central and Eastern Europe: the transition and beyond*, Oxford: University Press; 53 – 76.

Falkingham, Jane (1999) *Welfare in transition: Trends in poverty and well-being in Central Asia*. Centre for Analysis of Social Exclusion (CASE) paper CASE/20. London School of Economics, London. 54 pages.

Falkingham, Jane (2005) The end of the rollercoaster? Growth, inequality and poverty in Central Asia and the Caucasus. *Social Policy & Administration, 39*(4), 340 – 360.

Forrat, Natalia (2012) *The authoritarian welfare state: a marginalized concept.* Northwestern University Working Paper No. 12-005. Comparative-Historical Social Science (CHSS) Working Paper Series. Retrieved from http://buffett.northwestern.edu/documents/working-papers/CHSS-12-005-Forrat.pdf.

Franke, Anja, Gawrich, Andrea & Alakbarov, Gurban (2009) Kazakhstan and Azerbaijan as post-Soviet rentier states: Resource incomes and autocracy as a double 'curse' in post-Soviet regimes. *Europe-Asia Studies, 61*(1), 109 – 140.

Freyka, Tomas and Tomas Sobotka (2008) 'Fertility in Europe: diverse, delayed and below replacement', *Demographic Research* 19(3); 15 – 46.

Fukuyama, Francis (1992) *The End of History and the Last Man.* New York: Free Press.

Guardiancich, Igor (2004) 'Welfare State Retrenchment in Central and Eastern Europe: the case of pension reforms in Poland and Slovenia', *Managing Global Transitions* 2(1); 41 – 64.

Hann, Chris (ed.) (2002) *Postsocialism: ideals, ideologies and practices in Eurasia*, London: Routledge.

Hoffmann, Dražen et al. (2017) *Croatia's Captured Places: research report on the quality of local governance in Croatia*, Zagreb: GONG, web: https://www.researchgate.net/publication/319416737_CROATIA%27S_CAPTURED_PLACES_Research_report_Case_Studies_on_the_Quality_of_Local_Governance_in_Croatia (accessed 19 May 2018).

ISSC, IDS and UNESCO (2016) *World Social Science Report 2016, Challenging Inequalities: pathways to a just world*, Paris: UNESCO.

Ivanova, Vyara and George Bogdanov (2013) 'The Deinstitutionalization of Children in Bulgaria: the role of the EU', *Social Policy & Administration* 47(2); 199 – 217.

Jensen, Carsten. (2014) *The Right and the Welfare State*, Oxford: University Press.

Kornai, Janos (1997) 'Reforming the Welfare State in Postsocialist Societies', *World Development* 25(8); 1183 – 1186.

Lendvai, Noémi and David Bainton (2013) 'Translation: towards a critical comparative social policy agenda', in Patricia Kennett (ed.) *A Handbook of Comparative Social Policy*, Second edition, Cheltenham: Edward Elgar; 115 – 134.

Lendvai, Noémi and Paul Stubbs (2009) 'Assemblages, Translation, and Intermediaries in South East Europe: rethinking transnationalism and social policy', *European Societies* 11(5); 673 – 695.

Lendvai, Noémi and Paul Stubbs (2015) 'Europeanization, Welfare and Variegated Austerity Capitalisms—Hungary and Croatia', *Social Policy and Administration* 49(4); 445 – 465.

Lendvai, Noémi (2007) 'Europeanization of Social Policy? Prospects and challenges for South East Europe', in Bob Deacon and Paul Stubbs (eds.) *Social Policy and International Interventions in South East Europe*, Cheltenham: Edward Elgar; 22 – 44.

Lesay, Ivan (2006) *Pension Reform in Slovakia: the context of economic globalisation*, Brussels: ETUI-REHS.

Luong, Pauline Jones & Weinthal, Erika (2010) *Oil is not a curse: Ownership structure and institutions in Soviet successor states.* Cambridge University Press.

Maglajlić Holiček, Reima Ana and Ešref Kenan Rašidagić (2007) 'Bosnia and Herzegovina', in Bob Deacon and Paul Stubbs (eds.) *Transnationalism and the making of social policy in South East Europe*, Cheltenham: Edward Elgar; 149 – 166.

Maltseva, Elena (2008) *Policy implementation in post-Soviet states: A comparison of social benefits reform in Russia and Kazakhstan.* Paper presented at the 81 CPSA Annual Conference, Carleton University.

Matković, Gordana (2017) *The Welfare State in Western Balkan Countries: challenges and options*, Belgrade: Center for Social Policy, web: http://csp.org.rs/en/assets/publications/files/The_Welfare_State_in_Western_Balkan_Countries_Position_Paper.pdf (accessed 19 May 2018).

Milanović, Branko (1990) 'Poverty in Poland, Hungary, and Yugoslavia in the Years of Crisis, 1978 – 87', *Background Paper for the World Development Report WPS 507*, Washington: World Bank, web: http://documents.worldbank.org/curated/en/684501468750273473/pdf/multi0page.pdf (accessed 10 April 2018).

Mishra Ramesh (1981) Society and Social Policy. Theories and Practice of Welfare. 2nd ed. London Macmillan.

Mujanović, Jasmin (2018) *Hunger and Fury: the crisis of democracy in the Balkans*, London: Hurst.

Müller, Katarina (1999) 'Pension Reform Paths in Comparison: the case of Central-Eastern Europe', *Czech Sociological Review* 7(1); 51 – 66.

Müller, Katarina (2002) 'Between State and Market: Czech and Slovene pension reform in comparison', in Elaine Fultz (ed.) *Pension Reform in Central and Eastern Europe Volume 2*, Budapest: ILO.

Müller, Martin (2017) 'What About the Global East?' SSRN Paper, Web: https://ssrn.com/abstract=2881296 (accessed 22 March 2018).

Myant, Martin & Drahokoupil, Jan (2008) International integration and the structure of exports in Central Asian Republics. *Eurasian Geography and Economies*, 49(5), 604 – 622.

Myant, Martin & Drahokoupil, Jan (2010) *Varieties of capitalism in transition economies.* University of Mannheim—Mannheim Centre for European Social Research (MZES). Working Paper Series.

Myles, John & Quadagno, Jill (2002) Political theories of the welfare state. *Social Service Review*, 76(1), 34 – 57.

Novokmet, Filip (2017) 'Between Communism and Capitalism: essays on the evolution of income and wealth inequality in Eastern Europe 1890 – 2015', PhD thesis, *Ecole des Hautes Etudes en Sciences Sociales,* Paris, web: http://piketty.pse.ens.fr/files/Novokmet2017.pdf (accessed 17 June 2018).

Obradović, Nikolina (2016) 'War Veteran's Policy in Bosnia and Herzegovina', *Revija za socijalnu politiku* (Croatian J. of Social Policy) 24(1); 93 – 106, web: http://www.rsp.hr/ojs2/index.php/rsp/article/view/1367/1360 (accessed 19 May 2018).

O'Brien, Clare (2015) Introduction: Poverty and social justice in Central Asia. *The Journal of Poverty and Social Justice, 23* (2): 83 – 88.

OECD (2003) Labour Market and Social Policies in the Baltic Countries.

Orenstein, Mitchell (2011) 'Shock Therapy in Latin America, Russia and Eastern Europe, *Wilson Center, Global Europe Program*, no. 155, web: https://www.wilsoncenter.org/publication/155-shock-therapy-latin-america-russia-and-eastern-europe (accessed 23 March 2018).

Paas Tiiu, Marit Hinnosaar, Jaan Masso, Orsolya Szirko (2004) *Social protection systems in the Baltic states*. Tartu University Press, 2004

Pomfret, Richard (2010) *Constructing market-based economies in Central Asia: A natural experiment?* Keynote speech at the European Association for Comparative Economic Studies annual conference in Tartu (Estonia). *The European Journal of Comparative Economics, 7* (2), 449 – 467.

Pop, Luana (2013) 'The Decoupling of Social Policy Reforms in Romania', *Social Policy & Administration* 47(2); 161 – 181.

Ruminska-Zimny, Ewa (1997) *Human poverty in transition economies:* Regional overview for UNDP HDR 1997. Retrieved from http://hdr.undp.org/en/reports/global/hdr1997/papers/.

Shin, Hyun Bang, Loretta Less and Ernesto Lopez-Morales (2016) 'Introduction: locating gentrification in the Global East', *Urban Studies* 53(3); 455 – 470.

Sipos, Sandor (1994) 'Income Transfers: family support and poverty relief', in Nicholas Barr (ed.) *Labor Markets and Social Policy in Central and Eastern Europe: the transition and beyond*, Oxford: University Press; 226 – 259.

Solioz, Christophe and Paul Stubbs (2012) 'Regionalisms in South East Europe and Beyond', in Paul Stubbs and Christophe Solioz (eds.) *Towards Open Regionalism in South East Europe*, Baden-Baden: Nomos; 15 – 48.

Spivak, Gayatri Chakravorty (1988) 'Subaltern Studies: Deconstructing Historiography', in Ranajit Guha and Gayatri Chakravorty Spivak (eds.) *Selected Subaltern Studies*, New York: Oxford University Press; 3 – 32.

Standing, Guy (1996) 'Social Protection and Eastern Europe: a tale of slipping anchors and torn safety nets', in Gosta Esping-Andersen (ed.) *Welfare States in Transition: national adaptations in global economies*, London: Sage; 225 – 255.

Stubbs, Paul (2007) Community development in contemporary Croatia: Globalization, neoliberalism and NGO-isation. In L.Dominelli (Ed.), *Revitalising communities in a globalising world* (pp. 161 – 174). Aldershot: Ashgate.

Stubbs, Paul and Reima Ana Maglajlić (2012) 'Negotiating the Transnational Politics of Social Work in Post-Conflict and Transition Contexts: reflections from South-East Europe', *British Journal of Social Work* 42(6); 1174 – 1191.

Stubbs, Paul and Noémi Lendvai (2016) 'Re-assembling and Disciplining Social Europe: turbulent moments and fragile f(r)ictions', in Zlatan Krajina and Nebojša Blanuša (eds.) *EU, Europe Unfinished: mediating Europe and the Balkans in a Time of Crisis*, London: Rowman & Littlefield; 31 – 55.

Stubbs, Paul and Siniša Zrinščak (2009a) 'Rescaling emergent social policies in South East Europe', *Social Policy Review* 21; 285 – 307.

Stubbs, Paul and Siniša Zrinščak (2009b) 'Croatian Social Policy: the legacies of war, state-building and late Europeanisation', *Social Policy & Administration* 43(2); 121 – 135.

Stubbs, Paul and Siniša Zrinščak (2015) 'Citizenship and Social Welfare in Croatia: clientelism and the limits of 'Europeanisation'', *European Politics and Society* 16(3); 395 – 410.

Sušova-Salminen, Veronika (2012) 'Rethinking the Idea of Eastern Europe from Postcolonial Perspective: coloniality, Eurocentrism, border thing and Europe's Other', in Kari-Falt Alenius and K Olavi (eds.) *Vieraan Rajalla*, Rovaniemi: Societas Historica Finlandae Septentrionalis; 191 – 209, Web: https://www.academia.edu/28095985/Rethinking_the_Idea_of_Eastern_Europe_from_Postcolnial_Perspective_Coloniality_Eurocentrism_Border_Thinking_and_Europes_Other (accessed 22 March 2018).

Szikra, Dorrotya (2018) 'Welfare for the Wealthy: the social policy of the Orban regime, 2010 – 2017', *Analysis*, Budapest: Friedrich Ebert Stiftung, web: http://library.fes.de/pdf-files/bueros/budapest/14209.pdf (accessed 14 May 2018).

Thrift, Nigel (2005) *Knowing Capitalism*, London: Sage.

UNDP (2014) *Poverty, inequality, and vulnerability* in the transition and developing. economies of Europe and Central Asia. *UNDP* Regional Bureau for Europe and CIS. Retrieved from http://www.eurasia.undp.org/content/dam/rbec/docs/Poverty Inequality and Vulnerability.pdf.

UNICEF (1999) *After the Fall: the human impact of ten years of transition*, Florence: IRC, web: https://www.unicef-irc.org/publications/pdf/afterthefall.pdf (accessed 10 April 2018).

UNICEF (2001) *A Decade of Transition*, Florence: IRC.

Vanhuysse, Pieter (2014) 'Intergeneration Justice and Public Policy in Europe', *European Social Observatory Opinion Paper* No. 16, web: https://papers.ssrn.com/sol3/papers.cfm?abstract_id=2416916 (accessed 15 May 2018).

Verdery, Katherine (1996) *What Was Socialism and What Comes Next?*, Princeton: University Press.

Wilensky, Harold L. (1975) *The welfare state and equality. Structural and ideological roots of public expenditures*. University of California Press. Berkley and Los Angeles, California.

World Bank (2004) *Kazakhstan. Dimensions of poverty in Kazakhstan*. (In two volumes). Volume I: Policy Briefing. Poverty Reduction and Economic Management Unit. Europe and Central Asia Region. (Report No. 30294-KZ).

PART TWO:
POVERTY AND INEQUALITY:
From Theory to Everyday Life

CHAPTER 2:
POVERTY REDUCTION THROUGH SOCIAL PROTECTION AND LABOR POLICIES IN THE FORMER SOVIET UNION

Esuna Dugarova

INTRODUCTION

The chapter aims to analyze the role of social protection and active labor market policies (ALMPs) in reducing poverty in five former Soviet Union (FSU) countries—Russia, Belarus, Kazakhstan, Kyrgyzstan and Uzbekistan. The focus on these countries is explained by the fact that over the past decade they introduced a range of ALMPs aiming at promoting productive employment and addressing poverty more effectively. With variation in scope, tools and outcomes, these measures have become a social policy priority in the national settings under examination.

The structure of the chapter is as follows. Section 2 provides a brief profile of poverty and unemployment in the countries in question. Section 3 introduces a conceptual framework within which different types of ALMPs are distinguished. Sections 4 and 5 review major ongoing social protection and labor market programs in these contexts, respectively. The implications of these programs for poverty reduction are discussed in section 6, with some suggestions for moving forward.

POVERTY AND UNEMPLOYMENT TRENDS IN THE FSU COUNTRIES

Following the collapse of the Soviet economy, the centralized social protection system in the countries under examination was broken. The Soviet universalist principle of providing social support to the population at large had been largely replaced in favor of means-tested assistance targeting the most needy groups in the Central Asian republics and more recently in Russia and Belarus. Responsibility for supporting these people shifted away from the state to families themselves who had to rely on mutual assistance by intensifying intergenerational transfers (Dugarova, 2016a).

Drastic changes in the economy and social protection in the 1990s resulted in sharp increases in poverty, deeply affecting the living conditions of the populations in these settings. In the 2000s, however, due to economic growth and investments in the social sphere, poverty was decreasing steadily in the five countries, albeit at a different pace (figure 1).[1]

Figure 1   Poverty rate in selected former Soviet Union countries, 1992 – 2016, %

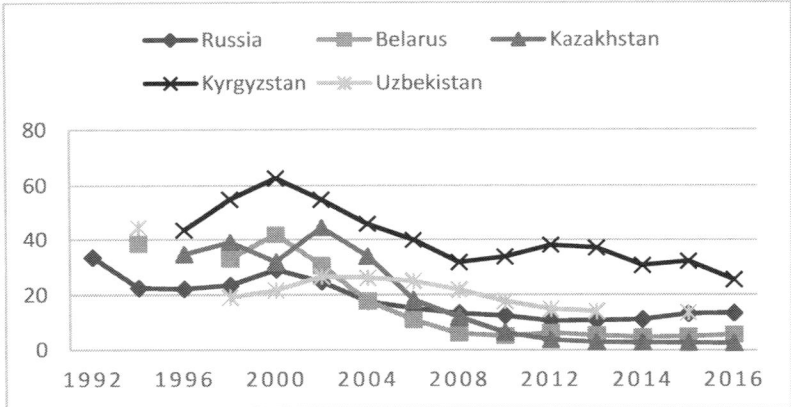

Source: Federal State Statistics Service of the Russian Federation; National Statistical Committee of the Republic of Belarus; Committee on Statistics, Ministry of National Economy of the Republic of Kazakhstan; National Statistical Committee of the Kyrgyz Republic; State Committee of the Republic of Uzbekistan on Statistics.

The formation of the labor force in the selected FSU countries takes place in the context of an increasing number of older people and shrinking working-age populations.[2] These trends will have significant implications not only for the supply of the workforce but also for the provision of services and resources to support the ageing populations (Dugarova et al., 2017).

Since the late 1990s up until 2014, the unemployment rate was falling in Russia and Kazakhstan, while in Belarus, Kyrgyzstan and Uzbekistan, it remained relatively stable throughout the transition period (figure 2).

---

[1] The national data on poverty should be treated and compared with caution due to different definitions of poverty, its measurements and methodology, as well as population coverage in these countries. Unless indicated otherwise, all data provided are obtained from official government websites.

[2] https://esa.un.org/unpd/wpp/Download/Standard/Population/ accessed 30 January 2018.

Figure 2   Unemployment rate in selected former Soviet Union countries, 1991 – 2016, %

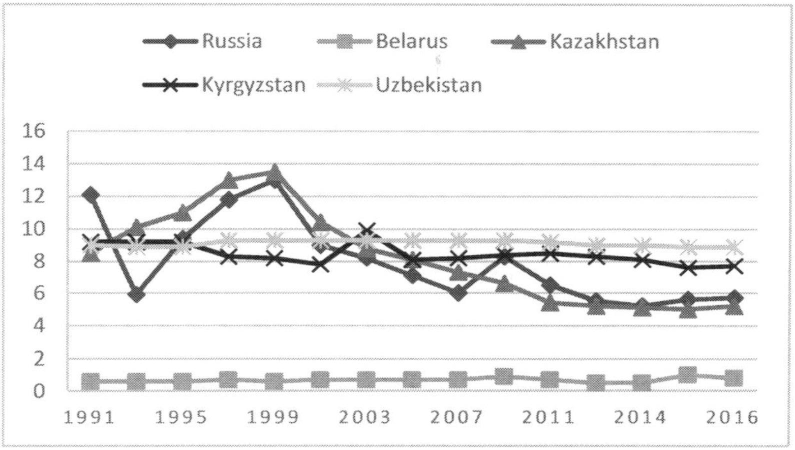

Source: ILO STAT

In recent years, due to the economic downturn there has been a reversal or slowdown in the poverty reduction trend in the region. Amid budgetary constraints, respective governments enhanced targeted support to selected groups while preserving basic social guarantees. To address poverty more effectively, the countries under examination adopted a new approach to social protection by introducing a range of programs that promote the activation of citizens' labor potential and the development of their economic self-reliance (Dugarova 2016a, b).

CONCEPTUAL FRAMEWORK

Social protection has emerged as an important strategy to protect people from livelihood risks and reduce vulnerabilities, while developing human capital and encouraging economic growth (ILO, 2012; UNDP, 2016). It has been recognized by the 2030 Agenda for Sustainable Development as a key tool in ending poverty.

Providing decent employment is the basis of social protection and is often seen as an important condition for reducing poverty and a main way to improving the quality of life (ILO, 2012). In practice, productive employment is promoted through ALMPs which are used to increase employment opportunities of jobseekers and improve the earnings capacity of workers. While ALMPs are not aimed at reducing poverty directly, they can contribute to reducing unemployment and hence decrease the risk of poverty by helping jobless people find paid work.

Bonoli (2010) provides a nuanced categorization of ALMPs and identifies four types. The first type—incentive reinforcement—refers to strengthening (positive and negative) work incentives for beneficiaries through, for example, making benefits conditional on participation in work schemes (positive) or through the use of sanctions (negative). The second type is employment assistance, which is aimed at removing obstacles to labor market participation. Relevant measures here include placement services, job search services (in particular labor market information which is usually collected in job banks), job counselling and coaching, job subsidies and, in some cases, help in finding (and paying for) suitable day care services for parents. These interventions allow beneficiaries to put their human capital to good use, although improvements in the human capital of beneficiaries can be modest, mostly in terms of shaping better soft skills. The third form—occupation—includes measures such as job creation and work experience programs to keep jobless people active and to prevent the depletion of human capital. These measures are generally aimed at increasing demand for labor. The fourth form—human capital investment—is about upskilling, which includes vocational training for jobless people. The idea here is to offer a chance to people—who were not able to profit from the training system or whose skills have become obsolete—in order to ultimately increase labor supply. Bonoli's (2010) analysis of ALMPs is based on government expenditure on relevant programs such as public employment services, employment subsidies, job rotation schemes, start-up incentives, training, and direct job creation.

The post-Soviet countries in the current study adopt different types of ALMPs, and the databases of governments or international organizations do not provide detailed and comprehensive information on expenditure data on various types of labor market policies and programs. Nonetheless, Bonoli's (2010) framework serves as a useful tool to understand the nature of ALMPs and analyze how they work in the countries under consideration.

THE SOCIAL PROTECTION SYSTEM IN THE FSU COUNTRIES

The social protection system has undergone considerable evolution in the FSU countries during the transition period. While all these countries reformed their social protection systems, some have remained with the initial mix of policies or redesigned specific programs, whereas others reformed the whole system or experimented with different schemes. Kyrgyzstan, for example, introduced a guaranteed minimum income whose value has been gradually increasing, rising from KGS 310 in 2010 to KGS 900 per month in 2016, but still falling well below the poverty line (which amounted to KGS 2,595 in 2016). Uzbekistan revitalized and strengthened the traditional *mahalla* system, which provides decentralized benefit-targeting using local communities as a main vehicle of social assistance to the poorest groups (Alam and Banerji, 1999). While Kazakhstan advanced substantially with pension reforms, with private pension funds accounting for nearly 45 percent of all contributions, public social assistance transfers have been generally low and poorly targeted (ibid.).

The provision of universal welfare, full employment with work being both a right and an obligation, and a comprehensive range of benefits were an essential part of the Soviet social contract. Following the collapse of the Soviet economy, government support in the five countries was severely cut back and the national welfare systems were reorganized involving the decentralization of health and education, introduction of privatization and insurance mechanisms, and elimination of subsidy programs. In contrast to the Central Asian republics which introduced targeting in the early transition period, in Russia and Belarus the structure of the universalist system remained, and despite cuts to many benefits and in some cases means testing, all existing guarantees were initially preserved (Cook, 2007). Recently, however, there has been a gradual and steady move towards targeted assistance to selected vulnerable groups rather than society at large in both countries.[3] Among priority groups for social assistance in the region are large families and children, people with disabilities and the elderly.

The social protection system in the FSU countries has traditionally consisted of social insurance, social assistance and social services. Over the past decade, there has been a shift in the relationship between the

---

3   In Russia, for example, the government reaffirmed its approach to social provision based on targeting and means testing in the Federal Law 388 in 2015, despite the fact that the principle of universalism is embedded in the national constitution.

state and society in these countries (Dugarova, 2016a), which entails a move from 'helping those in need' (a passive mode) to 'helping those in need if they are willing to undertake active steps to overcome poverty' (an active mode). In line with this approach, one of the major social protection programs that is currently implemented in Russia is 'Social support of citizens' (2013 – 2020). Participants are provided with lump sum cash payments (amounting to RUB 36,800 on average in 2016) to increase their income. The support is provided on the basis of a social contract, which entails assisted job search, participation in public works, vocational training, self-employment and other activities that can help participants to overcome 'a difficult life situation'. As part of the program, 65,400 social contracts were signed in 2016, covering 230,700 people. As a result, in 2016 the average *per capita* income of participating families increased by an estimated 1.4 times, and 46.7 percent of these families are claimed to have improved their living standards. While this kind of social protection mechanism has provided an opportunity to improve the living conditions of many low-income families in Russia, it has not been effective in eradicating poverty and making families self-sufficient. Most of the activities are oriented towards supporting families through a difficult life period through the provision of domestic services, food, medical treatment and leisure rather than developing their economic activity. Furthermore, in some regions, the payment hardly corresponds to the level of the subsistence minimum, whereas many targeted families have unemployed members such as children and the elderly who require care, and this constrains women's participation in the labor market due to limited state care services (Prokofieva et al., 2014).

To increase the competitiveness of the economy and improve the living conditions of the vulnerable population, the Belarusian government strengthened the targeted system of social protection through the 2012 Presidential Decree 'On state targeted social assistance' intended for low-income groups. In 2016, 290,400 people were covered by social assistance, which is nearly half of the total low-income population, with the main beneficiaries being large and single-parent families. In view of the country's sparse population, the social protection of families in Russia and Belarus are aimed at encouraging childbirth and reducing the costs of children. A notable example is the Maternal Capital program in Russia (2007 – 2018) and the Family Capital program in Belarus (2015 – 2019). Both programs provide a non-cash allowance to large families with children, regardless of the family's income status, which can be used for improvement of housing conditions, children's education or as a contribution to a mother's pension. In 2017, the value of the benefit constituted RUB 453,000 in Russia and USD 10,000 in Belarus. During the period of 2007–2017, over 8 million families in Russia received the benefit, the vast majority of which were used for housing.

Since 2002, Kazakhstan has been carrying out the Targeted Social Assistance (TSA) program, the country's key anti-poverty program focused on citizens with incomes below the poverty line. As poverty has been declining steadily since the early 2000s, so has the number of recipients of the TSA. Over the past decade, the number of TSA beneficiaries decreased by 95 percent, from 516,900 persons in 2005 to 28,500 in December 2016. The government of Kyrgyzstan has also undertaken measures to support the most vulnerable categories of the population by implementing the 'Program on development of the social protection system of the population in the Kyrgyz Republic for 2015 – 2017.' The number of recipients of state benefits has been decreasing steadily, falling from 510,600 in 2005 to 360,200 in 2017. In view of the poverty reduction trend in recent years in the country, this can point to the decreasing number of people in need of social assistance. At the same time, it can be the result of enhanced targeting of benefits implemented by the government as part of the program. Within the framework of the state program 'The year of the healthy mother and a child,' the year of 2016 in Uzbekistan was focused on the support of families, mothers and children through the provision of social benefits, improving health services and overall living conditions of low-income beneficiaries. In 2016, nearly UZS 7.5 trillion were allocated to the implementation of the program, which tripled the amount of expenditure on the 2015 program under 'The year of attention and care about the older generation' aimed at enhancing the social protection of senior citizens.

It is certain that the social protection programs in question contributed to poverty reduction in the respective countries. However, they covered only a limited proportion of the population and had little sustained impact on poverty levels. One of the key factors that can explain poor outcomes is the low government spending on social protection programs. Russia, for instance, spent 12.1 percent of GDP on social protection in 2015, Belarus 13.6 percent in 2016, Kazakhstan 3.2 percent in 2015, Kyrgyzstan 5.8 percent in 2015, and Uzbekistan 12.8 percent in 2015.[4] Another factor

---

[4] The expenditure data on social protection should be treated with caution, as countries adopt different definitions and measurements of social protection. While

in the poor results is the low monetary value of benefits compared to the income deficit of beneficiaries. A monthly childcare allowance, for example, in Belarus, Russia and Kazakhstan constitutes around 40 percent of the average wage of a child carer (who is primarily a mother). In Kyrgyzstan, while the size of monthly benefits for low-income families has been steadily increasing, amounting to KGS 870 in 2016, its value is barely half of the extreme poverty line. Furthermore, the flawed design and administration of programs result in their insufficient effectiveness due to a substantial leakage of funds and a large exclusion of the targeted population (UNDP 2016). Nonetheless, without social assistance the situation would be even worse with higher poverty rates. Despite their low generosity, social assistance transfers remain essential for poor families, as they can counter the uncertainty associated with earnings and compensate for costs, including those of childcare. In Belarus and Kyrgyzstan, for example, cash transfers accounted for 24.2 percent and 16.5 percent, respectively, in the structure of disposable income of the population in 2016, thus constituting an important source of people's livelihoods.

LABOR ACTIVATION IN THE FSU COUNTRIES

While the state in the FSU countries provided certain job security guarantees to its citizens since the early years of transition which included free vocational (re-)training, paid public works, assistance with job search and free evening schools for workers, their scope remained limited, and it was not until the late 2000s – early 2010s that these countries started to adopt ALMPs. Such an approach is aimed at activating people's labor potential and developing their economic self-reliance in order to improve their living standards and ultimately reduce poverty.

Russia

The Russian government launched the 'Promotion of population's employment' program (2013 – 2020) targeted at young people, unemployed citizens, as well as those at risk of dismissal. With a total estimated budget of RUB 579 billion, the program is aimed at developing

---

exact figures may vary, the scale of spending on social protection by the governments is clear. It should also be noted that all the data presented are obtained from official government websites unless indicated otherwise.

an effective labor market. The key services provided include vocational training and further professional education, paid public works, promotion of self-employment, temporary employment for young people, professional orientation, job subsidies, and assistance with relocation of unemployed citizens and their families to another area to obtain employment. In addition, the government provides financial assistance including unemployment benefits, stipends during (re-)training, and pensions until retirement age.

In 2016, state employment services received a total of 4 million applications from citizens seeking assistance in job search, of which 64.4 percent found employment. The same year 164,500 unemployed people underwent vocational (re-)training or upgraded their qualifications; 83,100 people, or 2.9 percent of the total number of registered unemployed, received assistance in self-employment; and nearly 328,000 contracts for temporary employment were issued, of which 86 percent were paid public works.

To increase the labor productivity of the population and that of women in particular, the Russian government increased the availability of preschool institutions, enhanced flexible forms of employment, and vocational training for women during their childcare leave. In 2016, 18,500 women on childcare leave completed vocational training, upgraded their qualifications or received support on professional orientation.

Despite these positive results, there are still a large number of people who were not able to find a job. Since 2014 the unemployment rate has been growing, reaching 5.7 percent in 2016, which amounts to around 4.3 million people. At the same time, real wages have been falling over the past three years. While professional (re-)training is an important source of replenishment of human capital in Russia, it tends to be selective, oriented towards skilled workers in large enterprises, higher education holders and young people. Yet those who are in greatest need of (re-)training are often not able to access it. Low technological level of production and weak competition reduce incentives for investing in (re-)training. As a result, the overall level of human capital is below optimal (Gimpelson et al., 2017). These trends in the Russian labor market have taken place amid a decline in the GDP growth rate, which has led to a slowdown in the growth of labor productivity.

Belarus

Within the labor activation approach, Belarus has implemented the 'State program on social protection and the promotion of population's employment for 2016 – 2020.' With an estimated budget of BYR 23.9 billion, it is designed to stimulate economic activity, improve the competitiveness of the unemployed, and reduce the imbalance between labor demand and supply. Similar to Russia, this is addressed through professional (re-)training, paid public works, provision of temporary jobs (notably to young people), assistance with self-employment, and relocation of the unemployed to a new place of residence and employment. During the period of job search or training, unemployed citizens are provided with financial support. The program also involves professional (re-)training for women (and men) on childcare leave and provides pregnancy and childbirth allowances. In 2016, 239,000 people applied for assistance with job search were registered as unemployed, of whom 67 percent found employment. An important element of state measures in the labor market is support for entrepreneurial initiatives. Since 2011 over 12,000 unemployed people received government support in the form of subsidies for business activities, agro-ecotourism, and crafts.

Belarus is the only country in the post-Soviet space which introduced a tax on 'parasitism' through the 2015 Presidential Decree 'On prevention of social dependency' aimed at reducing hidden unemployment and illegal labor activities, and stimulating active job search among citizens. According to the decree, citizens who have been unemployed for 183 days in a calendar year must pay a tax of 20 basic units where one unit amounts to BYR 210,000. Tax-exempt are people with disabilities, minors and seniors, as well as parent(s) with a child under the age of seven (only if the child is not attending a preschool), a disabled child under 18, or three or more small children. Non-payment of the tax is penalized with a fine or community service. The government estimates that around 400,000 people, or 7 percent of the total labor force, can be considered 'parasites'—that is people who do not have official income, are not registered as unemployed, not self-employed, not on maternity or childcare leave, and not in education. While the government justified this measure by the growing number of people in the grey economy (that takes place amid an economic downturn in the country and the increase of insurance contribution rates), the decree received various criticisms from local experts and NGOs who argue that it undermines the constitutional rights and freedoms of citizens and see it as state intervention in private life. This measure officially serves to reduce the scale of 'social dependency' and address unregistered employment; in practice it can be seen as a way to replenish the state treasury in view of increasing budget pressure, instead of providing the population with quality jobs and decent salaries.

Kazakhstan

In 2011, Kazakhstan adopted the 'Employment Roadmap 2020,' which is arguably the first large-scale national employment program in Kazakhstan aimed at improving people's incomes through sustainable and productive employment, particularly among low-income citizens, unemployed women with children and young people in rural areas. In line with the state objective to develop economic self-reliance among citizens, the key focus of the program is the creation of jobs through the promotion of self-employment and entrepreneurial activities and, where necessary, assistance in relocation to more economically active regions. The program also helps graduates obtain relevant work experience through internships up to six months in companies, which are paid by the government in the form of subsidies. During 2011 – 2016, about 800,000 people participated in the program, of whom 76 percent obtained permanent jobs, 6 percent received microcredits, and 20 percent underwent training. Of those young people who underwent an internship, 60 percent obtained employment after its completion. In 2016, the government replaced the 'Employment Roadmap 2020' with the 'Program for the Development of Productive Employment and Mass Entrepreneurship (2017 – 2021)' which enhances measures to ensure employment with further emphasis on entrepreneurship. These include the provision of professional education and training in line with labor market needs; financial support of entrepreneurial projects and teaching entrepreneurial skills; assistance in finding employment through professional orientation, public works, job subsidies, and internships for young people. In 2017, the estimated state expenditure on the program was KZT 40.3 billion. The state has played a key role in generating jobs (mainly in the public sector) by accounting for 20 percent of the increase in employment in 2010 – 2015.

Despite the positive developments, the labor market as a whole remains unstable and unequal in Kazakhstan. Four key factors account for this. The first one is the poor quality of labor resources. For instance, the share of the labor force with higher education was only 37 percent in 2015. The second factor is unproductive employment. Of the self-employed—who constituted 2.2 million people in 2015—16 percent were unproductively employed, with the majority engaged in low-productivity agricultural activities with poor incomes. A third problem is related to regional and demographic imbalances. The southern part of the country is more densely populated and has a larger share of working-age population compared to the northern one, which reflects the unequal distribution of labor resources. Lastly, generation of jobs in the economy is not sufficient. The main sector that generated jobs and contributed to economic growth in 2010 – 2015 was the service sector. In particular, trade contributed almost a third of the total economic growth during this period, another 15 percent was provided by transport services, and 13 percent by information and communication. The production of goods, however, contributed only 17 percent to the growth of the economy and is gradually decreasing.

Kyrgyzstan

A distinctive feature of Kyrgyzstan's labor market is the mass outmigration of its workers triggered by the lack of adequate job and income opportunities and low living standards in the country. An estimated 350,000 to 500,000 Kyrgyz citizens carry out labor activities abroad throughout the year, with primary destinations in the region being Russia and Kazakhstan. In contrast to other FSU countries under consideration, remittances from external labor migration constitute an important source of income for families in Kyrgyzstan reaching up to 18 percent of disposable income in some parts of the country, with the volume of these transfers increasing from 0.2 percent of GDP in 2000 to 30.1 percent of GDP in 2016.

In 2013, Kyrgyzstan introduced the 'Program to promote population's employment and regulate internal and external labor migration until 2020,' which includes (re-)training programs that teach skills and professions to meet demands in the labor market, temporary employment through paid public works, the provision of microcredits to support small and medium-sized enterprises, business incubators, and job search assistance.

Despite these measures, the results are quite poor. While the official unemployment rate in the country stood at 7.7 percent in 2016, some analysts estimate that in reality it reaches up to 30 percent (Fakhrieva 2017). In 2015, the total number of unemployed people amounted to 192,200 people (that is, 7.6 percent of total labor force), with only 50,700 people, or 26.4 percent, having found employment. One of the key problems in Kyrgyzstan's labor market is its labor surplus. In recent years, for example, the growth of the working-age population exceeded the growth of employment by more than two-fold, while labor supply exceeded demand by nearly 30 percent. Thus, it appears that a large number of unemployed are competing for a very limited number of jobs, many of which are low-paid and low-skilled. Although the number of unemployed per one vacancy constitutes on average 14 people, there are around 15 percent of unfilled vacancies every month. This indicates that despite excess supply in the labor market, the jobs offered remain unattractive to jobseekers. The situation is further exacerbated by widespread informal and part-time employment. The share of the employed in the informal sector as a percentage of the total employed population amounted to 71.7 percent in 2015.

In the context of the demand-deficient labor market, the Kyrgyz economy faces a big challenge of creating the necessary number of quality and well-paid jobs. In fact, while productivity growth is mainly driven by the small formal sector, job creation in Kyrgyzstan has primarily occurred in the large informal economy (Schwegler-Rohmeis et al., 2013). As the Kyrgyz population is projected to increase further, low wages and lack of decent jobs will continue to cause external labor migration. Seeing labor migration as a form of employment, the government of Kyrgyzstan integrated it into its state policy to make use of global employment through expanding employment opportunities for Kyrgyz citizens in domestic and international labor markets. However, as international markets, both in the FSU and beyond, experience economic downturn and uncertainty, incomes from external labor migration will likely fall as a result, thus affecting the living standards of the population back in the home country. Furthermore, while Kyrgyzstan has relatively high labor force participation rates, it also has some of the largest shares of working poor, migratory and vulnerable employment in the region, which raises concerns about the quality and quantity of employment opportunities (UNDP, 2016).

Uzbekistan

Similar to Kyrgyzstan, Uzbekistan saw a rapid growth of the working-age population which determined the growth of its labor force and thus increased the demand for new jobs. In particular, the labor market in Uzbekistan features a significant proportion of young people, with half a million graduates every year in need of employment. Since 2009, the government of Uzbekistan has consistently implemented the 'Program on job creation and employment provision,' particularly for vulnerable groups including youth and those living in rural areas. In 2017, the program was focused on creating 345,300 new jobs; supporting entrepreneurship through loans from commercial banks; providing seasonal and temporary jobs, as well as paid public works; and promoting self-employment particularly among women, people with disabilities and returning labor migrants. Special attention has been given to the employment of graduates who account for over 500,000 people. In line with this, in 2018 the government introduced the program 'The year of support of active entrepreneurship, innovative ideas and technologies' with a view to improving living standards through creating new jobs by entrepreneurs. The new elements of this program include exempting relevant enterprises from all types of taxes and allowing people to work in any region of the country regardless of their residency status.

In 2016, around 726,000 people obtained employment, of whom 60 percent were graduates. Furthermore, as a result of the government's emphasis on the development of small businesses, farming enterprises and various forms of home-based work, nearly 350,000 people were provided with relevant jobs in 2015. In particular, entrepreneurial activities—seen as a driver of Uzbekistan's economic growth—produced over 300,000 jobs, accounting for 78 percent of total employment in 2015 and thus contributing a major part to the country's regional development. In 2016, the amount of credits allocated to support small businesses alone amounted to UZS 15.9 trillion. Furthermore, as part of growing private entrepreneurship, in recent years there has been a rapid development of home-based work, including crafts and family businesses. This is viewed as particularly suitable for women as it allows them to earn an income and provides protection under labor law, while enabling them to fulfil their domestic and childcare duties. In 2015, home-based work contributed to the employment of more than 200,000 people, the majority of whom were women.

Despite steady and substantial employment generation, the labor market in Uzbekistan is characterized by several weaknesses. The level of unemployment in Uzbekistan remains higher than in other FSU countries under examination. In its efforts to create jobs 'at any cost,' the government of Uzbekistan has not paid due attention to their stability. A large part of these jobs is generated in financially unstable sectors such as agriculture and textiles, which does not allow the self-financing of new jobs (CER, 2013). In 2014, for example, the number of people engaged in irregular employment amounted to 4.4 million people, which included temporary jobs and unregistered businesses, while only 55 percent of 780,000 jobs created in 2014 had a fixed (stable) contract. Furthermore, the number of new jobs is not sufficient to absorb the annual increase of the working-age population. In fact, the level of the employed population relative to the working-age population has been decreasing gradually over the past two decades, falling from 82 percent in 1991 to 67 percent in 2011 (CER, 2013). Finally, while home-based work has provided income opportunities for many women, it has not addressed the structural causes of women's lower economic activity and competitiveness.

DISCUSSION AND CONCLUSIONS

While social protection and labor activation programs implemented by the respective governments have contributed to improving living conditions of the population, poverty is still widespread in these countries, especially among large families with children, young people, as well as those living in rural areas, who remain at the highest risk of poverty. In Russia, for example, the number of people with income below the subsistence minimum constituted 19.8 million in 2016, an increase from 15.4 million, or 28.6 percent, in 2012. In Kyrgyzstan, over 67 percent of the total low-income population resided in rural areas in 2015.

While unemployment is an important cause of poverty, it is not the most critical one. In fact, the majority of those living below the poverty line in the region are employed. In Russia, for example, 61.2 percent of the low-income population was employed in 2016. In essence, three major problems can be identified with regard to the nature of employment in the FSU countries amid governments' efforts to generate jobs. Firstly, many of these jobs are low paid, which is not sufficient or effective in providing adequate support to vulnerable families and lift them out of poverty. The low pay could be attributed to the redundancy of jobs and / or to the low value of minimum wages in relative terms. In Russia, for example, the minimum wage accounts for about 20 percent of the average wage (RUB 7500 vs. 36750 in 2016), and nearly 5 million people received a salary below the minimum wage in 2017. Together with weak enforcement, this implies that minimum wages are unlikely to be binding, which allows companies to maintain low-paid jobs and thus contribute to wage dispersion (World Bank, 2005).

At the same time, financial assistance does not compensate for low earnings and is not enough to help the unemployed in the FSU countries. While passive labor market measures such as unemployment benefits can be an important instrument to support those without income, their level is inadequate. In Russia, for example, the minimum size of unemployment benefits amounted to RUB 850 and the maximum size to RUB 4,900 in 2016 (without increase since 2009). The low value of unemployment benefits provides little incentive for the unemployed to register, which can explain the relatively low official unemployment rate in these countries.[5] The coverage of the unemployed is also limited, accounting for only 1.7 percent in Kyrgyzstan and 5.8 percent in Kazakhstan (ILO World Social Protection Database).

Moreover, women in these countries tend to be more vulnerable to poverty than men due to lower participation in the labor market, gender wage gap (which in Russia and Kazakhstan, for example, amounts to around 30 percent), higher unemployment (notably in Kazakhstan and Kyrgyzstan), and continuous burden of unpaid domestic and care work particularly in rural areas. In addition, the shortage of preschools undermines women's participation in the labor market and can result in

---

5   The official unemployment rate may not necessarily reflect the real extent of unemployment. A large number of people can be engaged in shadow and illegal employment. In Russia, for example, an estimated 18 million of economically active people were working illegally in 2015.

significant losses of welfare and increase the risk of poverty (Dugarova, 2016a).

Another issue with jobs that contributes to persistent poverty in the region is their low quality and low productivity. In Central Asia, the rural economy is still quite large, and a significant proportion of the working population is employed in the informal sector concentrated in agriculture. In Kyrgyzstan, for example, around 70 percent of the active labor force is employed informally (Gassmann and Trindade, 2016). In Russia, 13.5 million people, or 18.5 percent of the total number of employed, were estimated to be engaged in the informal sector in 2015. In fact, Russia has one of the highest rates in the number of average annual hours worked per worker in Europe (amounting to 1974 hours in 2016),[6] but labor productivity is almost half the European average, which can primarily be attributed to inefficient production and the use of outdated technology amid the lack of qualified personnel and limited funding.

From this it follows that activation of labor potential alone is unlikely to raise people out of poverty, while stimulating labor demand without paying due attention to the nature of jobs is insufficient to address the needs of vulnerable groups. Amid the economic downturn and deteriorating living standards in the region, labor market policies should aim not only to protect existing jobs or generate new ones, but more importantly they should support incomes which would allow workers to maintain their earning ability and ensure a decent quality of life.

To address poverty and unemployment in these countries more effectively, it is important to strengthen policy linkages between social protection and labor market policies. From the labor market perspective, this foremost involves ameliorating the quality of jobs, which implies adequate income, security in the workplace, and social protection for workers and their families. It also includes improving employment programs through better coordination between professional (re-) training and the demands of the economy and labor market, and developing better gender-sensitive policies such as flexible forms of employment, paid paternity leaves, and promotion of shared responsibility within the family. From the social protection point of view, more efforts are needed to expand the coverage of social assistance especially for vulnerable groups, and increase the level of social benefits,

---

6   https://stats.oecd.org/Index.aspx?DataSetCode=ANHRS accessed 30 January 2018.

including unemployment benefits. In addition, it is essential to scale up care service provision by improving access and quality of social services for children and the elderly, especially in view of the growing ageing populations in all these FSU countries. Finally, to increase effectiveness of both labor market and social protection interventions, it is vital to allocate more fiscal resources, which should be seen as an investment into human capital and economic development.

In the context of ongoing economic uncertainty at the national, regional and global levels (Dugarova and Gulasan, 2017), it is particularly important to ensure that the negative effects of the economic downturn would not have a persistent impact on people's livelihoods. All these measures should therefore be treated as part of a comprehensive social protection system, which plays a critical role in reducing poverty, protecting the population against existing risks and improving the quality of life.

In view of the active labor market programs implemented by Russia, Belarus, Kazakhstan, Kyrgyzstan and Uzbekistan, the model in these countries under Bonoli's (2010) typology of ALMPs, can be considered hybrid. Russia, Belarus and Kyrgyzstan focus on human capital development through (re-)training and skill upgrading, and on employment assistance such as job subsidies in Russia and microcredits in Kyrgyzstan. Belarus is the only country here that uses sanctions as negative incentives to make people work. All these labor market measures seem to be primarily oriented towards increasing labor supply and improving the quality of workforce, while adapting it to existing jobs. Instead, the countries could consider focusing on increasing demand for labor. This can be done through the creation of good quality jobs within the productive sectors of the economy that could ultimately improve labor productivity. Somewhat in contrast to Russia, Belarus and Kyrgyzstan, the main element of the labor market model of Kazakhstan and Uzbekistan is occupation. It places emphasis on creating jobs and supporting entrepreneurship, while aiming to increase labor demand in order to accommodate a relatively large share of young populations. The promotion of entrepreneurship and self-employment, however, may not constitute a sustainable solution to problems in the labor market amid economic slowdown. In all these national settings, it is crucial to ensure that everybody, regardless of their work situation, age, location or income level, has access to basic income security and essential goods and services to which they are entitled.

REFERENCES

Alam, Asad and Arup Banerji (1999) *Uzbekistan and Kazakhstan: a tale of two transition paths?* (Washington, DC: World Bank).

Bonoli, Giuliano (2010) "The Political Economy of Active Labor-Market Policy" in *Politics & Society* 38(4).

CER (Center for Economic Research) (2013) *Employment in Uzbekistan: Challenges and Prospects* (Tashkent: CER).

Cook, Linda (2007) *Postcommunist Welfare States: Reform Politics in Russia and Eastern Europe* (Ithaca, NY: Cornell University Press).

Dugarova, Esuna (2016a) *The Family in a New Social Contract: The Case of Russia, Kazakhstan and Mongolia* UNRISD Research Paper (Geneva: UNRISD).

Dugarova, Esuna (2016b) "Implementing SDG 1: poverty eradication through family support policies and social protection measures in transition countries". Paper prepared for Expert Group Meeting "Family policies and the 2030 Agenda" (New York: United Nations).

<http://www.un.org/esa/socdev/family/docs/egm16/EsunaDugarova.pdf> accessed 30 January 2018.

Dugarova, Esuna et al. (2017) *Ageing, Older Persons and the 2030 Agenda for Sustainable Development* Issues Brief (New York: United Nations, HelpAge International and AARP).

Dugarova, Esuna and Nergis Gulasan (2017) *Global Trends: Challenges and Opportunities in the Implementation of the Sustainable Development Goals* (New York and Geneva: UNDP and UNRISD).

Fakhrieva, Natalia (2017) *Public policy in the employment sphere of the Kyrgyz Republic* (in Russian) Vestnik KRSU 17(2)

Gassmann, Franziska and Lorena Trindade (2016) *The effect of means-tested social transfers on labour supply: heads versus spouses. An empirical analysis of work disincentives in the Kyrgyz Republic* UNU-MERIT Working Paper 2016–030.

Gimpelson, Vladimir, Rostislav Kapelyushnikov, and Sergei Roschin (eds.) (2017) *The Russian Labour Market: Trends, Institutions, Structural Changes* (in Russian) (Moscow: National Research University Higher School of Economics).

ILO (International Labour Organization) (2012) *Social security for all: building social protection floors and comprehensive social security systems* (Geneva: ILO).

Prokofieva, Lidia, Irina Korchagina, Anna Mironova, and Ekaterina Tarnovskaya (2014) "The Social Contract as a Mechanism of Overcoming Poverty in Russia" *Journal of Social Policy Studies* 13(1).

Schwegler-Rohmeis, Wolfgang, Annette Mummert and Klaus Jarck (2013) *Study on "Labour Market and Employment Policy in the Kyrgyz Republic"* (Bonn: GIZ).

UNDP (United Nations Development Programme) (2016) *Progress at Risk: Inequalities and Human Development in Eastern Europe, Turkey, and Central Asia* Regional Human Development Report (Istanbul: UNDP).

CHAPTER 3:
EQUALITY AND INEQUALITY IN SOCIAL SCIENTIFIC STUDIES IN RUSSIA, 2000 – 2015

Natalia Grigorieva

INTRODUCTION

As a result of the social reforms of the late twentieth century, Russia went through the transition from a planned economy (the USSR) to a market economy (Chubarova et al., 2012, 2013). The collapse of the old social structure of Russian society in the course of transformation led to dramatic changes in social stratification. New social groups emerged, such as entrepreneurs, and the unemployed; at the same time 'old' ones remained, while their roles and status changed. As a result, Russian society was structured on new grounds with new social problems emerging, making it necessary to also develop new areas of research (Grigorieva, 2016).

One of the most striking post-Soviet developments is the emergence of inequality and, consequently, studies of it. Concepts of equality and inequality are fundamental to the social sciences, with generations of researchers studying various aspects of inequalities. The main focus of these studies has been the question of how justified are the inequalities existing in different types of societies. Policy relevant research has asked what governments can do to minimize inequalities, and how life chances can be equalized, ensuring that all can lead a decent life corresponding to their abilities and aspirations (Gorshkov, 2013). Recently, the influential World Social Science Report (WSSR, 2016) highlighted significant gaps in research on social inequalities worldwide, whilst emphasizing the enormous potential of social science research in the quest for sustainable development and social progress globally.

This chapter addresses the state of research on inequality in Russia, focusing on its main priorities and challenges. A review of the literature sheds light on the current state of analytical work and the main gaps, from an inter-disciplinary perspective, that need to be addressed in future research. The study reviews diverse publications—including monographs, research reports, and articles in scientific journals—

devoted to problems of inequality in Russia between 2000 and 2015. The chapter focuses primarily on research on income inequality, disparities between regions, and gender inequality. It also briefly discusses research on public opinion and media interest in inequality.

REVIEWING THE LITERATURE

An initial literature review found some 211 texts, published between 2000 and 2015, authored by Russian researchers, and which had inequality as a main topic, chapter, section heading or keyword. Journal articles, books and book chapters, working papers and project reports were found using internet-based search engines including Russian databases. From the initial search, 47 texts contained the word 'inequality' in their title, but the content did not reflect inequality as a subject, so they were discarded. In the end, 69 texts were chosen which focused on the aspects of inequality noted above.

The texts chosen fall into three broad categories. The first category includes theoretical studies of socio-economic equality, discussing income-based, regional and / or gender-based inequalities using a new approach, including those with a focus on the construction and forecasting of income and consumption of the population (Shevyakov, 2002, 2004, 2008) or on the identification of the causes, contributing factors and consequences associated with new socio-economic inequalities (Rimashevskaya, 2003, 2007, 2008, 2010). A number of texts in this category developed new methodological insights into the relationship between economic inequality and economic development in the context of general economic theory (Anisimova et al., 2016; Shkaratan, 2012, Greenberg et al., 2004; Kislitsina, 2005). In many ways, these fundamental studies formed the foundation for the work of other authors who used their theoretical, conceptual and methodological insights in their own work (cf. Bobkov, 2014, 2016; Lyubimov, 2016 and others); these studies also tend to be amongst the most cited articles on the topic of inequality within the Russian scientific citation index.

The second category is composed of primarily empirical studies carried out by teams of researchers from leading research and higher education institutions, including: the Institute of Sociology of the Russian Academy of Sciences, the Institute of Economics of the Russian Academy of Sciences, the Institute of Independent Social Policy, Lomonosov

Moscow State University, the Higher School of Economics (University), the Institute of Socio-Economic Population Problems of the Russian Academy of Sciences and others. These institutions are under the leadership of research specialists whose names are well known in the Russian scientific community, such as Gorshkov, Zubarevich, Kalabikhina, Rimashevskaya, Tikhonova, Chubarova, Yarskaya-Smirnova and others, including the author of this chapter. Of particular importance here are four large-scale research projects, all of which include an extensive meta-review of the relevant literature. Two focus on gender-based inequalities and two are major sociological surveys devoted to the study of poverty and inequality. The 'Gender Problems in Russia in National Publications 2004 – 2014' project analyzed 835 books and reports, and addressed the legal framework on gender equality and its implementation.

The third category includes broad studies of social transformation whose main focus is on changes in social structure, and processes of social disintegration that include inequality as one of the themes (Golenkova, 2001; Lokosov, 2002, Gofman, 2004). Studies here analyze the transformation processes at the national (Gorshkov, Tikhonova) and regional (Zubarevich, Shabunova, Narskaya) levels. There are a number of regional studies of inequality, focusing on one or more Russian regions. However, the results of these studies are not widely known, as they are mostly published in regional journals that are not easily available nationwide. Some of these are included in the analysis (Dylnova, 2004; Narskaya, 2014; Shabunova et al., 2012).

There are very few texts which focused on health care inequalities (Chubarova and Grigorieva, 2012, 2013, 2015; Rimashevskaya et al., 2005; Kislitsyna, 2005), educational inequalities (Liberman, 2002; Osipov, 2006; Ivanova, 2007; Konstantinovskiy, 2010), or on inequalities in access to social services (Iarskaia-Smirnova, 2012). As discussed above, the rest of this chapter concentrates on four aspects of inequality deriving from the extensive literature review. The first topic discussed is that of income inequality, with around 80 percent of the sample concentrating on this. The second topic discussed is regional inequality, given that Russia is a very big country divided into 85 regions which differ substantially from each other in socio-economic development, ethnic composition, and so on. The third topic is the relatively new area of research on gender inequality, first addressed in the literature in the mid-1990s. Finally, the fourth topic is research on public perceptions and media portrayals of inequality.

INCOME INEQUALITY RESEARCH: FROM INCOME DIFFERENTIATION TO SOCIAL INEQUALITY

One of the most important aspects of modern research on inequality in Russia is income inequality. Research has shown that incomes have been falling in recent times and that the most significant negative trend concerns income from wages. The second main component of income—pensions—has also been decreasing. During the 2000s, poverty in Russia, measured in real monetary incomes, was decreasing, at least according to official statistics, while inequality grew.

On the whole, a consensus is emerging amongst researchers that it is not income inequality *per se* that is the main challenge but the way in which socio-economic disparities hinder development. Using the Theil index (Theil, 1967), it is possible to unpack inequality into different components including the part of inequality which is a result of inequality between regions. The Thiel index is also well suited to distinguishing between within-group and between-group inequality.

A conference presentation in 2012 used the Thiel index to chart between-group inequality by different components between 1992 and 2010. It found that regional differences, i.e. place of residence, was consistently the greatest contributor to inequality, growing rapidly in importance from 1995 and reaching its peak in 1998 (Figure 1).

Figure 1   Factors of inequality in Russia 1992 – 2010

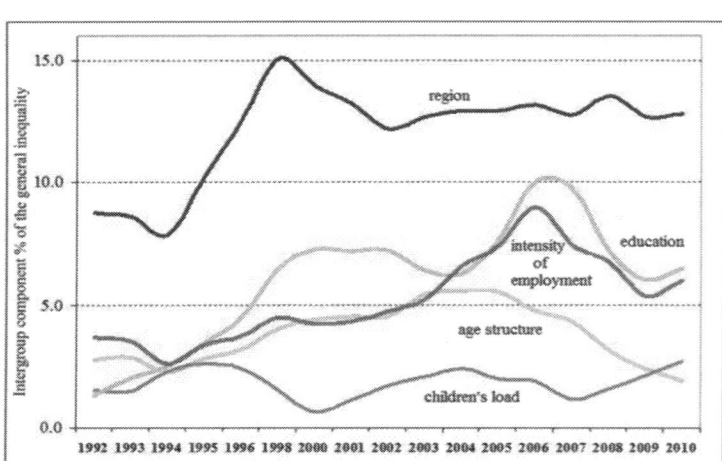

Source: Ovcharova (2012)

Research shows that, in the early 2000s, the most significant growth in real income occurred amongst rich or super rich Russians so that the growth of incomes did not contribute to the prosperity of Russian society as a whole. Moreover, the income gap between the richest and the poorest continued to grow such that the pre-crisis years (before 2008 – 2009) were marked by economic growth in favor of the rich. According to Rosstat, between 2000 and 2007, the income gap between the richest and poorest deciles of Russians increased from 13.9 times to 16.7 times (Milovzorov, 2008). In the crisis years (2008 – 2010), the decile coefficient index stabilized at the level of 16.6 times, and in subsequent years fell slightly to 16.2 times in 2013. Figure 2 shows similar large variations by quintile group.

Figure 2   Dynamics of real incomes by 20% income groups, % to 1991, comparable prices

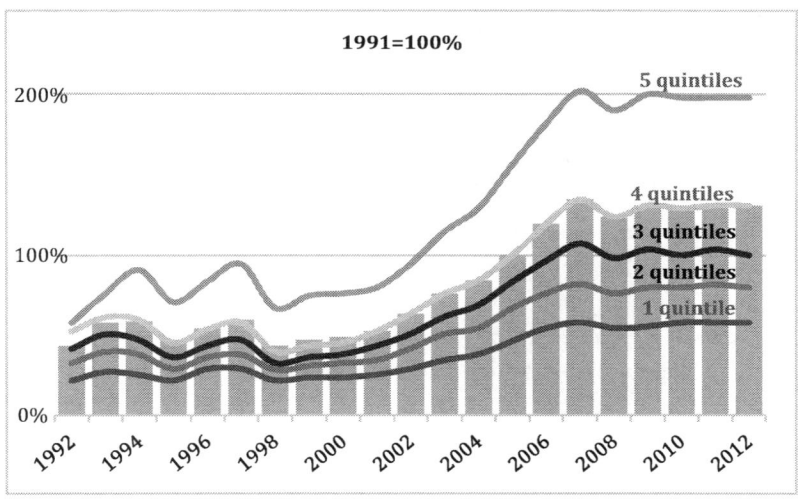

Source: Ovcharova L. IISP

A landmark study, 'The Rich and Poor in Modern Russia,' conducted by The Institute of Sociology of the Russian Academy of Science in 2003, used a sample of 2,118 people drawn from 11 regions, as well as Moscow and St. Petersburg. A representative quota sample of respondents from 11 socio-economic groups were interviewed, and the survey was conducted in 58 settlements, covering megacities, regional centers, district cities and villages. The share of respondents living in poverty was a quarter of the total.

In Russia, poverty is measured in absolute terms via subsistence minimum, namely the per capita consumer basket, the level of consumer prices for food and necessary services, and the inflation rate are taken into account. The country average is fixed by the federal government in accordance with the federal law, while regional averages are fixed by regional governments. The subsistence minimum is reviewed every six months. In Russian regions, the subsistence minimum may slightly differ from the country average. In accordance with Rosstat's methodology, 'income poor' include those whose per capita household incomes are lower than the subsistence minimum, calculated for certain population categories (working age, elderly, children).

In this study, poverty was determined based on respondents' listing of the main poverty characteristics (deprivation poverty) to include poor nutrition, inaccessibility of new clothing, poor housing conditions, inaccessibility of quality medical care, inability to get good education, meet priority needs without debts, free time, etc. (Tikhonova 2014; 7 – 19)

A follow-up study 'Poverty and Inequality in Modern Russia: 10 Years Later' was conducted in 2013. The total sample included 1,900 people from 21 regions including an experimental group of 300 people selected according to the poverty criterion. The main goal of both studies was to assess the real scope, causes and indicators of poverty in Russia, the attitude of Russians towards poverty in general, towards different groups of the poor, and towards social inequalities. These two studies, conducted ten years apart, provide the most reliable results in terms of scale and sample size, and allow for an analysis of trends over time.

The main contribution of the authors of the studies was to suggest that any assessment of living standards must include assessment not only of well-being, but of deprivation as well, including lack of access to a generally accepted set of consumer goods. Goods possessed and hardships experienced together give a real picture of people's standard of living (Tikhonova, 2013). A standard of living index should include not only what people have but also what they do not have. The studies showed how the polarization of poverty and wealth is one of the most acute manifestations of social inequality in contemporary Russia.

In terms of trends, the later study showed changes in the comparative significance of the main types of social inequalities; overall they deepened, with an increased awareness of the problems of inequality by the general population and its prioritization alongside poverty alleviation. Although not a particularly sensitive indicator, and relating to two different entities, the extent of the 'shock' can be seen by the fact that, in 1990, based on Human Development Index (HDI) rankings, the USSR was in 26th place, with a HDI of 0.920 (National HDR, 1990; 129), whereas by 2013, the Russian Federation was in 55th place, with a HDI of 0.788 (Human Development Index 2013).

REGIONAL INEQUALITY

By land mass, Russia is the largest country in the world, occupying one-seventh of the total world land mass, at 17,098,246 sq.km. The Russian population at the beginning of 2017 was 146,838,993, ranked 9th in the world. It is composed of 85 regions that are divided into Republics formed on a national basis (22); by *oblast* (46), or by *krai* (9)[1], together with three cities of federal significance, one autonomous province and four autonomous districts. Russia is built on a combination of regional and national-territorial principles as a voluntary association of its members. This association was formalized in the Federal agreement signed on 31 March 1992, and later incorporated in the 1993 Constitution. In 2000, in an attempt to improve the effectiveness of the federal government, nine federal administrative districts were formed that do not have the status of territorial subjects. In addition, Russia is a complex, multinational, state, inhabited by a number of nations and ethnic groups.

Researchers have noted significant disparities in the development of Russian regions as well as a low level of interregional cooperation (Khakimov (ed.), 2002; Lapina, 2006; Larina, 2006; Vereshchagina, 2008; Bochkaryova 2009; Zhuravskaya, 2010; Chirikova, 2011; Zubarevich, 2013; Chubarova et al., 2015) These disparities grew further in the 1990s as the differences in the social and economic situation across the regions increased. In the early 2000s, the federal government undertook a number of measures to prevent their further growth. In terms of the level and depth of regional differences, Russia exceeds levels found not only in developed countries but also in some developing countries (Novikov,

---

[1] The terms *oblast* and *krai* are sub-national scales of governance, the differences between them being more historical than administrative.

2013). The ratio between maximum and minimum regional GDP is 25.4 (Tsimbalist, 2009).

The literature addresses regional inequalities through diverse theoretical lenses. Among the indicators utilized by researchers to assess levels of inequality by region are: life expectancy; incomes and expenditures; GDP per capita; the ratio of the subsistence minimum to average monthly wage; regional financing of social programs; population dynamics; economically active and employed population; and levels of migration. The uneven distribution of population is often mentioned by researchers as one of the main factors influencing regional development (Bochkaryova, 2009; Podgornay, 2012; Novikov, 2013) According to official statistics (Rosstat) in Russia the average population density is about 8.4 people / sq. km. The lowest population density is in Chukotka (0.1 person / sq. km), the highest in Moscow (4,554.1 people / sq. km). The search for better living conditions and unregulated processes of population resettlement have led to the swelling of the metropolitan area; as a result, one in every eight citizens live in the capital or in the wider Moscow region (Novikov, 2013).

Zubarevich considers the concentration of economic advantages in certain regions to be the main cause of economic inequality (Zubarevich, 2005, 2008, 2010, 2012, 2015). Among such advantages, she distinguishes first order factors (richness of natural resources, favorable geographic location) and second order factors (levels of human capital development, favorable institutional environment, agglomeration effects, and so on).

Income inequality in Russia largely depends on region (Figure 3); as noted above, the incomes of those living in a rich region can exceed the incomes of those living in a poor region by 25 times (Grabar, 2013).

Figure 3   The Gini coefficient for regional inequality

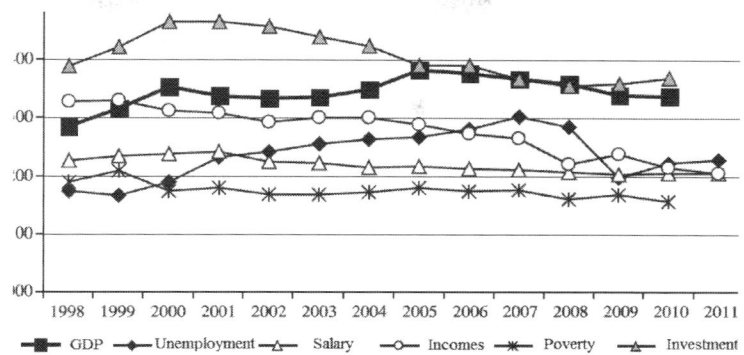

Source: Zubarevich and Safronov (2013:20)

At the same time, researchers have noted a decline in regional inequality since the mid-2000s. However, negative institutional factors have weakened this trend. The literature notes that regional policy instruments are ineffective in overcoming regional inequality and need to be strengthened (Vereshchagina, 2008; Boochkareva, 2009; Zubarevich et al., 2013; Novikov, 2013).

GENDER INEQUALITY IN RUSSIA

Gender studies began to develop in Russia in the late 1980s and early 1990s, when the first feminist groups and independent women's organizations emerged, and the first publications and translations of articles by foreign authors on gender issues were published in scientific journals. A laboratory for gender studies was opened in the early 1990s (the word 'gender' was first used in the official name), at the Institute of Social and Economic Problems of Population of the Academy of Sciences of the Russian Federation, and, from this base, the Moscow Center for Gender Studies was established in 1994. This saw not only the birth of a new research stream in Russian social science, but also the institutionalization of gender studies as similar centers were opened in other regions (Ivanovo, Tomsk, St. Petersburg and elsewhere). There followed a real boom in gender-related publications with the first review of publications on gender studies emerging in 2004, entitled 'Gender Problems in Russia (in National Publications 1993 – 2003)'. The text analyzed 1,248 publications published in Russia during the period in question. A period of active promotion of gender issues followed, in terms of research, training and advocacy in the political arena.

A follow-up survey of publications on gender equality in Russia, entitled 'Gender Problems in Russia in National Publications 2004 – 2012' analyses 835 publications and discusses gender equality across numerous domains: legislation and law enforcement practice; education; access to healthcare, health standards and life expectancy; employment; politics; and domestic violence. Each chapter includes recommendations on promoting gender equality in the given field.

Both surveys were conducted according to the same methodology and are based on a comprehensive analysis of documents and publications on the status of women and men in various spheres of life, assessing gender inequality as measured by a number of indicators in health, education, employment, the labor market, legislation and politics, providing a complete overview of gender inequalities in Russia for a 20-year period.

The studies found no significant change in key areas of gender equality in the two periods (see Table 2). The situation improved in demography (life expectancy of women and men, maternal mortality and abortions) but worsened in the field of political institutions promoting gender equality.

Table 1   Changes in various areas of gender equality in 2004 – 2012 compared to 1994 – 2003.

Gender equality in:		Changes 2004 – 2012 / 1993 – 2003
Legislation	Legislation	0
	Law enforcement practice	0
Education	Access to education	0
	The content of education	0
Health	Female and male expectancy of life	+
	Gender gap in expectancy of life	0
	The reduction of abortion and maternal mortality	+
	Women's health	0
	Health of women of special groups	0
Employment and poverty	Segregation and discrimination	0
	Hazardous jobs for men	0
	Gender gap in wages	0
	Female poverty	0
	Family-Work balance	0
Politics	Representation	0
	The role of institutions for gender equality	–
Domestic violence	The prevalence of violence	0

Notes:
0 = no significant changes
– = the deterioration of gender equality;
+ = the improvement of gender equality
Source: Kalabikhina I. (ed.) Grigorieva, N., Lukhovitskaya, E., Davtyan, M. (2012; 79).

Income inequality between women and men, gender segregation in the labor market, and women's poverty are the most developed areas of research in gender inequality (Rimashevskaya, 2003, 2010; Kalabikhina (ed.), 2012; Kislitsina, 2007). Research documents a significant gender wage gap in various regions of Russia. For example, the gap in pay for men and women in the country is on average 35 – 40 percent for work of equal value[2]. However, the Rosstat data show that in some regions, such as the Republic of Ingushetia, the salaries of men and women are approximately equal. In Moscow, women receive on average three-quarters of the wages of men. The biggest difference in salaries is in the regions of the Far East,

---

2   Rosstat (2016) 'Women and Men in Russian Federation'. http://www.gks.ru/bgd/regl/B16_50/Main.htm (In Russian).

where women on average receive only half of male wages. Women in Russia have a high level of education—about 60 percent of students in higher education are women—however, this does not allow them to easily overcome gender differences in the labor market.

To understand and assess the problem of gender inequality in Russia, researchers suggest more studies on topics such as: 1) *de jure* and *de facto* rights of women and men; 2) the persistence of gender stereotypes on women's role in society; 3) analysis of the distribution of gender roles in the socio-economic sphere; 4) analysis of gender issues at the macro-level; and 5) gender aspects of law enforcement practice[3].

There seems to be a correlation between research and publications on gender issues and political and legislative cycles. For example, 2003 was the peak year of active legislative work with the draft law 'On state guarantees of equal rights and freedoms of men and women and equal opportunities for their implementation in the Russian Federation' submitted to the State Duma. However, after a successful first reading, the draft was put aside for many years. The theme of gender equality then shifted to the margins of social research until a second peak between 2010 and 2012; this was just before the second reading of this, by now significantly modified, law in 2013. However, at the last moment, the second reading was postponed indefinitely. After the adoption of the National Strategy for Women for 2017 – 2022 in March 2017, another increase in the number of publications on gender issues is observed although the phrase 'women and men' rather than the term 'gender' is more often used in publications and public debates.

---

3   Gender studies are based on the premise that all social phenomena and processes have a gender dimension. At the macro level, large public structures and social relations are studied, for example, 'group – society' or 'personality – society.' At the meso level intergroup relations are studied, for example, 'group – group'; at the micro level, researchers focus on people's interactions with each other. In any social context, elements of all levels are combined. Everyday communication between family members takes place at the micro level. At the same time, the family is a social institution that is studied at the macro level, where it is connected with the labor market, the legislative system and social classes.

PUBLIC OPINION ON POVERTY, JUSTICE AND INEQUALITY AND MASS MEDIA IN RUSSIA

The studies of the Institute of Sociology of the Russian Academy of Sciences (2003, 2013), noted earlier, also document changes in attitudes towards the poor in modern Russia. Between 2003 and 2013, the share of those who did not care about the poor has grown threefold while the number of those who treated them with sympathy, or even with respect, decreased by 150 percent. At the same time, the public tended to associate poverty with drunkenness and drug addiction or general risk behavior, that is, personal behavior. An analysis of public opinion on causes of poverty and state policy towards the poor shows that people are more concerned with the consequences than the causes of poverty (Gorshkov and Tikhonova (eds.) 2014; 157).

What social and economic inequalities are currently perceived by Russians as the most painful for society as a whole, and for them personally? The results of sociological research show that income inequality is the major concern (47 percent and 71 percent of respondents, respectively, across the two studies), followed by inequality of access to medical care (38 percent and 47 percent) and housing conditions (28 percent and 38 percent). Interestingly, if inequality in access to good jobs is discussed, respondents consider it more important for them rather than for society as a whole (32 percent and 28 percent). This problem of inequalities in employment is acute for the poor in modern Russia, especially those of working age (VCIOM, 2013).

The answers of respondents who are in poverty show that a strong percentage is not opposed to significant differences in income if they result from differences in talent or effort (31 percent of respondents). At the same time, 42 percent of respondents in this group believe that inequalities will exist in any society and recognize this as fair (Gorshkov et al., 2014). The results of the study suggest that the poor is not a homogeneous group when it comes to evaluating inequality. Equality and inequality are evaluated positively or negatively depending on the notion of justice. It is assumed that if inequality is just, then it must be preserved, but it is necessary to eliminate inequality that is unjust.

In the framework of the project 'Construction of Inequality in the Rhetoric of Social Policy' (2013), the authors analyzed how social inequality and social policy are presented in print media in contemporary

Russia. In total, 1,205 publications between 2005 – 2012 dealing with poverty and inequality were selected. The peak year of relevant publications in the sample was in 2008 with a subsequent decline back to levels of interest found in 2005 (Figure 5). According to the authors, the frequency of referring to the topic of inequalities is closely correlated with election campaigns, and hence with increased or decreased attention to the issue by the country's leadership. In addition, interest in the topic of inequality tends to grow during a period of economic recovery and decrease during crisis times. Some researchers explain this in terms of the paradox of public consciousness, with poverty more acutely recognized when a country is growing in terms of wealth (Yarmiev, 2008).

Figure 5   Distribution of publications on social inequality, 2005 – 2012, the number of units per year

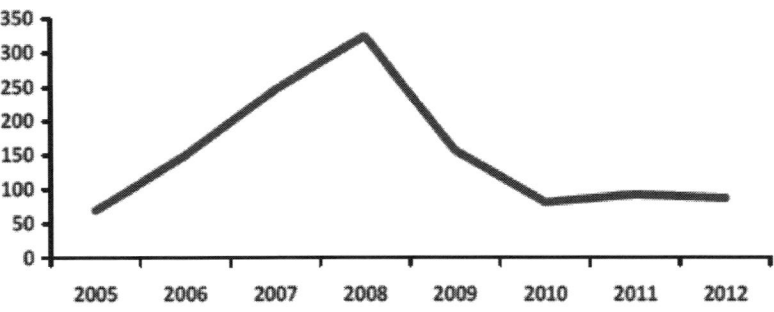

Source: Iarskaia-Smirnova E., Prisyazhnyuk D. (2013; 172)

Most often, the blame for social inequality in Russian media rests with the state (59 percent of the sample), followed by businesses (16 percent) and individuals (16 percent). The authors note that many problems are associated with ineffective government, 'anti-social' business policies, corporate egoism, and with the fact that some groups of citizens have not been able to adapt to a market economy.

CONCLUSIONS

This chapter has offered an overview of research publications on inequality in Russia over the period of 2000 – 2015. More specifically, this analysis mapped out research focusing on income inequality, regional inequality, and gender inequality in Russia as well as publications on public and media attitudes toward poverty and inequality in Russia.

It is emphasized in the research that the steady increase in incomes of a certain part of society is not related to efficiency growth in the economy, and is not in any way a measure of the prosperity of the country as a whole nor its regions. Differentiation is manifested not only in the polarization between the immensely wealthy 'top' and low-income 'bottom,' but in growing social stratification based on sphere of activity, profession, and place of residence. Unfair distribution of income leads to unequal access to goods and services for different social strata, directly or indirectly contributing to inequalities in health outcomes, access to education and to a decent life.

This overview of Russian research on various aspects of inequality shows that income inequality has attracted the most attention. There is a general consensus that in the early 1990s there was a sharp increase in income differentiation as a result of Russia's transition to a market economy. Researchers record an increase in income inequality for various social groups in the period 2000 – 2015. The peculiarity of the Russian situation is the fact that in the period 2010 – 2015 incomes grew, but inequality in income also increased.

Income inequality is a cross-cutting theme for all the studies analyzed in this chapter. Researchers have drawn attention to the fact that incomes depend, to a large extent, on place of residence and the level of socio-economic development of a given region. These studies point to the need for active policies aimed at reducing regional differences and achieving more equitable access to public services. In contemporary gender studies, the issue of income inequality between men and women has grown in importance as a research theme. Researchers agree that there have been no significant changes in gender inequality in the period from 2004 to 2012 compared to the decade from 1993 to 2003.

Surveys of public opinion demonstrate changes in the attitudes of the general public toward poverty and inequality, as Russians have become less sympathetic toward the poor, while their acceptance of inequality has grown over time. Many Russian respondents acknowledge the very existence of income inequality, but on condition that high incomes are the result of personal efforts and professional achievements.

Such inequality is considered fair by respondents. But they are critical of the wealth that was obtained as a result of privatization in the early 1990s.

Studies on the representation of inequality in the mass media demonstrate that heightened interest depends on political cycles, electoral campaigns, and the socio-economic situation in society. In most news items, the state tends to be blamed for social inequality and at the same time is primarily held responsible for its alleviation. Between 2000 and 2005, there was a major focus on linking social inequalities with ineffective social policies. Between 2006 and 2012, social inequality in Russian society tended to be explained more in terms of corporate greed, and is associated with individual behavior. Such studies are very important because the mass media are influential in framing the evaluation of social policy and the public's notions of social justice.

Overall, a review of publications on equality and inequality in Russia for the period between 2000 and 2015 shows that few studies go beyond a focus on income and wealth. Not enough attention has been paid to inequalities in the social sector, in access to health care and education and to health and educational outcomes. Thus, it is important to promote an interdisciplinary approach to the study of inequalities, and to this end, to draw on the results of studies across the different social science disciplines, as well as research by those for whom the study of inequalities is not the main topic, but one that is relevant to their work. This is necessary to provide evidence to government to develop more effective policies for sustainable development, given the significant challenge that high inequality presents to Russian society and the Russian state.

REFERENCES

Anisimova Galina, Voeykov Michael (2016). *The political economy of equality and inequality*. Report. Institute of Economy, Russian Academy of Sciences (Moscow).

Bobkov V. N., Anikeev S. D., Loktyukhina N.V., Rozhkov V.D., Pirovzhenko Ya. A., Demidov I.F. (2015). "On the state and forecast of the development of the labor market and employment of the population of the Russian Federation (2006 – 2017)". *The Standard of Living of the Population of Russian Regions*. (Moscow) No. 1(195).

Bobkov Vyacheslav, Gulyugina Aleftina (2015). "Monitoring of incomes and living standards". *The standard of living of the population of Russian regions (4th quarter 2014)*. No. 1(195). http://www.rea.ru/ru/org/employees/pages/bobkov-vjacheslav-nikolaevich.aspx.

Bochkaryova Valentina (2009). "Geographical dimension of efficient health care system". *Health Management*. (Moscow) No. 3.

Chirikova Alla (2011). "Regional social policy: actors and motivation". *Russian World.* (Moscow) No. 4.

Chubarova Taniana and Grigorieva Natalia (2015). "The Russia Federation". In: Katherine Fierlbeck and Horward A. Palley (eds.) *Comparative Health Care Federalism.* Routledge Taylor & Francis Group.

Dylnova Tatiana (2004). "Social Justice and Social Inequalities in Modern Russia: Problems of Integration". *RUDN Journal of Sociology.* (Moscow) No. 6 – 7.

Gofman Alexander (2004). "March theses on the sociology of equality and inequality." *SOCIS.* (Moscow) No. 7.

Golenkova Zinaida (2001). *Main Trends in the Transformation of Social Inequalities in Russia: a Transforming Society.* (Moscow).

Gorshkov Michael (2014). "Social Inequalities as an Object of Sociological Analysis." *Sociological Studies.* (Moscow) No. 7.

Gorshkov Michael (ed.) (2012). *Russian Society and Modern Challenges.* Moscow.

Gorshkov Michael, Tikhonova Natalia (eds.) 2014. Poverty *and the Poor in Modern Russia* Moscow.

Gorshkov Michael, Krumm Reinhard, Tikhonova Natalia (ed.) (2013). *What Russians Dream About: Ideal and Reality?* Moscow.

Grabar Yakov (2013). Bogach—poor: the world was unjust. URL: http://top.rbc.ru/economics/17/07/2013/866357.shtml.

Grigorieva Natalia (2016). "Social justice and equality / inequality issues in modern-day Russia". World Social Science Report 2016: Challenging Inequalities: Pathways to a Just World. UNESCO Publishing, (Paris) http://unesdoc.unesco.org/images/0024/002458/245825e.pdf.

Grigorieva Natalia and Chubarova Tatiana (2005). *Social Policy: Gender Aspect.* (Moscow: Olita).

Grigberg Ruslan, Chubarova Tatiana (2004). "Democratic Values and Inequality, or Democratic Inequaluties?" *Ekonomski pregled* (Moscow) No. 55 (1 – 2): 157 – 180.

Human Development Index (2013). http://www.undp.org/content/undp/en/home/librarypage/hdr/human-development-report-2013.html.

Human Development Report (1990). New York: United Nations Development Programmer.

Iarskaia-Smirnova Elena and Prisyazhnyuk Daria (2013). "Representations of the Inequality and Social Policy in public sphere: content analyses of Press." In Iarskaia-Smirnova E., Romanov P. (eds.) *Public sphere: theory, methodology, case studies.* (Moscow).

Ivanova Victoria (2007). "Social inequality in the Russian higher education: staging problems". *Higher education in Russia.* (Moscow). No. 1 (145).

Kalabikhina, Irina (ed.) Grigorieva Natalia, Lukovitskaya, Elena, Davtyan Maria (2012). *Gender issues in Russia. An overview of 2004 – 2012 national publications.* (Moscow).

Kalabikhina Irina, Tyndik Alla (2014). "Does Current Demographic Policy in Russia Impact on Fertility of Different Educational Groups? Results from Quantitative and Qualitative Studies". Working Paper Series. *Social Science Research Network.* (Moscow) February 18.

Khakimov Raphael (ed.) (2002). *Federalism in Russia.* Tatarstan Sciences Academy. (Kazan).

Kislitsina Olga (2005). *Inequality in the distribution of income and health in modern Russia.* (Moscow).

Konstantinovsky David (2008). *Inequality and Education: The experience of sociological research on the life start of Russian youth (1960s – early 2000s).* (Moscow).

Konstantinovsky David (2010). "Inequality in education: the Russian situation". *Monitoring of public opinion and social changes.* (Moscow). No. 5 (99).

Kosova, Ludmila (2012). "About equality and inequality". *Otechestvennie zapiski.* (Moscow) Vol. 5, No. 50.

Lapina, Natalia (2006). "Centre-regions in Post-Soviet Russia: History, Relationships and Future". *Politex: Political Expertise.* (Moscow) No. 2.

Larina, Natalia (2006). *State Regulation of Regional Development: Spatial Structure of Government and Regional Economic Policy.* (Novosibirsk).

Liberman Alexander (2002). "Stratification of society: the tasks that the school must solve in this situation." *Journal of the Head of the School.* (Moscow) No. 9.

Mareeva Svetlana and Tikhonova Natalia (2016). "Public Perceptions of Poverty and Social Inequality in Russia." *Mir Rossii.* (Moscow) No. 2.

Milovzorov Alexander (2008). "The world again becomes bipolar." URL: http://www.utro.ru/articles/2008/04/07/ 728835.shtml.

Narskaya Natalia (2014). "Health and social inequality in Russia." *Bulletin of the South Ural State University. Series: Social sciences and the humanities.* (Ekaterinburg) No. 1.

National Human Development Report in the Russian Federation, (2015). *Russia in 2015: the goals and priorities of development* (Moscow).

National Report on Human Development in the Russian Federation, (2014). Moscow.

Nikonov Vyacheslav (2017). *Leadership in Russian* (Moscow).

Novikov Alexander (2013). "Regional disparities in the Socio-economic development of Russia." E-journal Naukovedenie. (Nizhny Novgorod) No.1. URL: http:publ.naukovedenie.ru.

Osipov Alexander (2006). "Mechanisms of social stratification in education". *Education and Society.* (Moscow). No. 2 (37).

Ovcharova Lily (2008). "Poverty and Economic Growth in Russia." *The Journal of Social Policy Studies.* (Moscow). Vol. 6, No. 4: 439 – 456.

Ovcharova Lily (2009). *Theoretical and Practical Approaches to Evaluation of Level, Pattern, and Factors of Poverty: Russian and International Experience* (Moscow).

Oxfam (2014). *Signs of inequality: The inequality problem and solutions in modern-day Russia. Doklad* OKSFAM [Oxfam report]. http://fom.ru/Economika/11089.

Podgornaya Elena (2012). "Regional policy in the context of socio-economic differentiation of the subjects of the Russian Federation." Abstract for the degree of candidate of economic sciences. (St. Petersburg).

Rimashevskaya Natalia (2003). *Man and Reforms: Secrets of Survival* (Moscow).

Rimashevskaya Natalia (2006). "Poverty in the context of a social state." In: *Social state and Problems of poverty.* (Moscow).

Rimashevskaya Natalia (ed.) (2007). *Health and Health Care in the Gender Dimension.* (Moscow).

Rimashevskaya Natalia (2010). "Risks of poverty in modern Russia." *Population.* (Moscow) No. 2 (48).

Rimashevskaya Natalia and Lunyakova Larisa (2009). *Gender stereotypes in a changing society: the experience of a comprehensive social study* (Moscow).

Rosstat (2013). *Socialnoe Polozhenie i Uroven Zhizni Naseleniya v Rossii, 2012. Statisticheskiy Sbornik.* [Social Status and Standards of Living in Russia in 2012: Statistical Yearbook].

Shabunova Alexandra, Gulin Konstantin, Lastochkina Maria, Solovyova Tatiana (2012). *Modernization of the economy of the region: socio-cultural aspects.* (Vologda).

Shevyakov A.Yu. (2008). "Inequality and formation of a new social policy of the state." *Bulletin of the Russian Academy of Sciences.* (Moscow) Volume 78, No. 4: 304 – 331.

Shevyakov Alexey (2004). "Economic Growth and Inequality." *Society and Economics.* (Moscow) No. 2.

Shevyakov Alexey, Kiruta Alexander (2002). *Measurement of economic inequality* (Moscow).

Shilov Vladimir (2010). "Social Equality as the Purpose of the Policy and Modern Russia." *Belgorod State University. Series: History. Political science. Economy. Informatics.* (Belgorod) No. 13 (84).

Shishkin Sergei (ed.) (2003). *Problems of accessibility of higher education.* (Moscow).

Shkaratan Ovsy. (2012). *Sociology of Inequality. Theory and Reality* (Moscow: Home of the Higher School of Economics).

Teminka Anna (2012). "The gender issue in modern Russia." *Polit.ru*, June.

Theil Henri (1967). Economics *and Information Theory* (North-Holland).

Tikhonova Natalia (2014). "Poverty phenomenon in modern Russia." *SOCIS.* (Moscow). No. 1: 7 – 19.

Tsimbalist Alexander (2009). "Social stratification of society and its impact on the formation of the middle class in Russia." Abstract of doctor dissertations.

UNESCO (2016). *World Social Science Report 2016: Challenging Inequalities: Pathways to a Just World.* UNESCO Publishing, Paris.

VCIOM. (2013). "Social justice and how we understand it." July 15, N 2346. http://wciom.ru/index.php&uid+114297.

Vereschagina, Anna (2008). *European Territorial Cooperation: Influence on Decision-making in EU (1980 – 1990s)*. (Moscow).

Yarmiev Mansur (2008). "Representation of Poverty as a Social Problem in the Russian Media." *Sociological Research*. (Moscow). No. 4: 67 – 72.

Zhuravskaya, E. (2010). "Federalism in Russia." Working Paper, no 141 CEFIR. ES Working Paper series. Centre for Economic and Financial Research. New Economic School. April.

Zubarevich Natalia (2008). "The Regional Social and Economic Development: Myths and Actual Progress in Equalization." *SPERO*, (Moscow) No. 9.

Zubarevich Natalia (2015). "The Relations between the Center and the Regions." In: Petrov N, Lipman M (eds.) *The State of Russia: What Comes Next?* (Palgrave Macmillan).

Zubarevich Natalia (2010). "Regions of Russia: inequality, crisis, modernization." URL: http://gtmarket.ru/laboratory/expertize/5279.

Zubarevich, Natalia and Safronov Sergei (2013). "The inequality of the social and economic development of Russia's regions and cities in 2000s: Growth or decline?" *Social Sciences and Modernity*. (Moscow) No. 6: 15 – 20.

CHAPTER 4:
INEQUALITY OF ACCESS TO THE HEALTH SYSTEM IN RUSSIA: THE CASE OF OUT-OF-POCKET PAYMENTS

Tatiana Chubarova

INTRODUCTION

At present, inequality is high on the health system research agenda, including perspectives for future research which were set out in the latest World Social Science Report (2016). It is important to expand knowledge on inequalities in health care in order to inform public policy decisions. The focus on out-of-pocket-payments (OOP) is justified as they constitute a significant and growing share of health care financing in Russia. The aim is to use the data available to clarify the role of OOPs as financial barriers to access to medical treatment in the Russian health system, taking into account its specific features, both financial and institutional.

In this chapter, a brief overview of inequality of access to health care from a conceptual perspective is presented, which aims to provide a methodological basis for the study and to define research questions. The main features of the organization and financing of the Russian health care system are outlined to show how the public / private mix works in the Russian context. OOPs are then discussed in more detail and the available evidence is analyzed to evaluate their impact on inequality of access to health care. Some tentative conclusions are suggested to inform public policy decisions.

LITERATURE REVIEW AND METHODOLOGICAL FRAMEWORK

The data available documents rising inequalities on a global scale, to say nothing about the dramatic increase in income inequality observed in the former USSR and Eastern European countries that experienced transition from a centrally planned to a market economy. Research on inequality is traditionally dominated by income issues; however, there is a growing consensus that inequality is a multi-faceted phenomenon and recent debates have shifted to other dimensions, namely opportunities, power, education and health care (WB, 2006; Aaberge and Brandolini, 2014). It is generally accepted that there is likely to be a link between inequality and access to health care (Davis, 1991; Kislitsina, 2003). However, the literature mostly focuses on inequalities in health status according to income, demonstrating that poor people generally have worse health status than the better-off (Pickett and Wilkinson, 2015). A substantial correlation has been confirmed between income inequality, educational inequality, and health inequality (Deaton, 2003). There is also strong evidence that without specific government policies, greater economic inequality leads to worse health outcomes.

High income inequality in Russia is a well-documented fact (Kislitsina, 2003; Gerasimova, 2014). However, much less is known about other types of inequality, such as inequality of access to health care, and its causes and consequences. The aim of the present study is to single out how inequality manifests itself in Russian health care, paying special attention to financial barriers to access. The chapter tries to establish a connection between OOP and access to health care, to understand if the recent growth in OPP in Russia is leading to increased inequality in access to health care.

The chapter is based on a number of methodological premises. Firstly, it adheres to the 'determinants of health' approach stating that health status is, to a large extent, determined by social and economic factors. It suggests that inequalities in the health system mainly result from the unequal distribution of health determinants between people occupying different social positions in society. Secondly, inequality in health care must be discussed *vis-a-vis* equality, implying equal access to available care for equal needs and the same quality of care for all (Leenan, 1985). Health policy should aim to reduce or eliminate those inequalities that result from the distribution of health determinants that are considered both avoidable and unfair. In public policy, the aim of the health system is usually formulated as securing equality rather than eliminating inequalities.

Thirdly, access can be defined as the ability of a citizen to timely receive appropriate medical treatment according to need, and is very much dependent on the organization and financing of the health care system. Measuring access to health care faces a number of methodological challenges that have been widely discussed by researchers. The population coverage, the content of the health package, cost-sharing, geographical and organizational barriers and the level of utilization of available services are commonly used in research as the key indicators of access. Availability and affordability (cost) are considered as the most common reasons for variations in access to health care (Goddard and Smith, 2001). Access is often defined negatively as 'the absence of barriers'—territorial, financial and cultural. Financial barriers imply that access is dependent on the ability to pay rather than need.

The fairness of any financial contribution and financial risk protection are two basic concepts that are used in analyzing financial barriers to access. The fairness of financial contribution reflects the redistributive effect of health care finance, meaning differences in payments for health care as a share of income for various income groups. Financial risk protection indicators are developed within the framework of WHO Universal Health Coverage (UHC) monitoring to measure the incidence of catastrophic health expenditures (the number of households of all income levels who suffer financial hardship because of relatively large health payments in a given time period). UHC monitoring also measures impoverishment, when OOPs push a household below the poverty line.

OOPs are defined by WHO as direct payments made by individuals (or households) to health care providers at the time of service use. It includes non-reimbursable cost sharing, deductibles, co-payments and fee-for service (WHO). The OECD definition of OPPs also notes that they are 'paid directly by private households, irrespective of whether the contact with the health care system was established on referral or on the patient's own initiative' (OECD, 2001).

User fees have been introduced in the public sector for a number of reasons, including symbolism, preventing abuse, deterrence and prioritization (Glennester, 1992). OOPs are often referred to as barriers to access to medical treatment. First, there is a danger that they lead to a refusal or delay in receiving medical treatment with resulting negative consequences for people's health. According to OECD data, unmet need as an indirect indicator of financial barriers to access is higher amongst the poor compared to rich people (OECD, 2015). Second, in theory, there should be a shift in health financing towards those who use services more, namely to low income households as they have lower health status and greater needs. However, research on equity in health financing and delivery in low- and middle-income countries over the past decades indicates that the rich tend to benefit more from the health system than the poor and that the burden of financing also falls more on the rich (Asante et al., 2016). In addition, poor people might not seek medical care if they have to pay for it. As a result, the share of medical expenditures in poor households' budgets is lower that it would be if all their health needs were met. This suggests that the impact of OOPs on equality of access depends considerably on the institutional context.

In this context one of the most debated issues is the expansion of fee for services in publicly owned health services. Some researchers suggest that an increase in OOPs is inevitable under the conditions of budgetary restraint and stress their positive role as an expression of choice, with those with the ability and willingness to pay receiving better quality services (Kochkina et al., 2015). However, this implies that services rendered in state-owned health services free of charge are of an inferior quality and ignores the fact that people will find ways to pay for medical treatment for a number of reasons (uncertainty, pain, life threatening conditions, caring about family members) even if they do not truly have the ability to pay. Other experts suggest that increases in OOPs coupled with low public spending and the restructuring of the health delivery network is likely to hamper access to medical treatment for the low-income population.

The idea of a public-private mix stresses the importance of engaging all stakeholders and enhanced collaboration among them in various settings. In modern health policy, it is accepted that private money can be attracted into the health system to meet the challenges it faces globally—population ageing, rapid advances in technology, including new drugs and information technology, rising patients' demands and expectations, and so on. However, some prepayment mechanisms are necessary to secure redistribution from the rich to the poor (WHO, 2010).

This chapter is based on official statistics from the Russian statistical agency (Rosstat) on health outcomes and health finance, including household expenditures on medical treatment by income deciles, and international statistical databases, mainly WHO and OECD. Survey data includes the Rosstat comprehensive survey on population living conditions, two rounds of which were conducted in 2011 and 2014. It provides information on health services' utilization, infrastructure and expenses as well as population health status. Public opinion surveys on health issues are also conducted by independent agencies, such as the Levada center.

Data availability and its quality is one of the main limitations of health inequality research, as some health data is discontinuous and subjective (O'Donnell et al., 2008). Official statistics in Russia are incomplete and fragmented, so the bulk of information comes from surveys on population living conditions that include sections on health status and health services, as well as on payments for medical treatment. However, only a few surveys contain information on respondents' income to allow us to establish a link between income and access to health care. In addition, reports from NGOs that are actively involved in health issues were studied to gain more qualitative insights into the health system, including a review of patient organizations' websites.

OOPs AND THE NEW PUBLIC-PRIVATE MIX IN RUSSIAN HEALTH CARE

The Soviet health care system was known around the world as the *Semashko* model. It was a budget-funded system based on a network of state-owned health services provided to the population free of charge at the point of delivery. Transition to a market-based economy led to dramatic changes in the health system, with the main trend being the introduction of compulsory health insurance (CHI) and the emergence of a private sector in health care finance and delivery. However, universal access to timely and quality medical treatment was declared as the main aim of health policy in Russia and the right to free health care was guaranteed in the 1993 Constitution.

At present health care in Russia is financed from two sources, public and private.

Table 1   Selected health expenditures indicators in Russia

Selected indicators	1995	2000	2005	2010	2012	2014
Total health expenditures, % GDP	5.36	5.42	5.21	6.83	6.88	7.07
Total government health finance, % total health expenditures	73.88	59.88	61.98	54.12	55.18	52.20
Total private expenditures, % total health expenditures	26.12	40.12	38.02	45.88	44.82	47.8
Government health expenditures, % total government expenditures	9.14	12.67	11.75	9.72	10.18	9.49
Social security expenditures, % total health expenditures	34.52	40.35	42.01	34.17	43.75	53.12
Private OPP, % private health expenditures	64.66	74.70	82.39	94.39	94.92	95.92
Private OPP, % total health expenditures	16.89	29.97	31.32	43.30	42.55	45.85
Private prepayment plans, % private expenditures	6.0	8.06	8.24	4.58	4.3	3.50

Source: WHO, World health statistics, respective years. Date of retrieval: 17.03.2017

As can be seen from Table 1, public expenditures, which include budget appropriations and compulsory health insurance (CHI) contributions amounted to only 3.5 percent of GDP in 2014, or 52 percent of total health expenditures. Two comments are necessary here. The role of regions in health financing is set to increase. In 2014, federal budget expenditures on health amounted to 0.7 percent of GDP while expenditures of the consolidated regional budgets reached 1.8 percent of GDP.

The CHI system is a rather complex financial and organizational arrangement. Money comes from employers' contributions (5.1 percent of payroll) for those employed, and from payments of regional governments for those who are not employed (pensioners, children, the disabled, the unemployed). Special CHI funds were created in regions that collect money and distribute then to health services to cover their expenses via health insurance organizations. Low public expenditures on health have resulted in people having to mobilize private means. These include private voluntary health insurance and out-of-pocket payments. In Russia, the share of private spending on health is quite significant. In 2014, it accounted for almost 48 percent of total health expenditures. Private expenses in Russia mostly consist of OOP, i.e. people paying cash at the moment of receiving medical treatment. The share of OOP in private health expenditures increased to 96 percent in 2014 compared to 65 percent in 1995. As a result, they amounted to about 46 percent of total health expenditures in 2014, a rise from about 17 percent in 1995. The increase in private health expenditures has not been accompanied by the development of prepayment mechanisms, for example voluntary private health insurance (PHI) is underdeveloped in Russia. Its share in health financing was only 3.5 percent in 2014, showing a declining trend. PHI is typically provided by large foreign and domestic employers as a supplement to public entitlements.

The health care delivery network is dominated by public providers (mostly health centers) although the number of private providers both in primary and hospital care is gradually increasing, especially in urban areas and in certain segments of health care (laboratory tests and diagnostics, dentistry, plastic surgery, obstetrics). For example, the share of private hospitals in the total number of hospitals increased from about two percent in 2010 to three percent in 2014. The number of private hospital beds grew even faster—from 4,000 in 2010 to 11,000 in 2014, an almost threefold increase. Starting from the beginning of the 2000s, the Russian federal government put substantial financial and administrative efforts into modernization of the public health delivery network to secure effective use of resources, improve quality of care and save on administrative expenses. Reforms included network restructuring, a reduction, via closure or consolidation, in the number of hospitals and changing patient flows, together with promoting modern technologies including IT. However, the impact of these measures on access is controversial as the spatial factor is important in Russia where the share of the population living in rural and remote areas is quite high.

OOP IN THE RUSSIAN HEALTH SYSTEM: AN INSTITUTIONAL PERSPECTIVE

In Russian official discourse the term 'OOP' is not used. Direct patients' payments to health care providers are divided into two streams, namely official payments via cashier both in public and private settings (*platnye meditzinskiye uslugi*, or services rendered for fee) and informal payments in the public sector both as a condition to get a particular treatment, and as a gratuity (a voluntary payment, usually after treatment is received). Informal payments are often referred to as 'envelope' money, referring to cash handed over in an envelope. Informal payments became widespread in Russia in the early 1990s leading to the formation of a 'shadow health economy' (Lewis, 2007). Payments include institutional or individual payments to suppliers, in kind or in cash, made outside official channels or paid for services that should be covered by the health care system. Envelope money was typically paid directly to a doctor and / or to other medical staff. The dramatic drop in public spending coupled with low salaries made these payments quite common in the 1990s and early 2000s (Shishkin et al., 2007).

At that time, official payments were charged only in private health services that emerged in the course of transition and covered the full cost of treatment. The situation changed when state health services became actively involved in provision of medical treatment for money. Government regulations stipulate what types of medical treatment can be subject to fees in state health services, namely treatment not covered by the program of state guaranteed free medical care that is annually adopted by the government starting from 1999 and funded through CHI contributions and the state budget (taxes). In addition, fees are paid when a patient does not have a CHI policy or is not officially referred to a hospital from a health center; when treatment is provided anonymously, or when the patient is a foreign citizen not otherwise covered. In addition, patients may opt to pay for additional services that are not included in the medical and economic standards (MEAs) for particular diseases.

It should be noted that when patients pay for treatment this does not mean that they are no longer eligible for free health care. A common practice is partial payments meaning than a patient may get some procedures free while paying for others, most often lab tests and diagnostics. Paying for better quality medical devices, especially for surgery, than those that are provided through CHI is also quite widespread in Russia. There are several requirements that a state health service should fulfill to be able to charge fee for service, including: obtaining informed consent from a patient, informing a patient about possibilities to receive free care, having a license for the treatment in question, signing an appropriate agreement and providing a receipt.

In early 1990 the provision of medical services rendered for a fee was regulated primarily by the norms of the civil law as fixed in the Civil Code and consumer protection legislation. The first special regulation—a federal government decree—adopted in 1996 still failed to regulate the conditions under which services could be provided for a fee. It was stated that the regulation applied to all health services regardless of form of ownership. The Fundamentals of Citizens' Health Protection were adopted in 2011 and included a special section on fee for service. It stipulated that people can pay a fee for any services they wish. Following this law, more detailed rules on rendering services for a fee were adopted in 2012. Prices in state health services are fixed by the relevant government bodies while private health services are unregulated in this matter. Revenues received go to the health service that can dispose of them at its discretion. However, in 2015 a limitation was imposed prohibiting spending more than 60 percent of the money raised from charging fees on salaries.

To provide fee-based services and taking into account the demand and availability of resources, a health service can organize a separate structural unit as well as open new staff positions or invite consultants from other organizations. The competition between the public and private sector for patients' money is quite strong, especially in big cities. Imperfect competition on the part of state health services should also be mentioned as state health services with a good reputation attract patients that prefer them to private clinics that are relatively new and less well-known.

OOP AND INEQUALITY OF ACCESS TO HEALTH CARE

Assessing the link between OOP and inequality of access to health care in Russia is a difficult task, as there are factors that contribute to reducing as well as widening inequality. The main factor that works against inequality of access is that every Russian citizen is covered by compulsory healthy insurance (CHI). The network of state-owned health services that provide health care free at the point of delivery is well developed. Surveys conducted by different agencies (*Levada tsentr*, 2016) demonstrate that the majority of respondents still seek medical treatment in the public system. It can be argued that OOPs increase patients' choice and give them the possibility to gain faster access to health care, to overcome waiting lists and visit specific doctors for whatever reason. However, according to the 2000 WHO World Health Report (WHO, 2000), Russia was in the 185th position on the list of countries ranked by the index of fairness of financial contributions. The increase in private payments in health care indicates that public money is not enough to fully cover the population's needs. Though universal access is guaranteed at least politically and legally, the public system is not adequately funded, and it is likely that people experience problems with access to free medical care. OOP should be discussed from the standpoint of the ability to pay rather than as a social right. In Russia, OOPs are increasing against the background of high income inequality and high levels of poverty.

The Gini coefficient reached its peak of 0.421 in 2007 and then slightly decreased to 0.415 in 2015. The ratio of the highest to the lowest income deciles followed the same dynamic, 16.7 and 15.7, respectively. Also, the Gini is quite high for the distribution of wages. It shows that there are significant differences in the socio-economic status of households. The number of people living in poverty is also quite significant. The lowest level since the start of transition was in 2012 at 10.7 percent of the population with the rate increasing to 13.3 percent, or about 20 million people, by 2015. However, as poverty in Russia is measured relative to a subsistence minimum, fixed by the government via consumer basket, the real numbers are likely to be higher. The number of the working poor is also quite significant—in 2015 more than 10 percent of those employed received wages lower than the subsistence minimum.

According to a selective observation of the behavioral factors affecting population health status conducted by Rosstat in 2013, indicators of self-assessment of health status vary considerably by income group. Seventy percent of respondents with high incomes compared to only 18 percent of respondents with low incomes rated their health status as 'very good' or 'good'. Accordingly, only seven percent of respondents with high incomes compared to 32.9 percent of those with low incomes consider their health 'bad' or 'very bad'. A similar tendency can be traced in relation to morbidity. Only 18.6 percent of respondents with low income compared to 52.6 percent with high income noted the absence of disease. For all ten types of diseases included in the survey, the proportion of respondents with low incomes who had a particular disease, is higher, and in some cases quite significantly so, being most pronounced in relation to diabetes, being 5.6 times higher amongst those with low incomes compared to those with high incomes.

Official statistics also show an increase in medical expenditures in Russians' household budgets. The share of health care in total household expenditures increased from 2.5 percent in 2005 to 3.6 percent in 2014. The highest rises were recorded for expenses on medical devices and medication, rising from 1.3 percent to 2 percent, and on ambulatory care, rising from 0.7 percent to 1.3 percent. The share of hospital expenses slightly decreased in 2014 to 0.3 percent, having been about 0.4 percent from 2010 to 2013. The share of medical treatment in the total volume of services rendered for fee is also growing, from 4.8 percent in 2005 to 6.4 percent by 2014. This indicates that the scope of medical treatment provided for fee is growing faster than total paid services. In per capita terms in current prices it increased for the period of 2005 – 2014 by over four times (see Table 2).

Table 2   Fee for service medical treatment in Russia

Selected indicators	2005	2010	2011	2012	2013	2014
Services rendered for fee, total, mln rbls	109756	250474	286058	333895	416227	474432
Services rendered for fee, per capita, total, rbls	15828.8	34606.2	38756.4	42156.2	48272.8	51115.7
including medical treatment	764.7	1753.4	2001.0	2331.6	2900.4	3247.5
Share of medical treatment in total fee for service, %	4.8	5.1	5,2	5,5	6.0	6.4

Source: Rosstat, 2015 (a), 2015 (b).

Official statistics indicate that on average Russian households of all income groups have an experience of paying for health care at some point. Rich people spent a bigger share of their household expenditures on medical care than the poor—3.3 percent for the 10th decile compared to 2.5 percent for the 1st decile in 2014.

The data on *per capita* household expenditures on services by income groups show that rich people spent more both in absolute and relative terms. The share of medical treatment in total expenditures on services of the 1st (lowest) decile increased for the period in question from 1.14 percent to 1.2 percent, and of the 10th (highest) decile from 5 percent to 7.4 percent. The ratio of health expenditures on medical treatment of upper to low income deciles increased from 33 times in 2004 to 43 times in 2014. In absolute terms, per capita household expenditures on medical treatment of the rich are growing faster than the poor—they increased by 6 times for the 1st decile and by 8.5 times for the 10th decile.

Sociological research suggests that the growth of OOP might mean not only an increase in the average bill but also growth in the number of people who end up paying for medical care. According to Public Opinion Foundation (FOM), in 2015 46 percent of respondents noted that they had to pay for medical treatment, an increase from 2007 (42 percent). Accordingly, the proportion of respondents who did not pay declined, from 57 percent to 53 percent, respectively (Public Opinion Fund, 2015).

Interestingly, in the 2015 survey, the majority of those who paid did it officially, through a cashier at a health service—34 percent of respondents mentioned that they always paid officially while 6 percent of respondents said they paid officially more often than informally. In the 2007 survey the numbers were 25 percent and 6 percent, respectively. This means that more than 75 percent of those respondents who paid for health care did it officially.

The number of respondents who paid only informally decreased from 4 percent in 2007 to 2 percent in 2015 as well as the number of those respondents who said that they paid more often informally than officially—7 percent and 3 percent respectively. This means that official fee for service is becoming more widespread while informal payments are gradually decreasing. At the same time, 29 percent of respondents paid when visiting state health services, and 22 percent when visiting private ones.

The possibilities of alternative means of funding medical care are limited. Only 6 percent of Russians have voluntary health insurance. Approximately the same number of Russians (7 percent) have the opportunity to regularly go to private clinics. In other words, only 13 percent of the population uses paid medical services. Among the high-income group this share reaches 23 percent.

Sociological research reveals the following paradox: the majority of respondents (75 percent) go to public health services but think that quality care can be obtained only if one pays. In the Levada center survey, 86 percent of respondents admit that only those who have money can get high-quality medical care in Russia. This opinion is shared by respondents of all groups, regardless of the wealth or size of the settlement. This indicates a belief that there is a strong link between the quality of medical care and money spent, however; steps towards increasing mandatory official payments are not accepted by the bulk of the respondents (Levada 2016, 21).

Two rounds of the comprehensive Rosstat population survey on standards of living, undertaken in 2011 and 2014, provide information on respondents who consider the need to pay as an obstacle to obtaining medical care (see Table 3).

Table 3   The reasons for not seeking medical assistance in health services and receiving medical care from other sources if there is a need for medical treatment

	2011	2014
Did not seek medical treatment in health services in case of need, % of all respondents	42.7	33.6
Including, the necessary treatment could be obtained only for fee		
all respondents, %	5.7	11.0
urban population	6.1	11.0
rural population	4.5	11.0
working age	5.7	10.0
young people (16 – 26 years)	5.1	7.4
elderly	5.9	12.5
working people	5.3	9.8

Source: compiled by the author based on: Rosstat. Comprehensive survey of population living conditions, 2011 and 2014.

The survey data shows that the proportion of those who did not seek medical help, because necessary treatment could be obtained only for money, almost doubled from 2011 to 2014, especially in groups such as the rural population and the elderly. However, in general, the number of people who did not seek necessary medical care decreased for the period in question from 42.7 percent to 33.6 percent Substantial financial problems arise in access to medicines—in 2011 95.2 percent of respondents bought drugs at their own expense while 17 percent of respondents noted the lack of funds for the purchase of drugs. 29.5 percent of respondents failed to complete a course of treatment or went through it only partially because they were asked to pay for treatment for which they had no money.

However, an increase in OOP *per se* need not result in increased inequality. As mentioned above, people do not necessarily need to pay for medical treatment as they can seek care in the public sector that is well-developed in Russia. According to survey data, more than 75 percent of Russians obtain medical treatment in state polyclinics / hospitals. However, the lower the income, the more often free medical care is sought in state owned health services—80 percent of respondents from the group with a low-income status compared to 66 percent of the higher-income group.

It is argued here that institutional barriers are important to understand the relation between OOP and inequality of access. There is a big concern, supported by evidence from the field, that state health services might increase inequality of access by using highly bureaucratic management procedures and providing medical staff with a perverse stimulus to make patients pay for services that should be provided free of charge. When both for free and fee for services are provided in the same facility, by the same doctors, using the same equipment, it is likely to tempt medical personnel to 'force' a patient to pay, especially for laboratory tests or tertiary care. When somebody pays to overcome a waiting list, s / he is just jumping over the heads of fellow taxpayers which is unfair to those on the waiting list.

As public funds are scarce, OOPs are considered by both health authorities and medical personnel in health services as a source of additional funding. For a patient it is often very difficult to evaluate his / her medical need. Thus, patients can be easily manipulated into paying to receive medical treatment as soon as possible. An information problem should also be mentioned, as in many cases people do not know exactly what should be provided free under CHI. In a situation of discomfort and uncertainty, they often are ready to pay for that which should be provided free.

The role of the primary care doctor (*terapevt*) as a gate keeper was strengthened in the course of the recent health reforms. This is a rationing mechanism that also pushes the patient towards paying for medical treatment. To visit a consultant, a patient needs to be referred by a *terapevt*, otherwise s / he can get access only for a fee. Recently a norm was set that a doctor should allocate about 12 minutes per patient. Together with increased administrative load, such a brief visit limits the time a doctor spends with patients and, often, that is not enough, especially in the case of a patient with multiple health issues.

The situation of 'exit' seems to be relevant in the Russian context as people prefer to opt for fee-for-services as they are more responsive to their needs (although this does not automatically mean a better quality) instead of fighting for their rights for free treatment. Under the present system they might complain to either a special government agency (*Roszdravnadzor*) or their CHI company. Both have special mechanisms, first of all financial, to deal with such problems. However, people prefer to pay or to change polyclinic rather than complain or fight for their rights.

CONCLUSIONS

The general conclusion is that the increase in OOP in the Russian health care system is likely to contribute to widening inequality in access to health care. However, the analysis demonstrates that the situation is complicated, as there are also factors that mitigate inequality. Health financing indicators are indirect, and much depends on institutional context, and the organization of the health care system in the country. Against a background of high income inequality and low public spending, the expansion of fee-for-service in state-owned health services is likely to contribute to inequality of access via the formation of a two-tier health system: good care for the rich and lower quality care for the poor. The role of individual health finance seems to be institutionalized, an important consequence of which is that virtually no redistribution happens in health financing. This undermines the basis of social solidarity, where the rich pay for the poor and the healthy pay for those who are ill.

In Russia quality health care is often considered as a service for those who can pay rather than as a citizen right. Well-off people in Russia *de facto* are opting out of free health care thus contributing to the deterioration of the quality of treatment provided for free. Free medical care is shrinking and losing its potential to become a leveling force in a divided society. It is suggested here that the state should introduce mechanisms to control private health expenditures. Several policy options have been discussed in the course of public sector reforms, yet the choice has not yet been made. As it is unlikely that public health financing will increase substantially in the near future, developing prepayment schemes (voluntary or employer-based insurance) might help to ease the burden of costs of direct payments and to level inequalities in access to health care. However, as recent Russian government initiatives show, inequality—unlike poverty—is not openly mentioned among strategic social and economic priorities.

REFERENCES

Aaberge R., Brandolini A. (2014). *Multidimensional Poverty and Inequality* (September 26, 2014). Bank of Italy Temi di Discussione (Working Paper) No. 976.

Asante A, Price J., Hayen A., Jan S., Wiseman V. (2016). "Equity in Health Care Financing in Low- and Middle-Income Countries: A Systematic Review of Evidence from Studies Using Benefit and Financing Incidence Analyse". *PLoS One.* Apr 11; 11(4).

Bychkova S. G. (2016). "Problemy i vozmozhnosti statisticheskoj ocenki neravenstva i bednosti v Rossijskoj Federacii i regionah". *Vestnik universiteta (Gosudarstvennyj universitet upravleniya)* № 1: 226 – 232 (Problems and possibilities of statistical evaluation of inequality and poverty in Russian Federation and its regions).

Chubarova T., Grigorieva N. (2013). Patterns in Health Care Reforms in Economies under Transition: a Case of Russia. In: *Health Reforms in Central and Eastern Europe. Options, Obstacles, Limited Outcomes.* Bjorkman J., Y. Nemec, eds. Eleven Publ., Hague.

Chubarova T.V. (2016). "Finansovo ehkonomicheskie aspekty dostupnosti medicinskih uslug v Rossii". *Byulleten Vostochno Sibirskogo nauchnogo centra SO RAMN.* T. 1. №5 (111); 84 – 89. (Financial and economic aspects of access to medical care in Russia).

Davis K. (1991). "Inequality and Access to Health Care." *Milbank Q.* 69(2); 253 – 73.

Deaton A. (2003). "Health, Inequality, and Economic Development." *Journal of Economic Literature*, 41(1); 113 – 158.

HOPE (2015). *Out-of-pocket payments in healthcare systems in the European Union.* European Hospital and Healthcare Federation Publications, September 2015.

ISSC, IDS and UNESCO (2016). *World Social Science Report 2016. Challenging Inequalities: Pathways to a Just World.* UNESCO, Paris.

Gerasimova E.A, Gerasimova I.V. (2014). "Neravinstvo denezhikh dokhodov v Rossii". *Mir Rossii*, №2; 38 – 74 (Inequality of monetary incomes in Russia).

Glennester H. 1992. *Paying for welfare.* The 1990s. Haverster Wheatsheaf: Hemel Heampstead.

Goddard M, P and Smith P. (2001). "Equity of access to health care services: theory and evidence from the UK." *Soc Sci Med.* Nov; 53 (9); 1149 – 62.

Grigorieva N. (2016). Social justice and equality / inequality issues in modern-day Russia. ISSC, IDS and UNESCO, World Social Science Report 2016. Challenging Inequalities: Pathways to a Just World. UNESCO, Paris; 93 – 96.

Grinberg R., T. Chubarova (2004). "Democratic Values and Inequality, or Democratic Inequality?" *Ekonomski pregled*, 55 (1 – 2); 157 – 180.

Hsiao W. (1995). "Abnormal Economics in the Health Sector". *Health Policy*, № 32; 37 – 49.

Kalashnikov K. N. and Kalachikova O. N. (2014). "Dostupnost i kachestvo medicinskoy pomoschi v kontekste modernizacii zdravoohraneniya". *Ekonomicheskie i socialnie peremeni: fakti, tendencii, prognoz*. № 2 (32); 130 – 142 (Access and quality of medical care in the context of health care modernization).

Kislitsina O.A. (2003). *Income Inequality in Russia during Transition: How Can It Be Explained?* Moscow: EERC.

Kochkina N.N., M.D. Krasil'nikova, S.V. Shishkin. (2015). *Dostupnost' i kachestvo meditsinskoy pomoshchi v otsenkakh naseleniya*. Preprint WP8 / 2015 / 03 Seriya WP8. Gosudarstvennoye i munitsipal'noye upravleniye (Availability and quality of medical care in population estimates).

Krasnova L. S. (2015). "Sostoyaniye zdorov'ya kak faktor sprosa na platnyye meditsinskiye uslugi". *Vestnik RLMS*, vypusk 5:123 – 140 (Health status as a factor of demand for paid medical services).

Kulkova V.Yu. (2014). "Gosudarstvennie rashodi na zdravoohranenie v OESR i Rossii: potencial i metodika sravnitelnogo analiza" *Finansoviy zhurnal*. 3 (21) iyul-sentyabr 2014: 35 – 46 (State health expenditures in OECD and Russia: potential and methodology of comparative analysis).

Le Grand, J. (1987). "Equity, Health and Health Care". *Social Justice Research*, 1; 257 – 74.

Leenan H. (1985). *Equality and equity in health care*. Paper presented at the WHO / Nuffield Centre for Health Service Studies meeting, Leeds, 22 – 26 July 1985.

Levada tsentr (2016). "'Protivostoyaniye logic': vrach, patsiyent i vlast' v usloviyakh reformirovaniya sistemy zdravookhraneniya". Svodnyy analiticheskiy otchet Levada tsentr. ("Opposition Logic": a doctor, a patient and authorities in the context of reforming health care system).

Lewis M. (2007). "Informal Payments and the Financing of Health Care in Developing and Transition Countries". *Health Affairs*. Jul – Aug, 26(4); 984 – 97.

Mackenbach J.P., W.J. Meerding, A.E. Kuns (2007). *Economic implications of socio-economic inequalities in health in the European Union*. European Commission, Health and Consumer Protection Directorate, July 2007.

Mackenbach J.P., Meerding W.J., Kunst A.E. (2011). "Economic costs of health inequalities in the European Union". *J Epidemiol Community Health*. 2011 May, 65(5); 412 – 9.

OECD (2001). *Health Data 2001: A Comparative Analysis of 30 Countries*. OECD, Paris.

OECD (2015). *Health at a Glance 2015: OECD Indicators*, OECD Publishing, Paris.

OECD (201. *Income inequality update*. Income inequality remains high November.

Paul P. and H. Valtonen (2016). "Health inequality in the Russian Federation: An examination of the changes in concentration and achievement indices from 1994 to 2013". *Int J Equity Health*. 15; 36.

Pickett K.E. and Wilkinson R.G. (2015). "Income inequality and health: a causal review". *Soc Sci Med.* Mar, 128; 316 – 26.

Public Opinion Fund (2015). Dominanti. Pole mneniy. Zdorovie. *Sociologicheskiy byulleten.* Zdravoohranenie. Opros. (Dominants. Field of Opinions. Healthcare).

Rosstat (2015a) *Zdravoohranenie v Rossii.* 2015. Stat.sb. / Rosstat-M. (Health care in Russia).

Rosstat (2015b) *Socialnoe polozhenie i uroven zhizni naseleniya Rossii* 2015. Stat.sb. / Rosstat-M. (Social status and living standards of people in Russia 2015).

Rosstat. *Itogi kompleksnogo nablyudeniya usloviy zhizni naseleniya. 2011 i 2014 gg.* (Results of the comprehensive of population living conditions 2011 and 2014) http://www.gks.ru/free_doc/new_site/inspection/itog_inspect1.htm.

Savedoff W. (2003). "How Much Should Countries Spend on Health?" Discussion paper number 2-2003. World Health Organization. Geneva.

Sen A. (2002). "Why Health Equity?" *Health Economics* 11(8); 659 – 66.

Shishkin S. (ed.) (2007). *Analiz razlichij v dostupnosti medicinskoj pomoshchi dlya naseleniya Rossii.* M., Nezavisimyj Institut social'noj politiki. (Analysis of differences in access to health care for Russian population).

Wagstaff A. (2002). "Reflections on and alternatives to WHO's fairness of financial contribution index". *Health Econ.* Mar; 11(2); 103 – 15.

Walters S. and M. Suhrcke (2005). *Socioeconomic inequalities in health and health care access in Central and Eastern Europe and the CIS: a review of the recent literature.* WHO European Office for Investment for Health and Development Working paper 2005 / 1 November 2005.

Whitehead, M. (1992). "The Concepts and Principles of Equity and Health". *International Journal of Health Services* 22(3); 429 – 45.

World Bank (1993). *World Development Report. Investing in Health.* Washington, DC: World Bank Group.

World Bank (2006). *World Development Report. Equity and Development,* Washington, DC: World Bank Group.

World Bank (2008). Analyzing health equity using household survey data: a guide to techniques and their implementation / Owen O'Donnell et al., The International Bank for Reconstruction and Development / The World Bank, Washington, DC: World Bank Group.

WHO (2000). *World Health Report 2000. Health Systems: Improving Performance. WHO,* Geneva.

WHO (2010). *World Health report 2010. Health Systems Financing: the path to universal coverage. WHO. Geneva.*

WHO (2013). *Monitoring Progress towards Universal Health Coverage at Country and Global Levels: A Framework Joint WHO* / World Bank Group Discussion Paper, December 2013.

WHO. Health financing. Out-of-pocket payments, user fees and catastrophic expenditure. https://www.who.int/health_financing/topics/financial-protection/out-of-pocket-payments/en/.

CHAPTER 5:
THE HIDDEN REALITY OF DAY-TO-DAY STRUGGLES OF THE WORKING POOR IN LITHUANIA

Natalija Atas

INTRODUCTION

This chapter investigates the problem of in-work poverty (also referred to as working poverty) because it represents a modern form of poverty that is rapidly becoming one of the most pressing issues not only in Lithuania, but across all capitalist countries. According to the most recent Eurostat statistical data, 9.5 percent of employees in the European Union (EU27) were living at-risk-of-poverty in 2014 (in comparison to 8.3 percent in 2007). This means that millions of men and women are currently facing the risk of poverty despite being active members of the labor market. The financial crisis of 2007 – 08 has influenced the surge in working poverty rates since cuts in working hours, lower salaries and suspension of pay were common practices of employers and institutions in dealing with the crisis (Gottfried and Lawton, 2010). In 2010, at 12.6 percent, the level of in-work poverty in Lithuania had not only reached a record high but also was one of the highest in the EU (Eurostat, 2017). Women were disproportionally affected by the increase (14.3 percent of working women faced risk of poverty in comparison to 10.6 percent of men). Even though in the following years, the level of poverty among working people in the country decreased, as this study will reveal, it had a destructive impact on the lives of those affected.

Despite a growing body of literature analyzing statistical patterns, characteristics and causes of in-work poverty (Lohmann, 2008; Ponthieux, 2010; Frazer and Marlier, 2010; Fraser et al., 2011; Maitre et al., 2012; Meulders and O'Dorchai, 2013; Pradella, 2015), the knowledge about the day-to-day realities of the working poor is largely neglected by scientific communities across Europe. Nevertheless, as Sidel (1992; xxiv) once sensibly said about statistical accounts of poverty, 'statistics are people with the tears washed off.' Therefore, in order to gain a comprehensive and accurate understanding of in-work poverty, it is necessary to look at what hides behind these statistical trends. This could not only facilitate a scientific understanding of what it means for an employed person to live in poverty, but also help to track the individual and structural roots of this problem. Hence, this chapter addresses gaps in in-work poverty knowledge existing in the literature, on both national and regional levels, by depicting first-hand experiences and realities of lives of those who live in working poverty in Lithuania. It aims to discuss strategies that are commonly applied among the working poor in order to manage their hardship. A concept of strategy in this context refers to a set of predetermined actions that help the poor to manage their income and spending disparities. Poverty here is understood in terms of relative deprivation as initially proposed by Townsend (1979; 31):

> Individuals, families and groups in the population can be said to be in poverty when they lack the resources to obtain the types of diet, participate in the activities and have the living conditions and amenities which are customary, or are at least widely encouraged or approved, in the societies to which they belong. Their resources are so seriously below those commanded by the average individual or family that they are, in effect, excluded from ordinary living patterns and activities.

This chapter will begin with an overview of the literature on first-hand experiences of poverty. Next, it will introduce the qualitative methodological approach that was utilized to obtain data for this study. The following sections will present empirical data depicting first-hand accounts of challenges and strategies related to employment, spending, prioritizing and borrowing that enable employed people living in poverty in Lithuania to make ends meet. It will reveal how in-work poverty is reflected in people's lives and, consequently, affects their daily experiences.

This chapter demonstrates that poverty represents a daily struggle, one that manifests itself in a number of ways and requires a relentless response.

FIRST-HAND EXPERIENCES OF POVERTY

Numerous studies have revealed that there is a clear pattern of poverty experience shared by different groups of people. To begin with, being poor does not only mean lack of fiscal or material resources, but also being disadvantaged in areas of health, education and housing conditions is a part of the overall poverty experience (Ellwood, 1999; Toynbee, 2003;

Munger, 2007; Shildrick et al., 2012). People living in hardship often emphasize that in order to lead a dignified life they require four key necessities, namely: education; health; housing; and employment (MRC, 2006). In other words, people see poverty as more than material deprivation. Nevertheless, material deprivation defined as 'having insufficient physical or material resources—food, shelter and clothing—necessary to sustain life in either an absolute or relative sense to some prescribed standard' is always at the epicenter of poverty (Baldock et al., 1999; 129). Poverty affects all three core dimensions of human life, that is, individual, family and social. Concerns about the management of household budgets and areas related with housing and nutrition are often identified as the most pressing among those who live in poverty (Kempson, 1996; Farrell and O'Connor, 2003; Attree, 2004). Furthermore, this constant hardship and struggle not only creates an immense psychological pressure, but also may lead to some other health issues (Sharpe and Bostock, 2002; Gould, 2006). Finally, stigma has been identified as a by-product of poverty that has a significant effect on people's lives (Beresford and Croft, 1995; Riggins, 1997; Oliver, 2001; Pickering, 2001; Lister, 2004).

A number of studies conducted in the UK showed that people living on low incomes were pressured to adopt specific 'survival' strategies in order to cope with their challenging living circumstances (Dean, 2007; Green, 2007; Power, 2007; Maynard and Clewett, 2009; Lister and Strelitz, 2008; Patrick, 2014). The strategies enabling people to keep their heads above water are complex and versatile, but often range between conditions of living in shortage and living in debt (Kempson et al., 1994; McKendrick et al., 2003). The first strategical pattern, cutting back on expenses in order to make ends meet, is inevitably adopted by everyone who lives in poverty. Often people have to cut back not only on social activities, but also on the necessities, such as food and heating, in order to avoid the stigma of debt. Careful budgeting is an essential part of managing on a low income. Individuals not only have to prioritize their purchases, but also be aware of ways and means in order to make budget purchases. This involves a great deal of researching, planning and accessing the budget products which requires substantial time and effort. Constant detailed planning can be a demanding and time-consuming activity that for some may became a full-time occupation (Kempson et al., 1994; McKendrick et al., 2003). Therefore, setting up priority areas and distributing income according to these expenses is an initial step of managing the low income for many. Leisure and recreation activities are usually not making it even to the bottom of the list (Ghate and Hazel, 2002). Purchasing food and paying utility and housing bills are considered to be the most pressing expenses that are the top priority for many low-income families. However, many have to compromise even with these two essentials.

The second strategy, applied by people experiencing poverty, is borrowing. This kind of debt manifests as 'bank overdrafts, credit and store cards, kinds of debt including rent, council tax and utility bill arrears, overpayments of tax credits, catalogues, social fund loans, loans from family, friends and children, and high interests doorstep loans' (Hooper et al., 2007; 25). Debts taken on to pay basic household bills are most common; however, low-income families might turn to borrowing and debts for a number of other reasons (Kempson, 1996). People are falling into debt in order to cover the cost of basic necessities, such as food, clothing and utility bills. Unexpected expenses and late or cancelled benefit / tax credits are other reasons why some people fall into debt. Besides, some people fall into debt in order to improve their quality of life and to maintain living standards prevailing in their community. For instance, the study showed that some extra money was needed by many in order to afford such social necessities as 'a large TV, Sky, birthday and Christmas presents, a car, a holiday, to have friends around' (Hooper et al., 2007; 25). Inability to maintain living standards and behavioral patterns accepted in society creates a psychological tension that sometimes can be momentarily relieved by taking on a debt. Some families do not have any extra money to participate in religious and cultural celebrations and, therefore, have to make a Hobson's choice between falling into debt or seeing their children denied their rights of being a part of such celebrations (Maynard and Clewett, 2009).

Although the above-mentioned strategies enable people to make ends meet, and normally are the only ways of managing life with a low income, they also place a number of constraints on people. All of the above strategies have one common feature: decision-making. Although making decisions is a normal feature of everyone's life, for people who live with rather limited options it can be a very frustrating and stressful experience for a very simple reason: with a limited income you are faced with only very limited choices.

METHODOLOGY

The data in this chapter derive from analysis of 36 semi-structured interviews conducted with the working poor of Lithuania. The field work was conducted in Vilnius, the capital of Lithuania, in 2012. This research followed a purposive sample procedure (Maxwell, 1997). The study participants were selected in the following way: a) the individual had to be employed for more than 6 months; b) the person's income had to be below the official at-risk-of-poverty threshold that is measured across the EU Member States as 60 percent of median equivalized income. Lithuania has one of the lowest at-risk of poverty thresholds in the EU. In 2012, the poverty threshold for two adults with two children younger than 14 years was just below 5.50 Euros per year, which made it the third lowest poverty threshold in the EU (Eurostat, 2017b). In other words, the selection criteria of the participants mirrored the 'in-work poverty' statistical indicator utilized by the European Commission (European Commission 2009; 11). Semi-structured interviews were used in the study in order to maximize the flexibility of the interviewing process (Saidman, 1998; May, 2002).

Demographic characteristics of participants revealed the following patterns. Of the 36 research participants, only 8 were male. On the one hand, this can be explained by fact that after the group of people who could have been identified as working poor was accessed, the selection process transformed to convenience (or availability) sampling 'where respondents selected simply because they are close at hand, or easy to access' (Pole and Lampard, 2002; 35). In other words, anyone who lived in in-work poverty and agreed to participate in the research was included in the sample (regardless of their other characteristics). Also, it must be noted that, due to the domestic gender division of labor, women living with a male partner were more likely to be the ones responsible for collection of food donations. However, at the same time, the over-representation of women in this sample is not random as in-work poverty among women at the time of research (in 2012) in Lithuania was more widespread than among men (Eurostat, 2017).

Without exception, all sample members were part of families with children. There were two household types in the sample, namely married couples and lone mothers. To be more precise, there were 18 married people, 16 single mothers (including those divorced or widowed) and 2 cohabitating couples. Predominantly, families consisted of 1 – 3 children, with only a few larger families. The sample included people with four educational backgrounds: secondary, vocational, technical and higher. The majority of the people with vocational and technical qualifications were not working according to the level of their qualification. Just a few people had a higher education and were in the minority compared to other groups.

CHALLENGES AND STRATEGIES FOR MAKING ENDS MEET

Employment strategies

Managing living on a low income is a significant challenge—and one that requires strategic thinking, a high level of organization and time (McKendrick et al., 2003; Dean, 2007; Green, 2007). However, time is a commodity that working individuals lack. Combining work and executing poverty survival strategies requires extra effort on the part of employees. Regardless, the participants of this study proved to be very resourceful in developing their survival strategies. The priority strategy for the majority of the participants was attempting to maximize their earning potential. A common practice that enabled participants to make ends meet was taking on additional jobs in order to increase their overall income. A number of participants had more than one job, at one point or other, during the last few years. Additional work usually took the form of unregistered employment. However, having additional employment does not always mean a notable increase in living standards, as one of the participants had noticed, 'There was a time when I had three jobs. But it didn't provide me with good money. Although, at that time, I could eat meat 3 – 5 times a week. Now I am not able to do that.'

Participants occasionally made an attempt to improve their position in the labor market. Some of them spoke about their effort to improve their skills or to gain new qualifications. However, they emphasized the insufficiency of qualification courses offered by the Labor Exchange. A forty-six year-old mechanic said:

> I was registered as a job seeker and I was offered to attend a course to improve my qualification. I have done it, but I can't say that it was very useful. Yes, I got a certificate. But it did not give me much in the way of skills.

A participant, who had been trying to gain some new skills, after her technical qualification became irrelevant in the contemporary labor market, told about her struggle to gain some relevant skills that would help her to increase her employability:

> I don't want anything extraordinary; I understand my abilities, as I am considered an unqualified worker. To be honest, I even am hiding my technical qualification because I was told that I will not get any additional training if I have any qualification. Therefore, I had to hide from the Labor Exchange the fact that I graduated technical school in order to be able to attend any course. Once I attended sewing course. But this course did not give me such skills that would enable me to do this type of job professionally. I was not able to become a tailor, because my speed is not as it supposed to be in order to work in factory; and my vision is not the best. And now, I can't take any courses for two years, because I was enrolled in the previous one.

Her experience shows that there are some systematic obstacles preventing people getting a new set of skills. On the one hand, there are some eligibility restrictions preventing enrolment in the free training courses offered by the Labor Exchange. On the other hand, these courses do not always provide the outcome expected initially, that is, of gaining a specific skill that is in demand in the current labor market.

Lack of satisfactory jobs was often identified as a key aspect preventing a change in working position. Workers emphasized that low pay often comes with a high work load and distant job location:

> Offers are not good, they are offering positions where you have to work a lot, but the wage is very small. You have to work night shifts and double shifts too. Or they are offering jobs far away and you have to travel a long distance. Therefore, you will spend all your money on travelling. (Male, builder)

Furthermore, single mothers were often pushed into part-time employment as they had to compromise between childcare and income because of inflexible working hours. Therefore, they had limited options for a full-time employment that could fit around their childcare responsibilities. It was an especially common problem. One interviewee, like a number of other single mothers, reported that she was forced to stay in part time employment because she did not feel that she had another choice:

> I am working part time, because I am always asking them to offer me a job that starts at 8am because I need to send my son to school. And they only offer me a full-time position that starts at 6am. And I can't start at 6am. And everywhere in agencies they are offering this time. Women that are my age, and have children are not able to start their work at 6am. Many are working 4 hours on one site, having a break, and going to another site. When I am in a bus, I can see all these women with grey faces, you can see them immediately. It is not a life.

Part-time employment for the single mothers inevitably meant immense financial restraints. Very often it jeopardized their livelihood. Therefore, people in this situation were looking for alternative means of support.

Unofficial employment that supplements the official part-time employment is a very common strategy of coping. Jobs such as 'cleaning the houses of rich people' were one of the most common unofficial earnings. Unofficial employment is considered advantageous because it is tax-free. Also, it allows flexibility in a working schedule, which is a major issue for many working lone mothers who struggle to adjust their working schedules to the working hours of the institutions that their children attend during the day, especially school (majority of participants of this study had children attending schools and not child care facilities). Although such income has immediate financial benefits and is absolutely essential for survival of the families, it has serious negative consequences. Several respondents admitted that they have insufficient official work experience, as a significant part of their employment was unregistered. This will affect their prospect of a pension and financial wellbeing after retirement. Although, interviewees realized it, they did not feel like they have another choice, as they are focusing on fulfilment of the immediate needs of their families.

Spending strategies: decisions, dilemmas and day-to-day sacrifices

The pattern of spending across the sample was very similar. Spending on food and utility bills was often said to consume the total income of a household. Respondents often described their spending in the following way: 'we are paying bills first, and everything else is going on food.' It was repeatedly emphasized that during the winter season a significant part of total income is devoted to covering heating bills. Respondents who are renting property said that they are legally prevented from receiving compensation for heating even though their revenue for family members is below the established national poverty line. Families with school age children also identified the constant financial pressure experienced from the school related expenses and clothing needs of children. Neglecting the needs of adults of a family is a common approach taken by participants. Indeed, often parents, normally on their own cost, have to make harsh choices with regards to items that are conventionally considered necessities (Kempson, 1994; Middleton et al., 1997; Women's Budget Group, 2008). Commonly parents, particularly mothers, prioritize their children's needs, especially in terms of providing adequate nourishment and clothing. Often, they decide to go without personal necessities in order to ensure that needs of their children are satisfied (Ghate and Hazel, 2002). Attitudes such as 'our biggest concern is our children, we are not important anymore' or 'I would rather buy nothing for myself, but I will get what is necessary for the children' were dominant across the interviews within this study. Frequently, interviewees expressed uneasiness about their inability to satisfy their children's needs:

> It is more difficult when we need to buy clothes, then usually we are going to *Humana* (second hand shop) and buying something there. Even though our children are already at this age that they don't want to wear second-hand clothes, we are buying it there anyway. Then we are lying that we bought it from a good shop. (Female, name withheld, shop assistant)

Items such as clothing for adult family members were as a rule identified as luxury items that were only occasionally purchased and exclusively in second-hand shops. Moreover, meeting basic needs for food was a constant struggle for those interviewed. Respondents also often had to compromise on their nutritional intake. A man who was working as a system administrator said: 'we are limiting our food expenses as much as we can. We are buying discounted things. We are buying the cheapest products.' Such limited spending on food rations is negatively affecting the nutritional needs of the participants:

> When I am in a shop, there are some products that I even will not look at because they are out of reach for us. I just look what have a bigger discount. We are not able to buy fruits as often as we want. I even was not able to buy cheese not so long ago, although my children really wanted it. We are eating modestly. Just basic, but it is enough for us. If I could, I would pay more attention to quality of the food. We became sort of vegetarians. We buy fish just at big celebrations. We would buy it more frequently if we could. (Female, teacher)

Poor nutrition is likely to affect all people who live on a low income for more than a few months (Dowler et al., 2001; Seeley and Lobstein, 2004). Spending on food is considered to be the most flexible part of the household budget by many. Therefore, it is the most vulnerable part of household expenditure. Restricted food budgets for many mean poor diet and inadequate nutritional intake, either caused by intake of cheap, low quality food or a reduced quantity of consumed food, or both (Beresford et al., 1999; Seeley and Lobstein, 2004).

Furthermore, poverty has a strong impact on housing conditions (Reynolds et al., 2008; Tunstall et al., 2013). Low income leaves people with limited housing options. Moreover, it constrains people's ability to sustain their accommodation. The main concerns regarding housing repeatedly brought up by people living with low income include availability of affordable housing, a low quality of accommodation, inadequate living space and inability to pay housing costs (MRC, 2006). Similarly, in order to survive with given incomes, participants of this study had to compromise on the quality of housing. Commonly, respondents gave up conventional comfort in order to reduce spending on rent and bills. Some chose accommodation without facilities that are considered normal in the society, such as water and centralized heating systems. Others even decided to move to summer houses with very limited facilities, usually located out of the city, in order to minimize their spending on utilities and housing.

Nevertheless, the ability to control the amount spent on some facilities, such as centralized heating, is essential for many. The winter season in the country usually starts in October and finishes in April. For people on low incomes, who live in accommodation that is connected to the central heating, this period of the year is the most challenging. A single mother who was working as a cleaner said, that 'the most important thing is that we are able to control heating in this flat. Therefore, we are not using heating in order to save money. Otherwise I don't know what we would do.' Fuel poverty was a big issue among the cohort. Many had to choose accommodation of poorer quality because they hoped to reduce their heating expenses. Another strategy of coping with high utility costs was merging households with close relatives, such as parents or siblings. However, this was often just a temporary solution. A number of respondents expressed dissatisfaction and concern about their housing. The poor quality of accommodation was one of the biggest concerns for many families in the sample. A full-time sales assistant, who lives in a home of four, said that her accommodation is not only unsatisfactory visually, but also endangers the health of her child. She revealed that:

> Furniture and kitchen equipment need to be renewed. We didn't have any redecoration for 20 years. It is in a pretty bad condition right now. Our roof is constantly leaking, it is cold, and my daughter is coughing all the time.

The Hidden Reality of Day-to-Day Struggles of the Working Poor

Parents expressed concern over raising children in their current accommodation because of its poor state. Factors such as structural defects, excess dampness and mold, insufficient insulation and excess cold, were commonly defined as the main issues. A male participant, who is working full-time in a private company, described the dreadful condition of a rented studio where he is living with his wife and two children aged six and one and a half:

> We even wanted to invite someone from television to look at our living conditions. But they refused to come. We have a horrible window, but we can't afford to change it. And the wall is horrible, mold everywhere. I don't know what to do, where to go to seek help. Our living situation is very harsh, and we are raising our children there.

People reported their inability to invest in any form of home repair. Even though some faults in a house may be significant and may cause some health hazards, respondents have to make a sacrifice in order to make any change. One female participant spoke about the dilemma that she had to face on a daily basis. She had to choose whether to prioritize spending on food or maintenance of her house:

> My family needs more space. We are living in a one room apartment. My younger son needs to prepare his homework, so does my older one. The flat is in a wooden house, no one else is living in that house. Therefore, I have to heat it on my own. Heating is getting too expensive; to eliminate mold also costs money. And then you have to choose between buying means to eliminate mold or buying food to top up the empty fridge. And you don't know what to do. Therefore, maintenance of the house requires money and the quality of accommodation is very poor. And renovation is an unreachable option for us although we really need it. We have been renting this accommodation for a long time.

When personal means are not enough

With a few exceptions, the majority of the participants disclosed that they were not able to devote any of their family income to saving, even for emergencies: if someone from us would die, we even wouldn't have money for funeral, because we have absolutely nothing' (Nurse Assistant, mother-of-one). Due to an absence of money set aside, low-income families often turn to borrowing and, therefore, tumbling into debts. For many participants of this study falling into debt was one of the most unpleasant experiences that could happen to them. Borrowing money, especially from non-family members, meant personal defeat and symbolized the last step before falling into 'real' poverty. Therefore, most people tried to do everything in their power to avoid it. Consequently, some extreme savings techniques were a better option for many. Families chose to limit their family's intake of food instead of borrowing money. One of the participants said that 'we had better eat less in order to avoid debts.' A lone mother of two children who worked as a part-time manager revealed that she had to undermine the quality of even the most essential food products: 'you are going to shop and looking for the cheapest products. When I am going to shop, I am never buying fresh bread, always discounted one. Because paying 2.50 litas (Euro 0.72) for a piece of bread is too expensive for us.'

However, even though some people tried to minimize their spending as much as possible, they had to borrow money at the end of the month as their wages ran out. For some participants, it was a common practice to borrow some money a week short of the pay date in the end of the month and then give it back after getting their salary at the beginning of the next month. One interviewee called this situation 'a vicious circle.' Nevertheless, the people who were not able to survive by their own means and therefore had to borrow money often called it a 'horrendous' experience. It was disclosed that without extended family support, many would not be able to scratch out a living. Occasional or periodical support from family members, predominantly retired parents, is a common support structure identified during interviews. This support can be financial, but more often it is expressed through food or living arrangements. Food is commonly received from relatives living in villages where they are growing their own food. Other ways of dealing with the situation is the merging of the households of older and younger generations. There were some examples when younger families had to move in with their parents, usually retired mothers, in order to reduce their spending on housing and utility bills.

The majority of interviewees identified the assistance from the Food Bank[1] as the last resort that they approached in order to make ends meet. For many their decision to come to the Food Bank was determined by their limited income and inability to keep up with rising food prices. Some people reported that their household faced hardship after one of the breadwinners lost their job, had to downgrade to a part-time position or

---

1   Food Bank is a charitable NGO, collecting food donations and distributing them to people in need. It has been distributing food to a number of locations across Lithuania.

experienced a wage cut. Some said that the only thing that prevented them seeking help from the Food Bank earlier was lack of awareness of its existence and their eligibility for this support.

CONCLUSION

This chapter has highlighted that in-work poverty represents, or is, a struggle—and one that manifests itself in a number of ways. Consequently, in order to face this struggle, people living in poverty have to develop a strong agency emerging through robust willingness, resilience and resourcefulness. Nevertheless, their agency is often constrained by structural obstacles that prevent them from improving their living conditions. Working people who struggle to make ends meet appear to have rather pessimistic life outlooks. If some unemployed people may have hope that their life could improve once they find a job, working individuals often feel that they have exhausted their options. Therefore, individuals who participated in this study were rather skeptical about the potential for improvement of their well-being—and maybe rightly so. They had jobs, they worked hard, budgeted carefully, spent wisely (and rather modestly) but none of these things mattered. Although they exercised their agency to full measure, this failed to improve their chances of progression, and, therefore, did not count. They were convinced that they would not receive any substantial outside help because they did not matter.

Qualitative analysis of realities and issues faced by the working poor takes this study to the heart of the phenomenon as it sheds light on issues that are rarely discussed and often concealed by statistics. It illustrates challenges faced by this group of people and shows the ways they deal with and adapt to the resulting situation. And, most importantly, it gives voice to a group of people that rarely get heard either in academic or political sphere in Lithuania. However, this study does not go without limitations. Even though interviews conducted for this study provided an important and unique understanding of experiences of those living in in-work poverty, the interviewing process also had its shortcomings. Due to time, financial and access restrictions, the researcher was not always successful in building 'a level of trust so that the participant feels safe enough to share' (Dickson-Swift et al. 2007; 338). It is likely that some respondents withheld some relevant details that could potentially have contributed to an even better understanding of the issue. Even though some authors have argued that lack of a closer relationship may actually increase the level of disclosure (Brannen, 1988; Patai, 199; Reinharz, 1992), the author of this chapter believes that such strategies as organizing an introductory meeting prior to interviews or follow-up interviews could have helped to improve the quality of data obtained. Furthermore, whilst the sampling strategy (purposive-convenience) used in this study contributed to gaining access to people belonging to the group of the working poor, unintentionally, it excluded certain representative voices within the group (e.g. younger and older workers). In other words, every person who was identified as working poor and who agreed to participate in the research was included in the sample regardless of their demographic characteristics. Consequently, some demographic groups were not adequately represented. Future researchers would benefit from using quota sampling, which is characterized by more inclusive properties and would help to reveal experiences of people with a wider range of characteristics (such as age, gender, marital status, etc.). Also, future studies could expand the focus of the questionnaire and include a wider spectrum of questions, bringing up such themes as the way the working poor construct their identities or define and conceptualize poverty.

REFERENCES

Attree, Pamela (2004). "Growing up in Disadvantage: A Systematic Review of the Qualitative Evidence" in *Child: Care, Health and Development*, Vol. 30, No.3. In <http://onlinelibrary.wiley.com/doi/10.1111/j.13652214.2004.00480.x/abstract> accessed 2 May 2014.

Attree, Pamela (2005). "Low-Income Mothers, Nutrition and Health: A Systematic Review of Qualitative Evidence" in *Maternal and Child Nutrition*, Vol. 1, No. 4. In <http://onlinelibrary.wiley.com/doi/10.1111/j.17408709.2005.00022.x/abstract> accessed 2 May 2014.

Baldock, John, Manning, Nick, Miller, Steward and Vickerstaff, Sarah (eds.) (1999). *Social Policy* (Oxford: Oxford University Press).

Bennett, Fran and Daly, Mary (2014). *Poverty through a Gender Lens: Evidence and Policy Review on Gender and Poverty* (Oxford: Department of Social Policy and Intervention).

Beresford, Peter (1999). *Poverty First Hand* (London: CPAG).

Beresford, Peter and Croft, Suzy (1995). "It's Our Problem too! Challenging the Exclusion of Poor People from Poverty Discourse" in *Critical Social Policy*, Vol. 15, No. 44 – 45. In <http://journals.sagepub.com/doi/abs/10.1177/026101839501504405> accessed 2 May 2014.

Brannen, Julia (1992). *Mixing methods: Qualitative and Quantitative Research* (Aldershot: Avebury).

Cohen, Ruth, Coxall, Jill, Craig, Gary and Sadiq-Sangster, Azra (1992). *Hardship Britain: Being Poor in the 1990's* (London: CPAG).

Dean, Hartley (2007). "Tipping the Balance: The Problematic Nature of Work-Life Balance in a Low-Income Neighbourhood" in *Journal of Social Policy*, Vol. 36, No. 04. In <http://eprints.lse.ac.uk/3452/1/Tipping_the_balance.pdf> accessed 10 April 2015.

Dickson-Swift, Virginia, James, Erica, Kippen, Sandra and Liamputtong, Pranee (2007). "Doing Sensitive Research: What Challenges do Qualitative Researchers Face?" in *Qualitative Research*, Vol. 7. No. 03. In <http://journals.sagepub.com/doi/abs/10.1177/1468794107078515> accessed 2 Janury 2015.

Dowler, Elizabeth, Turner, Sheila and Dobson, Barbara (2001). *Poverty Bites: Food, Health and Poor Families* (London: Child Poverty Action Group).

Ellwood, David (1999). "The Plight of the Working Poor" in *Children's Roundtable Report*, No.2. (Washington: The Brookings Institution).

European Commission (2009). *Portfolio of Indicators for the Monitoring of the European Strategy for Social Protection and Social Exclusion—2009 Update* (Brussels: Employment, Social Affairs and Equal Opportunities DG).

Eurostat (2017). "In-work at-risk-of-poverty rate by age and sex" in *EU Statistics on Income and Living Conditions (EU-SILC)*. In <http://ec.europa.eu/eurostat/en/data/database> accessed 10 April 2017.

Eurostat (2017b). "At-risk-of-poverty threshold" in *EU Statistics on Income and Living Conditions (EU-SILC)*. In <http://ec.europa.eu/eurostat/en/data/database> accessed 10 April 2017.

Farrell, Christopher and O'Connor, William (2003). "Low-Income Families and Household Spending" in *DWP Research Report*, No.192 (Leeds: Corporate Document Services).

Frazer, Hugh and Marlier, Eric (2010). "In-Work Poverty and Labour Market Segmentation in the EU: Key Lessons" in *Synthesis Report* (Brussel: European Commission).

Ghate, Deborah and Hazel, Neal (2002). *Parenting in Poor Environments* (London: Jessica Kingsley Publishers).

Gottfried, Glenn and Lawton, Kayte (2010). *In-Work Poverty in Recession* (London: IPPR).

Gould, Nick (2006). *Mental health and child poverty* (York: Joseph Rowntree Foundation).

Green, Mhoraig (2007). *Voices of People Experiencing Poverty in Scotland: Everyone Matters?* (York: Joseph Rowntree Foundation).

Harvey, Lee (1990). *Critical Social Research* (London: Unwin Hyman).

Hooper, Carol-Ann, Gorin, Sarah, Cabral, Christie. and Dyson, Claire (2007). *Living with Hardship 24/7* (London: Frank Buttle Trust).

Kempson, Elaine (1996). *Life on a Low Income* (York: Joseph Rowntree Foundation).

Kempson, Elaine, Bryson, Alex and Rowlingson, Karen (1994). *Hard Times? How Poor Families Make Ends Meet* (London: Policy Studies Institute).

Lister, Ruth (2004). *Poverty* (Cambridge: Polity Press).

Lister, Ruth and Strelitz, Jason (2008). "Parents Speak Out" in: Jason Strelitz and Ruth Lister, (eds.) *Why Money Matters: Family Income, Poverty and Children's Lives* (London: Save the Children).

Lohmann, Henning (2008). "Welfare States, Labour Market Institutions and the Working Poor: A Comparative Analysis of 20 European Countries" in *European Sociological Review*, Vol. 25, No. 4. In <http://www.diw.de/english/products/publications/discussion_papers/27539.html> accessed 2 April 2012.

Maitre, Bertrand, Nolan, Brian and Whelan, Christopher (2012). "Low Pay, In-Work Poverty and Economic Vulnerability: A Comparative Analysis Using Eu-Silc" in *The Manchester School*, Vol. 80, No.1. In <http://onlinelibrary.wiley.com/doi/10.1111/j.1467-9957.2011.02230.x/abstract> accessed 2 May 2014.

Maxwell, Joseph Alex (1997). "Designing a Qualitative Study" in Bickman, Leonard and Rog, Debra J. (eds.) *Handbook of Applied Social Research Methods* (Thousand Oaks: SAGE).

May, Tim (2001). *Social Research. Issues, Methods and Process* (Buckingham: Open University Press).

Maynard, Kim and Clewett, Naomi (2009). *From Crunch to Crisis: Winter hardship for families in the UK* (Essex: Barnardo's).

McKendrick, John Holland, Cunningham-Burley, Sarah and Backett-Milburn, Kathryn (2003). *Life in Low Income Families in Scotland* (Edinburgh: CRFR).

Meulders, Daniele and O'Dorchai, Sile (2013). "The Working Poor: Too Low Wage or Too Many Kids?" in *American International Journal of Contemporary Research*, Vol. 3, No.7. In <http://www.aijcrnet.com/journals/Vol_3_No_7_July_2013/6.pdf> accessed 2 April 2012.

Middleton, Sue, Ashworth, Karl and Braithwaite, Ian (1997). *Small Fortunes: Spending on Children, Childhood Poverty and Parental Sacrifice* (York: Joseph Rowntree Foundation).

MRC (2006). *A Stronger Voice. Report of the Workshops Carried out by the Anti-Poverty. Get Heard project* (London: Migrants resource Centre).

Munger, Frank (ed.) (2007). *Laboring Below the Line* (New York: Russell Sage Foundation).

Oliver, Kelly (2001). *Witnessing: Beyond Recognition* (Minneapolis: University of Minnesota Press).

Oppenheim, Carey and Harker, Lisa (1996). *Poverty: The Facts* (London: Child Poverty Action Group).

Patai, Daphne (1991). "US Academics and Third World Women: Is Ethical Research Possible?" in Gluck, Sherna and Patai, Daphne (eds.) *Women's Words: The Feminist Practice of Oral History* (London: Routledge).

Patrick, Ruth (2014). "Working on Welfare: Findings from a Qualitative Longitudinal Study into the Lived Experiences of Welfare Reform in the UK" in *Journal of Social Policy*, Vol. 43, No.4. In <https://doi.org/10.1017/S0047279414000294> accessed 10 April 2016.

Pickering, Michael (2001). *Stereotyping: The Politics of Representation.* Houndmills, Basingstoke, Hampshire: Palgrave.

Ponthieux, Sophie (2010). *In-Work Poverty in the EU* (Luxembourg: Publications Office of the European Union). In <http://epp.eurostat.ec.europa.eu/cache/ITY_OFF PUB/KS-RA-10-015/EN/KS-RA-10-015-EN.PDF> accessed 15 Jun. 2011.

Power, Anne (2007). *City Survivors: Bringing up Children in Disadvantaged Neighbourhoods.* (Bristol: Policy Press).

Pradella, Lucia (2015). "The Working Poor in Western Europe: Labour, Poverty and Global Capitalism" in *Comparative European Politics*, Vol.13, No. 5. In <http://link.springer.com/article/10.1057%2Fcep.2015.17 > accessed 2 April 2017.

Reinharz, Shulami (1992). *Feminist Methods in Social Research* (Oxford: Oxford University Press).

Reynolds, Liam, Parsons, Hazel, Baxendale, Anne and Dennison, Abigail (2008). *Breaking Point. How Unaffordable Housing is Pushing us to the Limit* (London: Shelter).

Riggins, Stephen Harold (ed.) (1997). *The Language and Politics of Exclusion* (Thousand Oaks: SAGE).

Saidman, Irving (1998). *Interviewing and Qualitative Research: A Guide for Research in Education and Social Science* (London: Teacher College Press).

Seeley, Annie and Lobstein, Tim (2004). *Going Hungry: The Struggle to Eat Healthily on a Low Income* (London: NCH Action for Children).

Sharpe, Jane and Bostock, Janet (2002). *Supporting People with Debt and Mental Health Problems* (Northumberland: Northumberland Health Action Zone).

Shildrick, Tracy, MacDonald, Robert and Webster, Colin and Garthwaite, Kayleigh (2012). *Poverty and Insecurity. Life in Low-Pay, No-Pay Britain* (Bristol: The Policy Press).

Sidel, Ruth (1992). *Women and Children Last* (New York: Penguin Books).

Sung, Sirin and Bennett, Fran (2007). "Dealing with Money in Low- to Moderate-Income Families: Insights from Individual Interviews" in Clarke, Karen, Maltby, Tony and Kennett, Patricia (eds.) *Analysis and Debates in Social Policy 2007—Social Policy Review 19* (Bristol: The Policy Press).

Townsend, Peter (1979). *Poverty in the United Kingdom* (Berkeley: University of California Press).

Townsend, Peter, Davidson, Nick, Black, Douglas and Whitehead, Margaret (1988). *Inequalities in Health* (Harmondsworth: Penguin).

Toynbee, Polly (2003). *Hard Work: Life in Low-pay Britain (*London: Bloomsbury).

Tunstall, Rebecca, Bevan, Mark, Bradshaw, Jonathan, Croucher, Karen Duffy, Stephen, Hunter, Caroline, Jones, Anwen, Rugg, Julie, Wallace, Alison and Wilcox, Steve. (2013). *The Links between Housing and Poverty: An Evidence Review* (York: Joseph Rowntree Foundation).

Women's Budget Group (2008). *Women and Poverty: Experiences, Empowerment and Engagement* (York: Joseph Rowntree Foundation).

PART THREE:
POLICY ACTORS AND INSTITUTIONAL CHANGE

CHAPTER 6:
IGOs' STRATEGIC FRAMEWORKS AND POVERTY ALLEVIATION IN MACEDONIA[1]

Maja Gerovska Mitev

INTRODUCTION

The role and impact of international governmental organizations in the social policies of South East Europe has been widely discussed in the academic debates. Most notably, Deacon and Stubbs conclude that 'no analysis of social policy is complete without the role of international actors being understood' (2007; 238). In this respect, the case of Macedonia has been frequently added to this type of analysis, confirming that 'the policy of excessive use of external financial and technical support prohibited customized and country specific reforms and agendas' (Gerovska Mitev, 2007; 145). While such impact could be detected more on the central governmental level, international authority has been less visible in the local governance in Macedonia (Pickering, 2010). An earlier attempt to depict the type of influence of international organizations in social policy in Macedonia shows that it is more a regulative and institutional type of influence rather than the cognitive and discursive shifts that can be indicated (Gerovska Mitev, 2006). The analysis below focuses more on direct visible impacts in relation to International Governmental Organizations' (IGOs) impact on poverty reduction and measuring systems, in order to provide a general assessment about the effectiveness of specific IGOs' policy mechanisms and approaches to poverty and social exclusion.

POVERTY TRENDS IN MACEDONIA

Poverty as a socio-economic phenomenon has been on the rise since Macedonia's independence in 1991. More visible poverty reduction trends have been noticeable as of 2012, although the latest chosen methodology used for poverty measurement may not provide a realistic

---

[1] Throughout the book, the official name 'Macedonia' is used. Just prior to publication, this was changed to 'North Macedonia'.

outlook. Systematic and comprehensive periodization of poverty trends and poverty profiles in Macedonia for the period 1991 – 2017 are hampered due to changes in methodologies and survey instruments of poverty measurement.

In the period 1991 – 1996, the State Statistical Office did not measure poverty. For this period, there are World Bank assessments, which determine poverty as consumption below 60 percent of median annual adult equivalent. According to these estimates, poverty increased significantly in the period 1991 – 1996, from 4 percent of the population in 1991 to approximately 20 percent in 1996. More particularly, poverty increased sharply between 1993 and 1995, mainly because of a decline in real consumption. The incidence of poverty increased further between 1995 and 1996, and analysis indicates that as real consumption remained roughly constant over this period, the main reason for poverty growth was growing inequality in the distribution of income (World Bank 1999, ii). The composition of poor people also changed during the transition period. In 1990, the majority of the poor resided in rural areas, in mixed (43 percent) or agricultural households (32 percent). In 1996, this changed, and although poverty was still predominantly rural, those with non-agricultural source of income represented the majority among the poor (66 percent). Additional groups that were affected by poverty during the first years of transition included: unemployed / social assistance beneficiaries; households headed by the employed; and younger household heads. Also, the number of children has a strong impact on the poverty status of a household. In particular, households with three or more children have the highest poverty rates relative to households of other family size and composition. These households comprised almost half of all the poor in 1996. Common factors among those experiencing poverty in this period were: low education attainment, labor force status, poor living conditions and vulnerable health status (ibid.; iii).

Figure 1 Growth of Poverty and Inequality, 1993 – 1996

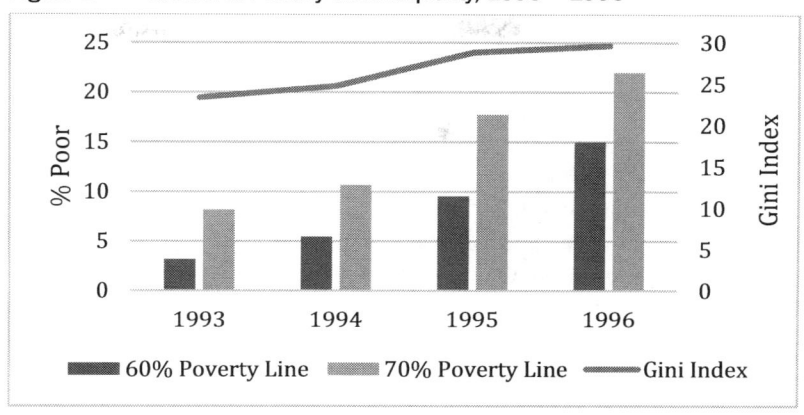

Source: World Bank, 1999

According to the World Bank assessment (1999) the rise in inequality in the early transition years is a result of movements in the upper tail of the distribution of wages. The main reason behind growing wage inequality is the emergence of the private sector. Wages were far more unequally distributed in the private sector than in the public sector. Within each sector, education (though less so in the private sector) and inter-industry and occupational wage differences are also important in explaining the growing wage inequality (1999; 25).

Official calculations of poverty in Macedonia have been initiated in 1996, and the State Statistical Office has provided poverty data, based on the expenditure method, since 1997. During 1997 – 2010, the poverty line was defined as 70 percent of median equivalent expenditures. The choice of measuring poverty as 70 percent of median expenditure (not comparable with the international standard of 60 percent of the median) was a peculiar arbitrary policy choice at the time, which might have been connected also with the small sample of households obtained through the Household Budget Survey. According to Novkovska, the reasons for using expenditure rather than incomes as the basis for poverty calculation in Macedonia included:

> great variations in households' income, especially when salaries are received with delays up to few months; social transfers not reported by the households; households whose head works abroad, do not report the incomes received as private transfers; expenditures show greater stability over time; in the current social-economic conditions, the households' incomes are insufficient to cover all the households' expenditures. (2002; 6)

Throughout this period, poverty was on continual rise, reaching its peak in 2010 and 2011, with more than one-third of the population living below the poverty line. Most affected by poverty were: households with three and more children (with a poverty rate of 55.8 percent in 2010); children aged 0 to 6 (37.9 percent in 2010); children and households living in rural areas (43 percent and 47.1 percent respectively); as well as those without education or incomplete primary education (62.3 percent and 49.6 percent respectively). The alarming fact remains that during 2004 – 2008, five years in which the country experienced continual real GDP growth of 4.7 percent to 6.4 percent, poverty decreased only negligibly, by 1.3 percentage points. This confirmed not only that economic growth does not benefit everyone in the society (already acknowledged by the rising income inequalities data), but also that the prevailing national economic approach—seeing growth as a panacea for unemployment and poverty issues—should be redefined and reconstructed.

Figure 2   Relative poverty rate and poverty gap, by years*

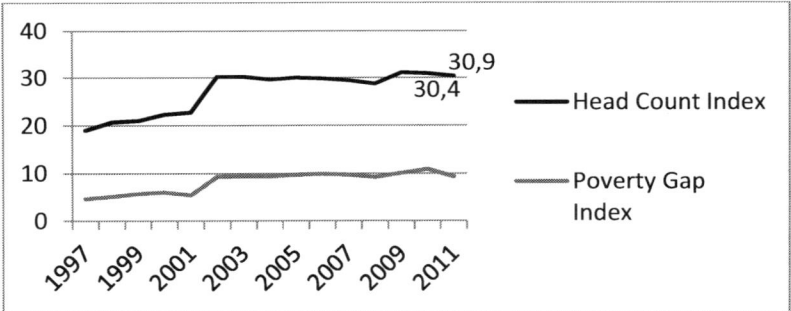

Source: State Statistical Office, MAKStat database, accessed April 2017
*Source for calculation of relative poverty is Household Budget Survey. Poverty line is defined as 70 percent of median equivalent expenditures. Change between 2001 and 2002 is mostly due to changes in the survey instrument and sampling methods (i.e. the introduction of daily recording sheets).

The latest phase of poverty measurement in Macedonia started in 2010, when the State Statistical Office initiated the Survey of Income and Living Conditions (SILC), and changed the methodology for poverty measurement from expenditure to income-based (60 percent of median national equivalized income). This change was inspired by the country's aspirations towards the European Union, and the need to harmonize national statistical methodologies with the EU ones. However, the introduction of this measurement was very convenient for political reasons as well, as the income data showed lower poverty levels. While the new method showed a different poverty rate (21.5 percent in 2015), poverty profiles remained the same. Currently, the most vulnerable categories include: households of two adults with three or more dependent children (52.2 percent); unemployed people (39.7 percent); and those with children aged 0 – 17 (28.6 percent).

Figure 3 At risk of poverty rate, 2010 – 2015, percent of the population

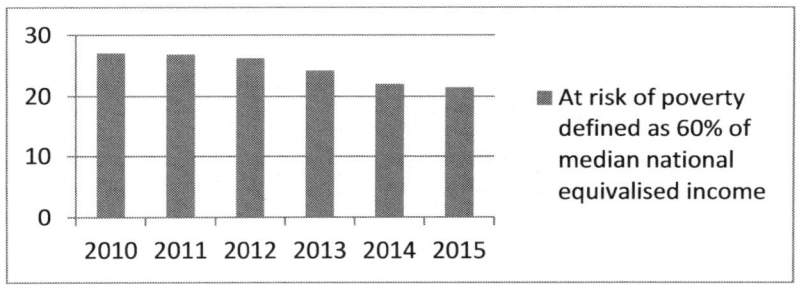

Source: State Statistical Office, MAKStat database, accessed April 2017
*Source for calculation of at-risk-of-poverty rate is Survey on Income and Living Conditions.

Despite different methodological approaches used for measuring poverty, all of them seem to capture the same poverty profiles. However, increased statistical capacity to identify and measure poverty according to different methodologies is not fully utilized in the policy process. Despite well-defined and identified statistical categories (at risk of poverty and social exclusion), they do not seem to be translated into targeted or tailor-made policy measures.

NATIONAL POLICIES ON POVERTY AND SOCIAL EXCLUSION

Social policy creation in the first decade of Macedonian independence (1991 – 2000) was not evidence-based, and was predominantly focused on generic goals and declarative descriptions. During this period, social policy and social protection measures were not based on strategic documents nor on identified targets for improving the social profile of the country. It may be even speculated that the heavy borrowing portfolio with the international financial organizations was among the leading reasons why certain prioritization and goals in the social sector were identified. Hence, some of the social objectives in the first transitional period included:

> placing key social sector programs on a long run fiscally sustainable path, increasing labor market efficiency by reducing labor market distortions inherent in social sector programs and the labor code, as well as reducing poverty by improving the quality of social sector programs and their targeting (Government of the Republic of Macedonia, 1998)[2].

However, all this was not accompanied with quantifiable targets and impact assessments. One of the major obstacles towards this end was the lack of poverty data from the national statistical office based on harmonized international methodologies. In general, the main national instruments for tackling poverty were the social protection transfers, including social financial assistance, permanent financial assistance, as well as pensions. However, as these 'passive' transfers were not part of a more comprehensive or integrated policy approach for poverty alleviation, they have either negligibly improved poverty among vulnerable populations, or even created a 'poverty trap' for many of its beneficiaries.

A first step towards more quantifiable and measurable social goals was the introduction of the poverty line in 1996. This again was done as part of the wider international support, and more particularly through the World Bank, which stated that 'to equitably and efficiently target the poor, the borrower needs to establish a poverty line' (World Bank, 1995; 9).

First poverty calculations showed worrying results, with poverty reaching up to one-third of the population in the years 2002 and 2003. However, these calculations provided a good base for the creation of the first Anti-Poverty Strategy in the country in 2001. Of course, preparation of this Strategy did not result only from the sudden political will to tackle growing poverty trends, but was also an obligatory requirement for all countries using the Poverty Reduction and Growth Facility (PRGF) arrangement from the International Monetary Fund (IMF). It was a comprehensive document, involving a multi-disciplinary approach, as well as perceptions of people living in poverty. However, the document

---

2   Letter signed by the Minister of Finance and Minister of Labour and Social Policy accompanying 1998 Social Sector Adjustment Credit Project for the World Bank.

was adopted at the end of the term of the Government in power, and was not sufficiently addressed in the following years.

The second decade of Macedonian independence is associated with an increase in strategic documents, operational and action plans, namely the soft legislation for tackling poverty. The Government adopted one more Poverty Strategy (the National Strategy for Reducing Poverty and Social Exclusion 2010, and its revised version in 2013). The newer strategic approach increased the focus from poor to socially excluded people. As in the past, the main shortcoming of these strategic documents was lack of precise budget allocations for their implementation. In Macedonia, the strategic documents in relation to poverty only serve to identify and update poverty profiles and trends. Direct measures for tackling poverty rely solely on the traditional social protection system, comprised of social financial assistance (the amounts not being sufficient to lift people out of poverty), and limited and underfinanced social service provision.

On the whole, the Macedonian approach towards tackling poverty may be identified as strongly economically determined, as during the last two decades it was predominantly based on expectations that economic growth would deliver more jobs and hence reduce poverty. Even an examination of the latest budget items stipulated as anti-poverty measures shows that they are placed in the category—active labor market support. Lack of innovation and integrated policy approaches between the educational, health, employment and social protection systems left national anti-poverty policy without clear prioritization or goals. In addition, dependence on the international governmental organizations' (IGOs) financing as well as their political support, led to implementation of external policy proposals that were not rooted in the tradition, capacity and expectations of the social protection system. As a result, anti-poverty policy in Macedonia may be characterized as sporadic, inadequate and not evidence-based, producing continuing high rates of people experiencing poverty and ongoing social exclusion.

IGOs' INSTRUMENTS AND AGENDAS AND THEIR INFLUENCE ON POVERTY IN MACEDONIA

National approaches to poverty and social exclusion showed a lack of capacity to look beyond the economic paradigm of poverty alleviation. Also, there was no readiness for innovation or social experimentation. This vacuum of comprehensive approaches related to poverty policy brought the IGOs into play. While there is a large number of international agencies that have contributed with different support mechanisms to alleviating poverty, social inclusion and inequality in Macedonia, this chapter focuses only on three international actors whose instruments have continuously and substantially dominated the national social policy agenda. Their impact on poverty policy in Macedonia may be seen through: the introduction of direct financial transfers targeted towards low income families; support for the introduction of internationally harmonized methodology for poverty measurement; and setting of anti-poverty goals on the national agenda.

Conditional cash transfer (CCT) and its impact on poverty among vulnerable households in Macedonia

The implementation of the CCT program was initiated in 2010, as part of the World Bank Loan (IBRD, Loan no. 7735-MK). Among a number of CCT programs suggested by the World Bank (World Bank, 2007), the Government decided to go only with the CCT program for secondary education. Among others, this was convenient for them as a support tool, for the initiative of making secondary education obligatory, which was introduced in 2008 / 09. The CCT program is aimed at students in secondary education who come from households that are receiving social financial assistance (minimum income). The payment of 1,000 denars per month (or 12,000 denars per year) is given on the condition of regular attendance of at least 85 percent of the time during the school year. Monthly CCT in general is very low, considering real costs of schooling (i.e. transport, books, equipment, etc.). However, taking into consideration that the amount of social financial assistance is very low as well, this represents an important top-up for the beneficiary households with children in secondary education. As a comparison, the amount of the monthly CCT represents 20 percent of the social financial assistance for a three-member household, and 10 percent of the monthly minimum net wage. Hence, it is not much, but for some families it may represent important financial support. Personal stories of CCT beneficiaries indicate that this money was mostly spent for their school supplies, clothing, food and school excursions, which increased their confidence and most importantly decreased the family burden for these costs (World Bank, 2015).

During the first years of its implementation (2010), there were around 9,100 children benefiting from this program, while in December 2016 this number dropped to 4,348 beneficiaries. The decline corresponds with the general decrease of the households' beneficiaries of the social financial assistance. According to the Bank's internal documents in 2016, this program had been evaluated as satisfactory, as it reached almost all of it targets. However, from Table 1, it may be seen that the attendance rates are little above the required level of 85 percent, enrolment is around 75 percent (although secondary education is obligatory), and that not all eligible households (only 84 percent) have participated in the program.

Table 1   Beneficiaries and Performance indicators of Conditional Cash Transfer Program

	December 2016
Number of beneficiaries	4,348
Attendance rates (%) of children aged 15 – 18 in CCT beneficiary households	89.74
Enrolment rates of children aged 15 – 18 in CCT beneficiary households	75.90
Female beneficiaries (%)	48
% of SFA beneficiary children aged 15 – 18 that have been registered with CCT	84

Source: World Bank, 2016

After seven years of its implementation, some important outcomes challenge the CCT program, particularly in relation to its visible impact among vulnerable students in secondary education. According to the comprehensive evaluation of the CCT program in Macedonia undertaken by Armand and Carneiro: 'the CCT was successful in its central goal of improving secondary school enrolment among poor adolescents' (2016; 20). However, the evaluation also showed that the CCT program had: 'limited impact on school attendance, very mild impact on poverty as measured by household expenditure, and no significant effect in terms of relative school performance, defined as the end-of-the-year average grade of the students' (2016; 40). These important results show that while on the micro level the CCT program may have improved the educational attainment among some beneficiaries, in general it has not contributed toward decreased poverty rate nor improved educational performance among children from low income households.

These results are also in line with similar international evidence (Table 2). CCTs as a policy program have been widely used and implemented in Latin America. In relation to educational outcomes, the evidence shows that the program has been effective in increasing school enrolment and school attendance, as these were the explicit conditions and objectives of the program design. However, as indicated by Lomelí (2008), CCT is less successful in relation to effects on actual learning. Other studies have also shown that CCTs are unable to document positive results on learning, and that without effects on learning and quality of education, CCTs cannot be considered efficient (Villatoro, 2005; Morley and Coady, 2003).

Table 2 Effect of CCT programs on educational outcomes in Latin America and Macedonia

Country	Overall assessment	Cases with significant effects	Cases with minor or non-existent effects
Nicaragua	General increase in school attendance and school enrolment, no positive effect on learning.	RPS* (up to 30 percentage points increase in school enrolment; increased school enrolment of 22% among cohort aged 7 – 13)	No effects on school learning
Colombia	General increase in school attendance and school enrolment, no positive effect on learning	FA* (up 5% rural, 13% urban increase in school attendance)	No effects on school learning
Mexico	General increase in school attendance and school enrolment, some positive results on school leaving, no positive effect on learning.	PROP (increase in school enrolment of 12% in transition to secondary, more for girls and for high school)	PROP—Less significant effect on school enrolment in primary education because subsidies are concentered on the groups already in school; No effects on school learning
Macedonia	Strong impacts on school enrolment of children in secondary school age, but not impacts on school attendance.	Strong impacts of paying the mother vs. the head of household on food expenditure at the end of the second year of the program.	No significant effect in terms of relative school performance, defined as the end-of-the-year average grade of the student divided by the average grade of all students in the same school program.

Source: Lomelí (2008), Armand and Carneiro, 2016.
*Red de Protección Social (RPS), Familias en Acción (FA), Progresa/Oportunidades (PROP) (Social Protection Network (RPS), Families in Action (FA), Progress / Opportunities (PROP).

The context and the baseline indicators in Macedonia differ from those where the CCT program was previously implemented. A report commissioned by the European Commission on the impact of CCTs on children indicates that:

> even if there might be a need for conditional transfer, when engaging in policy transfer, policy makers need to be careful in addressing differences in the institutional context, cultural context and policy context of these programmes in the country of origin and the country of destination (European Commission, 2014; 89).

Taking into consideration the local profile of poverty among children, as well as social protection system specifics (i.e. take up, coverage, etc.), it may be argued that lack of a more visible impact of the CCT program in Macedonia is due to several factors: a) its explicit focus on social financial assistance households (instead of involving also community-based targeting); b) conditioning only the school attendance (instead of adding school performance as well); and c) low benefit, which does not lift households out of poverty.

Other international organizations such as the EU and UNICEF were not visibly critical to the implementation of the CCT program in Macedonia, and have not provided alternative recommendations or proposals.

Further redefinition of the CCT program or its replacements with a similar program is worth considering. Having in mind that the social assistance does not cover all people living in poverty or all low-income households, educational grants could be provided by schools who would apply for them, on behalf of enrolled children from low income families. In addition, municipalities can also play a role in this, providing assistance to those socially vulnerable households whose school-aged children are not in education. Also, a condition on school performance should also be attached, as to incentivize students to achieve more than just attending school. The top-up CCT benefit could also increase each school year, thus improving the household's chances to escape the cycle of poverty.

In general, the CCT program is one of the most direct instruments related to poverty reduction the World Bank has applied in Macedonia. The majority of the Bank's projects in the social sector in Macedonia were focused on legislative and administrative reforms, thus having more macro impact on the general welfare agenda (i.e. pension reform with the introduction of the compulsory second fully funded pension pillar, unemployment assistance and redefinition of the criteria and duration of its receipt, and the health sector). The main value of the CCT program in Macedonia may be seen in its integrated character (combination of social assistance plus education grant). Further restructuring of social assistance schemes in Macedonia should consider such an integrated approach, where low income households would benefit not only from a singular financial transfer, but from a 'package' based on their needs (basic benefit plus housing, health, education or similar grants or services).

European Union 2020 agenda and its impact on measurement and renewed strategic approach towards poverty in Macedonia

Macedonia gained the status of a European Union (EU) applicant country in May 2004, and candidate country in December 2005. During this period, a greater alignment of national legislation and policy approaches towards the EU style of tackling poverty was initiated. The contribution of the EU may be seen in extending the policy approach on poverty with a focus on improving social exclusion. This was particularly important for Macedonia, as official documents usually perceived poverty mainly through monetary and economic constraints (i.e. National Strategy for Economic Development of Macedonia, 1997). The first steps towards a different policy approach were undertaken as a result of the participation in the EU exercise of preparing a Joint Inclusion Memorandum (JIM). This is when Macedonia started to widen the strategic approaches towards vulnerable categories, to include not only those on low incomes, but other groups as well. Hence, in 2004, Macedonia adopted the National program targeted at socially excluded groups, which, albeit somewhat arbitrary, defined four categories as socially excluded: drug users and their families; street children and their families; victims of family violence; and the homeless. These categories were identified on the basis of lacking more systematic and targeted support from the social protection system (Ministry of Labour and Social Policy, 2004). During the period 2005 – 2009, and in consultation with the European Union, the Ministry of Labour and Social Policy prepared the National Strategy for Reducing Poverty and Social Exclusion (2010). This Strategy was revised and adopted three years later (2013), mainly to comply with the Europe 2020 Strategy for smart, sustainable and inclusive growth.

At the same time, the government also aligned its official poverty measurement methodology to correspond with the one used at the EU level.

Hence, as of 2010, the State Statistical Office undertook the Survey of Income and Living Conditions (SILC), on the basis of which it produced data related to poverty and social exclusion. Notwithstanding the fact that the previously used expenditure approach of measuring poverty may be more relevant for Macedonia, as a country with a significant share of informally employed (around 19.9 percent in 2015, according to the 2016 publication of LFS), the newly introduced poverty measurement methodology, as well as the obligation to regularly provide data to Eurostat, improved the quantitative and disaggregated data on poverty and social exclusion. The data was also used as a basis for the revised National Strategy for Reducing Poverty and Social Exclusion (2010 – 2020), where the national poverty target was set to be at or below 21.5 percent, to be achieved by 2020. However, the Strategy does not clearly indicate whether the target refers to those actually living in poverty and social exclusion, or to people living at risk of poverty.

The contribution of the European Union may also be seen in its persistence in prioritizing poverty more visibly on the national agenda, both in the country economic pre-accession documents (i.e. Economic Reform Programme) and in the social policy pre-accession documents (i.e. Employment and Social Reform Programme). Also, in a context where access to data from official and administrative sources is complicated due to complex bureaucratic procedures, but also due to lack of timely and disaggregated data provision, the obligation to submit statistical data to Eurostat provides national researchers and policy advocates with a significant tool for comprehensive and evidence-based analysis. Hence, on child poverty, the State Statistical Office provides public data related only to children's gender and age, and also poverty among some household types (State Statistical Office, 2016). More disaggregated data related to child poverty may be easily accessed through Eurostat, which provides data on poverty among different household types, as well as according to different variables (income poverty, material deprivation, poverty and social exclusion, as well as children in (quasi-)jobless households.

Table 3 People at risk of poverty or social exclusion by household type, 2015, %

	EU	MK
Single person with dependent children	48.0	71.2
Two adults with one dependent child	17.6	40.9
Two adults with two dependent children	18.1	38.1
Two adults with three or more dependent children	31.5	65.9
Two or more adults with dependent children	22.6	41.8
Three or more adults with dependent children	30.1	40.6
Households with dependent children	25.1	42.3

Source: Eurostat, http://appsso.eurostat.ec.europa.eu/nui/show.do?dataset=ilc_peps03 &lang=en Accessed April 2017

On the basis of Eurostat data for people living at risk of poverty and social exclusion by household type in 2015 (Table 3), it may be seen that in Macedonia, most at risk are children living in single parent households, whose poverty rate is 71.2 percent, closely followed by households with two adults and three and more children (65.9 percent). In addition, almost half of children aged 0 – 17 are at risk of poverty or social exclusion (Table 4), while one third of children are affected with severe material deprivation.

Table 4 Children (0 – 17) and whole population who are at risk of poverty or social exclusion (AROPE), at risk of poverty (AROP), severely materially deprived (SMD), or (quasi-)jobless (QJ), 2015, %

	Children 0 – 17				Whole population			
	AROPE	AROP	QJ	SMD	AROPE	AROP	QJ	SMD
EU	26.9	21.1	9.3	9.5	23.7	17.3	10.6	8
MK	46.1	28.6	18	31.6	41.6	21.5	17.4	30.4

Source: Eurostat, http://ec.europa.eu/eurostat/web/income-and-living-conditions/data/database?node_code=ilc_mdm Accessed April 2017

Comparison between different risks that children are facing (Table 5) shows that children in Macedonia are mostly affected by the risk of severe material deprivation (12.8 percent), followed by the risk of income poverty (7.3 percent). The risks faced by the children in the whole of the 28 EU countries differ, as most at risk in the other EU states are those living at risk of income poverty (11.6 percent), followed by the risk of living in jobless households (3.7 percent). Also, while 9.4 percent of all children in Macedonia suffer from all three problems (income poverty, material deprivation and living in jobless households), only 2.7 percent are faced with all three risks in the EU 28.

Table 5   Intersections of Europe 2020 Poverty Target Indicators

	EU27	MK
Children (0 – 17) at risk of poverty but not severely materially deprived and not living in a (quasi-) jobless household	11.6	7.3
Children (0 – 17) at risk of poverty, not severely materially deprived but living in a (quasi-) jobless household	3.7	3.8
Children (0 – 17) at risk of poverty, severely materially deprived but not living in a (quasi-) jobless household	3.0	8.0
Children (0 – 17) at risk of poverty, severely materially deprived and living in a (quasi-) jobless household	2.7	9.4
Children (0 – 17) not at risk of poverty, not severely materially deprived but living in a (quasi-) jobless household	2.1	3.4
Children (0 – 17) not at risk of poverty but severely materially deprived and not living in a (quasi-) jobless household	3.1	12.8
Children (0 – 17) not at risk of poverty but severely materially deprived and living in a (quasi-)jobless household	0.7	1.3
Children (0 – 17) neither at risk of poverty, nor severely materially deprived nor living in a (quasi-) jobless household	73.1	53.9
Children (0 – 17) suffering from 'only' one problem	16.8	23.5
Children (0 – 17) suffering from exactly two problems	7.4	13.1
Children (0 – 17) suffering from all three problems	2.7	9.4

Source: Eurostat, http://appsso.eurostat.ec.europa.eu/nui/show.do?dataset=ilc_pees04&lang=en, and http://appsso.eurostat.ec.europa.eu/nui/submitViewTableAction.do

Finally, the EU can also be credited for insisting on extending the focus on poverty policies in Macedonia from cash to include also community-based services.

Notwithstanding the fact that 'EU pressure is not sufficient to transform informal institutions and behavioral practices' (Borzel, 2011; 13), it may still be argued that the EU accession process has provided additional sources of guidance and support towards a more comprehensive social policy orientation. More particularly, through the pre-accession instruments and processes, such as the former JIM exercise, as well as the Employment and Social Reform Program (ESRP), the EU is supporting more anticipatory, transparent and integrated social policy governance in the country. While such support is still not yielding the desired results, nonetheless it has encouraged more visible and straightforward political commitment towards comprehensive and integrated tackling of poverty and social exclusion.

United Nations Sustainable Development Goals and poverty setting in Macedonia

The UN Sustainable Development Goals (SDGs—agreed in 2015) as well as the previous Millennium Development Goals (MDGs—agreed in 2000) offered national leaders an additional platform and further opportunities to commit to ending poverty. However, it is worth nothing that the MDG of eradicating extreme poverty and hunger, and the official measure for its assessment on the global level (i.e. less than US $1 a day) was not the most appropriate measure for the countries from the European continent. Also, the MDGs have been criticized as a retrenchment due to the 'focus on targeting the poorest of the poor' (Deacon, 2007; 77).

Adoption of the first National Report on the Millennium Development Goals (2005) came at the time when Macedonia was using the expenditure method for poverty calculation. Hence the poverty target for Macedonia to be achieved by 2015 was set at 9.5 percent, which was simply constructed as halving the poverty rate from 1997 (19 percent). Regardless of the fact that the poverty target might not have been carefully planned and developed, it is important to note that this was the first document in which there was a quantified goal to reduce poverty. Previous documents, such as the National Strategy for Economic Development of Macedonia (1997), as well as the National Strategy for Poverty Reduction in the Republic of Macedonia (2002) did not identify a national poverty target, according to which progress could have been planned and measured. The second National Report on Progress towards the Millennium Development Goals (2009) acknowledged the shortcomings in the setting of the poverty target in 2005, and recommended a redefinition 'at an ambitious, but achievable level' (UNDP, 2009; 24). Due to the change in poverty measurement methodology, progress towards achievement of the national MDG target is not possible. Although poverty has not been halved, it did decline by 5.5 percentage points in the period 2010 – 2015.

The United Nations Development Programme (UNDP) is the UN Agency with the mandate on a global level to monitor the progress towards the achievement of the Millennium Development Goals. Yet, the UNDP country office in Macedonia has not succeeded in pushing this agenda more vigorously on the national level. While the UNDP country office was more successful in relation to self-employment and activation support of Governmental policies, they have not been as visibly successful with their poverty and social inclusion portfolio.

The SDGs, agreed in 2015 and due to be achieved by 2030, enhance the previous MDG framework by adding more goals and targets. Deacon and St. Clair (2015) noted that, in relation to poverty, the most important addition relevant for the policy context may be SDG target 1.3: 'Implement nationally appropriate social protection systems and measures for all, including floors, and by 2030 achieve substantial coverage of the poor and the vulnerable' (UN, 2015). This explicitly provides a number of opportunities for restructuring the social protection system, including the introduction of the national adjusted basic income, accompanied with social protection support.

The first phase of national consultations related to the SDGs has resulted in a Report on 'Gap Analysis in Addressing the Sustainable Development Goals into the National Strategic Documents of the Republic of Macedonia.' This preliminary document (November 2016) indicates that the 'SDG targets 1.2; 1.3; 1.4 and 1.5 are a priority, while the SDG target 1.1 needs localization of the global indicators' (Government of Republic of Macedonia, 2016; 6).

However, this preliminary document does not provide data related to allocated resources for achieving the identified challenges and targets, nor do any other publicly available documents. Analysis undertaken by Chongcharoentanawat et al. (2016) for five low and lower-middle income countries from Asia, Africa and Latin America, show that budget implications for achieving the SDGs in the areas of income poverty, health and education will have a different magnitude in different countries. In addition, they find that, 'high expenditure does not equal high outcomes, as efficiency also plays an important role' (2016; 19).

Overall, the UN strategic framework for poverty reduction through the MDGs has been beneficial for Macedonia in relation to advocating and pushing forward a measurable target of the poverty policy. The renewed SDG agenda, particularly SDG 1.3, provides additional external impetus for instigating much needed restructuring of the traditional social protection system in Macedonia, along the principles of ensuring adequate incomes and integrated social service provision.

CONCLUSIONS

The case of Macedonia shows that IGOs have a significant contribution to make towards promoting, incentivizing and supporting instruments, measurements and goal-setting for countries to tackle poverty and social exclusion. In countries where the welfare state does not have a strong tradition, and where economic conditions are limited, initiatives coming from IGOs related to social measurement and target-setting encourage more measurable and accountable social policy making. On the basis of this, we can identify an additional form or dimension of global social policy making, a 'global social measurement,' that is complementary with the other three global social policy mechanisms identified by Deacon— regulation, redistribution and rights (Deacon with Hulse and Stubbs, 1997; Deacon, 2000).

On the whole, national approaches to tackling poverty and social exclusion in Macedonia have failed to prioritize identified poverty profiles, and have been unsuccessful in making the welfare system more effective in tackling poverty. Lack of clear poverty priorities and goals led towards the adoption of instruments offered by the IGOs that were not of highest priority for tackling poverty, nor did these instruments have much identified impact on poverty. The main factors that have contributed towards the lack of success of different IGO instruments in improving poverty trends in the country could be described as their limited coverage and design, low benefit level, the lack of integration with the general social protection scheme, a lack of enforcement on the national level, as well as the fact that most of them are partial solutions. Therefore, countries with higher poverty rates require a policy of prioritization of the most impoverished categories, rather than sustaining generic or non-integrated poverty instruments.

REFERENCES

Armand, A. and Carneiro, P. (2016). *Impact evaluation of the conditional cash transfer programme for secondary school attendance in Macedonia, 3ie Grantee Final Report.* New Delhi: International Initiative for Impact Evaluation (3ie).

Borzel, T. (2011). "When Europeanization Hits Limited Statehood: The Western Balkans as a Test Case for the Transformative Power of Europe", KFG, Working Paper Series, No. 30, September 2011, Kolleg-Forschergruppe (KFG) *"The Transformative Power of Europe"*, Freie Universität Berlin.

Chongcharoentanawat, P., Kebede, K.H., Deters. B.K., Kool, T.A. and Kwadwo, V.O. (2016). "The affordability of the Sustainable Development Goals: A myth or reality?", *UNU-MERIT Working Papers*, Maastricht: Maastricht University.

Deacon, B. with Hulse M. and Stubbs, P. (1997). *Global Social Policy; International Organisations and the Future of Welfare*, London: Sage.

Deacon, B. (2000). "Globalization and Social Policy: the threat to Equitable Welfare", *UNRISD Occasional Papers on Globalization*, No. 5, Geneva: UNRISD.

Deacon, B. (2007). *Global Social Policy and Governance*, London, Sage.

Deacon, B. and Stubbs, P. (2007). *Social Policy and International Interventions in South East Europe,* Cheltenham: Edward Elgar.

Deacon, B. and St. Clair, A. (2015). "End Poverty in All Its Forms Everywhere" in *Review of Targets for the Sustainable Development Goals: The Science Perspective*, Paris: International Council for Science (ICSU) and International Social Science Council (ISSC).

European Commission (2014). *Study on Conditional Cash Transfers and Their Impact on Children, Final Report*, Volume 1, Brussels: European Commission.

Eurostat, Children (0 – 17) and whole population who are at risk of poverty or social exclusion (AROPE), at risk of poverty (AROP), severely materially deprived (SMD), (quasi)-jobless (QJ), 2015, http://ec.europa.eu/eurostat/web/income-and-living-conditions/data/database?node_code=ilc_mdm, accessed April 2017.

Eurostat, Intersections of Europe 2020 Poverty Target Indicators, http://appsso.eurostat.ec.europa.eu/nui/show.do?dataset=ilc_pees04&lang=en, and http://appsso.eurostat.ec.europa.eu/nui/submitViewTableAction.do, accessed April 2017.

Eurostat, People at risk of poverty or social exclusion by household type, 2015, http://appsso.eurostat.ec.europa.eu/nui/show.do?dataset=ilc_peps03&lang=en, accessed April 2017.

Gerovska Mitev, M. (2007). "Macedonia" in Deacon, B. and Stubbs, P. *Social Policy and International Interventions in South East Europe,* Cheltenham: Edward Elgar (pp. 130 – 149).

Gerovska Mitev, M. (2004). "Effects of Europeanisation on social policies of Slovenia and Macedonia: convergence vs. disparity?" in *Proceedings of the 1st Annual SEERC Doctoral Student Conference—DSC 2006.*

Government of the Republic of Macedonia (1998). Letter signed by the Minster of Finance and Minister of Labor and Social Policy accompanying *Social Sector Adjustment Credit Project* for the World Bank, Skopje.

Government of the Republic of Macedonia (2002). *National Strategy for Poverty Reduction in the Republic of Macedonia*, Skopje: Government of the Republic of Macedonia.

Government of the Republic of Macedonia (2005). *National Report on Millennium Development Goals*, Skopje: UNDP.

Government of the Republic of Macedonia (2009). *National Report on Progress towards Millennium Development Goals*, Skopje: UNDP.

Government of the Republic of Macedonia (2016). "Gap analysis in addressing the sustainable development goals into the national strategic documents of the Republic of Macedonia", Skopje: UNDP.

International Bank for Reconstruction and Development (2009). Loan Agreement, *Loan no. 7735-MK*, Conditional Cash Transfers Project, Washington DC: World Bank.

Lomelí, V. (2008). "Conditional Cash Transfers as Social Policy in Latin America: An Assessment of their Contributions and Limitations" in *Annual Review of Sociology*, Vol.34: 475 – 499, DOI: 10.1146/annurev.soc.34.040507.134537.

Macedonian Academy for Science and Arts (1997). *National Strategy for Economic Development of Macedonia*, Skopje: MANU.

Ministry of Labor and Social Policy (2004). Programme for Socially Excluded Groups, http://www.mtsp.gov.mk/WBStorage/Files/socijalna_inkluzija.pdf, accessed April 2017.

Ministry of Labour and Social Policy (2013*). National Strategy for Reducing Poverty and Social Exclusion*, http://mtsp.gov.mk/WBStorage/Files/revidirana_str_siromastija_eng.docx, accessed April 2017.

Morley, S. and Coady, D. (2003). *From Social Assistance to Social Development. Targeted Education Subsidies in Developing Countries*, Washington, DC: Center for Global Development, International Food Policy Research Institute.

Novkovska, B. (2002). "Measurement of the welfare in transition countries: conditions and perspectives in the Republic of Macedonia", Paper presented at the *International Association for Research in Income and Wealth 27 General Conference*—Djurhamn, Sweden—18 to 24 August 2002.

Pickering, P. (2010). "Assessing International Efforts to Promote Good Local Governance in the Western Balkans," *Democratization*, Vol. 17, pp. 1021 – 1046.

State Statistical Office (2016). *Labour Force Survey 2015*, Skopje: State Statistical Office.

State Statistical Office, MAKStat database, Relative poverty rate and poverty gap, by years, http://makstat.stat.gov.mk/PXWeb/pxweb/en/MakStat/MakStat__Zivoten Standard__AnketaZaPotrosuvackaDomakinstva/325_ZivStand_mk_HBSPOV_en.px/?rxid=46ee0f64-2992-4b45-a2d9-cb4e5f7ec5ef, accessed April 2017.

United Nations (2015). *Transforming our world: the 2030 Agenda for Sustainable Development,* http://www.un.org/ga/search/view_doc.asp?symbol=A/RES/70/1&Lang=E, accessed April 2017.

Villatoro, P. (2005). *Estrategias y programas de reduccion de la pobreza en America Latina y el Caribe,* Presented at XXXI Reunion Ordinar, Sistema Economico Latinoamercano, Caracas.

World Bank (1995). Staff Appraisal Report, the Former Yugoslav Republic of Macedonia, *Social Reform and Technical Assistance Project,* Washington DC: Word Bank.

World Bank (1999). *Former Yugoslav Republic of Macedonia, Focusing on the poor, Main Report,* Washington DC: World Bank.

World Bank (2007). *Macedonia—Conditional Cash Transfers Project,* Washington, DC: World Bank. http://documents.worldbank.org/curated/en/860711468270553016/Macedonia-Conditional-Cash-Transfers-Project, accessed April 2017.

World Bank (2009). *Macedonia—Conditional Cash Transfers Project,* Washington, DC: World Bank. http://documents.worldbank.org/curated/en/666201468270921750/Macedonia-Conditional-Cash-Transfers-Project, accessed April 2017.

World Bank (2015). A Little Cash Goes a Long Way for Macedonian Students, http://www.worldbank.org/en/results/2015/07/15/little-cash-goes-long-way-for-macedonian-students, accessed April 2017.

CHAPTER 7:
BETWEEN MODERN DESIGN AND OLD POLITICAL HABITS: THE KOSOVAR PENSION SYSTEM UNDER THREAT

Igor Guardiancich

INTRODUCTION

Kosovo falls within the broader family of Mediterranean welfare states that are characterized by GDP *per capita* levels lower than in most advanced political economies, relatively underdeveloped social protection, a higher proportion of the population at risk of poverty, and higher levels of economic inequality.

These states share common socio-economic and historical idiosyncrasies:

> Late industrialization, labor market segmentation and a large shadow economy, a recent memory of colonial rule or non-democratic regimes and weak central states with ineffective public bureaucracies have implications for the funding, structuring and functioning of welfare states (Gal, 2010: 283).

They are, moreover, characterized by three dominant cultural traits: a prominent role of religion, the traditional family and patron-client relations.

All of these are present in Kosovo. However, due to the presence of the international community following the conflict with Serbia in 1998—99, under the aegis of the United Nations Interim Administration Mission in Kosovo (UNMIK) acting as an international civilian administration, several social security institutions have been externally imposed.

One of them is the multi-pillar pension system, designed by consultants funded by the United States Agency for International Development (USAID), with involvement from representatives of UNMIK, the European Union (EU), the International Monetary Fund (IMF), the World Bank, the UK's DFID (Department for International Development) and the International Labour Organization (ILO).

Its zero pillar—a universal non-means-tested basic pension for the whole resident population aged 65 and above—is an administratively very simple system, created to supplant the country's adverse labor market conditions. Its universal character is unique within the Mediterranean cluster. Here, pension schemes usually display extreme fragmentation (for example, in Italy there were dozens of micro-schemes), itself the result of clientelistic party competition, which thrives on the targeting of specific groups in exchange for political gain (Ferrera, 1996).

As the international community gradually withdrew after Kosovo declared independence in 2008, so-called benefits clientelism, i.e. the exchange of monetary rewards for political support (Taborda, 2017), started affecting all publicly financed sectors. A number of special pension schemes have proliferated, and benefits to narrow constituencies, *in primis* the independence war veterans, have ballooned. These represent one of the most burdensome legacies of the Yugoslav wars that several of the countries involved in the conflicts still have to bear (Bartlett, 2013; Guardiancich, 2013).

Consequently, the new schemes and soaring benefits attracted harsh criticism from the IMF (2015; 2016), which demanded cutbacks to comply with the Stand-By Arrangement (SBA) agreed in 2015. Despite the early admonishments, the Ministry for Labor and Social Welfare proposed to partly dismantle the universal basic pension in order to free up resources to finance these additional schemes. The draft legislation included the introduction of means testing (and, possibly, a separate administrative unit), which would weaken the pension system's Beveridgean objectives.

As retrenchment of welfare schemes is often a politically risky affair (Weaver, 1986; Pierson, 1994), this contribution explains why such a universal and efficient scheme has been targeted to free up resources. Drawing on up-to-date literature on blame avoidance and employing official documents as well as interviews with practitioners, the study shows that the low political salience of Kosovar basic pensions makes them vulnerable to potential cuts. By definition, the universal scheme can be used for benefits clientelism only at a high cost (by disbursing rewards to everyone) and with uncertain results (as there is no or excessively widespread targeting). Consequently, they represent a 'path of least resistance' to free up readily available resources (Bonoli, 2012).

This chapter argues that the Labor Ministry's planned intervention is unnecessary, potentially harmful to the poorest strata of the elderly population and out of touch with Kosovo's socio-economic reality. In response, the author recommends a radical change in reform strategy.

THE KOSOVAR PENSION SYSTEM: GENESIS, DESIGN AND EVOLUTION

There are several reasons why Kosovo underpinned its multi-pillar pension reform with a universal non-means-tested pension. Specific problems relative to the Yugoslav pension system and the conflict rendered the existing institutions unusable (Gubbels et al., 2007). More importantly, the unfavorable labor market conditions hardly allowed for the *ab ovo* introduction of contributory pensions. Finally, a lack of trust in Kosovo's newly established political institutions prompted the international community to lock in the reforms as quickly as possible.

Starting with the historical legacies, Kosovo inherited unviable retirement institutions. The Serbian 1990 Labor act for extraordinary circumstances dismissed 145,000 Kosovar Albanians from civil administration posts, public services, and economic enterprises. The Yugoslav pay-as-you-go (PAYG) system covered fewer than half of the *circa* 110,000 persons over the age of 65. Moreover, during the conflict, not only almost half of the population was displaced, but also the Serbian authorities stopped paying benefits to ethnic Albanians. Finally, during the NATO intervention, a cruise missile and the ensuing fire partly destroyed the contributory records of working age Kosovars.

The extremely precarious situation of the labor market affected the pension system's design (see Table 1). Given the low employment and high unemployment rates, few regularly contribute to the social security system and many suffer from contributory gaps.

Table 1   Labor market indicators for Kosovo (2012 – 14), in %

	2012	2013	2014
Employment rate total (20 – 64)	29.7	33.0	31.3
Employment rate men (20 – 64)	46.6	51.5	48.4
Employment rate women (20 – 64)	12.4	14.9	14.5
Unemployment rate total	30.9	30.0	35.3
Unemployment rate men	28.1	26.9	41.6
Unemployment rate women	40.0	38.8	33.1

Source: Eurostat.

The magnitude of the phenomenon increases when own-account and family workers are included in the picture (some 31.8 percent of all employed persons in Kosovo in 2014, according to Eurostat). These groups often lack social security coverage and proper labor and fiscal records.

In sum, Kosovo has a large informal economy, which provides the means for self-subsistence to the population but limits the access to formal types of social insurance and reduces government revenues. Several reasons account for the large levels of informality (Krasniqi and Topxhiu, 2012).

First, the demographic composition of the population is anomalous in the European context. According to the 2011 census (KAS, 2013), over 47 percent of the population was younger than 25, leading to an estimated 35,000 new job seekers each year, which the labor market cannot absorb (Bertelsmann Stiftung, 2016). Hence, in the late 2000s, social security did not cover up to two-thirds of workers.

Second, the characteristics of post-socialist transition economies (the rapid distancing from self-management and low salaries in the formal economy) generate informality. The Kosovar informal sector's size was estimated at 27 – 35 percent of GDP in 2004 – 2006 (Schneider, Buehn and Montenegro, 2010).

Finally, Kosovo witnessed large-scale outflows of working-age people due to the conflict and economic difficulties. So, remittances and visits by members of the diaspora support families, seasonally boost consumption, but at the same time make it difficult to identify households in need and distort the structure of fiscal revenues (Feher et al., 2016).

In sum, the autonomous province had too fragile welfare institutions to build upon and a dysfunctional labor market. Additionally, Kosovar leaders were not eager to re-implement the Yugoslav pension system, as it was associated with the repression of the Milošević period. Under such conditions, the international community designed a set of original social policies: the basic pension was the first law passed by the Provisional Institutions of Self-Government (PISG) in the newly created Kosovo Assembly.

The UN administration had very little trust in the newly established Kosovar institutions, including the PISG (Héthy, 2005). The IMF feared that the reforms would have been probably debated, delayed and altered had Kosovo not been under international governance (Gubbels et al., 2007). Hence, legislation was passed before a Kosovar government was in place, thereby ensuring independence from local political involvement (Cocozzelli, 2009).

On the one hand, the international community's concerns were not unfounded: despite the efforts to develop a responsible and accountable administration, only those parts insulated from political influence did not suffer from low competence or develop extensive patronage networks (Skendaj, 2014). Similarly, it was expected that pensions, once the authority was definitively transferred to the PISG, would have become vehicles for benefits clientelism. On the other hand, the hasty adoption generated tensions between social welfare reforms that are still unresolved.

The current design

The current pension system is the result of several amendments, the latest one through the 2014 Law no. 04 / l-131 on pension schemes financed by the state. Originally, the multi-pillar design was simpler, a textbook version of what was advocated by the World Bank (1994) in the 1990s. It consisted of a first pillar comprising a universal basic old-age pension and a disability pension narrowly focused on total and permanent disability, a second mandatory fully-funded defined-contribution contributory pillar, managed by the Kosovo Pension Savings Trust (KPST) and voluntary private third pillar schemes.

Focusing on state-financed pensions, the 2017 budget covered 12 different schemes, meaning that the system's fragmentation has been rising in recent years. This trend fits perfectly with what the literature on the clientelistic political competition in the Mediterranean welfare cluster predicts (Ferrera, 1996; Gough, 1996). Additionally, two schemes are not yet active (the work disability pension and the family pension) for budgetary reasons. The IMF (2015) has been extremely critical of their ill-conceived design and unsound targeting. Table 2 gives a succinct description.

Table 2   Selected Kosovar old-age and disability pension schemes

Scheme	Target group	Age	Earnings tested	Pension tested	Benefit type and amount
Basic age pension	All	65+	No	Yes	Flat (€75 / month)
Contributory pension	Beneficiaries based on law from before 1999	65+	No	Yes	Education-linked (€158 – 230 / month)
Disability pension	100% disability	<65	Yes (categorical)	Yes	Flat (€75 / month)
Work disability pension	Work accident or professional disease	<65	Yes (categorical)	Yes	Flat (€75 / month)
Family pension	Beneficiaries based on law from before 1999 or family of work disabled	Spouse <65	Yes (categorical)	Yes	Flat (€50 / month + 20% per eligible child)

Source: Feher et al. (2016; 32).

Two old-age pension schemes constitute, together, the Kosovar zero pillar (using more recent World Bank terminology, see Holzmann and Hinz, 2005). The basic age pension is still a tax-financed universal flat benefit, covering all citizens aged 65 and over, who do not qualify for other budget-financed schemes and who are residents of Kosovo.

Individuals have to report to an office designated by the Ministry at least every six months to qualify for continuous benefit receipt. The Ministry of Labor and Social Welfare administer the plan. Between its inception in 2002 and the end of 2015, the scheme has become more generous (benefits increased from 28 to 75 Euro / month) and beneficiaries climbed from 93,000 to 132,000.

Until 2015, the Ministry of Finance annually determined the pension benefit, based on the minimum consumption food basket. Indexation was unsystematic (neither linked to prices, wages or GDP) and conditional on the budget. With the Law no. 04 / l-131, the Finance Minister is still in charge and again determines the amount depending on the budget and the inflation rate. The cost of the program in 2015 was a bit less than 2.1 percent of Kosovar GDP, that is, circa 11 percent of total Government's expenditures and circa 40 percent of all expenditures on social contributions and benefits, as shown in Table 3.

Table 3   Selected national and government accounts

	2010	2011	2012	2013	2014	2015
GDP (million €)	4,402.0	4,814.5	5,058.7	5,326.6	5,567.5	5,771.5
GDP per capita (€)	2,480	2,672	2,799	2,935	3,084	3,258
Govt revenues (% of GDP)	25.9	27.2	27.3	25.5	24.2	29.6
Govt expenditure (% of GDP)	27.7	28.3	28.6	28.0	27.2	27.9
Social protection spending						
—as % of GDP	3.9	3.7	3.9	4.3	5.1	5.3
—as % of govt exp.	14.1	12.9	13.7	15.3	18.7	19.0

Source: KAS (2016).

The contributory pension was introduced in 2007 (Decision of the Government no. 13 / 277), in part due to the pensioners' dissatisfaction with a basic pension that does not take into account previous contributions (arguably some of the old records are intact) (Loxha, 2012). It is budget-financed and targeted to citizens aged 65 and over with at least 15 years of contributions prior to 1999 into the social security scheme of Yugoslavia (Table 4).

Here as well, benefits and beneficiaries increased over time. In 2008, it amounted to a top-up of 35 Euro / month over the basic pension disbursed to circa 28,000 pensioners. In 2015, the over 40,000 eligible individuals were entitled to a flat benefit of 140 euros, with the same residence and administrative procedures in place as for the basic pension. The total budgetary cost amounted to almost 1.2 percent of GDP.

Table 4   Basic and contributory pension indicators

	Basic age pensions			
Year	No. retirees	Monthly rate	% of per capita GDP	Annual budget (mio €)
2010	109,585	€45	21.8%	63.641
2011	107,145	€45	20.2%	61.192
2012	113,043	€50	21.4%	69.204
2013	117,042	€60	24.5%	87.340
2014	125,883	€75	29.2%	-
2015	132,000	€75	27.6%	-
	Contributory pensions			
Year	No. retirees	Monthly rate	% of per capita GDP	Annual budget (mio €)
2010	30,641	€80	38.7%	30.900
2011	32,415	€80	35.9%	31.670
2012	34,722	€101	43.3%	42.038
2013	36,015	€112	45.8%	49.413
2014	38,651	€140	54.5%	-
2015	40,365	€140	51.6%	-

Source: KAS (2016).

In 2014, there have been several changes to the contributory pension. First, various non-contributory periods count towards eligibility, such as years of work in the parallel health, education and other sectors in Kosovo between 1989 and 1999. Second, all eligible beneficiaries are granted an extra 25 years of notional earnings history, rewarded with a 0.5 percent increase per service year. So, the benefit increased to 158 Euro / month as of 2016. Third, there will be benefit differentiation according to the individual beneficiary's education attainment to restore some of the lost earnings-related nature via a proxy.

International comparison

Given Kosovo's status as a lower-middle income country and labor market problems, the situation begged for a different approach to its pension system than in the rest of the post-socialist countries. Kosovar reforms are part of a wider trend, where contributory pensions are combined with non-contributory ones (the basic pension), to increase coverage in developing countries with large informal labor markets (ILO, 2017). Universal non-means-tested pensions are perceived to have many advantages over targeted ones. They are 'probably the best way to provide poverty relief to the elderly. Considering the difficulty of identifying who among the elderly is poor, the principal merit of the program is that its universality avoids the targeting issue' (Holzmann and Hinz, 2005; 95).

Such unconditional schemes are, however, rare (see Willmore, 2007). Kosovo is the only transition post-socialist country that adopted one. Additionally, the basic pension stands out in international comparison due to a number of features. If the qualifying age is average (it ranges from a low of 60, e.g. in Mauritius, to 75 in Nepal), Kosovo is the only country where current residency is the only additional requirement. Elsewhere, the prospective beneficiary has to demonstrate to either have resided there for a number of years, to be a citizen or both.

Regarding the coverage, the Kosovar basic age pension has slightly expanded in the past few years, thereby paying benefits to *circa* 7.4 percent of the population in 2015. This is relatively high in international comparison: in the mid-2000s, only New Zealand and Mauritius registered more beneficiaries.

In terms of costs, the Kosovar basic age pension has been often depicted as excessively generous. Initially, benefits totaled 45 percent of *per capita* GDP, higher than the recommended and non-distortionary 15 – 20 percent (Palacios and Sluchynsky, 2006). However, the benefit being adjusted *ad hoc*, its value has fluctuated substantially; at times, it has not distanced itself excessively from the recommended values (see Table 4).

With regards to administrative costs, Kosovo's plan, despite being the least expensive per member in absolute terms, is relatively inefficient when costs are adjusted for income (Sluchynsky, 2009). That is surprising, given that operationally it is the simplest program: a) it pays a flat benefit to an easily discernible group; b) the civil register identification is the sole and sufficient proof of identity, age and residence; c) disbursement of all payments happens through an automated centralized process with a combination of easy-to-read bank coverage maps, joint account options and complementary mobile bank services.

Clientelism and fragmentation

The brief Kosovar political experience is replete with instances of clientelistic party competition, which manifests in all its forms such as benefits, patronage, and corruption. With regards to benefits clientelism, the government of PM Hashim Thaçi (2008 – 14) of the Democratic Party of Kosovo (PDK) increased public sector wages and all non-contributory pensions by some 25 percent prior to the 2014 elections, at the expense of public investment projects. The hike in old-age retirement benefits alone cost the budget more than 40 million Euro in 2015, and the annual bill is bound to increase to 66 million by 2017. The move has to be seen as a one-off event, as its cost was excessive and the targeted population too heterogeneous.

Thaçi, now Kosovo's President, and a (former) member of the inner circle of the Kosovo Liberation Army (KLA) and the PDK constituted from its political wing, made sure the subsidization of veterans was high on the agenda. In particular, the Kosovar Assembly passed Law no. 03 / L-100 on the pensions for Kosovo Protection Corps members in 2008, Law no. 04-L-84 on pensions for members of the Kosovo Security Force in 2012 (the KPC, later KSF, were the civilian successors to the KLA) and Law no. 04-L-261 on Kosovo Liberation Army veterans in 2014.

In each case, the IMF has been extremely critical. The KPC and KSF are non-contributory, earnings-related, final salary schemes, whose eligibility is relaxed and benefits generous (members can retire as early as 45 / 50 in KPC / KSF, and benefits are not lower than 50 / 60 percent of the final salary). Worse even, the war veterans' pension (plus additional benefits paid to KLA war invalids, martyrs' families and the families of civilian victims of the war) was set to become the most expensive special benefit program in Kosovo, due to its generosity, ease of access and extension, thereby exacerbating the safety net's inequities (Feher et al., 2014; 18 – 23).

Although the government led by PM Isa Mustafa of the Democratic League of Kosovo (LDK), in coalition with PDK, vowed to cap veteran benefits at 50 million Euro in the 2017 budget, these have soared to almost double that. The main reason, again in line with theoretical expectations, is that over 46,000 people are eligible, which more than doubles the IMF's initial estimate of 18,000. The number swelled partly because the paramilitary organization Armed Forces of the Republic of Kosovo (FARK) was LDK's military wing, which also requires its share of the welfare pie, in fierce (and bloody) competition with the KLA. Such cronyism spurred the protests of senior members of the War Veterans' Association, which complained that the list includes people who never saw the front lines, thereby enabling associates of both ruling and opposition parties to claim welfare (Quirezi, 2016).

Dismantling the basic pension

The costly fragmentation of the Kosovar pension system obviously requires additional resources, which could be carved out from schemes that are ill-suited to be further exploited as a source of benefits clientelism, such as basic pensions. As cutting welfare is politically costly, a rich literature sprung up in the mid-1990s, explaining that reforms nonetheless succeed when politicians successfully deploy blame-avoidance strategies. These include obfuscation (through the low visibility of cutbacks), division (creating a wedge between otherwise homogeneous groups), compensation (ranging from direct financial pay-outs to exclusion from reforms) and justification tactics (convincing the public of the reforms' necessity) (Weaver, 1986; Pierson, 1994; Green-Pedersen, 2003).

Plenty of governments, e.g. Berlusconi in Italy or Juppé in France in the mid-1990s, have been wrecked by public opposition to welfare cuts. When losers to a proposed change are veto players, a government may search for viable options instead of using blame avoidance. By choosing the safer path of least resistance, the costs are concentrated on marginal groups, such as widows, younger pensioners, temporary workers, etc. These groups are less likely to mobilize effectively, especially when complementary reforms are pursued through long phasing-in periods and liberalization at the margin.

Given the basic age pension's cost, universalistic objectives and particular demographic characteristics, the scheme offered a path of least resistance to retrenchment. Indeed, during the spring of 2016, the Kosovar Ministry of Labor and Social Welfare started a process that would have turned the universal scheme into an income-targeted scheme.

This chapter contends that this was an ill-conceived reform, and that the policymaking process was deeply flawed. The few gains achieved would likely be offset by the appearance of horizontal leakages and increased administrative costs. Consultation with civil society and the social partners almost did not take place. The scope of changes presumably exceeded those allowed by the chosen procedure. In addition, the content did not take into consideration any priorities other than redirecting the liberated funds towards politically more profitable schemes (KSI, 2016).

The proposed changes

A 2016 Concept Paper of the Labor Ministry envisaged three scenarios regarding the future of tax-financed pensions in Kosovo (Government RK, 2016). The no-reform scenario was deemed to be unfair. First, the basic age pension continues to be paid out to Kosovar citizens permanently living abroad (10 – 15,000 people) due to excessively lax residence requirements and to pensioners having additional sources of income, as there is no means test. Second, Kosovar citizenship as an eligibility criterion may be in breach of the European coordination regime (e.g. Regulation 883 / 2004) of social security schemes; hence, a better solution than bilateral agreements should be legislated.

An alternative scenario was to draft a new law regulating all pension and disability schemes financed by the state with a single bill. This would: a) introduce nuanced disability scales on which to calculate invalidity benefits; b) create a separate administration for all non-contributory Kosovar schemes (including the special ones for veterans, for the blind etc). The new administration would have a one-stop-shop in each Kosovar municipality. Although a new law was the preferred solution, the shortages in trained staff, time constraints, a dire labor market situation and the many uncovered citizens with disabilities (only 20 out of 200 receive a benefit) would make the solution exceed budgetary capabilities.

Hence, the favored option became amending the Law no. 04 / l-131. The basic age pension would be replaced by a social age pension, with substantially different characteristics. It is means-tested and implicitly taxed at a rate of 100 percent (so if one's income is less than the social pension, one receives just the top-up). Second, both Kosovar and foreign citizens can draw benefits, provided that they have resided in Kosovo for the past 10 years (and the last five as permanent residents). The benefit becomes non-exportable abroad in the absence of a bilateral agreement. The law would also regulate the main procedures, documents and requirements for the Labour Ministry to monitor the residence and income requirements. Additionally, the criteria for the application to a disability pension would be clarified.

Substance flaws

Two of the proposed reform's objectives are particularly problematic. First, the creation of an independent administrative body vis-à-vis keeping the Department for Pension Administration (DAP) within the

Labor Ministry clearly duplicates capacity. It is advisable to 'piggyback' on existing administrative structures, as several countries tend to centralize and automatize social security procedures and communication. For example, in Latin America, only Paraguay is reported to have an independent directorate in charge of non-contributory pensions. The others either manage them through the institutions responsible for the contributory pension system or for social assistance (Rofman, Apella and Vezza, 2015). Given the lack of trained staff and the unenviable record of patronage, the new administration would be used to appoint cronies and it is likely that there would be few administrative improvements (Skendaj, 2014).

Second, the introduction of an eligibility test takes away the core function of universal poverty alleviation. Introducing a generic means test is, in the Labor Ministry's conception, akin to linking the basic pension to the generic social assistance scheme, which have the same purpose but apply different eligibility criteria (according to the Ministry, the pension ones are soft and prone to abuse, whereas those related to social assistance are hard and solid) (Government RK, 2016).

A targeted system may reduce fiscal costs, it is horizontally more equitable (people who do not need a service / benefit do not get it) and the political support can be higher than for universalism (Grosh and Leite, 2009; Korpi and Palme, 1998). At the same time, however, it requires a complex and expensive targeting system, which, depending on the type (income, pension, proxy, etc.) has its own administrative, efficiency and equity problems. Although there have been advances in targeting in the past decades, this chapter advises against an ex-ante income test beyond testing against other pension benefits.

First, the experience with social assistance in Kosovo[1] is deemed to be relatively positive in terms of efficiency, but there are coverage gaps, e.g. poor children are excluded (Roelen and Gassmann, 2011). That several categories of the elderly fall off the income-tested scheme might have severe consequences on individual well-being. During the 1996 crisis in Russia, various households lost their entitlement to a public pension. Despite income replacement strategies, the event increased the

---

1 Social assistance benefits are targeted towards poor families on the basis of a hybrid form of targeting, including categorical targeting, a proxy-means (asset) and means (income) test.

probability of men dying from all causes within the next two years by five percent (Jensen and Richter, 2004).

Second, strengthening the residence test and the coherence of the pension system is likely to better improve financial sustainability. As means testing in Kosovo is problematic due to economic informality and large inflows of remittances, the required administrative capacity is substantial, and the operating costs are likely to partly offset the prospective savings.

Third, if testing against other pension income is sensible, general income and other means testing creates inactivity and poverty traps. The likely consequences are to severely limit gainful employment or self-employment in retirement and to create tangible disincentives for younger, lower income workers to save or formalize their employment status.

Lack of consultation, illegitimate procedures, political motivation

The amendment of Law no. 04 / l-131 affects every Kosovar citizen. As such, the revision should include an encompassing consultation process with civil society actors, thereby aiming at reaching consensus. Instead, the procedure has involved mainly the Labor Ministry staff and external (domestic and international) consultants. Public consultations lasted one week only from 22 to 29 January 2016 (Government RK, 2016).

Furthermore, the legal procedure applied by the Labor Ministry's working group was probably unsuitable. The amending and supplementing process allows for a maximum 40 percent change of a law. Exceeding that, a new law should be drafted. Although the number of articles affected falls within the remit, the amendment radically changes the nature of the basic age pension, which makes the procedure *de facto* inadequate (KSI, 2016).

Finally, the stated motives behind the proposed legislation were to harmonize the basic age pension to social assistance and to generate fiscal savings. Such policy objectives neither take into account the *raison d'être* of the Kosovar zero pillar, which is to protect from poverty, nor reveal that the funds would fuel well-targeted benefits clientelism. Rather candidly, the Finance Ministry inserted into the Concept Paper the recommendation to employ the saved funds to finance the family and work disability schemes that were legislated in 2014 but never implemented (war veterans are the other important group that would benefit, but they are not explicitly mentioned).

Such retrenchment represents for the government the path of least resistance for a number of reasons (Bonoli, 2012). First, Kosovo being a very traditional society, the gender imbalance is a fundamental trait of basic age pensions. Women represent almost two-thirds of recipients, due to short or inexistent contributory histories, compared to just 12 percent of those entitled to a contributory pension. A reform of the basic pillar would hence overwhelmingly affect women (mainly former family workers). Second, politics and civil society are uninterested in the defense of such a constituency. On the one hand, although there are some 6,000 registered Non-Governmental Organizations (NGOs) in Kosovo, there are only a few that actively deal with municipal policy, corruption and environmental issues rather than with social policy (Bertelsmann Stiftung, 2016). As for the social partners, neither the employers nor trade unions are particularly affected. Labor leaders often are themselves pensioners, who hold the belief that people with no contribution record should not be entitled to public pensions. Finally, the recipients of the basic age pension do not represent a major voting platform to be targeted through benefits clientelism, as opposed to the beneficiaries of other special schemes.

AN ALTERNATIVE REFORM STRATEGY

The Kosovar pension system shows several inconsistencies with regards to its various components. As the IMF notes, however, most complications are concentrated in special benefit schemes, family and disability pensions. In comparative terms, the zero pillar is less problematic. As advocated by the World Bank, a mixed strategy that tackles the problem on multiple fronts may sensibly improve the basic pension's design efficiency (Robalino and Holzmann, 2009). There are several ways of reducing the costs while preserving universality: taxing pensions as ordinary income; increasing the pensionable age; reducing the benefit ratio; and increasing administrative efficiency (Willmore, 2007).

Taxation

As universal basic pensions are financed from general revenue, a way of ensuring both vertical equity and fiscal sustainability is by applying a progressive Personal Income Tax (PIT). By doing so, retirees contribute to lowering the costs, with wealthier pensioners paying a proportionally higher share of the burden. This method is successfully implemented, for example, in the Nordic countries, but has not been applied in many lower- and middle-income countries, where administrative capacity is low.

In Kosovo, all social transfers are exempted from PIT. Except for the neediest recipients, beneficiaries should pay income tax and health contributions (Feher et al., 2016). Consequently, all sources of income would be similarly treated, thereby sharing the burden of social security among generations, and improving vertical and horizontal equity. This would, furthermore, create fewer distortionary effects on the labor market, reducing consequently inactivity and poverty traps. Of course, such taxation would hardly apply to recipients of zero-pillar benefits.

People engaged in dependent employment or self-employment who are also benefit recipients should be allowed to continue working. At the same time, they should be subject to a partial claw back of pension benefits as their income rises.

Eligibility

An effective way to contain costs and simultaneously increase the adequacy of benefits is raising the statutory retirement age (Barr, 2012). The advantages of age targeting are easy identification of the eligible population and administrative simplicity, important in countries with low implementation capacity. The disadvantages are vertical leakages (benefits flow to people who are not poor), the crowding out of funding to other groups at risk of poverty (e.g. children) and regressivity, as the poor die younger than the rich.

Despite Kosovo's population being the youngest in Europe, rapid ageing (also a result of sustained working-age population migration) might pose a challenge in the medium- and longer-term (Table 5).

Table 5   Aged as % of total population

Year	Age group	World	More developed	Less developed	Least developed	Kosovo
1980	+65	5.8	11.7	4.0	3.1	-
2015	+65	8.3	17.6	6.4	3.6	8.0
2050	+65	16.0	26.5	14.4	6.6	22.8

Sources: United Nations (2015); KAS (2016)[2].

---

2   The projections for Kosovo refer to the years 2016 and 2051. All projections are based to either the UN or KAS medium variants. The UN divisions into more, less and least developed countries apply.

A sensible solution is to link the statutory retirement age to life expectancy, which is precisely what the European Commission recommends. If this is done automatically, it also reduces the politicians' incentive to tinker with the system during periodical reviews (Schoyen and Stamati, 2013). As there is no silver bullet, beneficiaries have either to accept to save more, receive lower benefits, or work longer. The latter option is the most palatable, provided that the labor markets are ready to venture into uncharted territory.

Benefits

The Kosovar basic age pension was rather incorrectly categorized as ranking among the most generous. It errs on the profligate side, and yet, the disbursed benefits are only slightly higher than the recommended 15 – 20 percent of *per capita* GDP. So, it is not zero-pillar benefits that are problematic with regards to generosity. It is rather the other special pension schemes and inefficient disability assessment procedures that should be addressed first. As avoiding *ad hoc* increases by decree is paramount, all budget-financed benefits should be subject to systematic indexation.

An important point for future consideration is the recipients' general perception that the basic benefit is modest compared to the costs of living. Given the high levels of indigence (*circa* 29.7 percent of the population lived under the national poverty threshold in 2011, according to World Bank data), the pension system shall play a prominent role in poverty alleviation, once its remaining problems are resolved and compatibly with budgetary capacity.

Administration

The interventions that may improve the efficiency of the Kosovar pension system include stricter residency requirements (partly introduced in the amendment to Law no. 04 / l-131) and a consolidated social security database (more capacity duplication was instead recommended in the Concept Paper). First, although the basic and contributory pensions cannot be paid to the same person, the numbers do not add up. At the end of 2015, there were reportedly 172,365 recipients of basic and contributory pensions, against an estimated population aged 65 and above of *circa* 142,000. So, there may be as much as one-fifth of the cohort that are unlawfully receiving the basic pension. The IMF adduces four possible causes: individuals claiming both basic and contributory benefits; unreliable population estimates based on the 2011 census; non-declaration of deaths; and flaws in the concept of residency, both for benefit eligibility and for the census.

In order to improve the situation, residency requirements should be more rigidly enforced. This would mean that the recipients of old-age pensions should present themselves more often to the designated government agencies, lest they trigger a suspension of benefit disbursement, and that retroactive collection of benefits should be limited. As some NGOs deem this requirement as excessively burdensome, a partial solution may be to oblige, as some municipalities do, religious communities to report all burials, thereby enabling the immediate de-registration of all deceased from the lists of recipients (KSI, 2016).

Second, the administrative costs of the pension system should be reduced through a gradual integration of all social security payments, checks and tests with the tax administration as is the trend in many developing countries. Hence, a consolidated database of budget-financed cash transfers for individuals and households as well as of recipients, through the introduction of, e.g. a Danish-inspired Personal Identification Number (*CPR-nummer*) should be complemented by automated data exchange between the benefit database, the tax authority and financial service providers licensed to execute money transfers benefitting natural persons (Feher et al., 2016). This would serve the double purpose of reducing overall administrative costs and limiting the fruition of mutually incompatible benefits.

CONCLUSIONS

Consistent with the theoretical expectations on the clientelistic party competition in Mediterranean welfare regimes, the Kosovar budget-financed pension system has undergone steady fragmentation since the international community relinquished authority to local politicians. If the original, World-Bank-inspired, design espoused universalism as its defining feature, since 2008, a host of special schemes has sprung up, especially favoring the powerful constituency of war veterans.

In order to finance the costly and inequitable plans, the Labor Ministry planned to free up fiscal resources by limiting the coverage of the basic age pension. Due to its universalistic character, which reduces the potential for benefits clientelism, as well as low political and societal salience, the scheme represented a path of least resistance for retrenchment. The consequences of such reform would be dear: given Kosovo's socioeconomic reality, the planned measures might unnecessarily harm the poorest strata of the elderly population.

In line with the IMF's proposals and the World Bank's current orientation, a more sensible solution would entail a mixed reform strategy that simultaneously tackles issues of: eligibility (a progressive linkage of the statutory retirement age with life expectancy); taxation (treating pensions as all other income and allowing recipients to continue working); benefit structure (keeping benefit levels and introducing systematic indexation); and administration (more rigidly enforcing residency tests and consolidating social security databases).

At the time of writing, the reform of the basic age pension has been stalled for some months. The unofficial reason is that the governing coalition between PDK and LDK is increasingly antagonistic, and incapable of solving the distribution of rewards between FARK and KLA veterans. Only the external intervention of the IMF, which imposed a cap on war-related and other special schemes under the threat of discontinuing the Stand-By Arrangement, is holding back such detrimental benefits clientelism.

REFERENCES

Barr, Nicholas (2012). Economics of the Welfare State, 5th Edition (Oxford: OUP).

Bartlett, William (2013). "The Political Economy of Welfare Reform in the Western Balkans," in Ruggeri Laderchi, Caterina, and Savastano, Sara (eds.) *Poverty and Exclusion in the Western Balkans: New Directions in Measurement and Policy* (Springer: New York).

Bertelsmann Stiftung (2016). *BTI 2016—Kosovo Country Report* (Gütersloh: Bertelsmann Stiftung).

Bonoli, Giuliano (2012). "Blame Avoidance and Credit Claiming Revisited" in Bonoli, Giuliano and Natali, David (eds.) *The Politics of the New Welfare State* (Oxford: OUP).

Cocozzelli, Fred P. (2009). *War and Social Welfare* (New York: Palgrave Macmillan).

Feher, Csaba, Jirasavetakul, La-Bhus Fah and Jousten, Alain (2016). "Kosovo: Enhancing Social Protection Cash Benefits" *IMF Country Report No. 16 / 123*.

Ferrera, Maurizio (1996). "The 'Southern Model' of Welfare in Social Europe" in *Journal of European Social Policy*, Vol. 6, No. 1.

Gal, John (2010). "Is There an Extended Family of Mediterranean Welfare States?" in *Journal of European Social Policy*, Vol. 20, No. 4.

Gough, Ian (1996). "Social Assistance in Southern Europe" in *South European Society & Politics*, Vol. 1, No. 1.

Government RK (2016). *Drafti i konceptdokumentit për rregullimin e fushës e pensioneve* (Prishtina: Ministry of Labour and Social Welfare).

Green-Pedersen, Christoffer (2003). *The Politics of Justification: Party Competition and Welfare-State Retrenchment in Denmark and the Netherlands from 1982 to 1998* (Amsterdam: AUP).

Grosh, Margaret and Leite, Philippe G. (2009) "Defining Eligibility for Social Pensions: A View from a Social Assistance Perspective" in Holzmann, Robert, Robalino, David A. and Takayama, Noriyuki (eds.) *Closing the Coverage Gap: Role of Social Pensions and Other Retirement Income Transfers* (Washington, DC: The World Bank).

Guardiancich, Igor (2013). *Pension Reforms in Central, Eastern and Southeastern Europe: From Post-Socialist Transition to the Global Financial Crisis* (New York: Routledge).

Gubbels, John, Snelbecker, David and Zezulin, Lena (2007). "The Kosovo Pension Reform: Achievements and Lessons" *World Bank Social Protection Discussion Paper*, No. 707.

Héthy, Lajos (2005). *Kosovo Mission: Reconstructing the Labor and Social Welfare System* (Brussels: ETUI).

Holzmann, Robert and Hinz, Richard (2005). *Old-Age Income Support in the Twenty-first Century: An International Perspective on Pension Systems and Reform* (Washington, DC: The World Bank).

ILO (2017). *World Social Protection Report 2017 – 19* (Geneva: ILO).

IMF (2016). "Press Release No. 16 / 514. IMF Staff Concludes Visit to Kosovo with Agreement on Second and Third Review of the SBA Program" in https://www.imf.org/en/News/Articles/2016/11/18/pr16514-IMF-Staff-Concludes-Visit-to-Kosovo-with-Agreement-on accessed 20 January 2018.

IMF (2015). "Republic of Kosovo: First Review under the Stand-By Arrangement and Requests for Modification and Waivers of Applicability of Performance Criteria" *IMF Country Report*, No. 16 / 22.

Jensen, Robert T. and Richter, Kaspar (2004). "The Health Implications of Social Security Failure: Evidence from the Russian Pension Crisis" in *Journal of Public Economics*, Vol. 88, No. 1.

KAS (2013). *Kosovo Population Projection 2011 – 2061* (Prishtina: Kosovo Agency of Statistics).

KAS (2016). *Statistikat e mirëqenies sociale (2015)* (Prishtina: Kosovo Agency of Statistics).

Korpi, Walter and Palme, Joachim (1998). "The Paradox of Redistribution and Strategies for Equality: Welfare State Institutions, Inequality, and Poverty in the Western Countries" in *American Sociological Review*, Vol. 63, No. 5.

KSI (2016). *Don't Fix What Ain't Broke—II. Position Paper on Pensions in Kosovo* (Prishtina: Kosovar Stability Initiative).

Krasniqi, Florentina Xhelili and Topxhiu, Rahmije Mustafa (2012). "The Informal Economy in Kosovo: Characteristics, Current Trends and Challenges" in *Journal of Knowledge Management, Economics and Information Technology*, Vol. 11, No. 2.

Loxha, Arbëresha (2012). "Pension System in Kosovo: Review of Current State, Main Challenges and Gaps" *Group for Legal and Political Studies Policy Report*, No. 06 / 2012.

Palacios, Robert J. and Sluchynsky, Oleksiy (2006). "Social Pensions Part I: Their Role in the Overall Pension System" *World Bank Social Protection Discussion Paper*, No. 0601.

Pierson, Paul (1994). *Dismantling the Welfare State? Reagan, Thatcher, and the Politics of Retrenchment* (Cambridge: CUP).

Quirezi, Arben (2016). "Kosovo Budget Held up by Row Over Veteran Benefits" in *Balkan Insight*.

Robalino, David A. and Holzmann, Robert (2009). "Overview and Preliminary Policy Guidance" in Robert Holzmann et al. (eds.) *Closing the Coverge Gap* (Washington: The World Bank).

Roelen, Keetie and Gassmann, Franziska (2011). "How Effective Can Efficient Be? Social Assistance in Kosovo and What It Means for Children" in *Journal of European Social Policy*, Vol. 21, No. 3.

Rofman, Rafael, Apella, Ignacio and Vezza, Evelyn (2015). "Introduction and Overview" in Rofman, Rafael, Apella, Ignacio and Vezza, Evelyn (eds.) *Beyond Pension Reform. Fourteen Experiences with Coverage Expansion in Latin America* (Buenos Aires: The World Bank).

Schneider, Friedrich, Buehn, Andreas and Montenegro, Claudio E. (2010). "Shadow Economies All over the World: New Estimates for 162 Countries from 1999 to 2007" *World Bank Policy Research Working Paper*, No. 5356.

Schoyen, Mi Ah and Stamati, Furio (2013). "Political Sustainability of the NDC Pension Model: The Cases of Sweden and Italy" in *European Journal of Social Security*, Vol. 15, No. 1.

Skendaj, Elton (2014). "International Insulation from Politics and the Challenge of State Building: Learning from Kosovo" in *Global Governance*, Vol. 20, No. 3.

Sluchynsky, Oleksiy (2009). "Administration of Social Pension Programs" in Holzmann et al.

Taborda, Luis Ernesto (2017). *Sick Healthcare Systems: Clientelism and the development of healthcare systems in Italy and Colombia, PhD Dissertation* (Odense: University of Southern Denmark).

United Nations (2015). *World Population Prospects: The 2015 Revision* (New York: Department for Economic and Social Affairs, Population Division)

Weaver, Kent R. (1986). "The Politics of Blame Avoidance" in *Journal of Public Policy*, Vol. 6, No. 4.

Willmore, Larry (2007). "Universal Pensions for Developing Countries" in *World Development*, Vol. 35, No. 1.

CHAPTER 8:
THE TRANSFORMATION OF CHILD WELFARE INSTITUTIONS IN KAZAKHSTAN: LAYERING, HYBRIDIZATION AND MULTIPLE INSTITUTIONAL LOGICS

Sofiya An

INTRODUCTION

Over the past twenty-five years, welfare institutions in the former socialist and Soviet states have undergone major reforms as a part of political and socio-economic restructuring. Post-Soviet social policy reforms have been often constructed as a replacement of 'old', Soviet-style, and discredited welfare institutions and policies with 'new', global, and essentially, Western frameworks. Research shows that post-socialist and post-Soviet transformation of welfare institutions has been a complex, dynamic, and multidirectional process, and there has been no consensus among scholars of social policy on how to conceptualize change (e.g. Aidukaite, 2004; Beblavy, 2008; Deacon, 2000; Ferge, 1997). With a multitude of minor and major welfare reforms, the question remains of how to examine change and what changes indicate meaningful transformation. In this chapter, I examine the interplay of continuity and change through a case study of child welfare transformation in post-Soviet Kazakhstan. I seek to address the following research questions: (1) What types of changes characterize post-Soviet child welfare evolution in Kazakhstan? (2) To what extent have multiple changes introduced over the past two and a half decades transformed the dominant institutional logic underlying child welfare provisions in Kazakhstan?

After this introduction, I briefly review the literature on post-socialist and post-Soviet welfare provisions and then outline selected approaches to theorizing institutional change within historical institutionalist scholarship. Specifically, two theories are considered: Streeck and Thelen's (2005) typology of incremental institutional transformation and Thornton and Ocasio's theory of institutional logics (Thornton and Ocasio, 2012). The second, empirical, part of the chapter provides an overview of multiple reforms in the provision of child welfare in Kazakhstan since the country's independence, focusing on legislation, child welfare providers, and governing institutions. This analysis seeks to identify types of institutional change and tracks the evolution of the dominant institutional logics underlying welfare provisions. In the third section, I will summarize the case study findings, organizing the discussion around two themes: the continuity and incremental change in post-Soviet child welfare institutions and the shifting institutional logic underlying the evolution of welfare institutions.

UNDERSTANDING POST-SOCIALIST AND POST-SOVIET INSTITUTIONAL CHANGE

While Soviet and socialist social policy was largely excluded from mainstream welfare state analysis (Aidukaite, 2009), the end of state socialism twenty-five years ago gave rise to scholarship on post-socialist and post-Soviet social policy[1]. Initially, the social transformation occurring in the former Soviet socialist countries was theorized as a 'transition', a linear path from socialism to capitalism that entails structural reforms leading to market-oriented economies and Western-type pluralist democracies (Kuzio, 2001)[2]. Applied to social policy, 'transition' translates into a process of replacement of the discredited Soviet welfare system by modern, global, and essentially, Western-type welfare institutions (Esping-Andersen, 1996).

However, a growing body of research into transnational post-socialist policy points to the multiple, complex, and multidirectional processes that do not fit into the reductionist notion of 'transition' (e.g. Aidukaite, 2004; Beblavy, 2008; Deacon, 2000; Ferge, 1997). One stream of research emphasizes institutional continuity, arguing that post-Soviet and post-socialist states constitute a distinct welfare regime which has maintained its unique characteristics over time (Aidukaite, 2004; Burlacu, 2007). An alternative perspective points to the diversity of post-socialist and post-Soviet transformations and contends that 'transition' states

---

1 In this chapter, the term 'post-Soviet' refers to fifteen former Soviet Socialist republics and 'post-socialist' refers to the former socialist states in Europe. The terms are used, first, to suggest that these two families of states share a common past and, second, that they differ from one another. While this empirical study focuses on the case of post-Soviet social policy, it is located within a broader body of literature on post-socialist social policy.
2 Later, the concept grew to incorporate other dimensions transforming into a 'triple' and 'quadruple' transition (Kuzio, 2001).

follow multiple paths and cannot be aligned within a conventional welfare regime typology (Kuitto, 2011; Fenger, 2007; Ferge, 2001; Orenstein, 2008). Pointing to the complexity and multidirectionality of changes, scholars used the terms 'fuzzy' (Ferge, 2001) and 'unique hybrids' (Cerami, 2009) to describe post-socialist welfare institutions. As Hacker (2009) points out, changing welfare institutions in post-socialism is better described as 'hybridization,' rather than clustering.

The question of the relationship between institutional continuity and change is central to inquiry into post-Soviet and post-socialist welfare transformation. Historical institutionalist scholarship, emphasizing the maintenance of institutions and their resistance to change, has developed two different perspectives on institutional change (Hall and Taylor, 1996; Streeck and Thelen, 2005; Thelen, 2004). From one perspective, institutional change is viewed as a 'critical conjuncture,' with short periods of transformation interrupting long periods of stability and self-maintenance (Capoccia and Kelemen, 2007). Incremental changes, it is argued, serve the purpose of institutional adjustment and maintenance, while 'real' institutional change can only result from major, drastic restructuring (Streeck and Thelen, 2005).

Alternatively, Streeck and Thelen (2005) argue that institutional transformation can result from incremental changes. Their typology of institutional change includes five types of incremental institutional transformations: (a) displacement, which refers to the rise of subordinate institutions to replace the dominant ones; (b) layering, which refers to creating new institutions in addition to existing ones; (c) drift, a process of institutions losing significance due to inadequate maintenance; (d) conversion, that is, remodeling of institutions; and (e) gradual breakdown, which refers to institutions dying out (2005; 57). This typology of institutional change has been instrumental for examining complex institutional changes in various contexts (Bick, 2016; Carey, Kay and Nevile, 2017; Heijden, 2014; Rocco and Thurston, 2014).

Yet the question remains of when exactly incremental changes become (or can be interpreted as) transformative. What institutional dimensions can signify the 'turning point' in institutional change? In other words, how do we know that institutions have actually changed? To conceptualize institutional change, a promising approach is to incorporate ideas into institution-centered models (Beland, 2005; Beland,

2007; Hall, 1993; Steinmo, 2008). Different ways of analyzing the ideational dimension of social policy include, for instance, causal beliefs, concepts, language, sentiments, political ideologies, policy paradigms, language, or discourses (Beland, 2014; Hall, 2003). A more comprehensive approach to integrating ideational frameworks in the analysis of institutional change can be found in Thornton and Ocasio's (2008) institutional logics theory. Institutional logics refers to 'socially constructed, historical patterns of cultural symbols and material practices, including assumptions, values, and beliefs, by which individuals and organizations provide meaning to their daily activity' and 'frames of reference that condition actors' choices for sense-making' (Thornton, Ocasio and Lounsbury, 2012; 2). Institutional logics, therefore, can bridge the macro- and micro-levels of analysis, that is, individual and organizational actors and the institutional environments in which they operate.

METHODOLOGY

The question that has driven this study is how post-Soviet institutions change. Specifically, I seek to examine the interplay of continuity and change through a case study of child welfare transformation in post-Soviet Kazakhstan. I seek to address the following research questions: (1) What types of changes characterize post-Soviet child welfare evolution in Kazakhstan? (2) To what extent have multiple changes introduced over the past two and a half decades transformed the dominant institutional logic underlying child welfare provisions in Kazakhstan? For the study of child welfare restructuring in post-Soviet Kazakhstan, these two analytical tools are combined. Firstly, I apply Streeck and Thelen's typology of incremental institutional change to examine multiple reforms of child welfare institutions. Secondly, I employ Thornton and Ocasio's institutional logics perspective to track the shift in the institutional logic underpinning post-Soviet child welfare transformation. This analysis draws upon in-depth semi-structured interviews I conducted over the summer of 2012 with 30 individuals, including representatives of domestic NGOs, government organizations, agencies, and transnational organizations (TOs) involved in child welfare policy reforms in Kazakhstan. I also analyzed documents including relevant laws and regulations, policies and programs, organizational documents, media publications, and research reports. In the empirical section of the chapter, I examine multiple developments in child welfare provisions in Kazakhstan from 1991 to 2012 and trace the shifting dominant logic underlying these provisions. I begin by outlining the main characteristics of the Soviet child welfare system inherited by Kazakhstan. Then I proceed to an examination of the post-Soviet child welfare transformation, broken down into two periods: the phase of welfare retrenchment (1991 – 2000) and the phase of welfare revival (2000 – 2012).

THE SOVIET APPROACH TO CHILD WELFARE: THE LOGIC OF 'SOVIET WELFARISM'

Soviet child welfare was an integral component of the comprehensive Soviet welfare system, which encompassed full employment, generous maternity benefits, child allowances, sick leave and pensions, free education and health care, state housing, and subsidized goods and services (Deacon, 2000). In addition to universal programs available to all citizens, the state provided special categorical benefits, such as for families with four or more children, military personnel and their families, people with disabilities, and orphans (Maltseva, 2005). Since all sectors of the society—the economy, the political system, and welfare provision—were governed by the state, the entire society functioned as a welfare system.

Similarly, the child welfare system inherited by Kazakhstan was characterized by the key role the Soviet state played in planning, financing, and providing assistance to families and children. Child welfare was provided in three forms: cash transfers to families with children; public services, including child care and recreational programs for children; and government-run children's residential institutions. By the late 1980s, cash transfer programs encompassed a generous maternity leave program, child birth allowance, paid childcare leave in case of child sickness, pensions for widows with children, and allowances for children who were deprived of parental alimony (Teplova, 2007). Public social services for families with children were provided through nurseries, kindergartens, after-school centers, children's summer camps and resorts. Soviet child welfare was governed by the principle of universalism, ensuring wide coverage. The needs of selected special groups were addressed through categorical benefits in the form of cash transfers and in-kind programs[3].

The emphasis on universality in the Soviet child welfare system can be also found in the absence of (personal) social services and / or social work to address the specific needs of families with children (e.g. low-income families, families with many children, single mothers, parents with alcohol / drug addiction, parents with disabilities, and children with disabilities). The lack of personal social services and / or social work was tied to the well-known official denial of social problems intrinsic to the Soviet ideology and culture. The official discourse constructed a society without social problems, which effectively eliminated the need for social work (Iarskaia-Smirnova and Romanov, 2009; Iarskaia-Smirnova, 2011).

While personal social services were absent, children's residential institutions became the main approach to addressing the needs of families requiring special support. Throughout Soviet history, children's residential institutions were an institutional solution to the issue of children's deprivation caused by changing socioeconomic and political conditions (Kostina, 2003; Zezina, 2000). On the one hand, children's residential institutions symbolized the paternalistic state that cares for its children. On the other hand, institutions were used to remove social problems (e.g., abandoned, abused children, or children with disabilities) from the public eye and render them invisible. When a family failed to provide care to their children, the state would intervene by depriving parents of their parental rights and responsibilities and placing children in residential institutions. Kazakhstan (like other post-Soviet states) has inherited and maintained a variety of residential institutions for children[4], such as: infant houses; orphanages and boarding schools for children deprived of parental care; special correctional institutions for children with disabilities; boarding schools for children with deviant behaviors; centers for temporary isolation and rehabilitation of unattended children; family-type children's homes; children's villages, and youth homes for care leavers.

---

3   For instance, children with disabilities were entitled to monthly pensions and free medications and access to professional education, free use of public transportation and a 50 percent discount for travel within the Soviet Union.
4   Most of the institutions listed here were inherited from the Soviet system, but children's villages and family-type orphanages were introduced in the 1990s.

Thus, the main characteristics of the child welfare system inherited by Kazakhstan from the Soviet system included: a key role for the state; universality as the main principle of welfare provision; the family's responsibility for child care relying on state support; a major role for children's residential institutions; and the absence of personal social services and / or social work. These features, I argue, were interlinked with the logic of 'Soviet welfarism', the dominant institutional logic underpinning the massive Soviet child welfare infrastructure. In this chapter, the logic of 'Soviet welfarism' refers to the notion of the paternalistic, all powerful, all-encompassing, and supposedly benevolent Soviet welfare state, which played the major role in the provision of child welfare. While the family was viewed as the primary childcare provider, the state adopted supportive family policies through universal public programs, including state cash transfer programs and public services, while the needs of special categories of families and children were addressed through a wide network of government-run children's residential institutions.

POST-SOVIET TRANSFORMATION OF CHILD WELFARE INSTITUTIONS

Shaped by the shifting economic and political environment, the post-Soviet transformation of child welfare institutions in Kazakhstan has gone through two distinct phases: child welfare retrenchment (1991 – 2000) and child welfare revival (2000 – 2012).

Child Welfare Retrenchment 1991 – 2000

Cutting 'old' programs: Cash transfers and public services
In the 1990s, the government introduced structural economic reforms, such as privatization and liberalization, while drastically reducing social welfare expenditures on two pillars of child welfare: cash transfers and public services for families with children. Cuts in cash transfers were achieved by restricting the entitlement for welfare and monetization of in-kind categorical welfare benefits[5]. Real public expenditures on education

---

5   As ex-Minister of Labor and Social Protection G. Karagussova admitted in her interview, monetization allowed the government to cut costs of welfare programs because monetary compensation was overall lower than the costs of in-kind benefits (KAZINFORM, 14 December 2006).

in 1996 dropped to 28 percent of the 1991 level; similarly, real public expenditures on health care in 1997 fell to 35 percent of the 1991 level (Falkingham, 1999). Apart from cuts in existing universal and categorical programs, in 1994 a means-test was introduced to the main child allowance scheme, indicating a shift from universalism to selection (Maltseva, 2008; World Bank, 1998).

Reinforcing old institutions: Children's residential institutions

Surprisingly, the third major component of child welfare—children's residential institutions—was not only maintained but reinforced. The number of residential institutions for children without parental care increased by 50 percent and the number of children in institutions more than doubled between 1990 and 1999[6] (Kazakhstan, 2000). Residential institutions continued to be viewed as a legitimate response to children's deprivation in sharp contrast to a regional orthodoxy of 'deinstitutionalization'. As claimed by the government in the First National CRC Report (Kazakhstan, 2001a), 'this is the only network within the system of primary and secondary education that has not been optimized [cut]' because 'the least protected [groups] are considered orphans, children with limited developmental capacities [disabilities] and children from large and low-income families. State support for them is provided through the system of children's houses and boarding schools' (Kazakhstan, 2000). While maintaining Soviet-type children's residential institutions, the government made an attempt to introduce Family-Type Children's Villages and Youth Homes in 2000, modelled after SOS villages (SOS Kinderdorf Kazakhstan, 2017) with the aim of the 'gradual transformation of children's homes into children's villages' (Law on Family-Type Children's Villages and Youth Homes, 2000). However, rather than replacing Soviet-type children's residential institutions, children's villages have simply co-existed as yet another type of children's residential institution.

---

6   41 children's homes and boarding schools accommodating 4,700 children in 1990 and 65 institutions accommodating 10,961 children in 1999 (Kazakhstan, 2000).

Ideas underlying child welfare policies: The roles of family vs state re-interpreted

A number of legal acts in the area concerning child welfare that were adopted in the 1990s indicate an attempt to introduce new ideas of the family as the primary caregiver while largely preserving the logic of 'Soviet welfarism'. First, Kazakhstan ratified the Convention on the Rights of the Child (CRC) in 1992, symbolically, the first UN Convention ratified by a new state; but despite the importance of this gesture, the translation of the Convention into practice was slow (Kazakhstan, 2001b). Further, the new country's Constitutions, adopted in 1993 and 1995, declared that the family has the primary responsibility for caring for children with a smaller role for the state, as compared with the 1978 Constitution (the Constitution of the Republic of Kazakhstan, 1995). Similarly, a new Law on Marriage and Family (1998) placed the primary responsibility for children on parents. Yet, the Law maintained the Soviet child welfare approach to dealing with families failing to provide necessary care: the state intervenes by depriving parents of their parental rights and placing the child under the protection of state authorities.

Child Welfare Revival 2000 – 2012

Introducing new policy ideas: A children's rights framework

The economic recovery of the 2000s was accompanied by a steady increase in public spending on education, health care, and social welfare in absolute figures[7]. After a decade of being secondary to economic reforms, social policy shifted from the periphery to the center of the state agenda, and children re-gained their status as one of the primary target populations for welfare policy[8]. The revitalization of child welfare is evident from the visible increase in the number of regulations and state programs concerning children adopted in the 2000s. First, the Law on the Rights of the Child (2002) has symbolic significance as it had no analogous regulation in the Soviet welfare system and signifies an ideational shift in child welfare as the Law mirrors the CRC. The Law, however, made no

---

7   Public expenditure still lags behind as a percentage of GDP as compared to OECD countries[7] (UNICEF, 2007).
8   As the President of RK stated in his 2005 Address to the nation, 'An important issue for our strategy is the decent provision for the livelihood of the least protected member of the society—children, their mothers, and the older generation. The government will not save resources for the solution of these issues.'

attempt to change the system of child welfare provision, and its introduction was not accompanied by amendments to other laws. Rather, the Law re-instated the Soviet-era principles of child welfare provision, including the role of the state in child welfare provision and the dominant role of children's residential institutions, which were framed as 'organizations performing functions on the protection of the rights of the child.'

Institutional maintenance: Re-enforcing old welfare programs

In the 2000s, the government increased spending on 'traditional' welfare programs, such as income transfers and public services for families and children. First, the Law on Targeted Social Assistance adopted in 2001 replaced other cash assistance programs for the poor. Next, the Law on State Allowances for Families with Children (2005) introduced several family and maternity benefit programs, one means-tested and others universal.[9] Unlike the almost negligible cash benefits in the 1990s, the cash value of these allowances is sizable[10]. Importantly, children made up the majority of recipients of targeted social assistance (60 percent) in 2003 (ILO, 2004). The state also boosted its support for child care. From 2007 to 2009, 2,557 pre-school facilities were opened with capacity to accommodate 142,000 children, and in 2010 there were 4,972 pre-school facilities, covering 38.7 percent of eligible children (MoESc, 2010).

Layering: introducing new agencies in child welfare

In addition to four traditional Ministries (the Ministry of Education and Science; the Ministry of Labor and Social Protection; the Ministry of Health and the Ministry of Internal Affairs) that had their own areas of responsibility within the public child welfare system, new government agencies were established that represent a global, rights-based approach to child welfare. First, the National Commission on Family and Women's

---

9   The newly introduced programs include: (1) monthly cash transfers to families whose per-capita income is below the food basket value until the child reaches 18 years of age; (2) a single-payment child birth allowance (since 2003); (3) monthly childcare allowance until the child reaches one year; and (4) a monthly childcare allowance for parents / caregivers of children with disabilities.

10 In 2013, child birth allowance was 45,360 KZT (approximately, $300); monthly childcare allowance for children from birth to one year was 8,316 KZT ($55) for a woman who was not employed and 40 percent of the average monthly salary for working women.

Affairs, created in 1998 as part of the state's agenda of advancing gender equality, was also involved in child welfare reform. Another coordinating body was the Council on Youth Affairs, established in 2000, which played no more than a consulting and advisory role. Next, created in 2002 under the President, the National Commissioner for Human Rights (Ombudsperson) is responsible for monitoring human rights (including the rights of children) and dealing with citizens' complaints on government bodies. Finally, in 2006, the government created the Committee for the Protection of the Rights of the Child, a special body under the MoESc, which was tasked 'to realize government policy in the area of protection of rights and legal interests of children, as well as implementing and control functions in this area' (MoESc, 2011). However, the Committee's authority was limited because of its subordinate position within the MoESc.

Thus, new governing agencies represent a 'layering' strategy in child welfare governance. New institutions were established, while 'old' governing bodies continued to exist. Typically, new institutions were 'weaker' than old agencies: they were given fewer resources, smaller infrastructure, and limited authority[11]. While adding to the child welfare governance structure, new agencies have not changed the core principles of child welfare governance but rather contributed to greater institutional complexity.

Drifting away: Children's residential institutions

In the early 2000s, the total number of children in all residential institutions (including those with and without parents) rose. The numbers continued to grow until the mid-2000s and then stabilized (See Table 1, Children in residential care).

Table 1   Children in residential care, at the end of the year (in 1,000s)

1999	2000	2001	2002	2003	2004	2005	2006	2007	2008	2009	2010
58.0	67.2	69.2	76.2	82.5	87.0	84.6	79.5	79.0	82.9	78.5	77.4

Source: UNICEF (TransMonEE, 2012).

By the late 2010s, the overall number of children in all residential institutions appears to be rather stable, but the number of children deprived of parents in residential care started to shrink (See Table 2). A

---

11   Interviews with key informants (2012).

recent media release[12] reports that the government closed 17 children's residential institutions since 2010 due to the fall in the number of children without parental care. The government tends to attribute this development to state efforts aimed at de-institutionalization (Kazakhstan, 2012). Although this argument cannot be substantiated[13], the reduction in the number of children's residential institutions indicates that these welfare institutions are no longer viewed as legitimate modes of welfare provision in the national welfare system.

Table 2   Children in residential care by type of institution*

Type of children's residential institutions	2001	2003	2010
Infant homes	2,436	2,120	(data unavailable)
Boarding schools (for all children including those without parental care)	71,400	73,200	79,674
Children's houses and boarding schools for children without parental care	12,022	12,000	6,700

*Sources: Kazakhstan CRC Report #2,3,4; Ministry of Education and Science of Kazakhstan data (2012); UNICEF TransMONEE data (2012).

Layering and new modes of care: Social services for children

Absent in the Soviet child welfare system, social services are a new modality introduced over the past two decades. Social services are an alternative to children's residential institutions operating according to a different institutional logic: to provide individualized support to families with children in the community, without removing children from the family. Three pieces of legislation adopted in the 2000s created the legal basis for the development of social services for children in Kazakhstan. First, the Law on Social, Medical, and Pedagogical Correctional Support to Children with Special Needs (2002), launched the development of the governmental institutional network responsible for the detection and correction / treatment of disabilities and the provision of medical, educational, psychological, and social services to children with special needs. Second, the Law on State Social Contracting (2005) was introduced

---

12 Meeting the Ministry of Justice of the Republic of Kazakhstan on 16 June 2013, http://www.rfdeti.ru/news/7018-vstrecha-s-ministrom-yusticii-respubliki-kazahstan.
13 There was no respective increase in the use of alternative forms of family care, such as adoption, guardianship / tutelage, and foster care (*patronat*) (Kazakhstan, 2012).

as an institutional mechanism for state funding of NGOs as providers of social services. Third, the Law on Special Social Services (2008) regulates the provision of social services to individuals and families in ten types of 'difficult living situations' (five of them are children-only categories).

Overall, while the main characteristics of the child welfare system inherited by Kazakhstan from the Soviet welfare system have been largely maintained over the past twenty years, a number of incremental changes can be identified. The state continues to play a major role in planning and financing child welfare but through a number of recent legislative acts, it allowed non-state service providers to enter the welfare sector. Alongside old universal and categorical welfare programs, means-tested social assistance has been introduced for poor families. The answer to the question of who is responsible for children—the family or the state—has been revised to justify the reduction of public support for families with children. State-run children's residential institutions continued to play a significant role in child welfare provision but began to lose their legitimacy, while personal social services and / or social work have been introduced on a small scale. These changes, I argue, can be associated with the introduction of a new institutional logic based on children's rights.

Table 3   An overview of child welfare reforms in Kazakhstan (1991 – 2012)

Pre-1991 (Soviet child welfare)	1991 – 2000	2001 – 2012
Public services: education, health care, child care	Cuts in public services, partial privatization, removal of subsidies	Increase in state funding of public services
Income transfers: benefits for families and children	Cuts in income transfer programs, monetization of in-kind benefits	Increase in income transfer programs for families with children Introduction of means-tested family benefits
Children's residential institutions as a main response to families and children's deprivation / special needs	Increase in the number of children's residential institutions and the number of children in institutions Introduction of new types of children's institutions (family-type homes, children's villages, youth homes)	Maintenance of children's residential institutions until 2010. After 2010, reduction in the number of institutions. Maintenance of new types of children's institutions (family-type homes, children's villages, youth homes)

Alternative forms of family care: adoption, guardianship / tutelage, and *patronat* / foster care (the latter was cancelled in 1968).	Adoption and guardianship maintained	Re-introduction of alternative forms of family care (*patronat*), or their reinforcement through cash benefits (guardianship / tutelage)
No formal social services / social work	Introduction of social services provided by NGOs funded by TOs	Introduction of social services for children with special needs provided by governmental organizations and by NGOs
Governance of child welfare divided among four agencies: MoESc, MoH, MoLSP, and MIA	Governance of child welfare divided among four agencies: MoESc, MoH, MoLSP, and MIA Establishment of new agencies: National Commission of Women's and Family Affairs; National Commission for Human Rights (Ombudsman)	Governance of child welfare divided between four agencies: MoESc, MoH, MoLSP, and MIA Maintenance of new governance agencies.
'Soviet welfarism' as an underpinning institutional logic	'Soviet welfarism' as an underpinning institutional logic	'Soviet welfarism' and children's rights framework as competing and co-existing underpinning institutional logics

FINDINGS AND DISCUSSION

The post-Soviet transformation of child welfare institutions: Layering, hybridization and multiple institutional logics

This analysis of post-Soviet child welfare transformation in Kazakhstan was particularly concerned with tracing institutional continuity and change. Institutional continuity was conceptualized as the maintenance and reproduction of Soviet institutions. The evolution of child welfare institutions was examined using Streeck and Thelen's (2005) typology of incremental institutional transformation, while shifting ideas underlying child welfare provision were conceptualized through the lens of Thornton and Ocasio's (2008) institutional logics theory.

Post-Soviet child welfare transformation in Kazakhstan has been made subservient to the economic and political restructuring. This analysis points to two distinct phases in the evolution of post-Soviet child welfare: child welfare retrenchment during the first decade of the country's independence (1991 – 2000) and child welfare revival during the second decade (2001 – 2012). During the first post-Soviet decade of the dismantling of the Soviet welfare system, child welfare retrenchment included broad cuts in income transfers to families and public programs, such as education, health care, and child care. However, children's residential institutions not only survived cuts but also increased in number, indicating that the institutional logic underpinning child welfare was preserved: if the family fails to provide care for its children, the state steps in by placing children in residential institutions. While new types of children's institutions were introduced, they were maintained on a small scale, posing no threat to the dominance of Soviet-type children's residential institutions.

As this analysis shows, changes introduced during the second, child welfare revival, phase fall into two categories: (1) the reinforcement of old, traditional child welfare programs, as seen in the increase in public spending on traditional, pre-1991 welfare programs, including children's residential institutions, and (2) the introduction of new institutions under the children's rights framework, which was used increasingly by policy actors to frame desired policy changes or to legitimize their claims (Table 3). As a result, alternative forms of family care (e.g. *patronat* / foster care, guardianship / tutelage) were re-introduced or supported by public funds, while the legitimacy of children's residential institutions among policy actors started to fade, and the number of children's residential institutions began to contract ('drifting away', according to Streeck and Thelen's classification). Another new form of welfare provision, personal social services, was introduced and gained legitimacy. Funded by the state and provided by NGOs and by new or reformed state institutions, social services represent a different institutional logic of individualized and specialized support for the family and children. Furthermore, new child welfare governance institutions based on human and children's rights frameworks (e.g. the Committee on the Protection of Children's Rights, the Ombudsperson, the Commission on the Family and Women's Affairs) were established.

The examination of child welfare reforms points to 'layering' as the key element of institutional change in post-Soviet child welfare provision in Kazakhstan. While multiple welfare institutions (i.e. laws, welfare providers, and governing agencies) have been introduced over the past twenty years, much of the Soviet child welfare infrastructure has been maintained, including public cash assistance programs, public services, children's residential institutions, and the broad governance structure. Overall, the child welfare system shows remarkable resilience and an ability to change incrementally, mainly by adding new layers of institutions, while maintaining its core welfare institutions.

A crucial characteristic of post-Soviet child welfare transformation was that new welfare institutions did not replace old ones but were added to existing institutions (in Streeck and Thelen's typology, 'layering'). However, the newly introduced institutions have struggled (informant interviews, 2012). The provision of social services in the public sectors suffered from a lack of expertise, formalism, and a general confusion about their new roles and responsibilities. NGOs as new social service providers faced institutional barriers to accessing public resources. The development of alternative forms of family care became stagnant. Also, new governance institutions that are based on rights' frameworks (e.g. the National Commission on Women's and Family Affairs, the Committee on the Protection of Children's Rights) were given less authority than the traditional governing agencies (e.g., Ministries), that convey the logic of 'Soviet welfarism'.

Drawing upon the empirical study of post-Soviet welfare reform, this analysis confirms the value of examining the ideational dimension of institutional change (Beland, 2005). The post-Soviet transformation of child welfare institutions in Kazakhstan has been characterized by co-existing and competing institutional logics: the logic of 'Soviet welfarism' and the logic of children's rights. Both logics can be traced in existing, reformed, maintained, and newly introduced welfare institutions. While multiple institutional layers may not indicate an actual shift in institutional logic underlying welfare provisions, the shift in institutional logics may be indicative of a more profound institutional change that can ultimately lead to institutions drifting away and dying out.

To conclude, child welfare transformation in post-Soviet Kazakhstan can be understood as a dialectical interplay of institutional continuity and change. Institutional continuity can be found in the maintenance and revival of old welfare institutions. Institutional change has been incremental in the form of multiple layers of new institutions. At the core of the transformation of child welfare institutions in post-Soviet Kazakhstan, I argue, was the change in the dominant institutional logics: the logic of Soviet welfarism (paternalistic child protection) that fed the Soviet-type child welfare system did not go away but co-existed with the imported transnational logic of children's rights. Institutional layering along with the co-existence of multiple institutional logics produced a hybrid child welfare system which includes preserved Soviet welfare institutions and layers of newly introduced institutions.

REFERENCES

Aidukaite, Jolanta (2004). *The emergence of the post-socialist welfare state. The case of Baltic States: Estonia, Latvia and Lithuania*. Doctoral dissertation. Retrieved from DiVA portal.

Aidukaite, Jolanta (2009). "Old welfare state theories and new welfare regimes in Eastern Europe: Challenges or implications" in *Journal of Communist and Post-communist studies, Vol.* 42, No 1: 23 – 39.

Beblavý, Miroslav (2008). *New welfare state models based on the new member states' experience?* SSRN paper in <https://ssrn.com/abstract=2403764 or http://dx.doi.org/10.2139/ssrn.2403764> accessed 10 January 2018.

Béland, Daniel (2005). "Ideas and social policy: An institutionalist perspective" in *Social Policy & Administration Vol. 39*, No 1: 1 – 18.

Béland, Daniel (2007). "The social exclusion discourse: Ideas and policy change" in *Policy & Politics*, Vol. 35, No 1: 123 – 139.

Béland, Daniel (2014). *Mapping changing social policy ideas: A global, actor-centred approach*. Draft paper prepared for the UNRISD Conference New Directions in Social Policy: Alternatives from and for the Global South in <http://unrisd.org/80256B3C005BCCF9/(httpAuxPages)/1DD0172F83CDBA40C1257D080033E7C0/$file/Beland.pdf> accessed in January 2018.

Bick, Etta (2016). "Institutional layering, displacement, and policy change: The evolution of civic service in Israel" in *Public Policy and Administration*, Vol. 31, No 4: 342 – 360.

Burlacu, Irina (2007). "Welfare state regimes in transition countries: Romania and Moldova compared" in *CEU Political Science Journal*, Vol. 3, No 3: 302 – 318, in <http://epa.niif.hu/02300/02341/00008/pdf/EPA02341_ceu_2007_03_302-318.pdf> accessed in January 2018.

Capoccia, Giovanni and Kelemen, Daniel R. (2007). "The study of critical junctures: Theory, narrative and counterfactuals in institutional theory" in *World Politics*, Vol. 59, No 3: 341 – 369.

Carey, Gemma, Kay, Adrian and Nevile, Ann (2017). "Institutional legacies and "sticky layers": What happens in cases of transformative policy change?" in *Administration & Society*, online publication, published in April 2017.

Cerami, Alfio (2009). "Mechanisms of institutional change in Central and Eastern European welfare state restructuring" in Cerami, Alfio and Vanhuysse, Pieter (eds), *Post-communist welfare pathways: Theorizing social policy transformations in Central and Eastern Europe* (Palgrave Macmillan).

Deacon, Bob (2000). "Eastern European welfare states: the impact of the politics of globalization" in *Journal of European Social Policy*, Vol. 10, No 2: 146 – 161.

Esping-Andersen, Gosta (1996). "After the Golden Age? Welfare state dilemmas in a global economy" in Esping-Andersen, Gosta (ed.) *Welfare states in transition. National adaptations in global economies* (London: Sage).

Falkingham Jane (1999). "*Welfare in transition: Trends in poverty and well-being in Central Asia*" in Centre for Analysis of Social Exclusion (CASE) paper CASE / 20 (London: London School of Economics).

Fenger, H.J.M. (Menno) (2007). "Welfare regimes in Central and Eastern Europe: Incorporating postcommunist countries in a welfare regime typology" in *Contemporary Issues and ideas in Social Sciences*: 1 – 29.

Ferge, Zsuzsa (1997). "The changed welfare paradigm: the individualization of the social" in *Social Policy and Administration*, Vol. 31, No 1: 20 – 44.

Ferge, Zsuzsa (2001). "Disquieting quiet in Hungarian social policy" in *International Social Security Review*, Vol. 54, No 2 – 3: 107 – 126.

Hacker, Björn (2009). "Hybridization instead of clustering: Transformation processes of welfare policies in Central and Eastern Europe" in *Social Policy & Administration*, Vol. 43, No 2: 152 – 169.

Hall, Peter A. and Taylor, Rosemary C.R. (1996). "Political science and the three new institutionalisms" in *Political Studies, XLIV*: 936 – 957.

van der Heijden, Jeroen (2014). "Through Thelen's lens: Layering, conversion, drift, displacement and exhaustion in the development of Dutch construction regulation" in *RegNet Research Paper No. 2014 / 46* in SSRN: <https://ssrn.com/abstract=2497838> accessed in January 2018.

Iarskaia-Smirnova, Elena (2011). "Professional ideologies in Russian social work: Challenges from inside and outside" in Selwyn, Stanley (ed) *Social work education in countries of the East: Issues and challenges* (Hauppauge, New York: Nova Science Publishers, Inc.): 425 – 448.

Iarskaia-Smirnova, Elena and Romanov, Pavel (2009). "The rhetoric and practice of modernisation: Soviet social policy, 1917 – 1930s." in Hauss, Gisella and Schulte, Dagmar (eds). *Amid social contradictions. Towards a history of social work in Europe* (Opladen & Farmington Hills: Verlag Barbara Budrich): 149 – 164.

International Labor Organization [ILO] (2004). *The Republic of Kazakhstan. Final Report: Assessment of targeted social assistance scheme. Decent Work: Integrated approach to social sphere in Kazakhstan*. (ILO, Astana 2004).

Kazakhstan (2000). *National Report on Follow-up to the World Summit for Children: Kazakhstan* [NRFWS].

Kazakhstan (2001a). *Initial Report on the Implementation of the UN Convention on the Rights of the Child* in <http://daccess-dds-ny.un.org/doc/UNDOC/GEN/G02/446/05/PDF/G0244605.pdf?OpenElement> accessed in January 2014.

Kazakhstan (2001b). *Alternative NGO report commenting on the Initial Report on the Implementation of the UN Convention on the Rights of the Child* [CRC Report].

Kazakhstan (2012). *Fourth Periodical Report on the Implementation of the UN Convention on the Rights of the Child* [CRC Report].

Kostina, Yelena (2003). *Istoriya sotsialnoy raboty* [History of social work] (Dalnevostochny University. Vladivostok).

Kuitto, Kati (2011). More than just money: Patterns of disaggregated welfare expenditure in the enlarged Europe, in *Journal of European Social Policy*, Vol. 21, No 4: 348 – 364.

Kuzio, Taras (2001). "Transition in post-communist states: Triple or quadruple?" *Politics, Vol. 21*, No 3: 168 – 177.

Maltseva, Elena (2008). *Policy implementation in post-Soviet states: A comparison of social benefits reform in Russia and Kazakhstan*. Paper presented at the 81 CPSA Annual Conference, Carleton University.

Orenstein, Mitchell A. (2008). "Postcommunist welfare states" in *Journal of Democracy*, Vol. 19, No 4: 80 – 94.

Rocco, Philip and Thurston, Chloe (2014). "From metaphors to measures: observable indicators of gradual institutional change" in *Journal of Public Policy*, Vol. 34: 35 – 62.

Steinmo, Sven (2008). "Historical institutionalism". In Donatella Della Porta and Michael Keating (Eds.), *Approaches and methodologies in the social sciences* (pp. 118 – 138). Cambridge UK: Cambridge University Press.

SOS Kinderdorf Kazakhstan (2017). in http://www.sos-kazakhstan.kz/ru/page/o-nas accessed in December 2017.

Streeck, Wolfgang and Thelen, Kathleen (eds.) (2005). *Beyond continuity: Institutional change in advanced political economies* (Oxford: Oxford University Press).

Teplova, Tatyana (2007). "Welfare state transformation, childcare, and women's work in Russia" in *Social Politics: International Studies in Gender, State & Society*, Vol. 14, No 3: 284 – 322.

Thornton, Patricia H. and Ocasio, William (2008). "Institutional logics" in Greenwood, Royston, Oliver, Christine, Sahlin-Andersson, Kerstin and Suddaby, Roy (eds.) *SAGE Handbook of Organizational Institutionalism* (CA: Sage).

Thornton, Patricia H., Ocasio, William and Lounsbury, Michael (2012). *The institutional logics perspective: A new approach to culture, structure and process* (Oxford University Press).

UNICEF Kazakhstan (2007). Increasing social orientation of budgets and efficiency of public expenditures at national and local levels in the best interests of children and families in Kazakhstan. Presentations from the international conference in https://www.unicef.org/innovations/files/Kazakstan_increasing_social_orientation_kazak.pdf accessed in January 2018.

World Bank (1998). *Kazakhstan. Living standards during the transition.* Human Development Sector Unit Europe and Central Asia Region. (Report No. 17520-KZ) in <www-wds.worldbank.org/servlet/WDSContentServer/WDSP/IB/1998/03/22/000009265_3980623151019/Rendered/INDEX/multi_page.txt> accessed in January 2018.

Zezina, Mariya R. (2000). "The system of social protection of orphans in the U.S.S.R." [Systema sotsialnoy zashity detey sirot v SSSR] in *Pedagogika*, Vol. 3: 58 – 67.

CHAPTER 9:
THE IMPACT OF WOMEN'S AGENCY AGAINST POVERTY IN RUSSIA

Ann-Mari Sätre

INTRODUCTION

Post-Soviet transformation has created large income gaps and removed social safety nets for ordinary people across Russia. Societal structures have disappeared, and workplaces are no longer obliged to provide housing or child care, as in the Soviet time. Individuals have to pay for services that they did not previously pay for. The situation some people end up in is chronic poverty, where expenses are constantly higher than income. Many families are close to the edge of poverty, particularly younger families. Families with many children are even more vulnerable (Korchagina and Prokofeva, 2008; Moskovskii Finansovyi Forum, 2016).

This chapter examines developments in social policy in Russia, along with trends concerning women's work and engagement, to solve problems of poverty as a complement to state policies. Although there are general tendencies towards decreasing poverty levels since the turn of the century, certain elements of persistent poverty within some population groups are likely to remain, while inequality by and large also remains high and stable. Following the initial shocks in 1991 – 92 immediately after the Soviet Union collapsed, a major financial crisis in 1998 and the international economic crisis in 2008 – 09 represented setbacks to households and enterprises in Russia. Also, the economic crisis in Russia in 2014, following the falling price of oil and economic sanctions due to the Crimean annexation, has had consequences. Recent changes in directions of social policy further contribute to some worrisome developments and trends.

Section 2 outlines the theoretical and research basis for this chapter. Section 3 discusses the evolution of poverty in Russia and highlights the problematic nature of the chronic elements of poverty. Then state policies of social policies are analyzed in Section 4. It is argued that although resources devoted to social policy have increased, efforts appear insufficient to cover basic needs. The effect of the continuing responsibility of women for solving problems of poverty through their paid and unpaid work is analyzed in Section 5, before the conclusions are drawn.

THEORETICAL AND RESEARCH BASIS

The analytical framework is based on Douglass North's (1990) categorization of four main kinds of institutions which influence the way a society develops: legal rules; organizational forms; enforcement; and behavioral norms. Institutions are all the restrictions that humans have created to regulate interaction in society. While formal rules can be changed by political decisions, informal rules, such as behavioral norms that are rooted in society, are not so quickly changed.

Although North (1990) highlighted the need for 'agency' (action) for change, he did not incorporate the inter-relationship between agency and the institutional framework. In this chapter, the agency dimension is added, drawing on Sen's (1984) capability approach. Sen's analytical framework also connects agency to the issue of empowerment, and seeks not only to answer the actual needs for a resource (e.g. money, housing), but also to identify the kind of support needed to transform resources into goods and services (Sen, 1984). The core of the empowerment concept lies in the ability of the individual to control her own destiny, that is, the agency aspect.

The aim here is to highlight the impact of institutions on women's agency against poverty in Russia. The chapter pays attention to the relationship between socially-oriented NGOs and social work, given the assumption that resources devoted to social policy are insufficient relative to needs. A goal is therefore to identify when and how socially-oriented NGOs can contribute to empowerment processes involving poor people. The impact of two kinds of informal institutions are highlighted; firstly, the survival of a general hierarchical structure of organizations from the Soviet era (in both municipal agencies and NGOs), and secondly, the survival of the norm that women are responsible for the organization of social welfare.

Empirical data has been collected in 2002 – 2017, using semi-structured qualitative interviews; this is complemented by observation and in some cases by special methods like focus group meetings. Interviews are typically 40 – 80 minutes long, structured with basic questions but varying to a degree because of different places, work tasks and socio-economic features of the interviewees. The data has been collected during several projects focusing on local development and / or poverty. The most relevant part of data for this chapter was composed of over 250 interviews on policies on poverty collected in 2010 – 2017 from five Russian regions with social work experts, social workers, and social pedagogues (see Sätre, 2019). Interviews also took place with teachers, doctor's assistants, NGO representatives, local politicians and deputies of commissions or local village councils. Most of the respondents were women. Four of the regions are located in north-western Russia and one in the Volga region.

Formal versus informal institutions and the role of agency

An institution-centered approach to poverty takes aspects of a society as a cause of poverty rather than individual failings (Sen, 1984). According to this approach, slow-adapting institutions would explain why many people would be unable to support themselves; salaries that are too low are seen as an integral part of the functioning of the economic system (Gaddy, 2007; Kornai, 1980; North, 1990; Sätre, 1994; 2001). In effect, some features of the Soviet system have survived the reform measures from the 1990s, which explains why a large part of the Russian workforce is still employed in unprofitable large-scale enterprises. The tradition of low salaries in certain professions, such as for teachers and doctors who are employed in non-commercial organizations, seems to have survived. At the same time, privatization made it so that firms are not obliged to secure welfare for their employees as in the Soviet times, while individuals have to pay for services that they did not previously have to pay for (Lazareva, 2009). The situation some people end up with is living in chronic poverty, where expenses are constantly higher than income. Many of the poor are young people whose situation became worse as a result of their poor adjustment after the global economic crisis in 2008 (Rimashevskaya, 2010). The majority of the poor are working families with children (Moskovskii Finansovyi Forum, 2016; 14).

North (2005) argues that the post-Soviet experience highlights the wide gap between intentions and outcomes and the fragility of social order in the process of fundamental economic, political and social change. According to the general ideas in North (1990), although formal institutions in the form of laws and regulations have changed as a result of political decisions, informal institutions such as behavioral norms and organizational culture are not likely to have evolved to the same extent. Two main reasons for this can be identified. Either the informal institutions are more deeply rooted culturally and change slower than formal ones, or they barely change at all or in another direction than what was intended by policy-makers. Adding the agency dimension, effects of reforms as such need to be separated from consequences arising from the survival and evolution of informal institutions. All these aspects are related to how people react or adapt to reforms, and they are also connected with their faith in the enforcement of rules, organizational structures, norms, behavior and attitudes.

The capability approach to analyzing poverty highlights relational aspects rather than incomes or ownership as such. This means that a person's exchange entitlements are highlighted. The ability of people to get out of poverty thus depends on their ability to transform whatever income or assets they have into food and other necessities. Assets are, according to Sen (1984), classified into three categories: resources, including all kinds of capital (also social capital, human capital, cultural capital); rights, such as welfare entitlements; and relationships. This means that according to this approach, incomes or assets are not enough for people to overcome poverty; agency in one form or another is also required.

THE EVOLUTION OF POVERTY IN RUSSIA

Output was falling in Russia all through the 1990s until 1998 / 9 (Ericson, 2009; Leeson and Turnball, 2006; Roland, 2006). After that, high economic growth was registered from 1999 to mid-2008, when it was hit by the global economic crisis (Sutela, 2013). Since mid-2009, economies were recovering again until 2013, when falling oil prices started to cause problems. Poverty levels followed these trends quite closely. Federal law No 134-FZ, 'About a living wage in the Russian Federation' was adopted in 1997. This law established 'a legal basis for minimum wage definition, state guarantees and social protection'. The law was revised in May 2000, August 2004 and July 2009. The official poverty line (*prozhitochnyi minimum*) is defined as the minimum income necessary for physiological survival (Yates, 2004; 13).

Poverty is officially defined with an absolute 'subsistence minimum' based on the price of a basket of goods, which is assumed to cover basic needs. According to the resulting national poverty lines, while in the early 1990s on average a third of the Russian population was considered to be poor, poverty rates then started to decrease. In 2007 – 2013, poverty rates in Russia have remained rather stable at 11 – 12 percent (Rosstat, 2015). This is partly due to the indexation of poverty lines for inflation, but it does highlight that a section of the population lives in entrenched, chronic poverty. In Russia, poverty has, since 2014, started to increase again; in 2016, according to official figures, 13.5 percent of the population was poor. A sign of increasing poverty was that people were using increasing shares of their income for food (Ovcharova and Biryukova, 2015; 5 – 6).

Measuring poverty simply on the basis of income has, however, proven to be a problematic approach (Yates, 2004). One reason is due to irregular payments (Rimashevskaya, 2010). Another reason is the spread of the informal economy and hidden types of income (Gaddy and Ickes, 1998; Kim, 2002). A third reason is that peoples' subjective evaluations differ from the official definitions based on income (Chebankova, 2010; Rudenko, 2014). A fourth reason which is less commonly highlighted is that focusing on income does not adequately reflect the effects of changes in entitlements that people have experienced in the aftermath of the *perestroika* processes. The large number of people close to the poverty line means however that if this was set at a slightly different level, the percentage of official poor would change quite substantially (Ovcharova, 2008). Therefore, one should not focus on exact figures, but rather on tendencies.

Interviewees give the impression that the 'subsistence minimum' is far too low to provide a decent variety of food. Additionally, the poverty line is based on a political decision and it can be moved down or up according to the government's considerations. If the line is dropped down, the number of beneficiaries decreases. That can save budget expenditures but will also bring a bias in statistics.

State policies of social policy in Russia

Across Russia, the sudden emergence of large-scale poverty in the 1990s was exacerbated by the fact that the social welfare programs inherited from the Soviet Union were inadequately focused on deprivation. The Soviet authorities denied that social ills like poverty existed. Social benefits were generally universal, for example pensions, or else awarded to particular groups of the population on the basis of merit or special needs: for example, to military veterans, mothers of large families and disabled people. A significant amount of support was provided in-kind or as discounts on services, rather than cash. The notion of 'targeting' state financial resources to individuals on the basis of material need was unfamiliar, and existing welfare programs thus could not cushion shocks to income and well-being during the 1990s (Klugman, 1998; Lokshin and Popkin, 1999; Yates, 2004). Russia confronted the challenge of reforming its social protection systems in conditions of limited budgetary resources. Also, resistance to change has appeared from a range of stakeholders: public protests broke out across Russia in 2005 when the government attempted to replace a range of subsidies and free benefits for pensioners, veterans and other groups with cash payments.

The poverty phenomenon of the 1990s led to increased resources being allocated to social security but also laid the basis for the professionalization of social work (Iarskaia-Smirnova and Romanov, 2002). Russia has used budgetary reserves amassed from natural resources to raise pensions and social payments from time to time. Such moves as increasing pensions by 35 percent in 2010 have ensured that real disposable incomes actually rose, despite the economic downturn in the years of financial crisis (Zubarevich, 2015a). Wages for teachers, librarians and cultural workers have been raised, and—according to the government's plan from 2013—were to continuously rise until 2017. Regardless of their employment status, all individuals are eligible by law for a basic pension and free health care. This principle of universal coverage of the provisions is combined with a low level of provision. Welfare has been financed by oil and gas revenues rather than income tax revenues (Gaddy and Ickes, 2015).

Up until 2012, expenses for social policy in Russia were adjusted to inflation rates (Ovcharova et al., 2015; 2). From 2013 to 2015, adjustments were not done even if inflation rates were increasing (Biryukova and Bardanyan, 2015; 2 – 3). Nevertheless, despite the falling GDP, leading to considerable cuts in most budget expenses for 2015, the budget for social policy was increased in nominal values.[1] The formal conditions and procedures regulate who has the right to social services.

---

1   Budget spending on education, health and social policy has since 2013 decreased in a number of Russian regions, in 2015 spending decreased in eight regions (Zubarevich 2015b).

Some major reforms have been initiated, for example, the 'maternity capital' reform, the 'foster family' reform and the 'social enterprise' reform enabling delivery of social services by non-state actors. The 'maternity capital' reform (*Federal'nyi Zakon No.* 256-FZ 2006) came into force in Russia in 2007.[2] It is aimed to encourage women to give birth to a second or even a third child by providing families with a substantial financial incentive. In addition to the state support system are the regional programs, i.e. subsidies for families for their living and for education, and extra rubles for a third child. Families may also get land for free to build homes. It is important for the local administration to be active in order to get any federal funding. This funding is mostly based on the system of local co-financing. Consequently, local residents face different possibilities of benefitting from such programs, depending on how active their community is.

There are also documents demonstrating the size of the different benefits, and depicting their adjustment to compensate for price increases. Social services provide information to groups entitled to support about their rights. At the same time, it is evident that hierarchical structures in social service have many negative effects, among others that recipients maintain low trust in authorities (Shlapentokh, 2006). Also, there exist problems of enforcement as, for example, it appears that it is difficult for social services to allocate help to the most needy. The poor have to apply for benefits themselves, but many do not fulfil the requirements (interviews with social work experts, 2010 – 2013).

The financial distribution of social benefits has been the main means of regulating poverty. Resources allocated to poverty relief have generally, however, been insufficient when reflected against the fact that payments of social benefits do not cover basic expenditures. It appears that social policy has not been primarily devoted to combatting poverty. Birth grants are, for example, contingent on child-bearing only. The National Priority Programs and demographic policies have entailed new interventions in employment, housing and health care, in order to reach the state's demographic goals (Cook, 2011; Chandler, 2013). But there are also considerable subsidies distributed for housing and various forms of child

---

2   The maternity program was to be ended by the end of 2016, but has been extended to 2018. In a speech before the presidential election in March 2018, Vladimir Putin announced that it will be extended to 2021.

benefits. Many of the benefits are quite small, but gathering all of them together implies a contribution to family incomes, especially to families with three or more children. These are distributed according to category, and not based on needs, and as such not primarily to the poor. This is about solving the problem of social orphans by, on the one hand, increasing support to families in connection to the birth of children and, on the other, to increase support to families who step in to take care of bringing up children whose parents have lost custody.

Changing priorities?

Russian administration has two levels of socio-cultural expenses, those at the federal level and those by regions. Seventy-five percent of expenses for social policy are paid by the state, reflecting the fact that the state has to secure payments of pensions, while the regions have to finance the bulk of expenses for health and education by themselves. However, only a small part of benefits is targeted to low income families; this consists of a subsidy for accommodation plus a minor child benefit per child and, since 2013, additional monthly payments for families with three children or more (Zubarevich and Gorina, 2015; 51 – 52).

But there is somewhat of a contradiction here, which is due to the downturn of the economy implying restrictions on expenses directed to social policy. This is about the increased effort to also direct support to the poorest. Minimum subsistence level, along with its components and ways of calculation, is set by the federal level, while it is the regions that are charged with the responsibility to secure rights with their own budgets.

Some restructuring of priorities has been reflected through a few pieces of legislation in 2013 – 2015. According to new principles adopted in 2014, support should be reoriented from general support to support to those below the poverty line. The policy is implemented by regions, but due to financial deficiencies in 2014 – 2015, in order to fulfil the new regulations, other kinds of adjustments are required. In effect, the normative decisions regulating rights to support have been changed; the list of responsibilities that should be covered has changed. Conditions for measures have become stricter and decision-making concerning payments have also been altered (Gorina, 2017). The specific changes vary between regions, but in general terms this is about stricter conditions for actually being entitled to support aimed for the poor. In

Arkhangelsk region, for example, according to a social work specialist, the minimum subsistence level has been reduced from 13,500 to 10,000 rubles in 2016 (interview, social services, December 2016).

The change to targeted subsidies has meant a cut in social transfers, while also reducing the number of people entitled to support. In addition, inflation is no longer compensated for, as there is no indexation. Interviews with foster families indicate that even they are not protected from inflation (interview with foster family, Arkhangelsk *oblast*, April 2016). By and large, only a small percentage (seven percent) of total sums for social support go to targeted groups (*Moskovskii finansovyi forum*, 2016; 5). This is not surprising given the extremely small money that actually is paid in the form of child benefits and the like.

Russia has relied on income from oil when funding the general welfare system. In 2015, as the oil price went down, the Russian budget was running with a deficit. Although price decreases of oil did not affect the budget, it contributed to increasing inflation rates and consequently decreased the real value of social policy measures for individual families. The temporary solution of financing social policy through the reserve fund provides a warning; one should assume that there will be more cuts in social expenses to come, and that this could be harmful to parts of the Russian population.

The State and socially-oriented NGOs

Although the number of NGOs was indeed growing in the 1990s, many commentators have noted that doors have been closing again after Putin's access to power, which is reflected in a decreasing number of NGOs (Cook, 2011). Generally, after the Federal Law on 'foreign agents' was enforced (*Federal'nyi Zakon No.* 121-FZ 2012), NGOs became more dependent on domestic funding and the Presidential Administration increased its capacity to distribute presidential grants (Chebankova, 2012). In order to be able to get grants one has to make sure to enter the 'right' NGO list (interview with NGO leaders, Novgorod, May 2016).

In particular, increased control from above (as manifested in new legislation in 2006 and again in 2012 and 2014), suggest that it has become more difficult for bottom-up initiatives to provide social services, given that they are not likely to get support from the state (interview with a lawyer, Arkhangelsk, December 2016). Some of the larger NGOs with roots from the Soviet period, such as the non-governmental organizations 'for Deaf and Blind' and 'for the Disabled', provide an example of NGOs who are accepted and supported by the state (Interviews, Arkhangelsk, October 2012; December 2016).

The increased effort to engage people in the 'third sector' or socially oriented activities, is promoted by the Federal Law No 40-FZ 'On socially-oriented NGOs' (adopted in 2010). It appears that, rather than increasing tax payments to finance social policy, citizens are 'encouraged' to contribute to the fulfillment of social aims in various ways (*Obshchestvennaya palata*, 2012). First, there are general measures to redirect NGO activities from politics or human rights to social welfare, through new laws regulating the activities of NGOs promising tax relief measures, fewer audits and less control. NGOs should contribute to 'social help', emphasizing the importance of being an active citizen in the social sphere; that is, a special kind of activism is promoted. Secondly, there are raised expectations of voluntary work, mainly by women engaged in the social sphere. Third, voluntary contributions to charity by businesses are encouraged on the basis of ethics and moral values, rather than through the use of monetary incentives (ibid., 2012).

Women responsible for solving problems of poverty

It is well documented that female politicians were commonly responsible for social policies in the Soviet Union, and that women continue to take this responsibility at higher as well as at lower political levels in post-Soviet Russia (Lapidus, 1975; Moses, 2008). The same women are sometimes also the chairpersons in the women's councils which are registered NGOs, although they are not examples of bottom-up organizations. Kulmala (2013) and Phillips (2005) have observed that many of the organizational skills evident in NGOs were developed from women's experiences in Soviet organizations. As a result of the low priority given to female dominated sectors such as health and social services in state policy, women had to develop an ability to find practical solutions to everyday problems, and these skills have survived after the Soviet system (Sätre, 2001; 2016). Women use them in their formal positions as responsible for social policy and in informal positions, when taking responsibility voluntarily in social work. Interviews provide evidence of how social workers actually make their own judgements about whom to support, taking into account the inadequate resources they have at their disposal. Adhering to North, this is about the survival of informal institutions. Referring to Amartya Sen's framework of capabilities, to act they need to have access to some assets, and also to be able to use these assets.

Interviews were conducted with directors of children homes, rehabilitation centers, schools and other places in order to find out whether women helped to make possible increasing resources, rights or relations of the poor. Focusing on their agency facilitates distinguishing their potential roles of empowering the poor from their controlling roles. Interviews tell about how social workers, social pedagogues at schools, teachers, doctor's assistants, deputies of commissions or local village councils, local politicians and others have tried to help people take part in state programs and become classified to be entitled to support in one way or another (Sätre, 2014b).

Parallel hierarchies versus personal networks
Earlier research acknowledges that NGOs have been formed in order to address current social problems (cf. Cook and Vinogradova, 2006; Hemment, 2007; Kay, 2000; Salmenniemi, 2008; Sperling, 1999). Many of these have addressed the problems of poverty in one way or another; one example is distribution of food in rural areas (Sätre, 2000). It has been argued that many of these organizations adapt to changes and try to solve problems as they appear rather than trying to change something through open protests in society (Mendelson and Gerber, 2007). This is illustrated by an NGO representative (the director of a charity fund, interview 2011 and 2017). Six years after the first visit, the fund is still in place, and the leader is also the same, the former secretary of the Communist Party in the mono-town. On her list is 70 local people, these are people she knows. They are former party officials, from the trade union, those in administrative positions. The director of the fund knows what each of them can contribute: 'they all help, nobody refuses', she says. When somebody needs help, she makes the necessary phone calls, or she writes a letter.

It appears that female officials view women's organizations as potential allies in the social sphere, being potential providers of social services, and filling gaps in the badly shredded Russian safety net (cf. Sätre, 2014a). One aspect is also the continued reliance on help from voluntary organizations in one way or another (Kay, 2011; Salmenniemi, 2008). Interviews with professionals at state social services have revealed that they are dependent on NGOs in different ways.

It seems reasonable to assume that Soviet type systems aggravated the condition for bottom-up, empowering civil organizing (Rose, 1996). These legacies fulfill a function also in today's Russian society, since NGOs assisting the poor often are formed top down rather than bottom-up, and rather than working for empowerment, stand for charity.[3] Interviews from four Russian regions provided evidence of how social welfare institutions and NGOs seem to function as two parallel hierarchies of support that do not necessarily reach people most in need. It appears that state policies promote hierarchical top-down models, with both social welfare offices and NGOs providing charity rather than empowerment. There are no formal structures for collaboration, and therefore no regular means of co-operation. On the contrary, co-operation between NGOs and social services appears to be based on personal contacts or on *ad hoc* agreements. When something happens, resources are mobilized to meet the particular emergency situation.

Recent pressure from the state to engage socially oriented NGOs is compatible with developments at the local level. Women who were used to finding informal solutions to problems during the Soviet period continue to find ways to secure survival in post-Soviet Russia through their unpaid voluntary work (in addition to paid work). Local authorities are intertwined with traditional organizations, such as women's councils and veteran's councils, which are officially registered as NGOs (Kulmala, 2013; Sätre, 2014c). There are networks between women leaders, across state organizations and NGOs, as well as between leaders of informal clubs. Foster family clubs and networks of mothers with many children or single mothers are examples of the latter. A woman in charge at the administration of a small town says she as a member of the regional women's council, is a mentor to a child in a poor family (interview, Nizhny Novgorod *oblast*, April 2016).

Charity organizations are engaged in helping homeless children and young criminals, and also, to some extent, in 'bottom-up projects', such as helping individuals or groups with funds to start up various activities

---

3   See further Crotty (2009), who finds that social NGOs are hierarchical and they do not promote the development of civil society, but rather focus on one question.

(Granberg and Sätre, 2017). A local head of administration tells about how she had herself initiated all the ongoing TOS[4] activities in her area (interview Arkhangelsk *oblast*, December 2016). This implies a blurring of responsibilities, of roles and of tasks, so that it is difficult to see where the state's responsibility ends, and where the voluntary sector takes over.

Returning to the role of institutions, social work through women's paid and unpaid work resulted from the non-priority status of social work in the Soviet system. A combination of different strategies is important to overcome different kinds of deficiencies arising in the processes of transformation and decentralization in post-Soviet Russia, during which various combinations of women's formal and informal organizations have survived. Women continue to carry significant responsibilities for organizing social welfare within society, as well as for empowering voluntary work, given the gendered nature of the responsibility for social work in both state and non-state contexts.

CONCLUSIONS

Although social policy continues to be financed by the state to a major extent, new ways of organizing social welfare have been launched which are opening up opportunities for empowerment processes. Networks of women working and engaging in the social sphere provide hope for the poor in Russia. But it is still mostly about charity rather than empowerment. Despite all the problems with the functioning of the system there are local tendencies towards collaboration between women in different positions who try to find ways to go forward. It is usual that women who are responsible for social welfare have to find sponsors by themselves, for their regular activities. Being responsible for organizing social welfare, women working in the social sphere have created their own support networks for this. They use relations to create resources. Their agenda is often larger than the directives they might be subject to from above. They are also actively working to increase available resources by, for example, applying for projects, striving to participate in state programs and collecting charity. This means, however, that solutions are likely to be more heterogeneous than before. The empirical material

---

4   *Territorial'noe Obshchestvennoe Samoupravlenie*, in English 'self-managed local association' (see Granberg and Sätre (2017).

provides information about how this happens, how women continue to take responsibility for social welfare, how they react, and about their efforts. The broad picture supports the finding that Soviet culture taught women to find solutions which continue to be needed in contemporary Russia.

As to the Russian social policy, there is a risk that the state places too much reliance on women's unpaid work. No matter how active are women who take on responsibility for social welfare, whether they do this formally or informally, in any case, this activity will not be enough to solve the basic problems of poverty in Russia. Furthermore, stricter attitudes to NGOs are hindering initiatives and agency and provide additional difficulties. Agency is clearly not enough; stronger support from the government is needed as well.

REFERENCES

Biryukova, Svetlana and Elena Bardanyan. (2015). *Dinamika Detskikh i Semeinykh Byplat: Indeksatsiya i Inflyatsiya*, Moskva, Institut Upravleniya Sotsialnymi Protsessami.

Chandler, Andrea. (2013). *Democracy, Gender, and Social Policy in Russia. A Wayward Society.* Basingstoke, UK: Palgrave Macmillan.

Chebankova, Elena. (2010). 'Public and Private Cycles of Socio-Political Life in Putin's Russia.' *Post-Soviet Affairs* 26, 2: 121 – 148.

Chebankova, Elena. (2012). 'State-sponsored civic associations in Russia: systemic integration or the "war of position".' *East European Politics* 28, 4: 390 – 408.

Cook, Linda and Elena Vinogradova. (2006). 'NGOs and Social Policy Making in Russia's Regions.' *Problems of Post-Communism* 5: 28 – 41.

Cook, Linda. (2011). 'Russia's Welfare Regime: The Shift Towards Statism.' In *Gazing at Welfare, Gender and Agency in Post-socialist Countries*, edited by Maija Jäppinen, Meri Kulmala and Aino Saarinen, 14 – 36. Newcastle upon Tyne: Cambridge Scholars Publishing.

Crotty, Jo. (2009). 'Making a Difference? NGOs and Civil Society Development in Russia.' *Europe-Asia Studies* 61, 1: 85 – 108.

Ericson, Richard. (2009). 'The Russian economy in the year 2008: Testing the market economy.' *Post-Soviet Affairs* 25, 3: 209 – 231.

Gaddy, Clifford G. and Barry W. Ickes. (1998). 'Russia's Virtual Economy.' *Foreign Affairs* 77, 5: 53 – 67.

Gaddy, Clifford G. (2007). 'The Russian Economy in the Year 2006.' *Post-Soviet Affairs* 21, 1: 38 – 49.

Gaddy, Clifford and Barry W. Ickes. (2015). 'Putin's rent management system and the future of addiction in Russia.' In *The Challenges for Russia's Politicized Economic System*. Edited by Susanne Oxenstierna, 11 – 32. London and New York: Routledge.

Gorina, Elena. (2017). 'Sotsialnaya Poderzhka i Detstva v Rossii: v kontekste sovremennoi politika rasshireniya utcheta nuzhdaemosti.' Annual Conference on Economic and social Development, Higher School of Economic, Moscow, 11 – 14 April.

Granberg, Leo and Ann-Mari Sätre. (2017). *The Other Russia: Local Experience and Societal Change*. London and New York: Routledge / Taylor & Francis Group.

Hemment, Julie. 2007. *Empowering Women in Russia, Activism, Aid, and NGOs*. Bloomington and Indianapolis: Indiana University Press.

Iaroshenko, Svetlana. (2010). '"New" Poverty in Russia after Socialism. Summary.' *Laboratorium* 2, 3: 408 – 413.

Iarskaia-Smirnova, Elena and Pavel Romanov. (2002). 'A Salary Is Not Important Here: The Professionalization of Social Work in Contemporary Russia.' *Social Policy & Administration* 36, 2: 123 – 141.

Kay, Rebecca. (2000). *Russian women and their Organisations: Gender, Discrimination and Grassroots Women's Organisations, 1991 – 96*. Basingstoke: Palgrave Macmillan.

Kay, Rebecca. (2011). '(Un)caring Communities: Processes of Marginalisation and Access to Formal and Informal Care and Assistance in Rural Russia.' *Journal of Rural Studies* 27, 1: 45 – 53.

Kim, Byung-Yeon. (2002). 'The participation of Russian households in the informal economy: Evidence from the VTsIOM data.' *Economics of Transition* 10, 3: 689 – 717.

Klugman, Jeni. ed. (1997). *Poverty in Russia. Public Policy and Private Responses*. EDI Development Studies. Washington; D.C.: The World Bank.

Korchagina, Irina I. and Lidia M. Prokof'eva. (2008). 'Monetarnaya i sub'ektivnaya bednost': dinamika masshtabov i gruppy riska: Monitoring bednosti v Nizhegorodskoi oblasti: Itogi mezhdunarodnogo proekta po issledovaniyu problem bednosti v Nizhegorodskoi oblasti.' *Narodonaselenie*. 2.

Kornai, Janos. (1980). *Economics of Shortage*. Amsterdam, Netherlands: North Holland.

Kulmala, Meri. (2013). '*State and Society in Small-Town Russia—A Feminist-ethnographic Inquity into the Boundaries of Society in the Finnish-Russian Borderland*.' PhD diss., Helsinki: Publications of the Department of Social Research, University of Helsinki, 14.

Lapidus, Gail Warshofsky. (1975). 'Political Mobilization, Participation, and Leadership: Women in Politics.' *Comparative Politics* 8, 1: 90 – 118.

Lazareva, Olga. (2009). '*Labour Market Outcomes during the Russian Transition*.' PhD diss., Stockholm: Stockholm School of Economics.

Leeson, Peter T., and William N. Trumbull. (2006). 'Comparing Apples: Normalcy, Russia, and the Remaining Post-Socialist World.' *Post-Soviet Affairs* 22, 3: 225 – 248.

Ledeneva, Alena. (2008). 'Telephone Justice in Russia.' *Post-Soviet Affairs* 24, 4: 324 – 350.

Lokshin, Michael and Barry Popkin. (1999). 'The Emerging Underclass in the Russian Federation: Income Dynamics, 1992 – 1996.' *Economic Development and Cultural Change* 47, 4: 803 – 829.

Moses, Joel C. (2008). 'Who Has Led Russia? Russian Regional Political Elites, 1954 – 2006.' *Europe-Asia Studies*, 60, 1: 1 – 24, January 2008.

Moskovskii Finansovyi Forum. (2016). Edited by Vladimir Nazarov. *Effektivnaya Sotsialnaya Podderzhka Naseleniya Versiya 3.0: Adresnost*. Moskva: Nuzhdaemost i Universalnost.

North, Douglass. (1990). *Institutions, Institutional Change and Economic Performance*. Cambridge: Cambridge University Press.

North, Douglass. (2005). *Understanding the Process of Economic Change*, Princeton, New Jersey: Princeton University Press.

Obshchestvennaya Palata. (2012). *Doklad o Sostoyanii Grazhdanskogo Obshchestva v Rossiskoi Federatsii za 2012 god*. Moskva.

Ovcharova, Lilia N. (2008). 'Bednost i Ekonomicheskii Rost v Rossii.' *Zhyrnal Isleovanii Sotsialnoi Politiki* 6, 4: 439 – 456.

Ovcharova Lilia and Svetlana Biryukova. (2015). *Dokhody i Raskhody Naseleniya: Yanvar' 2014—Yanvar'*. Moskva: Institut Upravleniya Sotsialnymi Protsessami.

Ovcharova Lilia, Svetlana Biryukova, Elena Baranyan, Aleksei Rudberg and Sergei Ter-Akolov. (2015). *Dokhody i Raskhody Naseleniya: Osnovnye Izmeneniya*. Moskva: Institut Upravleniya Sotsialnymi Protsessami.

Oxenstierna, Susanne. (ed.) (2015). *The Challenges for Russia's Politicized Economic System*. London and New York: Routledge.

Phillips, Sarah D. (2005). 'Civil Society and Healing: Theorizing Women's Social Activism in Post-Soviet Ukraine.' *Ethnos: Journal of Anthropology*, 70, 4: 489 – 514.

Rimashevskaya, Natalia M. (2010). 'Riski Bednosti v Sovremennoi Rossii.' *Narodonaselenie* 2, 48: 4 – 9.

Roland, Gérald. (2006). 'The Russian Economy in the Year 2005.' *Post-Soviet Affairs* 22, 1:90 – 98.

Rose, Nikolas. (1996). 'The death of the social? Re-figuring the territory of government.' *Economy and Society* 3: 327 – 356.

Rosstat. Russian Federal Statistics, different years. Moscow: Goskomstat Rossii.

Rudenko, Dmitry Yu. (2014). 'A Comprehensive Approach to the Study of Poverty in the Region.' *Social Geography* 4, 3: 143 – 151.

Salmenniemi, Suvi. (2008). *Democratization and Gender in Contemporary Russia*. London & New York: Routledge.

Sen, Amartya. (1984). *Resources, Values and Development*. Oxford: Basil Blackwell Publisher Ltd.

Shlapentokh, Vladimir. (2006). 'Trust in Public Institutions in Russia: The Lowest in the World.' *Communist and Post-Communist Studies*, 39, 2: 153 – 74.

Sperling, Valerie. (1999). *Organizing Women in Contemporary Russia: Engendering Transition*. Cambridge: Cambridge University Press.

Sutela, Pekka. (2013). 'Economic Policy.' In *Return to Putin's Russia*, edited by Stephen K. Wegren, 173 – 188. Plymouth: Rowman & Littlefield Publishers, Inc.

Sätre, Ann-Mari. (1994). *Environmental Problems in the Shortage Economy: The Legacy of Soviet Environmental Policy*. Aldershot and Brookfield: Edward Elgar Publishing Limited.

Sätre, Ann-Mari. (2000). 'Women and the Social Economy in Transitional Russia.' *Annals of Public and Cooperative Economics* 71, 3: 441 – 465.

Sätre, Ann-Mari. (2001). 'Women's and Men's Work in Transitional Russia: Legacies of the Soviet System.' *Post-Soviet Affairs* 17, 1: 56 – 79.

Sätre, Ann-Mari. (2014a). 'Paid and Unpaid Social Work in Russia. Is Women's Social Work opening up Opportunities for Empowerment Processes?' *International Social Work* 57, 5: 523 – 534.

Sätre, Ann-Mari. (2014b). 'Policies against Poverty in Russia—a Female Responsibility.' *Debatte: Journal of Contemporary Central and Eastern Europe* 22, 3: 379 – 402.

Sätre, Ann-Mari. (2014c). 'Women in Local Politics in Russia: Coping with Poverty and Strategies for Development.' *Eastern European Countryside* 20, 1: 27 – 53.

Sätre Ann-Mari. (2016). 'Women's Entrepreneurs in Russia: Impacts from the Soviet System.' *Journal of Enterprising Communities*, 10: 1, pp. 53 – 69.

Sätre Ann-Mari. (2019). *The Politics of Poverty in Contemporary Russia*. London and New York: Routledge / Taylor & Francis Group.

Wegren, Stephen K. (2013). *Return to Putin's Russia. Past Imperfect and Future Uncertain*. New York: Roman & Littlefield Publishers.

Yates, Samantha. (2004). 'Living with Poverty in Post-Soviet Russia: Social Perspectives on Urban Development.' PhD dissertation, London School of Economic and Political Science.

Zubarevich, Natalia. (2015a). 'Regional Inequality and Potential for Modernization.' In *The Challenges for Russia's Politicized Economic System*, edited by Susanne Oxenstierna. London and New York: Routledge.

Zubarevich, Natalia. (2015b). 'Public Sector Finance Problems, Regional aspects.' Paper presented in UCRS seminar, University of Uppsala, Uppsala, 17 September.

Zubarevich Natalia and Elena Gorina. (2015). *Sotsialnye Raskhody v Rossii: Federal'nyi i Regional'nye Byudzhety*. Moskva: Institut Upravleniya Sotsialnymi Protsessami.

PART FOUR: WELFARE TRAJECTORIES AND ASSEMBLAGES

CHAPTER 10:
THE POLITICS OF PENSION REFORMS IN KAZAKHSTAN: PRESSURES FOR CHANGE AND REFORM STRATEGIES[1]

Elena Maltseva and Saltanat Janenova

INTRODUCTION

Following the dissolution of the USSR, Kazakhstan led the way amongst post-Soviet states by launching some of the most ambitious economic and welfare reforms (Dave, 2007). The government pursued a program of liberal economic reforms designed to establish a free market economy. In the social realm, dramatic changes in the economy and the failure of the Soviet pay-as-you-go (PAYG) system to provide for the proliferating number of pensioners, had led the government to the realization that Kazakhstan's collapsing pension system and rapidly growing pension arrears needed to be addressed (Maltseva, 2012). During this time, the international and regional policy contexts favored a liberal policy paradigm in the sphere of social security that was also promoted by major financial institutions such as the World Bank and the International Monetary Fund (IMF) as the only viable solution (Becker et al., 2009; Maltseva, 2012; Blackburn, 2016). As a result, in 1997, the Kazakhstani government went ahead with a radical pension reform (Maltseva, 2012). The Pension Law of 1997 replaced the PAYG system with a new pension system based on individual investment accounts to be maintained either with the State Accumulation Pension Fund (SAPF) or with non-state (privately-owned) pension funds (NSAPF) (Andrews, 2001; Maltseva, 2012). According to the original plan, an old state-supported PAYG pension system would remain in place for pensioners who had contributed to the system until 1998, with all workers who had accrued benefits under the old system retaining their entitlements. It was

---

1   Acknowledgements: We are grateful to the International Labour Organization for providing financial support to this study; to the Ministry of Healthcare and Social Development of the Republic of Kazakhstan and the Unified State Pension Fund (ENPF) for allowing access to the data used in this chapter; to the Federation of Free Trade Unions of Kazakhstan and civil movement 'For Fair Maternity Benefits,' as well as Sabit Khakimzhanov and Meiram Zhandildin for sharing their valuable insights on the implementation of the 2013 pension reform. All errors are our own.

expected that the new pension system would completely replace the old one between 2045 and 2050 (Seitenova and Becker, 2003).

Critics of this radical privatization model, primarily the International Labour Organization (ILO), long argued that the emphasis of the liberal reform on the technocratic elements of pension provision and the financial stability of the future pension system, without taking into consideration issues of inclusion, social justice and the adequacy of pension benefits, could lead to social protests and declining levels of old-age social security—thus undermining the system's overall sustainability (Frilander, 2012; Deacon, 2015). During the 1990s, when the World Bank / IMF model of pension provision was the dominant policy paradigm, this argument was rejected by most countries in transition, primarily because of their close co-operation with and financial dependency on international financial institutions (Frilander, 2012; Deacon, 2015; Blackburn, 2016). However, as time passed, it became increasingly difficult for the post-Soviet governments to overlook the institutional, social and economic deficiencies of private pension systems. Eventually, the IMF / World Bank model of old age security lost its appeal and the world witnessed the rise of several alternative policy solutions (Wang, Williamson and Cansoy, 2016; Koutronasa and Yew, 2017).

In Kazakhstan, the gradual transformation of the old age social security system unfolded in the context of a changing international policy paradigm in the area of pension provision. It was determined by the presence of lingering social, economic, demographic and financial pressures, which seemed to become more complex after the implementation of the liberal pension reform in 1998. Starting in 2005, the Government of Kazakhstan worked on adjusting the liberal pension system to fit Kazakhstani economic and labor market realities. An important ideational shift happened in 2012, when the President of Kazakhstan, Nursultan Nazarbayev, presented his vision of how the country should develop if it wanted to join the list of the 30 most developed countries in the world by 2050, echoing the East Asian developmental model. Titled the *Kazakhstan-2050 Strategy*, the program set ambitious developmental goals in the areas of economic development and diversification, good governance, education, public health, and others (Aitzhanova, Katsu, Linn and Yezhov, 2014). As part of this broad modernization effort, the president also ordered the development of a new concept for a pension system to align with the priorities of the *Kazakhstan-2050 Strategy* and tackle the deficiencies of the previous system (Mozharova, 2013).

Guided by these instructions, the new 2013 pension reform reflected the modernizing drive of Kazakhstani political elites. The reform reinstated a state monopoly in the sphere of pension provision, levied additional pension taxes on employers, and raised the retirement age for women from 58 to 63. Two years after the announcement of the 2013 pension reform, the government went ahead with targeting Kazakhstan's large informal labor market by linking the size of the basic pension payment to the length of one's formal employment, thereby establishing a quasi-funded pillar that would be maintained with employer contributions. Scheduled to come into force in 2018, the proposed change suggested that the announced pension reforms were the continuation of the broader transformation agenda set by the government in 2012.

This chapter offers insights into the causes and dynamics of Kazakhstani pension reforms since the 1990s. Using the theoretical framework of policy transfer, social learning and path-dependency, it is argued that the two distinct periods in the transformation of the Kazakhstani pension system during the last two decades are best explained by a combination of endogenous and exogenous factors. This includes an analysis of the shift in the global old age social security paradigm during the early 2000s, which at various stages of the reform process had a profound influence on the direction of Kazakhstan's pension reform.

OLD AGE SOCIAL SECURITY SYSTEMS IN COMPARATIVE PERSPECTIVE

The chapter will apply the policy transfer approach to study the origins of the government's decisions to reform the Kazakhstani pension system. Dolowitz and Marsh (2000) defined policy transfer as 'the process, by which knowledge about policies, administrative arrangements, institutions and ideas in one political system (past or present) is used in the development of policies, administrative arrangements, institutions and ideas in another political system' (5). Despite some legitimate criticism of this approach raised by such scholars as Stubbs (2002; 2005), Stone (2017) and several others, this approach allows researchers to explore the various dimensions of policy change, by answering such questions as why a particular policy was preferred to other policy options, who was involved in the policy transfer, what were the outcomes of policy transfer, and others (Greener, 2002).

According to Dolowitz and Marsh, policy transfer can be of a voluntary, negotiated or coercive nature (2000; 8; cf. Bender, Keller and Willing, 2014). Negotiated policy transfer occurs when, in exchange for loans or grants, policy actors agree to change their policies. Coercive policy transfer usually means that governments are forced to adopt certain policies by other actors, such as states or international or supranational organizations (Bender, Keller and Willing, 2014). Conditionality, which was frequently imposed on post-Soviet states during the 1990s, could be considered as one form of coercion (Bender, Keller and Willing, 2014). Finally, voluntary policy transfer is often compared to the process of policy learning, which presupposes that 'policies implemented elsewhere are examined by rational political actors for their potential utilization within another political system' (Bender, Keller and Willing, 2014; originally quoted in Evans, 2008; 7). In this sense, the concept of social learning is useful to explore how policymakers adjust their policies in response to past experience and new information (Bender, Keller and Willing, 2014).

Last but not least, to uncover the story behind Kazakhstan's pension reform, one should also pay attention to the considerable constraints that often prevent policymakers from implementing reforms as planned (Greener, 2002). Path dependency theory suggests that the choices available to actors at any given moment depend on the choices made in previous periods, and that once a path is chosen, it becomes increasingly difficult to change course because the processes become institutionalized (Rixen and Viola, 2009). This explains why radical policy change is so difficult to achieve despite the suboptimal performance of old institutions (Greener, 2002).

For several decades, research on social policy and pension reforms in Western Europe and North America was one of the most popular topics in policy research. Interested in issues of policy change and institutional inertia, scholars studied developments in mature capitalist societies facing growing demographic pressures and mounting fiscal costs. Works by Pierson (1994), Bonoli (2000), Hinrichs (2000), Taylor-Gooby (2001), Mattil (2006), Steenbeek and Lecq (2007), Marier (2008), Andersen and

Larsen (2009), Ebbinghaus and Gronwald (2009), Bengtsson (2010), De Santis (2012), and others examined the origins, dynamics and outcomes of welfare reforms, trying to understand the causes of change and stability in welfare institutions. Many of these studies explained social policy change (or the lack of it) through the prism of neo-institutionalist approaches, such as rational choice or historical institutionalism, arguing that there was a tendency for established institutions to create conditions for their own reproduction over time. In other words, in line with path dependency theory, many scholars argued that the policy options available to many Western governments when dealing with growing demographic and fiscal pressures were circumscribed by the presence of well-established institutions and constituencies, and the political risks associated with any attempts at welfare retrenchment or radical policy change.

In contrast, the welfare systems in developing and post-Soviet countries have been subject to more radical and more frequent policy changes, with governments reversing the course of earlier policies every time their priorities change. Starting in the 1980s, many developing countries in Latin America and other parts of the world, when faced with mounting economic and financial pressures, had no other choice but to agree to the implementation of drastic structural adjustment measures proposed by the IMF and the World Bank. As a result, during this time many developing countries switched to liberal private pension systems. The wave of neo-liberal pension reforms started in Chile, when in 1981 the right-wing government of General Augusto Pinochet replaced the old pension system with a privately-managed system of pension provision. Shortly after, several other governments followed. However, as time passed, the new pension systems displayed serious shortcomings and were either rolled back or adjusted to fit socioeconomic and demographic realities.

These developments offered scholars plenty of opportunities to study the weaknesses and limitations of private pension systems, and examine the origins and dynamics of pension reforms in unstable political and socioeconomic contexts. Scholars such as Paul and Paul (1995), Loayza and Palacios (1997), Schmidt-Hebbel (1999), Samwick (1999) and others analyzed Latin American pension systems after the reforms and pointed to a number of weaknesses in the operation of private defined-contribution pension models, and offered strategies for dealing with these problems. Several authors examined the dynamics of social policy change and obstacles to the implementation of liberal welfare reforms in transitional contexts of post-Soviet republics and Eastern Europe. Authors such as Cook (2000), Buckley and Donahue (2000), Andrews (2001), Chandler (2004), Seitenova and Becker (2003, 2004), Becker et al. (2009), Falkingham and Vlachantoni (2012), and others offered insightful accounts of welfare and old-age social security reforms in post-Soviet states during the 1990s and 2000s. Other scholars, such as Mitchell Orenstein (2008), provided important insights into the role that international actors played in facilitating policy transfer and driving liberal policy change in the area of old-age social security around the globe.

As time passed, and many countries reversed their liberal pension systems, scholars focused on explaining this, exploring the role of endogenous factors and changes in the international policy paradigm facilitating these reversals. Of particular interest are studies that tried to explain the recent reversals of private pension systems in Latin America (Bertranou, 2001; Mesa-Lago, 2002, 2006, 2008, 2009; Kay and Sinha, 2008; Calvo, Bertranou and Bertranou, 2010; Arza, 2012; Hujo and Rulli, 2014; Hujo, 2014), Central and Eastern Europe (Whitehouse, 2011; Hirose, 2011; OECD, 2012; Drahokoupil and Domonkos, 2012), Central Asia (Zhandildin, 2015) and Russia (Sokhey, 2017).

Utilizing relevant insights from the literature on policy transfer, social learning and path-dependency, this chapter aims to add important details to a central puzzle in public policy analysis, namely why and how policies change. The chapter contributes to a growing body of literature on the post-Soviet welfare state and policy reversals. The authors aim to highlight the importance of endogenous and exogenous factors in explaining the policy outcome, paying particular attention to the role of international financial institutions in setting the post-Soviet social policy agenda during the 1990s.

THE 1988 PENSION REFORM IN KAZAKHSTAN: THE PRIVATIZATION STAGE

Following the collapse of the Soviet Union, Kazakhstan underwent a dramatic socio-economic transformation that put great strain on the Soviet PAYG pension system. With nearly universal coverage, a low retirement age (60 for men and 55 for women), generous earnings-related benefits, and a high average replacement rate that often exceeded two-thirds of the workers' previous highest wages, the generosity of the Soviet pension system meant that the system was coming under pressure (Falkingham and Vlachantoni, 2012). During the 1990s, given the difficult economic situation, the aging population and negative trends in the pension system's dependency ratio, the question became especially urgent as to whether the PAYG system could and should be retained, or whether a completely new pension system should be adopted.

During this time, the major financial institutions such as the World Bank, the IMF, the Asian Development Bank (ADB), and donors such as the United States Agency for International Development (USAID) promoted a particular policy paradigm in the sphere of social security, pointing to its success in Eastern Europe and Latin America (World Bank, 1994). As a result, in 1997, the government of Kazakhstan presented its Concept of Pension Reform, developed under the guidance of the World Bank and built on the experience of the radical pension reform in Chile and the multi-level pension system model proposed by the World Bank in 1994 (Becker et al., 2009). It was hoped that the new system would avert an old-age social security crisis by promoting self-sufficiency instead of government dependence, help reduce government expenditures, improve the management of pension funds, encourage savings, and contribute to the development of the capital market (Bird, 1997; Kokovinets, 1998; Andrews, 2001; Seitenova and Becker, 2004; Becker et al., 2009). The proposed pension reform formed part of a broader package of socioeconomic transformation, including two other components: the privatization of state-owned enterprises (SOEs); and the development of a securities market (Becker et al., 2009).

Effective from 1 January 1998, the new pension law transformed Kazakhstan's pension system from a solidarity-based system to one based on individual accounts to be maintained either with the newly established state pension fund or with privately owned pension funds. It also raised the retirement age from 60 to 63 for men, and from 55 to 58 for women (Soloviev, 1997; Andrews, 2001). The new pillar, known as the mandatory accumulative pension scheme, was financed with a fixed 10 percent deduction from income. In addition to the mandatory pillar, the government also introduced a voluntary accumulative pension scheme that was based on voluntary pension contributions (VPC), with which all citizens could increase their savings and, thereby, secure a higher income after retirement (Hinz, Zviniene and Vilamovska, 2005). In regard to the old solidarity component, the reform recognized accrued rights earned up to 1998, but terminated solidarity pension benefits for all other population groups. This move meant that retirees continued to receive their benefits under the old solidarity pension system and that workers who had accrued benefits prior to 1998 retained the right to receive those benefits upon reaching retirement age in the future (Hinz, Zviniene and Vilamovska, 2005). In other words, according to the original plan, the mandatory, publicly funded pension would exist for as long as there were workers with accrued rights.

In short, the presence of various economic, fiscal, demographic and social problems motivated the government to launch the reform process, which, in turn, was heavily influenced by the ideology of neoliberalism and the advice of such powerful international policy actors as the IMF and the World Bank. However, as time passed, the deficiencies of the newly implemented pension system raised important questions about the applicability of fully privatized pension systems in the context of weakly developed political and economic institutions. Less than a decade after the implementation of the reform, it became evident that few of the government expectations pertaining to the development of the Kazakhstani fully-funded pension system had materialized due to deficiencies in the Kazakhstani labor and capital markets (Gorst, 2013; Zhandildin, 2015). One of the biggest obstacles to the successful implementation of the fully-privatized pension system was that the economic crisis of the 1990s was accompanied by serious problems on the labor market, with many people informally or only partially employed (Sziraczki, 1995). Since many people were paid unofficially, or received low official wages, they were prevented from amassing sufficient retirement savings, with many people making no contributions to the pension fund at all. The situation particularly affected women, who often had lower salaries than men, shorter or broken careers due to maternity leave, or entirely lacked an official employment record. To tackle the problems of these population groups, in 2005 the government introduced a basic social pension (*Bazovaia Pensia* in Russian) that was not dependent on private contributions or work history, and was provided to all persons reaching retirement age. The new initiative was seen by some as a positive development that guaranteed at least minimum income security to all citizens reaching old age, in addition to funds earned under the residual old solidarity system and fully-funded accounts (Kurmanov, 2011).

The situation on the Kazakhstani capital market was equally concerning. Affected by strict capital requirements and state restrictions on investments in foreign securities due to concerns about volatility on international markets, pension funds had failed to make a positive impact on the development of the Kazakhstani capital market, as was envisaged when the government launched the reform in 1998 (Gorst, 2013; Zhandildin, 2015). In addition, since the reform was implemented in the context of a weakly developed rule of law and underdeveloped financial markets, it came with a price in the form of non-transparent deals, weak governance in the private pension sector, and high service fees and operating costs (Yesirkepov, 2013).

Furthermore, the reform failed to achieve high replacement rates, or enhance pension coverage and compliance as expected. According to the World Bank World Development Indicators from 2011, 65 percent of the labor force in Kazakhstan did not contribute to a retirement pension scheme (Abdih and Medina, 2013). This especially concerned self-employed workers in the informal sector and / or unemployed people who remained in the socioeconomic shadows. For example, domestic services and subsistence farming were the two areas that grew rapidly in post-Soviet Kazakhstan and in which many people, especially women, worked unofficially (Semykina, 2014). Also, the low returns on investments, which averaged 3 – 4 percent, made the goal of attaining the 60 percent replacement rate stated by the government at the beginning of the reform highly unlikely (Yesirkepov, 2013). In the end, the insufficient performance by the second pillar and the limited presence of the first pillar contributed to low replacement rates, which stood at 27 percent in 2010 and 29 percent in 2013 (Zhandildin, 2015).

In other words, by the end of the 2000s, the realization was growing within government circles that it was problematic to focus on the development of a fully-funded pension system and not keep the parallel solidarity system to protect workers in the context of a deep economic crisis and weakly developed labor and capital markets. Therefore, a range of adjustments to the 1998 pension system were required.

REFORMING KAZAKHSTAN'S PENSION SYSTEM: FROM PRIVATIZATION TO NATIONALIZATION

The next stage in the transformation of the Kazakhstani pension system was preceded by mounting criticism of the dominant policy paradigm in the area of old age security (Orszag and Stiglitz, 1999; Kotlikoff, 1999; Barr, 2000; Heneghan, 2015). In addition to the growing academic literature questioning the outcomes of pension privatizations, perhaps one of the most significant reports was one published by the Independent Evaluation Group (IEG) of the World Bank in 2006. The report concluded that the World Bank's advice on pension reform had been based on political considerations rather than the optimal solution for each country; it concluded that in many developing countries, which had implemented the liberal pension reforms, the negative effects of reform outweighed the positive ones (IEG, World Bank, 2006). The research showed that in most countries studied, the reforms failed to significantly improve pension coverage, mainly because the poor did not have sufficient capacity to contribute to expensive private insurance systems. In addition, private pension fund companies had no interest in lowering administrative costs and making the system more affordable for the poor. Furthermore, the transition from one pension system to another proved to be prohibitively expensive, creating fiscal pressures on governments. Under conditions of the weak rule of law and weakly developed political and economic institutions, pensioners risked losing all their life savings if a country's financial markets collapsed. The report concluded that, in most countries, the reforms were driven by political elites without adequate social dialogue and the involvement of a range of stakeholders. Even though some positive effects of private pension systems on capital markets were reported, the ultimate goal of pension reform, namely creating an effective and sustainable old-age income support system, was not achieved (IEG, World Bank, 2006).

As a result, since 2008 the general trend has been that several countries with private pension systems, including Argentina, Bolivia, and Hungary, have either reversed earlier privatizations or offered citizens the option of returning under the umbrella of the public redistributive pension system, which was the case in Uruguay and Peru (Datz and Dancsi, 2013; Mesa-Lago, 2014, 2016; Olivera, 2016). Other countries, including Poland, Russia and Chile, have also experimented with their pension systems, often strengthening the public pension pillar rather than the private one (Sinha, 2000; Latorre-Artus, n.d.; Cohen and Cienski, 2014; Chłoń-Domińczak, 2016; Bertranou, 2016; Sokhey, 2017)[2]. In short, by the late 2000s, the global discourse on pension reform was no longer dominated by the ideas promoted by Western financial institutions, which contributed to the rise of alternative policy solutions to the problem of old age security.

In Kazakhstan, an important shift in welfare policy happened after the 2008 financial crisis, and the events in Zhanaozen (Stratfor Assessments, 2009; Anichshenko, 2009; Maltseva, 2017). The 2008 financial crisis revealed a troubling situation in Kazakhstan's banking sector and pointed to the need to restructure the country's financial system and diversify its economy. The importance of economic modernization was further reinforced during the early 2010s, when in response to growing external and internal pressures and falling oil prices, the country's economic development fell from 7.5 percent of GDP growth in 2011 to 4.1 percent in 2014 and 1.2 percent in 2015 (Asian Development Bank, 2016). However, economic modernization required the inflow of significant financial resources, which, given the slowing economy, were difficult to find. The situation was further complicated due to the events in Zhanaozen, when in December 2011 a conflict between a state-run oil company and a group of disgruntled oil workers turned violent, leaving 16 people dead at the hands of police, seriously challenging the legitimacy of the existing regime. The crisis highlighted the problems of Kazakhstani single-industry towns, and the need to invest in the reconstruction and development of cities like Zhanaozen (Human Rights Watch, 2012; Maltseva, 2017).

In the end, growing social and economic pressures motivated the government to launch an ambitious developmental project that aimed to address numerous problems including rule of law, state transparency and accountability, economic diversification, and social cohesion (Maltseva, 2017). The developmentalist turn happened in 2012, when President Nazarbayev declared in his address 'Socio-Economic Modernisation—The Main Vector of Kazakhstan Development' the beginning of extensive administrative, social, and economic reforms (Nazarbayev, 2012). The

---

2   See also Bretton Woods Project 2014. "Poland reverses World Bank-promoted pension scheme," 31 March 2014.

program known as 'Kazakhstan 2050' set out to transform Kazakhstan into a modern state with effective institutions and a knowledge-based diversified economy driven by the private sector (Nazarbayev, 2014). In line with the main goals of this strategy, the president gave an order to develop a new concept for a pension system that would fall in line with the proposed modernization goals and tackle the deficiencies of the previous old-age social security system (Mozharova, 2013). Already, reliance on Western advice had been replaced by a focus on the experience of the East Asian developmental states, especially Singapore (Stark and Ahrens, 2012; 2014; Roberts, 2016; Araral, 2016).

In April 2013, the government presented the public with a draft bill 'On Pensions in the Republic of Kazakhstan,' which reversed the process of liberal market and social reforms adopted in the late 1990s (Savchenko, 2013). With this move, the Kazakhstani government became the first Central Asian republic to follow in the steps of some Latin American and East European countries that introduced similar changes into their fully-funded, defined-contribution pension systems. This time, the process of policy formulation was relatively fast and initially involved only a limited number of policy actors. To be more specific, the reform process was led by the president, the government, the Ministry of Labor and Social Protection, and the National Bank of the Republic of Kazakhstan, whereas the involvement of civil society, private pension funds, and other stakeholders, including international policy actors, was minimal (Savchenko, 2013). The draft bill proposed the following changes to the 1998 fully-funded pension system: creation of a single pension fund under the name of the Unified Accumulative Pension Fund (UAPF, or ENPF in Russian) on the basis of the State Accumulation Pension Fund (SAPF); assigning of the management function of pension assets held by the ENPF to the National Bank; increasing the retirement age for women from 58 to 63 progressively between 2014 and 2024; and introducing mandatory 5 percent contributions paid by employers for workers employed in difficult and dangerous occupations (Medeusheyeva, 2013; Torebayeva, 2013).

The reform institutionalized a four-pillar pension system comprised of basic plus solidarity, mandatory, and voluntary levels. In 2013, no changes to the basic social pension were made, with the government providing it to all individuals who reached retirement age. Both the basic social pension and the solidarity pension were financed from the state budget. At the same time, changes affected the mandatory accumulative pension system, which was financed with a fixed 10 percent of mandatory pension deductions from workers' income (Government of Kazakhstan, 21 June 2013). To prevent some possible dissatisfaction and to compensate employers for the losses incurred as a result of these additional payments, the government promised tax deductions. It also urged employers to improve working conditions for employees, as this would allow them to obtain certificates confirming safe working conditions, and hence stop paying occupational pension contributions (Telemtayev and Adjivefayev, 2014).

The 2013 pension reform was driven by the imperfections of the 1998 pension system, domestic political and economic considerations, and the desire to make the existing old-age social security system, in particular its pension funds, an important element in the country's modernization process (Savchenko, 2013). The government and the president framed the issue, arguing that the poor performance of private pension funds, high fees that the private pension funds charged for their services, low returns from investments and frequent cases of corruption made it necessary for the state to intervene and rescue the accumulated pension funds from the deficiencies of financial markets (Alshanov, 2013). In other words, the new pension reform kept the individual pension accounts as the primary instrument of pension provision, but entrusted their administration to the state via the National Bank of Kazakhstan.

Of note, the decision of the government was met with limited criticism from international financial institutions and business actors. The general concern was that the nationalization of pension funds would result in the violation of the rights of depositors, the ineffective management of private pension assets, and the loss of jobs in the private pension sector. Some business actors were also concerned with how this move would affect the attractiveness of the Kazakhstani capital markets to international investors. Other observers pointed out that the nationalization of pension funds raised the risk that the fund's investment strategy would be decided by political priorities, rather than a balanced assessment of risks and likely returns.[3] Despite this legitimate criticism,

---

3   For more about investor reactions to these changes, please see "Kazakhstan Funds: Astana Merges Pension Funds," 2013. *The Economist: Intelligence Unit*, August 15.

the general dissatisfaction with the performance of the private pension system was evident not only in the statements of various policymakers, but also the critics of the new bill, who spoke not of preserving the private pension system, but rather criticized the hasty manner in which the bill was passed; they were concerned about possible negative outcomes of the state monopolization of pension funds (Galat, 2012).

The most negative reaction to the reform came from women's NGOs and women's rights movements, who openly criticized various aspects of the proposed increase in the retirement age for women from 58 to 63. To the surprise of many in the government, the scale of protests on the streets and social media was unprecedented for post-Soviet Kazakhstan. Peaceful demonstrations by women's groups took place across different regions in several major cities across the country, and a collective petition was signed by over 100,000 citizens including prominent female leaders in education, culture, sports and politics, all against the increased retirement age for women. The petition was passed to the president with alternative suggestions on how to improve the welfare system for women (Janenova, 2015).

Activists argued that the introduction of changes to women's retirement age should have been accompanied by comprehensive reforms of Kazakhstan's economy, labor market and healthcare system, as well as better access to childcare facilities for families with young children. It was argued that, even though Kazakhstani women live longer than men, they have numerous health problems that undermine their ability to work effectively after the age of 58, and are disproportionately affected by the deficiencies of the Kazakhstani labor market, including the difficulties for women aged 40 and over to find stable employment or to change jobs. Moreover, as some women argued, the introduction of a higher retirement age would dramatically affect the economic well-being and social fabric of many Kazakhstani families. Given the shortage of state-run pre-school childcare facilities, many young families have no other choice but to accept the traditional structure of Kazakhstani families and rely on their grandmothers for free babysitting services (Kuzhabekova et al., 2017). In the absence of timely developments in this area, respondents claimed that many young families would find it extremely difficult to balance their work and family obligations. In summary, they argued that Kazakhstan needed more jobs, a diversification of the economy to accommodate a greater number of female workers, better employment policies and their stricter enforcement, and significant improvements in the healthcare and education systems if the government wanted to move ahead with a higher retirement age for women.[3]

In light of the negative public reaction and the protests, the government was forced to respond. In an attempt to soothe public discontent, the government justified the reform with growing demographic and fiscal pressures, claiming that under the current system, although men were paying the bulk of money into the pension system, they could not benefit from it because they had a lower life expectancy and higher retirement age than women. Therefore, by increasing the retirement age for women, the government tried to create parity between the pension contributions of male and female workers, and also to increase the opportunities that would be available to women for receiving larger pensions (Mozharova, 2013). In addition, after discussions, the government pushed the start date of the retirement age hike from 2014 to 2018, with an annual increase of the retirement age by six months. They kept the right to early retirement for some groups such as women with five or more children, and several other categories were also left unchanged. In addition, the authorities promised to address the structural problems evident in the labor market and to introduce measures to improve the skills of women workers. A complex plan, *Initiative 50+*, was enacted to facilitate the employment of people over 50 years old within state and sectoral programs (Government of the Republic of Kazakhstan, 2013).

Two years after the implementation of the 2013 pension reform, in an attempt to reduce the informal market and motivate people to properly record their employment, the government decided to link the size of the basic pension payment to the length of service / employment and introduce the so-called quasi-funded pillar, in which each participant will have an individual retirement account (in addition to the already existing accumulative account) and to which employers will make contributions in the amount of 5 percent of the employee's income. Effective from 2018, this pension payment will be available to all citizens with work experience of no less than five years (Atabaev, 2014). Participants with at least 10

---

[3] Author interviews, June – July 2015.

years of contributions will be entitled to 50 percent of the subsistence minimum, and then, for every year worked, this figure will be increased by 2 percent (Urazova, 2014).

In summary, after 2013 the Kazakhstani pension system underwent profound changes that made the ENPF the sole organization responsible for the administration of pension funds and introduced a gradual retirement age hike for women starting from 2018. In line with the general governance trend, the reform process was swift, top-down and involved no real policy dialogue, with the government presiding over the process (Janenova and Knox, 2017). The reform was presented as an urgent matter, and framed as an indispensable component of the broader modernization program known as 'Kazakhstan-2050.' Driven by the Kazakhstani political elite in response to growing international and domestic pressures, the program was envisioned as an attempt at radical modernization of Kazakhstani society and the economy, akin to the experience of East Asian states. It aimed at transforming the structure of the Kazakhstani economy and its labor market, using the accumulated pension funds for investment in grand infrastructural and development projects.

KAZAKHSTAN'S PENSION SYSTEM AT A CROSSROADS: WHAT NEXT?

The Kazakhstani pension system went through two major reforms, which started in 1998 and 2013, and its transformation continues. The 1998 pension reform launched a radical overhaul of the old Soviet pension system to one based on fully-funded, privately managed pension accounts and defined contributions. During the 1990s, the decision to reform the Soviet PAYG pension system was made due to the presence of deep socioeconomic and demographic pressures affecting the country's transition. However, in line with the coercive policy transfer argument, the direction of the 1998 pension reform was largely determined by the broader international policy context, in which a particular policy paradigm in the sphere of old-age social security was favored and promoted by international financial institutions such as the IMF and the World Bank, and often reinforced through conditionalities. Pointing to the experience of other transitioning or developing countries which undertook similar reforms a decade before Kazakhstan, such as Chile, the World Bank justified the transition, arguing that the privatization of the pension system would help with keeping government social expenditures under control, increase workers' mobility and responsibility for their own fate, prevent the possible mismanagement of pension funds and have positive externalities for the financial sector as workers' savings would be invested in capital markets. Convinced by these arguments, the Kazakhstani political elites followed the advice and replaced the PAYG pension system with a private pension system (World Bank, 1994; Seitenova and Becker, 2004; Hinz, Zviniene and Vilamovska, 2005; Zhandildin, 2015).

However, as the negative outcomes of private pension systems in unstable socio-economic and political conditions became increasingly apparent, countries in Latin America and Eastern Europe started moving away from private pension arrangements and reintroducing or strengthening the publicly managed components of their pension systems (Whitehouse, 2011; Altiparmakov, 2017; Sokhey, 2017). Since 2008, some countries have reversed the earlier privatizations, while others have offered the possibility of returning to the public redistributive pensions system, or redirected the contribution rates allocated toward private individual accounts towards the pooled public pillar. Even Chile, despite not having reversed the policy of private pensions, has introduced a solidarity-based pension managed by the state and is currently discussing possible revisions (Arenas de Mesa et al., 2006; Altman, 2010). In other words, by the mid-2000s, the international policy environment in the field of old-age security had changed, offering countries like Kazakhstan an opportunity to re-evaluate the effectiveness of their private pension systems. In Central Asia, this process coincided with the strategic turn to East Asia, with governments using the experience of East Asian developmental states as a reference model for Eurasian countries, with Kazakhstan leading this (Stark, 2010; Roberts, 2016). Kazakhstan's fascination with the East Asian story of developmental success, and particularly Singapore, became especially noticeable in the last decade when the country adopted a series of wide-ranging reforms in the fields of education, health care, social security, research and development, IT, and others (Mahbubani, 2015; Araral, 2016).[4]

---

[4] See also "Why Kazakhstan Learns from Singapore—Analysis." 2016. *Eurasia Review: News and Analysis*, October 27.

The re-orientation of Kazakhstan to the East Asian developmental model could be described as a process of voluntary policy transfer and social learning, which came at a time when the old liberal social policy paradigm came under heavy criticism and the country was dealing with numerous problems. Following the onset of the 2008 financial crisis, the government was forced to come up with a comprehensive program of socio-economic transformation. The government declared its intention to strengthen the rule of law, actively invest in infrastructure, improve the management of natural resources, industrialize and diversify the economy, modernize the agricultural sector, and support employment mobility programs and entrepreneurship. The government also promised greater investments in education, research, professional training and retraining programs. Last, but not least, the new pension strategy was developed, which aimed to tackle the Soviet legacies and the deficiencies of the previous system, and also to assist the government with its ambitious modernization program. In other words, the 2013 pension reform, and the more recent 2015 changes to the basic pension, were developed by the government in the context of a global shift in pension policy discourse, albeit driven primarily by internal considerations and problems.

Still, despite the comprehensive economic and social reforms, several problems in the operation of the Kazakhstani pension system remain, including issues with the efficiency and transparency of the Unified National Pension Fund, low pension coverage and low pension levels, which especially concern women. Addressing these problems will require better integration of unemployed and self-employed people into the Kazakhstani pension system, diversification of the economy to ensure the faster growth of jobs in the formal sector, especially in rural areas, and better labor market policies and legal enforcement. Furthermore, to tackle the problem of gender inequality in the labor market and the gender wage gap, the government will need to ensure that its decision to increase the retirement age is accompanied by economic and labor market reforms and new social policies including financing paternity leave, improving child care facilities, introducing flexible working hours and working from home for women with young children. In the long run, these developments would facilitate a significant cultural shift in

Kazakhstani society, which would help advance the idea of gender equality in society and the workplace.

In conclusion, given the growing global and domestic social, economic and demographic pressures, the Kazakhstani government is likely to continue the complex transformation of the country's social and economic institutions, including its pension system. Carrying out these reforms undoubtedly poses a challenge to a regime whose legitimacy is primarily based on its ability to deliver high economic growth and provide adequate social protection for its citizens. To avoid a possible legitimacy crisis in the future, the government needs to more actively engage with civil society and establish a regular and effective policy dialogue with various stakeholders, especially women's groups.

REFERENCES

Abdih, Y. and L. Medina. (2013). *Measuring the Informal Economy in the Caucasus and Central Asia*. IMF Working Paper. Available at: www.imf.org/external/pubs/ft/wp/2013/wp13137.pdf.

Ahrens, Joachim and Manuel Stark. (2012). "Economic Reform and Institutional Change in Central Asia: Towards a New Model of the Developmental State?" Private Hochschule Göttingen, Research papers. Available at: https://www.pfh.de/fileadmin/Content/PDF/forschungspapiere/fp_2012_05_stark_ahrens.pdf.

Ahrens, Joachim and Manuel Stark. (2014). "Emulating Developmental States? The Institutional Foundations of Economic Transition in Kazakhstan," *Critique Internationale* 63 (2): 95 – 110.

Aitzhanova, A., S. Katsu, J. Linn, and V. Yezhov. (2014). *Kazakhstan 2050: Toward a Modern Society for All*. New Delhi: Oxford University Press.

Alshanov, Rakhman. (2013). "Pension *System Modernization to Promote Reliability and Efficiency*," *The Astana Times*, April 10. Available at: http://astanatimes.com/2013/04/pension-system-modernization-to-promote-reliability-and-efficiency/.

Altiparmakov, Nikola. (2017). "Another Look at Causes and Consequences of Pension Privatization Reform Reversals in Eastern Europe." *Journal of European Social Policy* (December), 1 – 18.

Altman, Daniel. (2010). "The Social Security Reforms in Chile: Can a Privatized System Work?" Undergraduate Honors Thesis, University of Redlands. Available at: https://inspire.redlands.edu/cas_honors/21.

Andersen, J.G., and C.A. Larsen. (2002). "Pension Politics and Policy in Denmark and Sweden: Path Dependencies, Policy Style, and Policy Outcome." Paper presented at XV World Congress of Sociology, Brisbane, July 7 – 13, 2002. Available at: http://www.dps.aau.dk/fileadmin/user_upload/ime/CCWS/workingpapers/2002-27-PensionpoliticsinDenmark-JGA.pdf.

Andrews, Emily S. (2001). "Kazakhstan: An Ambitious Approach to Pension Reform." World Bank, Social Protection Discussion Paper Series Nr. 0104. Available at: http://siteresources.worldbank.org/SOCIALPROTECTION/Resources/SP-Discussion-papers/Pensions-DP/0104.pdf.

Anichshenko, Valeriya. (2009). "The Impact of the Financial Crisis on the Banking System of Kazakhstan." *Central Asia Business Journal* 2. Available at: http://citeserx.ist.psu.edu/viewdoc/download?doi=10.1.1.519.5948&rep=rep1&type=pdf.

Araral, Eduardo. (2016). "Independent Kazakhstan Following Similar Path as Singapore toward Successful Development." *The Astana Times*, 5 December. Available at: http://astanatimes.com/2016/12/independent-kazakhstan-following-similar-path-as-singapore-toward-successful-development/.

Arenas De Mesa, Alberto and Jere R. Behrman, Olivia S. Mitchell, Petra E. Todd and David Bravo. (2006). "The Chilean Pension Reform Turns 25: Lessons from the Social Protection Survey." National Bureau of Economic Research: 1 – 42. Available at: http://www.nber.org/papers/w12401.

Arza, C. 2012. "Pension Reforms and Gender Equality in Latin America." UNRISD Research Paper. Available at: http://www.unrisd.org/80256B3C005BCCF9/(httpAuxPages)/3513162DF26920D5C12579CF0053534B/$file/Arza%20paper.pdf.

Asian Development Bank. (2016). "Sector Assessment (Summary): Finance." Manila. Available at: https://www.adb.org/sites/default/files/linked-documents/49076-005-ssa.pdf.

Atabaev, D. (2014). "Ocherednaya Pensionnaia Reforma: Ot Pessimizma do Nadezhdy" [Another Pension Reform: From Pessimism to Hope]. *Radio Azattyk*, July 26. Available at: http://rus.azattyq.org/content/pensionnaya-reforma-kazakhstan/25470850.html.

Barr, Nicholas. (2000). "Reforming Pensions: Myths, Truths, and Policy Choices." IMF Working Paper, August. Available at: https://books.google.ca/books?isbn=1451901194.

Becker, Charles M., Grigori A. Marchenko, Sabit Khakimzhanov, Ai-Gul Seitenova, and Vladimir Ivliev. (2009). *Social Security Reform in Transition Economies: Lessons from Kazakhstan*. New York: Palgrave Macmillan.

Bender, Katja, Sonja Keller and Holger Willing. (2014). "The Role of International Policy Transfer and Diffusion for Policy Change in Social Protection—A Review of the State of the Art." IZNE Social Protection Working Paper 14 / 1. Available at: https://www.h-brs.de/files/izne/policy_diffusion_1.pdf.

Bengtsson, Tommy. (2010). *Population Ageing— A Threat to the Welfare State? The Case of Sweden*. Berlin, Heidelberg: Springer-Verlag.

Bertranou, F.M. (2001). "Pension Reform and Gender Gaps in Latin America: What Are the Policy Options?" *World Development* 29 (5): 911 – 923.

Bertranou, Fabio. (2016). "Pension Benefits in Chile: Is It Possible to Improve Adequacy and Solidarity?" Presented at a joint ILO / IZA Conference in partnership with leading G20 think tanks, ILO headquarters, Geneva, Switzerland, 10 – 11 March. Available at: http://www.ilo.org/wcmsp5/groups/public/---dgreports/---inst/documents/meetingdocument/wcms_461932.pdf.

Bird, Chris. (1997). "Kazakhs Prepare for Sweeping Pension Reform." *Reuters News*, November 13.

Blackburn, Robin. (2016). "The Global Drive to Commodify Pensions." In Bryan S. Turner and Robert J. Holton (eds.), *The Routledge International Handbook of Globalization Studies*, 2nd edition, 344 – 367. New York: Routledge.

Bonoli, Giuliano. (2000). *The Politics of Pension Reform: Institutions and Policy Change in Western Europe*. Cambridge: Cambridge University Press.

Bretton Woods Project. (2014). "Poland Reverses World Bank-Promoted Pension Scheme." 31 March. Available at: http://www.brettonwoodsproject.org/2014/03/poland-reverses-bank-promoted-pension-scheme/.

Buckley, Cynthia and Dennis Donahue. (2000). "Promises to Keep: *Pension* Provision in the *Russian* Federation." In Mark G. Field and Judyth L. Twigg (eds.), *Russia's Torn Safety Nets: Health and Social Welfare during the Transition*, 251 – 270. New York: St. Martin's Press.

Calvo, E., F.M. Bertranou, and E. Bertranou. (2010). "Are Old-Age Pension System Reforms Moving Away from Individual Retirement Accounts in Latin America?" *Journal of Social Policy* 39 (2): 223 – 234.

Chandler, Andrea. (2004). *Shocking Mother Russia: Democratization, Social Rights, and Pension Reform in Russia, 1990 – 2001*. Toronto: University of Toronto Press.

Chłoń-Domińczak, Agnieszka. (2016). "Reversing the 2013 Retirement Age Reform in Poland." Available at: ec.europa.eu/social/BlobServlet?docId=15053&langId=en.

Cohen, Norma and Jan Cienski. (2014). "Poland Pension Reform Reversal Highlights Public Disillusion." *Financial Times*, February 5. Available at: https://www.ft.com/content/8ddeb5bc-6293-11e3-bba5-00144feabdc0.

Cook, Linda. (2000). "The Russian Welfare State: Obstacles to Restructuring," *Post-Soviet Affairs* 16 (4): 355 – 378.

Datz, Giselle and Katalin Dancsi. (2013). "The Politics of Pension Reform Reversal: A Comparative Analysis of Hungary and Argentina," *East European Politics* 29 (1): 83 – 100.

Dave, Bhavna. (2007). *Kazakhstan: Ethnicity, Language and Power*. New York: Routledge.

De Santis, Gustavo (ed.). (2012). *The Family, the Market or the State? Intergenerational Support under Pressure in Ageing Societies*. Springer Netherlands.

Deacon, Bob. (2015). "The International Labour Organization and Global Social Governance—The 100 Year Search for Social Justice within Capitalism." In Alexandra Kaasch and Kerstin Martens (eds.), *Actors and Agency in Global Social Governance*, 45 – 63. Oxford: Oxford University Press.

Dolowitz, D. P. and D. Marsh. (2000). "Learning from Abroad: The Role of Policy Transfer in Contemporary Policy-Making," *Governance* 13 (1): 5 – 23.

Drahokoupil, J., and S. Domonkos. (2012). "Averting the Funding-Gap Crisis: East European Pension Reforms since 2008." *Global Social Policy* 12 (3): 283 – 299.

Ebbinghaus, Bernhard and Mareike Gronwald. (2009). "International Policy Diffusion or Path Dependent Adaptation? The Changing Public-Private Pension Mix in Europe." Paper presented at ISA RC 19 Conference *Social Policies: Local Experiments, Travelling Ideas*, Montreal, August 20 – 22. Available at: http://cccg.umontreal.ca/RC19/PDF/Ebbinghaus-E_Rc192009.pdf.

Evans, Mark. (2008). "Policy Transfer in Critical Perspective." In Mark Evans (ed.), *New Directions in the Study of Policy Transfer*. Abingdon: Routledge.

Falkingham, Jane and Athina Vlachantoni. (2012). "Social Protection for Older People in Central Asia and the South Caucasus." In Sri Wening Handayani and Babken Babajanian (eds.), *Social Protection for Older Persons: Social Pensions in Asia*, 246 – 278. Mandaluyong City, Philippines: Asian Development Bank.

Frilander, Sonja. (2012). "Discussion between the World Bank and the International Labour Organization about Pension Policy Recommendations Concerning the Sub-Saharan-Africa during 1990 – 2010: Institutional Analysis in the Framework of Discursive Institutionalism." Master Thesis, University of Eastern Finland, Faculty of Social Sciences and Business Studies, Department of Social Sciences, Sociology. Available at: http://epublications.uef.fi/pub/urn_nbn_fi_uef-201202 35/urn_nbn_fi_uef-20120235.pdf.

Galat, Irina. (2012). "Kak Mozhet Vygliadet' Pensionnaia Reforma v Kazahstane" [The Possible Outlook of Kazakhstan's Pension Reform], *Vlast*, October 15. Available at: https://vlast.kz/obsshestvo/kak_mozhet_vygljadet_pensionnaja_reforma_v_ kazahstane-898.html.

Gorst, I. (2013). "Kazakhs Pension "Nationalisation" Plan Worries Fund Managers." *Financial Times*, January 25. Available at: http://blogs.ft.com/beyond-brics/ 2013/01/25/kazakh-pension-nationalisation-plan-worries-fund-managers/.

Government of Kazakhstan. (2013). Law of the Republic of Kazakhstan. On Pensions in the Republic of Kazakhstan. Astana, Akorda, 21 June, №105-V 3PK. Available at: https://eurasiangroup.org/files/Legislation_RUS/Kazakhstan/Zakon_RK_O_ pensionnom_obespechenii_v_RK_2013_god_.pdf.

Government of the Republic of Kazakhstan. (2013). "'Initiative 50+' Will Facilitate Addressing Employment Problems—Ministry for Labour of the RK." August 12. Available at: http://www.primeminister.kz/news/show/26/%C2%ABinitsiativa -50%C2%BB-budet-sposobstvovat-resheniju-problem-zanjatosti-naselenijamin truda-rk-/12-08-2013.

Greener, Ian. (2002). "Understanding NHS Reform: The Policy-Transfer, Social Learning, and Path-Dependency Perspectives," *Governance* 15 (2): 161 – 183.

Heneghan, Martin. (2015). "The Rise and Fall of the World Bank's Global Pension Model." Available at: http://speri.dept.shef.ac.uk/2015/12/01/the-rise-and-fall-of-the-world-banks-global-pension-model/.

Hinrichs, Karl. (2000). "Elephants on the Move: Patterns of Public Pension Reform in OECD Countries," *European Review* 8 (3): 353 – 378.

Hinz, R.P., A. Zviniene, A. Vilamovska. (2005). "The New Pensions in Kazakhstan: Challenges in Making the Transition." SP Discussion Paper No. 0537, The World Bank. Available at: http://siteresources.worldbank.org/SOCIALPROTECTION/Resources/SP-Discussion-papers/Pensions-DP/0537.pdf.

Hirose, K. (2011). "Pension Reform in Central and Eastern Europe in Times of Crisis, Austerity and Beyond." International Labour Organization. Available at: http://www.oit.org/wcmsp5/groups/public/---europe/---ro-geneva/---sro-budapest/documents/publication/wcms_171551.pdf.

Hujo, K. (ed.) (2014). *Reforming Pensions in Developing and Transition Countries*. Basingstoke: Palgrave Macmillan.

Hujo, K. and M. Rulli. (2014). "The Political Economy of Pension Re-Reform in Chile and Argentina: Toward More Inclusive Protection." Research Paper 2014 – 1. Available at: http://www.unrisd.org/80256B3C005BCCF9/(httpAuxPages)/13C947C84CC4FAFFC1257CAF004697A0/$file/Hujo%20and%20Rulli.pdf.

Human Rights Watch. (2012). "Striking Oil, Striking Workers: Violations of Labour Rights in Kazakhstan's Oil Sector." Available at: http://www.hrw.org/sites/default/files/reports/kazakhstan 0912ForUpload_0.pdf.

Independent Evaluation Group (Andrews, Emily S.; Wang, Debby Kim; Rofman, Rafael; Palmer, Ed; Fornero, Elsa; Ferraresi, Pier Marco; San Martino, Jorge; Valdes-Prieto, Salvador; Piggott, John; Bateman, Hazel). (2006). Pension Reform and the Development of Pension Systems: An Evaluation of World Bank Assistance. Washington, D.C.: The World Bank. Available at: http://documents.worldbank.org/curated/en/629861468166150111/Pension-reform-and-the-development-of-pension-systems-an-evaluation-of-World-Bank-assistance.

Janenova, S. (2015). "Pension Provision and Collective Action in Kazakhstan: The Case of 2013 Pension Law." Conference paper presented at IFEAC-KIMEP conference, Welfare State & Collective Action in Central Asia, 18 – 19 May, Almaty, Kazakhstan.

Janenova, S. and C. Knox. (2017). "Civil Service Reform in Kazakhstan: Trajectory to the 30 Most Developed Countries in the World?," *International Review of Administrative Sciences* (November): 1 – 21.

Kay, S. and T. Sinha (eds.). (2008). *Lessons from Pension Reform in the Americas*. New York: Oxford University Press.

Kokovinets, L. (1998). "Kazakhstan Prodolzhit Programmy MVF, Ne Ispol'zuia Kredity" [Kazakhstan Will Continue Its IMF Reforms, without Relying on Credits]. *Reuters*, May 28.

Kotlikoff, Laurence J. (1999). "The World Bank's Approach and the Right Approach to Pension Reform." Available at: https://www.kotlikoff.net/sites/default/files/adb.pdf.

Koutronasa, Evangelos and Siew-Yong Yew. (2017). "Considerations in Pension Reforms: A Review of the Challenges to Sustainability and Distributive Impartiality," *Malaysian Journal of Economic Studies* 54(1): 159 – 177.

Kurmanov, A. (2011). "Pension System of the Republic of Kazakhstan." *Pension Observer*, December 20. Available at: http://www.pensionobserver.ru/arxiv/4-4-oktyabr-dekabr-2010-g/v-czentre-vnimaniya-%28naczionalnyie-pensionnyie-sistemyi%29/pensionnaya-sistema-respubliki-kazaxstan?pg=all.

Kuzhabekova, Aliya, Saltanat Janenova, and Ainur Almukhambetova. (2017). "Analyzing the Experiences of Female Leaders in Civil Service in Kazakhstan: Trapped between Economic Pressure to Earn and Traditional Family Role Expectations." *International Journal of Public Administration* (October): 1 – 12.

Larsen, Christian Albrekt and Jørgen Goul Andersen. (2009). "How New Economic Ideas Changed the Danish Welfare State: The Case of Neoliberal Ideas and Highly Organized Social Democratic Interests," *Governance* 22 (2): 239 – 261.

Latorre-Artus, Remberto. (n.d.). "The World's Most Successful Pension Reform Based on Individual Choice Has Been Called for Reversal." Available at: http://www.austriancenter.com/the-worlds-most-successful-pension-reform-based-on-individual-choice-has-been-called-for-reversal/.

Loayza, Norman and Luisa Palacios. (1997). "Economic Reform and Progress in Latin America and the Caribbean." World Bank Policy Research working paper no. 1829. Washington, D.C.: The World Bank. Available at: http://documents.worldbank.org/curated/en/265401468766486590/Economic-reform-and-progress-in-Latin-America-and-the-Caribbean.

Mahbubani, Kishore. (2015). "The Unusual Partnership of Singapore, Kazakhstan." *The Straits Times*, July 25. Available at: http://www.straitstimes.com/opinion/the-unusual-partnership-of-singapore-kazakhstan.

Maltseva, Elena. (2012). "Welfare Reforms in Post-Soviet States: A Comparison of Social Benefits Reform in Russia And Kazakhstan." Ph.D. Dissertation, University of Toronto. Available at: https://tspace.library.utoronto.ca/bitstream/1807/35069/1/Maltseva_ Elena_201206_PhD_thesis.pdf.

Maltseva, Elena. (2017). "Cracks in the System: What the Zhanaozen Incident Says about Regime Performance in Kazakhstan." In John Heathershaw and Edward Schatz (eds.), *Paradox of Power: The Logics of State Weakness in Eurasia*, 184 – 199. Pittsburgh: University of Pittsburgh Press.

Marier, Patrik. (2008). *Pension Politics: Consensus and Social Conflict in Ageing Societies*. London and New York: Routledge.

Mattil, Birgit. (2006). *Pension Systems and Distributional Effects in Germany and the United Kingdom*. Heidelberg: Physica-Verlag.

Medeusheyeva, D. (2013). "UAPF JSC: Kazakhstan Embraces Pension Reform." *World Finance*, November 6. Available at: http://www.worldfinance.com/wealth-management/pension-funds/uapf-jsc-kazakhstan-embraces-pension-reform.

Mesa-Lago, C. (2002). "Myth and Reality of Pension Reform: The Latin American Evidence." *World Development* 30 (8): 1309 – 1321.

Mesa-Lago, C. (2006). "Private and Public Pension Systems Compared: An Evaluation of the Latin American Experience." *Review of Political Economy* 18 (3): 317 – 334.

Mesa-Lago, C. (2008). "Social Protection in Chile: Reforms to Improve Equity." *International Labour Review* 147 (4): 377 – 402.

Mesa-Lago, C. 2009. "Re-reform of Latin American Private Pension Systems: Argentinian and Chilean Models and Lessons." *The Geneva Papers* 34: 602 – 617.

Mesa-Lago, Carmelo. (2014). "Reversing Pension Privatization: The Experience of Argentina, Bolivia, Chile and Hungary." Geneva: International Labour Organization. Available at: http://www.ilo.org/gimi/gess/RessourcePDF.action?ressource.ressourceId=43277.

Mesa-Lago, Carmelo. (2016). "Suggestions for Pension Re-Reform in Peru," *Apuntes* XLIII (78): 41 – 60. Available at: revistas.up.edu.pe/index.php/apuntes/article/download/751/815.

Mozharova, V. (2013). "Pensionnaia Reforma v Kazakhstane: Novyi Etap" [Pension Reform in Kazakhstan: Another Step]. *Pravo.zakon.kz*, June 19. Available at: http://pravo.zakon.kz/4562981-pensionnaja-reforma-v-kazakhstane.html.

Nazarbayev, N. (2012). "Socio-Economic Modernization as Main Vector of Development of Kazakhstan." Annual Message of the President of the Republic of Kazakhstan to the people of Kazakhstan, January 27. Available at: http://www.akorda.kz/en/addresses/addresses_of_president/address-by-the-president-of-the-republic-of-kazakhstan-nursultan-nazarbayev-to-the-people-of-kazakhstan-27-01-2012_1341926486.

Nazarbayev, Nursultan. (2014). "Kazakhstan's Way—2050: Common Aim, Common Interests, Common Future." Annual Address, January 17. Available at: http://strategy2050.kz/en/page/message_text20141//.

OECD. (2012). *OECD Pensions Outlook 2012*. OECD Publishing.

Olivera, Javier. (2016). "An Assessment of a Proposed Multi-Pillar Pension Reform in Peru," *Apuntes* XLIII (78): 9 – 40. Available at: http://dx.doi.org/10.21678/apuntes.78.851.

Orenstein, Mitchell A. (2008). *Privatizing Pensions: The Transnational Campaign for Social Security Reform*. Princeton: Princeton University Press.

Orszag, Peter R. and Joseph E. Stiglitz. (1999). "Rethinking Pension Reform: Ten Myths About Social Security Systems." Presented at the World Bank Conference, "New Ideas About Old Age Security," September 14 – 15. Available at: http://www.ssc.wisc.edu/~scholz/Teaching_742/Orszag-Stiglitz.pdf.

Paul, S.S. and J.A. Paul. (1995). "The World Bank, Pensions and Income (In)Security in the Global South," *International Journal of Health Services* 25 (4): 697 – 726.

Pierson, Paul. (2000). "Increasing Returns, Path Dependence, and the Study of Politics." *American Political Science Review* 94 (2): 251 – 267.

Pierson, Paul. (1994). *Dismantling the Welfare State? Reagan, Thatcher and the Politics of Retrenchment*. Cambridge: Cambridge University Press.

Roberts, Sean R. (2016). "The Perils of the Autocratic Developmental State Leadership and Presidential Succession in Kazakhstan." *Georgetown Journal of Asian Affairs* 73: 72 – 81. Available at: https://asianstudies.georgetown.edu/sites/asianstudies/files/files/ upload/gjaa._2.2_roberts.pdf.

Rixen, Thomas and Lora Viola. (2009). "Uses and Abuses of the Concept of Path Dependence: Notes toward a Clearer Theory of Institutional Change." Prepared for Presentation at the International Summer School on the Logic of Self-reinforcing Processes in Organizations, Networks, and Markets, Freie Universität Berlin, 13 – 17 July. Available at: http://www.wiwiss.fu-berlin.de/forschung/pfadkolleg/downloads/summer_school_2009/Paper _Rixen_Viola.pdf.

Samwick, Andrew A. (1999). "Social Security Reform in the United States." *National Tax Journal* 52 (December): 819 – 842.

Savchenko, Katerina. (2013). "Kazakhstan Nationalises Pension Funds." *Open Dialog Foundation*, June 11. Available at: http://en.odfoundation.eu/a/1145,kazakhstan-nationalises-pension-funds.

Schmidt-Hebbel, Klaus. (1999). "Chile's Pension Revolution Coming of Age." Available at: http://citeseerx.ist.psu.edu/viewdoc/download?doi=10.1.1.587.3723&rep=rep1&type=pdf.

Seitenova, Ai-Gul S. and Charles M. Becker. (2003). "Kazakhstan's Pension System: Pressures for Change and Dramatic Reforms." Presented at the Institute of Economic Research, Hitotsubashi University, Workshop on Pension Reform in Transition Economies, Tokyo, Japan. Available at: http://cis.ier.hit-u.ac.jp/Common/pdf/dp/2002/dp142.pdf.

Seitenova, Ai-Gul S. and Charles M. Becker. (2004). "Kazakhstan's Pension System: Pressures for Change and Dramatic Reforms," *Hitotsubashi Journal of Economics* 45: 151 – 187. Available at: http://hermes-ir.lib.hitu.ac.jp/rs/bitstream/10086/14393/1/pie_dp142.pdf.

Semykina, Yu. (2014). "Chuzhie v Dome: Vsia Pravda o Domrabotnitsakh v Kazakhstane" [Foreigners in the House: All Truth about House Maids in Kazakhstan]. *365info.kz*, Dec 15. Available at: http://365info.kz/2014/12/chuzhie-v-dome-vsya-pravda-o-domrabtonicax-v-kazaxstane/.

Sinha, Tapen. (2000). *Pension Reform in Latin America and Its Lessons for International Policymakers*. New York: Springer Science + Business Media.

Sokhey, Sarah Wilson. (2017). *The Political Economy of Pension Policy Reversal in Post-Communist Countries*. Cambridge: Cambridge University Press.

Soloviev, D. (1997). "Ex-communist Kazakhs to Pioneer Pension Reform." *Reuters News*, July 8.

Stark, Manuel. (2010). "The East Asian Development State as a Reference Model for Transition Economies in Central Asia—An Analysis of Institutional Arrangements and Exogenous Constraints," *Economic and Environmental Studies* 10 (2): 189 – 210.

Steenbeek, Onno W. and S. G. Fieke van der Lecq. (2007). *Costs and Benefits of Collective Pension Systems*. Berlin, Heidelberg: Springer-Verlag.

Stone, Diane. (2017). "Understanding the Transfer of Policy Failure: Bricolage, Experimentalism and Translation." *Policy and Politics* 45 (1): 55 – 70.

Stratfor Assessments. (2009). "The Recession in Kazakhstan." Stratfor Assessments, June 18. Available at: https://worldview.stratfor.com/article/recession-kazakhstan.

Stubbs, Paul. (2002). "Globalisation, Memory and Welfare Regimes in Transition: Towards an Anthropology of Transnational Policy Transfers." *International Journal of Social Welfare* 11 (4): 321 – 330.

Stubbs, Paul. (2005). "Stretching Concepts Too Far? Multi-Level Governance, Policy Transfer and the Politics of Scale in South East Europe." *Southeast European Politics* 6 (2): 66 – 87.

Sziraczki, G. (1995). "Emerging Labour Market Policy in Kazakhstan." ILO Labour Market Papers, No. 3. Available at: http://www.ilo.org/wcmsp5/groups/public/---ed_emp/---emp_elm/documents/publi cation/wcms_126293.pdf.

Taylor-Gooby, Peter. (2001). *Welfare States under Pressure*. SAGE Publications.

Telemtayev, M., and V. Adjivefayev. (2014). "Subsoil Use: Additional Contributions to Unified Cumulative Pension Fund." *Lexology*, February 21. Available at: http://www.lexology.com/library/detail.aspx?g=38a54c25-c7f9-433b-8b3f-d0da2a9d89d2.

The Economist Intelligence Unit. (2013). "Kazakhstan Funds: Astana Merges Pension Funds." *The Economist: Intelligence Unit*, August 15, 2013. Available at: http://www.eiu.com/industry/article/790845063/kazakhstan-funds-astana-merges-pension-funds/2013-08-15.

Torebayeva, M. (2013). "Pension Reform in Kazakhstan: Conflicts about Age." *Deutsche Welle*, April 19. Available at: http://www.inozpress.kg/news/view/id/39254.

Towers Watson, Willis. (2015). "Kazakhstan: New Component Added to Old-Age Pension Entitlement Starting in 2018." November 9, 2015. Available at: https://www.towerswatson.com/en/Insights/Newsletters/Global/global-news-briefs/2015/11/kazakhstan-new-component-added-to-old-age-pension-entitlement-starting-in-2018.

Urazova, D. (2014). "Pension Reform Concept Approved in Kazakhstan." *Tengrinews*, July 16. Available at: http://en.tengrinews.kz/laws_initiatives/Pension-reform-concept-approved-in-Kazakhstan-254521/.

Wang, Xinmei, John B. Williamson, and Mehmet Cansoy. (2016). "Developing Countries and Systemic Pension Reforms: Reflections on Some Emerging Problems," *International Social Security Review* 69 (2): 85 – 106.

Whitehouse, Edward. (2011). "Reversals of Systemic Pension Reforms in Central and Eastern Europe: Implications." OECD Social Policy Division. Available at: http://www.ebrd.com/downloads/research/news/Whitehouse_Paper.pdf.

"Why Kazakhstan Learns from Singapore—Analysis." (2016). *Eurasia Review: News and Analysis*, October 27. Available at: http://www.eurasiareview.com/27102016-why-kazakhstan-learns-from-singapore-analysis/.

World Bank. (1994). *Averting the Old Age Crisis*. New York: Oxford University Press.

Yesirkepov, Zh. (2013). "O Prozrachnosti Nakopitel'nykh Pensionnykh Fondov Respubliki Kazakhstan" [About Transparency of Accumulative Pension Funds of the Republic of Kazakhstan]. *Delovaia Nedelia*, January 11. Available at: http://www.dn.kz/index.php?option=com_content&view=article&id=930:2013-01-11-05-59-30&catid=5:2011-10-23-11-45-05%20&Itemid=6.

Zhandildin, M. (2015). "Pension System Reform in Emerging Countries: The Case of Kazakhstan." *Global Journal of Emerging Market Economies* 7 (1): 65 – 88.

CHAPTER 11:
DIVERSE HEALTH CARE DEVELOPMENTS IN THE POST-SOVIET SPACE: THE ROLE OF NATIONAL AND INTERNATIONAL ACTORS

Gulnaz Isabekova

INTRODUCTION

Post-Soviet countries inherited the Semashko healthcare system from the Soviet Union[1]. The system is characterized by the paternalistic role of the state acting as financier, provider and regulator of healthcare services. Under this system, there was public ownership of healthcare institutions, and healthcare professionals were public employees. The paternalistic role of the state limited citizens' participation in decision-making. Twenty-five years after the collapse of the Soviet Union and independence for the post-Soviet states, some countries have retained an extensive role for the state in healthcare, while others have introduced market mechanisms and involved non-governmental institutions in service provision. This chapter argues that post-Soviet countries, also known as a region in 'transition' (Borisova, 2011), are diverse and although they all inherited the Semashko system, their reform paths in terms of healthcare developments differ considerably.

There is limited literature analyzing healthcare reforms across all fifteen post-Soviet countries. The majority of studies focus on Central Asia (McKee et al., 1998; McKee et al. eds., 2002; Klugman et al., 2002; Borowitz and Atun, 2007; Rechel et al., 2012; Ulikpan et al., 2014) or single country case studies (cf. Rechel and Khodjamurodov, 2010; Mirzoev et al., 2010; Tonoyan, 2004; Gordeev et al., 2011). The Baltic States are often excluded from the analysis as European Union (EU) member-countries (see Borisova, 2011; Balabanova et al., 2012). General overviews of the region either analyze healthcare financing, co-payments and public management (Leive, 2010; Kutzin et al., 2010; Antoun et al.,

---

[1] The system was founded in 1918 by Nikolai Aleksandrovich Semashko, who was the head of the Moscow Soviet's health department.

2011), or certain aspects of healthcare, such as primary healthcare or psychiatric care (Borisova, 2011; Polubinskaya, 2000). The studies rarely address the system as a whole. Those studies which do offer a broader overview of healthcare reforms in post-Soviet countries are now dated (cf. Belli, 2001). This chapter seeks to remedy this gap in the literature and aims to provide an overview of the healthcare systems in the fifteen post-Soviet countries and to explain their diverse development.

Diverse healthcare system developments in the region could be attributed to the interaction of national governments with external organizations. After the collapse of the Soviet Union, states faced a number of internal pressures. These included the deterioration of public healthcare systems and services, an increased incidence of infectious diseases, healthcare system inefficiency and a large proportion of hospital capacity having poor infrastructure (Savas et al., 2002; 81 – 82). Governments needed to change the healthcare system in a short period of time to address the new social realities. Multilateral agencies such as the World Bank and the International Monetary Fund (IMF) imposed pressures for adjustment and compliance (cf. Ferge, 1997; 302). However, the outcomes of this pressure and the precise nature of reforms depended on the interaction between the government and external actors. Hence, the stability of the healthcare reforms and the value of any capacity building rested on countries' ability to coordinate assistance (Rechel et al., 2012). There is an acknowledgement of external actors' influence on healthcare reform processes in some studies (Ulikpan et al., 2014; Rechel and McKee, 2009; Ancker et al., 2013). However, none of the studies have analyzed the role of external actors in the post-Soviet region as whole.

ANALYTICAL APPROACH

To analyze healthcare systems, this study applies the Rothgang-Wendt (RW) typology utilizing its systematic approach and broad focus. The framework builds on previous work evaluating various actors' roles in healthcare financing and service provision (Anderson, 1963; Field, 1973; OECD, 1987; Immergut, 1992; Freeman and Moran, 2000). It incorporates these dimensions and adds regulation. Although regulations have been mentioned before (Stevens, 2001), the RW typology was among the first to introduce a systematic approach to classification of healthcare systems

(Wendt et al., 2009: 71). It provides a useful framework for general analysis from a comparative perspective.

The typology groups countries according to actors' roles in healthcare. The framework focuses on the role of the state, society and private actors in healthcare financing, service provision and regulation (Rothgang et al., 2010). Depending on the influence of each actor, the typology posits three models or ideal types. In the first, a national health service, healthcare is publicly provided and financed through tax revenues (Rothgang, 2010b; 15 – 17). Healthcare facilities are owned by the state, and healthcare professionals are public employees. The state regulates financing, provision and conditions by ensuring equal access to all citizens (Rothgang, 2010b; 14 – 17). With the state dominating across all three dimensions, this model is similar to the Semashko system. In the second, a social insurance system, healthcare is financed through social insurance contributions and largely provided by private non-profit actors (Rothgang, 2010b; 15). Private non-profit institutions dominate financing, provision and regulation. The state retains control over the system, but there is the strong presence of social or corporatist groups, such as insurance funds and professional associations (Rothgang, 2010b). Access to healthcare in this model is based on the principle of solidarity. In other words, the contributions of employed citizens cover expenses for the unemployed and dependents (Schmid et al., 2010; 26 – 27). Both the national health service and social insurance systems have redistributive mechanisms ensuring access to services. In contrast, the third, a private healthcare system, has limited distributional capacity. The guiding principle of this system is the ability to pay for services (Rothgang, 2010b; 17). This model is characterized by the dominant role of the market. The main sources of funding are private insurance and out-of-pocket payments, and the main service providers are private for-profit actors (Rothgang, 2010b; 15). All three models represent ideal types and, in reality, healthcare systems combine features of all three. These models nevertheless provide a good proxy for evaluating change. Since all post-Soviet countries had a system similar to the national health service, the varying role of the state in financing, service provision and regulation, indicates changes to healthcare systems.

The RW typology is applied here with several modifications. The general typology attributes changes in healthcare to interactions between the state, society and private actors. However, this study focuses on the role of the state and external actors in healthcare reforms. It excludes private actors and the general population, including patients, due to their limited role in healthcare reforms. Initial policy development during the Soviet era without public participation resulted in the passivity of citizens as beneficiaries (Ferge, 1997; Rechel et al., 2012; Savas et al., 2002; Gedik et al., 2002). Hence, public participation is generally limited in all post-Soviet countries. Minor exceptions are civil society involvement in Moldova and Kyrgyzstan, and the cooperation of the state with professional associations in Kazakhstan (Footman and Richardson, 2014; 34; HiT Kazakhstan, 2012; 23 – 24). In an environment of limited financial and technical capacities, as well as experience of healthcare reforms, external actors have played a significant role in healthcare reforms.

Furthermore, a number of indicators used in the typology cannot be applied to post-Soviet countries, mainly because of a lack of comparative data. Therefore, the emphasis is on sources of healthcare expenditure (public, private and social insurance), the employment status of healthcare professionals, the ownership of healthcare facilities and benefit packages provided to citizens. In addition to data limitations, selection of indicators is driven by practical concerns. Coverage, as part of the regulations, refers to entitlement, and is often guaranteed in the constitution or in legislation. However, vague entitlement does not guarantee access to services in reality. Access could be measured by number of service providers and hospital beds per 1,000 population. Yet the physical presence of these facilities does not guarantee practical use. Therefore, this chapter focuses on benefit packages, as an object of regulation. In contrast to vague entitlements or the number of facilities, benefit packages list services provided free of charge. Consequently, usability of these services is higher. Table 1 summarizes the three dimensions of the RW typology used here:

Table 1   Operationalization of RW typology

Financing	Share of public and private spending, presence / absence of social / private insurance
Service provision	Ownership of healthcare facilities and healthcare professionals' employment
Regulation	Benefit packages

In addition, the study considers whether reforms were implemented in a coherent or fragmented way. This will help understand the outcomes of interactions between the state and external actors. The overall analysis is based on the secondary literature on healthcare reforms across the region and the European Observatory's Healthcare Systems in Transition reports for each country[2].

RESULTS

Financing

Depending on the share of tax revenues, social insurance and private funding, countries are divided into three groups. First, Estonia, Latvia, Lithuania, Russia, Moldova and Kyrgyzstan, have a mandatory health insurance system contributing to healthcare financing. Mandatory health insurance is a comparatively recent phenomenon in the region, and its share varies across countries. The existing database provides aggregated healthcare expenditures, without delineating the share of tax revenues and social insurance (cf. World Bank, 2017). This chapter groups countries implementing the insurance into one category (Graph 1). Independently of the share, adoption of this mechanism indicates change towards this system. Another group of countries are the states without health insurance, but with public health expenditure around 50 percent. These are Belarus, Kazakhstan, Uzbekistan, Ukraine and Turkmenistan (Figure 1). The large share of public financing in these countries suggests the dominance of the state in the healthcare system, although Uzbekistan is an outlier with an average share of public financing around 48 percent.

---

[2] Most recent Health Systems in Transition reports: Armenia (2006 and 2013), Azerbaijan (2004 and 2010), Belarus (2008 and 2013), Estonia (2008 and 2013), Georgia (2002 and 2009), Kazakhstan (2007 and 2012), Kyrgyzstan (2005 and 2011), Latvia (2012, 2008), Lithuania (2013, 2000), Moldova (2008, 2012), Russia (2003, 2011), Tajikistan (2010, 2016), Turkmenistan (2000), Ukraine (2010, 2015), Uzbekistan (2007, 2015).

Figure 1　　Average share (%) of public and private health expenditure (1995-2014)[3]

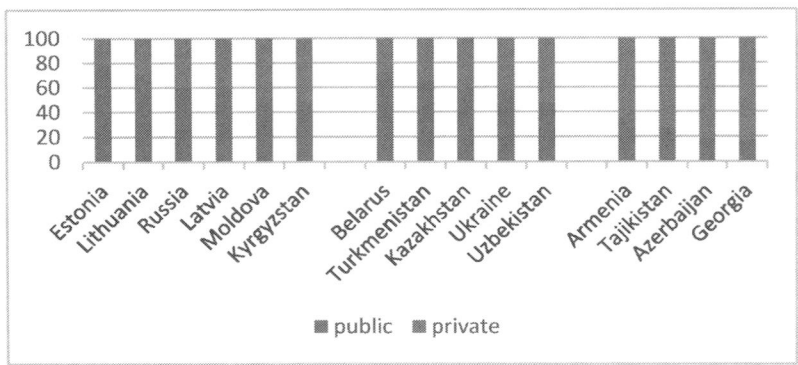

Source: World Bank, 2017

The third group of countries, namely Armenia, Azerbaijan, Georgia and Tajikistan, have a share of out-of-pocket payments (OOPs) over 60 percent of healthcare expenditure (Fig. 1). OOPs and private insurance as sources of funding point to a private healthcare system. Since the share of private or voluntary health insurance is low in all post-Soviet countries, private expenditures mainly refer to direct OOPs (Richardson, 2010; 54). In other words, patients' payments constitute the vast majority of healthcare expenditure. OOPs jeopardize equal access to healthcare by burdening poor households (Schmid et al., 2010; 29). As a result, access to healthcare services with high OOPs is uneven. Table 2 summarizes the groupings:

Table 2　　Main sources of healthcare expenditure

Tax revenues	Social insurance	Out-of-pocket payments (OOPs)
Belarus, Kazakhstan, Turkmenistan, Uzbekistan, Ukraine	Estonia, Kyrgyzstan, Latvia, Lithuania, Moldova, Russia	Armenia, Azerbaijan, Georgia, Tajikistan

---

3　Average percentages are calculated by the author (average% total expenditure = average% public + average% private for the period of 1995 – 2014) based on the information provided in the World Bank database.

Service provision

Healthcare service provision refers to the share of public and private institutions in terms of the ownership of healthcare institutions and the employment status of healthcare professionals (Schmid and Wendt, 2010). The post-Soviet countries largely retained state service provision, inherited from the Semashko model. Healthcare institutions are owned and administered by the government and healthcare professionals are civil servants. Privatization was limited to dental care, diagnostics and pharmacies, mainly located in capital cities (Footman and Richardson, 2010; 33). Hospital privatization was also insignificant. One exception is Georgia, where 40 percent of hospitals are owned by insurance companies, 30 percent by individuals and 20 percent by other enterprises (Transparency International Georgia, 2012; 4). The state nevertheless remains the main owner of healthcare facilities in the region. Regarding the employment of healthcare professionals, Armenia, Georgia, Estonia, Latvia and Lithuania introduced mixed service provision. In this model, healthcare providers have financial and administrative autonomy from the state. In Armenia, healthcare providers are state health enterprises, managing their finances, staff and prices for services outside the benefit package (HiT Armenia, 2006; 28 – 29). Healthcare facilities in Georgia have similar functions. Healthcare personnel in both countries are employed by healthcare facilities on a contractual basis (HiT Armenia, 2013; 18; HiT Georgia, 2009; 45 – 46). This change in employment status is important since it implies transition from public to contractual employment. Changes in the employment status of healthcare professionals are also visible in the Baltic States. Medical personnel in Estonia work under private labor regulations, while in Latvia they have the status of independent professionals or self-employed individuals (HiT Estonia, 2013; 23; HiT Latvia, 2012; 18). Lithuania has different payment regulations for state and private-employed specialists. State healthcare professionals are civil servants, whereas in the private sector employers define wage rates (HiT Lithuania, 2013; 69). Although retaining public ownership of healthcare facilities, diverse employment developments in post-Soviet countries suggests changes to healthcare systems.

Table 3   Healthcare service provision

State-dominated	Mixed	Private
Azerbaijan, Belarus, Kazakhstan, Kyrgyzstan, Moldova, Russia, Tajikistan, Turkmenistan, Ukraine, Uzbekistan	Armenia, Estonia, Georgia, Latvia, Lithuania	-

Regulations (benefit packages)

The range of benefit packages varies considerably across the post-Soviet states. Belarus has the most generous coverage in the region. It provides extensive access to health care and essential medicines free of charge (HiT Belarus, 2013; 35). Another group of countries retained a smaller share of benefits, although still larger than the basic package. The guiding principle of healthcare reforms in Estonia was ensuring access to healthcare, therefore health insurance provides a range of benefits (HiT Estonia, 2013; xxi, 53). Similarly, Moldova, Kyrgyzstan and Russia offer services in addition to the standardized benefit package. Moldova provides prophylactic dental care, care in the case of cardiovascular diseases, pediatrics and palliative care (HiT Moldova, 2012; 66 – 67). To improve access to medicines, Kyrgyzstan adopted the Additional Drug Package, while Russia introduced the State Program of Drugs Supply monetizing health benefits (HiT Kyrgyzstan, 2011; 100 – 104; HiT Russia, 2011; 137 – 138). However, the majority of countries in the region adopted basic benefit packages (BBPs) mainly covering primary and emergency care (see HiT Kazakhstan, 2012; HiT Uzbekistan, 2014; HiT Lithuania, 2013; HiT Latvia, 2012; Kukava, 2013). In some cases, such as Armenia and Ukraine, the range of guaranteed benefits depends on budget availability (HiT Ukraine, 2015; 46 – 47; HiT Armenia, 2013; 37). This creates uncertainties and confusion for patients and service providers. Tajikistan is the only country in the region without a benefit package. The government introduced a package in 2005 to formalize informal payments, but the initiative was cancelled after two months because of low public support (HiT Tajikistan, 2016; 46 – 47). At the same time, the list of benefits does not always guarantee access. Turkmenistan provides for a range of outpatient, inpatient, dental and sanatorium care (HiT Turkmenistan, 2000; 22 – 23), but the practical implementation is questionable. Furthermore, informal payments in healthcare are widespread in the region (see HiT Azerbaijan, 2010; Stepurko et al., 2015; Oka, 2015; Lewis, 2010; Polovinka, 2016). Therefore, there might be unofficial co-payments to services defined as free-of-charge. In general, depending on budget constraints, policy priorities and political volatility, the post-Soviet countries introduced various benefit packages (see table 4). The large number of countries opting out of the standardized benefit package suggests a decreasing role for the state in healthcare accessibility.

Table 4   Benefit packages[4]

Universal coverage	Standard benefit package	Unstable benefit package (budget availability)	No benefit package
Belarus, (Turkmenistan)	Azerbaijan, Estonia, Georgia, Kazakhstan, Kyrgyzstan, Latvia, Lithuania, Moldova, Russia, Uzbekistan	Armenia and Ukraine	Tajikistan

Table 5 summarizes changes in financing, service provision and benefits.

Table 5   Overview of healthcare systems in post-Soviet countries

Financing	Provision	Benefits	Countries
Tax	State	Universal coverage	Belarus, Turkmenistan (the Semashko healthcare system)
Tax	State	Standard package	Kazakhstan, Ukraine, Uzbekistan
Social insurance	State	Standard package	Kyrgyzstan, Moldova, Russia
Social insurance	Mixed	Standard package	Estonia, Latvia, Lithuania
OOPs	Mixed	Standard package	Armenia, Georgia
OOPs	State	Standard package	Azerbaijan
OOPs	State	No benefit package	Tajikistan

Russia is in the same group as Moldova and Kyrgyzstan, but it constitutes a case on its own. Diverse implementation of mandatory health insurance (MHI) across the country suggests dependence on the commitment of

---

4   Data on Turkmenistan is based on HiT report 2000, but its practical applicability is questionable given the limited data on the country.

regional authorities to reforms (HiT Russia. 2011; 146). Besides, there is a remarkable regional variation in access to healthcare (Borisova, 2011). Both size and regional diversity make it incomparable to other countries in the region. Therefore, Russia is analyzed as a separate case.

REFORMS AS AN INDICATOR OF INTERACTIONS

This section aims at explaining the changes described above by linking them to differences between post-Soviet countries in terms of interactions with external actors. External actors' assistance to healthcare reforms has been significant across the region. Newly independent countries could not finance the range of services provided under the Semashko system. At the same time, they lacked the finances, technical expertise and experience to implement healthcare reforms. Collaboration with external actors additionally defined the direction of healthcare reforms. The IMF, World Bank, USAID and other bilateral donors promoted neoliberal reforms and structural adjustment policies, which encouraged privatization, liberalization and deregulation (Rivkin-Fish, 2005; 76). These policies favored decentralization of the system across the region, weakening the regulative capacities of Ministries of Health and increasing regional inequalities. Some countries, notably Kazakhstan and Kyrgyzstan, recentralized their healthcare systems. In general, the policies promoted by external organizations fitted with national agendas. Given budget shortages, the delegation of healthcare financing, service provision and decreasing the number of health facilities were among the priorities for these countries.

Interaction serves as a better proxy for understanding the nature of external assistance than the amount of Official Development Assistance (ODA) as a percentage of total health spending. Three types of interaction with external actors are identified across the region: organizational membership, the Sector Wide Approach (SWAp) and the project-based approach. The Baltic States, implementing the EU's *acquis communautaire* and all the relevant regulations on healthcare, fit the first type of interaction. Moldova and Kyrgyzstan, mainstreaming financial and technical support of external organizations, have used SWAps. However, the majority of countries in the region have project-based interactions, limited to selected projects lacking an institutional platform for mainstreaming financial and technical resources for comprehensive reform of the system as a whole.

The amount of ODA, shown in Table 6, illustrates the presence of external actors in the post-Soviet region. The range of assistance across countries appears unrelated to the economic performance of the recipient states, the political regime nor the openness of the recipient country to external actors (Isabekova, 2016).

Table 6   Official Development Assistance (healthcare and general) per capita in USD[5]

Country	Healthcare	Period	General	Period
Armenia	258	1993 – 2013	707	1994 – 2013
Azerbaijan	245	1992 – 2013	1567	1991 – 2013
Moldova	206	1994 – 2013	2573	1991 – 2013
Georgia	204	1994 – 2013	3633	1991 – 2013
Estonia	196	1991 – 2004	1443	1991 – 2006
Kyrgyz Republic	151	1993 – 2013	2181	1991 – 2013
Tajikistan	132	1992 – 2013	1430	1991 – 2013
Latvia	110	1992 – 2007	2614	1991 – 2010
Kazakhstan	96	1993 – 2013	1712	1991 – 2013
Uzbekistan	95	1994 – 2013	740	1991 – 2013
Lithuania	75	1992 – 2007	1606	1991 – 2007
Turkmenistan	60	1992 – 2013	956	1991 – 2013
Belarus	29	1994 – 2013	467	1992 – 2013
Ukraine	22	1993 – 2013	1023	1991 – 2013
Russia	18	1990 – 2009	870	1990 – 2011

Source: Aiddata, 2017; World Bank, 2017

Another indicator is the percentage of external resources in total health expenditure (Fig. 2). External resources on average constitute around 10 percent of total health expenditure in Kyrgyzstan, about 9 percent in Armenia and Tajikistan, 6 percent in Moldova, 4 percent in Georgia and 3 percent in Uzbekistan).

---

5   The Official Development Assistance (healthcare and general) *per capita* is calculated by the author (development aid per country divided by average population for the relevant period). The results are rounded. Variations in the period are related to data availability.

Figure 2   Average share (%) of external resources in total health expenditure (1995 – 2014)[6]

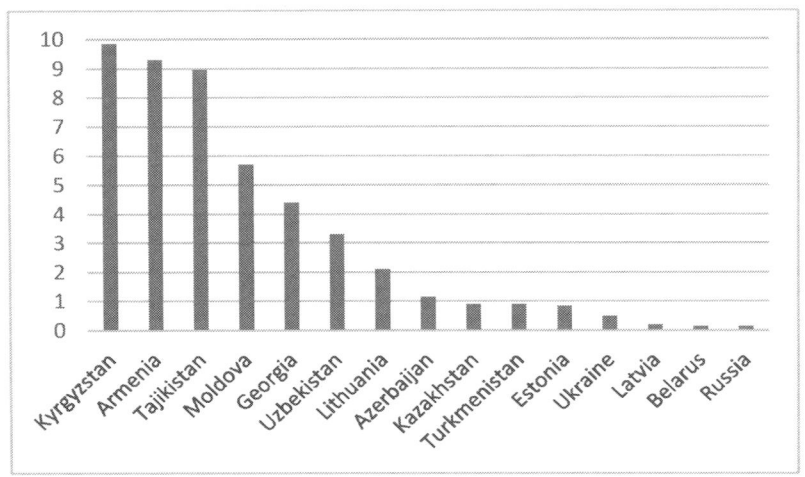

Source: World Bank, 2017

Not all countries receiving high ODA have a high percentage of external assistance in health expenditure. Assistance to healthcare could be irregular and / or its share in overall expenditure low. As noted above, our main focus is on types of interactions, be they organizational membership, sector-wide approaches, or project-based interactions. Countries implementing the first two types of interactions have managed to reform their healthcare systems by mainstreaming healthcare resources.

Organizational membership

In the case of the Baltic States, the major external actor involved in healthcare and other reforms was the European Union. Health system reform was part of EU accession requirements, with an additional emphasis on public health and safety (Rechel and McKee, 2009; 1187; HiT Estonia, 2008; 190). Countries implemented a number of reforms aimed at legislative harmonization. Certainly, the Baltic States cooperated with other external actors in reforming their healthcare systems. The World

---

6   Average percentages are calculated by the author for the period of 1995 – 2014 based on the information provided in the World Bank database. Percentages are rounded.

Bank's 'Health Reform Project' had a considerable influence in Latvia. The project provided a loan and additional financing for policy reform, institution building, skill development, primary healthcare (PHC) and hospital sector restructuring (HiT Lativa, 2008; 219). Even here, reforms were nevertheless shaped in terms of compliance to EU standards. As seen from Table 5, all three Baltic States changed to insurance-based systems. Reforms were driven by both interaction with external actors (organizational membership) and national actors' willingness to change the system. Thus, Lithuania was among the first to adopt a law on health insurances and decentralization (1991), followed by compulsory health insurance (1997) (HiT Lithuania, 2000). Similarly, healthcare reforms in Latvia in the early 1990s primarily aimed at changing from the Soviet-style Semashko system (HiT Latvia, 2008; 211). The role of national actors in the reform process is still considerable, however. Hence, despite the strong influence of compliance with EU standards, reforms in Estonia nevertheless followed the national plan (HiT Estonia, 2008; 190).

SWAp

The second type of interaction with external actors refers to the sector wide approach (SWAp). This framework channels government and donor activities towards the 'comprehensive' development of a particular sector (OECD, 2006; 36). The state and donor organizations collaborate to mainstream financial resources and technical skills and advance the system in general. SWAp is used in many sectors, including healthcare, education, water, and the like. According to this framework, the state and donor organizations agree on priority areas and a list of indicators. A SWAp is based on shared accountability, collective dialogue and long-term perspective (OECD, 2006; 36). Kyrgyzstan and Moldova are two countries implementing healthcare SWAp in the region. Both introduced social insurance reforms and retained state-dominated service provision with selective benefit packages. Interaction with external actors, based on SWAp, considerably shaped healthcare reforms in these countries.

Kyrgyzstan was among the first countries to implement SWAp in the region, with reforms shaped by national *Manas* and *Manas taalimi* programs. The *Manas* healthcare reform program (1996 – 2006) was developed in collaboration with the World Health Organization (WHO) (McKee et al., 1998; 138). To cut the number of healthcare facilities,

Kyrgyzstan initiated an optimization strategy. Hospital bed cuts contributed to PHC funding, while the strong commitment of the President mobilized the necessary resources from external actors (Gedik et al., 2002; 144; Vang and Haioff, 2002; 161; Savas et al., 2002; 86). The program aimed at retaining some of the benefits from the old system, but also prioritized prevention and cost-efficiency. Kyrgyzstan introduced family medicine and closed 43 percent of hospitals between 2000 and 2003 (HiT Kyrgyzstan, 2011; 100). The outcomes of the first program ensured external support for the follow-up *Manas taalimi* initiative (2006 – 2010). This aimed at strengthening PHC by additionally promoting public participation (HiT Kyrgyzstan, 2011; 104 – 109). The SWAp ensured the pooling of resources to the national budget from key development partners and increased the accountability of the national government over the use of resources.

Similar to Kyrgyzstan, Moldova implemented a SWAp in healthcare, supported by the WHO and the EU (WHO, 2017). Like other countries in the region, Moldova faced serious financial constraints while implementing healthcare reforms in early 1990s, but still emphasized a minimum package as a guiding principle for reforms (HiT Moldova, 2008; 111 – 112). Moldova cut the number of hospitals by half and focused on family medicine, increasing the number of family doctors from 57 to 2,096 between 1995 and 2004 (HiT Moldova, 2008; 114). All these reforms were implemented in collaboration with external actors. The World Bank's 'Health Investment Fund project' (1998 – 2005) aimed at restructuring medical services, strengthening PHC and introducing healthcare service packages according to the available budget (World Bank 2000 in HiT Moldova 2008; 114). Similar to Kyrgyzstan, national policies guided healthcare reforms in Moldova. The country adopted the 'Concept of reforming health-care system' (1997 – 2003), the 'Health system development strategy' (2007 – 2016) and the 'National Health Policy' (2007 – 2021), contributing to coherent reform of the healthcare system.

The healthcare reforms in both Kyrgyzstan and Moldova were shaped by interactions with external actors, not determined by them. Like the Baltic States, adherence to national strategies contributed to reform of the sector as a whole. Russia, to an extent, belongs to the same group of healthcare systems as Kyrgyzstan and Moldova (see Table 5). Although Russia did not implement SWAps, external actors nevertheless contributed to its healthcare reforms in similar ways.

Project-based interaction

Russia's interaction with external actors shifted from financial aid to technical assistance, initiating decentralization and privatization in the early 1990s. Decentralization reforms weakened the Ministry of Health's regulatory capacities, contributed to regional inequality and political tensions between regional and municipal authorities (Footman and Richardson, 2014; 37 – 38). The country's experience with decentralization, as in other post-Soviet countries, was ambiguous. In the late 1990s, the government gradually decreased adjustment loans. International support, by the World Bank and WHO for instance, mainly related to technical assistance (HiT Russia, 2011; 89). In 2007, Russia adopted the Concept Paper on 'Russia's Participation in International Development Assistance,' transforming the country from an aid recipient to an aid provider. All subsequent healthcare reforms were initiated and implemented by the state. The government adopted the 'National Priority Project—Health' (2005 – 2013), which prioritized major healthcare problems, including maternal and child care, PHC and disease prevention (HiT Russia, 2011; 139 – 140). However, the stated priorities nevertheless followed policies previously suggested by the World Bank and other external actors (Cook, 2007; 147). Compulsory health insurance introduced in 1993 faced a number of administrative challenges. The lack of support by the Ministry of Health restricted the development of a regulatory basis for a functioning Mandatory Health Insurance (MHI) (HiT Russia, 2011; 20). The initiative was later emphasized in the 'Further National Health Concept to the year 2020.' Nonetheless, many regions retain a combination of old (tax-based) and new (insurance-based) financing elements (HiT Russia, 2011; 18 – 19). MHI implementation in Russia is incomplete. Certainly, the role of external actors in healthcare reforms of the country is incomparable to those in Moldova and Kyrgyzstan. However, the country followed reform paths chosen in the late 1990s, although conflicts between regional and municipal authorities restricted their coherent implementation.

Two countries with a similarly small share of ODA and limited interaction with external actors are Belarus and Turkmenistan. However, the range and outcomes of reforms conducted in these two cases are considerably different. Belarus is the only country in the post-Soviet region providing healthcare benefits similar to the Semashko system. The country followed a gradualist approach to reforms and retained universal access to healthcare (HiT Belarus, 2013; 95). To decrease dependence on external supply, Belarus aimed at increasing the domestic production of pharmaceuticals (HiT Belarus, 2013; 97). The government additionally controls prices for essential medicines to ensure their accessibility. However, the sustainability of the system with increasing healthcare costs and economic underdevelopment is questionable (Balabanova et al., 2012; 843). The country implemented a number of reforms to optimize costs, including integration of parallel healthcare services (HiT Belarus, 2013; 97). Similar optimization reforms were initiated in Turkmenistan. The healthcare reform program (LUKMAN) was implemented aimed at rationalizing hospital beds and supporting PHC (Savas et al., 2002; 87; Gedik et al., 2002; 144 – 145; HiT Turkmenistan, 2000; 63 – 64). However, governmental decisions contradict the general healthcare program and slow down the reform process (Savas et al., 2002; 87; Vang and Haioff, 2002; 162). On paper, Turkmenistan provides a wide range of healthcare benefits to its citizens, although the literature reports that hospital rationalization led to closure of district hospitals (Horak and Sir, 2009; 81) and patients have to travel longer distance to access the system. Since compulsory health insurance does not cover the majority of costs, the use of traditional medicine increased (Horak and Sir, 2009; 80 – 81). However, estimating the true state of the healthcare system is difficult given data limitations.

Kazakhstan, Uzbekistan and Ukraine have tax-based financing, state service provision and selective benefit packages. All three countries collaborated with external actors, although their interactions were limited to ad hoc projects. Here, the state remains a decisive actor, responsible for the lack of healthcare reforms. In Uzbekistan and Kazakhstan, governments implemented a range of reforms. Uzbekistan cut 40 percent of hospital beds between 1991 and 1997 (Vang and Haioff, 2002; 163), collaborating closely with external organizations. The primary and secondary care reforms in the country were implemented within the World Bank's 'Project Health' (1998 – 2018), maternal and child health service improvement with the help of the Asian Development Bank (2005 – 2012) and EU grants (2009 – 2016) (HiT Uzbekistan, 2015). Kazakhstan is another country in the region where the state played a strong role in the reform process. Kazakhstan adopted the 'National program of Health Care Reform 2005 – 2010', reversing decentralization reforms implemented in the 1990s. Service provision is still administered by regional authorities, but the Ministry of Health is the main supervisory and regulating body. Similar to Uzbekistan, it introduced optimization reforms by cutting up to 45 percent of hospitals (1991 – 1998), emphasizing ambulatory care and PHC (Gedik et al., 2002; 144; Vang and Haioff, 2002; 160 – 161). The country piloted health insurance in several *oblasts*, but it was not rolled out at the national level (HiT Kazakhstan, 2007; 110).

Unlike Kazakhstan and Uzbekistan, the government of Ukraine did not play any active part in implementing healthcare reforms, although whether this was because healthcare was unimportant, or too important, is beyond the scope of this chapter to answer. Family medicine reforms in Ukraine are at an initial stage and PHC reforms are more formal than real (HiT Ukraine, 2010; 150 – 151). The country retained most elements of the Semashko system, except for the recent 'Economic Reforms Program' (2010 – 2014) (HiT Ukraine, 2015; 125). External actors have played an important role in the country's reform process. Thus, National Health Accounts were introduced in 2006 with technical support of international organizations (HiT Ukraine, 2010; 153). The overall contribution of external actors to total health expenditures is low, however, although there is strong pressure from the IMF, World Bank, WHO and USAID to reform the system (HiT Ukraine, 2015; 66, 125 – 126). Although the role of the state varies across the three countries, ranging from active to a passive reformer, all have largely project-based interaction with external actors, contributing to the fragmentation of healthcare reforms.

Reforms in Uzbekistan have focused on maternal and child care, PHC and emergency care, with no coherence across different initiatives (Savas et al., 2002; 87; Gedik et al., 2002; 145). In contrast to Uzbekistan, the incoherence of healthcare reforms in Kazakhstan has been attributed to external actors implementing projects on an ad hoc basis, inconsistent with national policies and marginalizing the Ministry of Health (Savas et al., 2002; 87). Interaction with external actors is at an early stage in Ukraine. The Ukrainian government secured funding form the Global Fund for HIV / AIDS and tuberculosis prevention program (2007 – 2011), later suspended because of a scandal over increased medication prices (HiT Ukraine, 2015; 66). Financing was granted only after an international non-governmental organization took over the project (HiT Ukraine, 2015; 67).

Armenia and Georgia received significant support for healthcare reforms, but external actors in both states pursued rather sporadic activities. Development assistance targeted small changes and 'ad hoc interventions' (Savas et al., 2002; 85). The healthcare organization in Armenia still resembles the Semashko system (Hovhannisyan, 2004; 4), although the country implemented privatization and decentralization reforms. Both contributed to the devastation of the referral system and weakened quality control mechanisms (HiT Armenia, 2006; 132 – 133). Privatization was most developed in Georgia, and was to the largest scale. According to the Development Master Plan, around 80 percent of hospitals were sold (HiT Georgia, 2009). Optimization and privatization policies in both countries significantly affected access to healthcare. As a result of privatization, visits to doctors fell by 30 percent and bed occupancy by 200 percent (HiT Armenia, 2006; 135 – 136; Tonoyan, 2004; 9 – 11). Both Armenia and Georgia received a large amount of ODA *per capita*, but the lack of a comprehensive national framework and ad hoc interactions with external actors, contributed to the fragmentation of reforms.

Azerbaijan and Tajikistan largely rely on OOPs in healthcare financing but have state-dominated service provision. Limited healthcare reforms in both countries are attributed to violent conflicts delaying the reform process (McKee et al., 1998; 138; Vang and Haioff, 2002; 162). Both countries are among the largest recipients of ODA, but external actors have mainly focused on humanitarian aid. A number of external actors, including USAID, EU, the UN and others, provided significant humanitarian assistance from the mid-1990s to the early 2000s to support internally displaced persons from the Nagorno-Karabakh region (HiT Azerbaijan, 2010; 31). Similarly, development assistance to Tajikistan initially focused on emergency assistance, due to significant destruction of infrastructure (Savas et al., 2002; 86; Gedik et al., 2002; 144). Both countries pursued project-based interactions with external actors. Healthcare reforms in Tajikistan are just beginning. The country initiated a program on family medicine (2011 – 2015) and piloted capitation-based financing to primary healthcare in two districts (2005 – 2006) (HiT Tajikistan, 2016; 85 – 88). In contrast to Tajikistan, Azerbaijan has implemented benefit packages. The laws 'About protection of health of the population' (1997) and 'Health Financing Concept' (2008) define state-guaranteed BBPs (HiT Azerbaijan, 2010; 24), but these have not been fully implemented. Therefore, despite formal entitlement, citizens often pay for healthcare services. Azerbaijan has adopted a number of presidential decrees, but their practical implications are restricted due to the lack of implementation mechanisms (HiT Azerbaijan, 2004; 55 – 56).

CONCLUSIONS

This study has several limitations. While providing an overview of healthcare developments in fifteen countries, it does not capture diversities within each state. These could be better captured by case studies. Furthermore, the categorization of countries is based on generalizations. Certainly, there are variations between the Baltic States (for variations regarding welfare systems see Ainsaar and Kesselmann, 2016; Aidukaite et al., 2016; Rajevska and Romanovska, 2016) and closer analysis of Russia would address its peculiarities more closely. Specific analyses of healthcare sectors, such as primary healthcare, maternal or child care, would also increase divergence in terms of the typology. The categorization produced in this chapter is not definitive, but contributes to understanding the diversity of the region and encouraging further research on healthcare reforms in post-Soviet countries.

Despite the Semashko healthcare system inherited from the Soviet Union, these fifteen states have followed different reform paths, largely explainable in terms of differences in interactions between the state and external actors. Three types of interactions have been proposed, namely: organizational membership, sector-wide approaches and project-based interactions. Countries implementing the first two types managed to reform their healthcare system by mainstreaming healthcare resources. The Baltic States, Moldova and Kyrgyzstan closely cooperated with external actors and introduced health insurance. Russia introduced similar reforms, although their practical implementation across the country is unclear. The majority of the states in the region have had project-based interaction, with healthcare reforms varying from retaining the Semashko system, to increasing reliance on out-of-pocket payments. Belarus has retained a broad range of benefits and the dominant role of the state in healthcare financing and service provision. The system in

Turkmenistan is unclear due to data limitations. Kazakhstan, Uzbekistan and Ukraine have implemented standardized benefit packages but retained the key role of the state in financing and service provision. On the contrary, Armenia and Georgia, have limited the role of the state by introducing mixed service provision and increasing out-of-pocket expenditures. In general, more social- and market-oriented systems, with some exceptions, have replaced the Semashko system.

REFERENCES

Aembe, Bwimana (2017). "Networked Health Sector Governance and State-building Legitimacy in Conflict affected Fragile States: The Variable Impact of Non-state Provision of Public Health Services in Eastern Democratic Republic of Congo" PhD Thesis Wageningen University the Netherlands in <http://edepot.wur.nl/411653> accessed 22 August 2017.

Aiddata, (2017). in <http://aiddata.org/> accessed 30 April 2017.

Aidukaite, Jolanta, Moskvina, Julija, Skuciene, Daiva (2016). "Lithuanian Welfare System in Times of Recent Crisis" in Schubert, Klaus, de Villota, Paloma, Kuhlmann, Johanna (eds.) *Challenges to European Welfare Systems* (Switzerland: Springer)

Ainsaar, Mare, Kesselmann, Liisa-Evi (2016). "Economic Recession and Changes in the Estonian Welfare State: An Occasion Not to Waste a Good Crisis" in Schubert, Klaus, de Villota, Paloma, Kuhlmann, Johanna (eds.) *Challenges to European Welfare Systems* (Switzerland: Springer).

Amsler, Sarah and Sanghera, Balihar (2007). "Introduction Post-Soviet Social Science: Reaching Beyond Neoliberalism and Neoconservatism" in Sanghera, Balihar, Amsler, Sarah and Yarkova, Tatiana (eds.) *Theorising Change in Post-Soviet Countries: Critical Approaches* (Bern: Peter Lang).

Anderson, Odin W. (1963). "Medical care: Its social and organizational aspects. Health Services Systems in the United States and Other Countries—Critical Comparisons" in *The New England Journal of Medicine* Vol. 269(16).

Antoun, Joseph, Phillips, Frank, Johnson, Tricia (2011). "Post-Soviet Transition: Improving Health Services Delivery and Management" in Mount Sinai Journal of Medicine Vol. 78.

Balabanova, Dina, Roberts, Bayard, Richardson, Erica, Haerpfer, Christian, and McKee, Martin (2012). "Health care reform in the former Soviet Union: beyond the transition" in *Health services research* Vol. 47, No 2.

Belli, Paolo (2001). "Ten Years of Health Reforms in Former Socialist Economies: Lessons Learned and Options for the Future" in <http://www.ces-asso.org/sites/default/files/belli.pdf> accessed 30 April 2017.

Bohm, Katharina, Schmid, Achim, Gotze, Ralf, Landwehr, Claudia and Rothgang, Heinz (2010). "Five types of OECD health care systems: Empirical results of a deductive classification" in *Health Policy* Vol. 113.

Borisova, Liubov (2011). "Health care systems as determinants of health outcomes in transition countries: developing classification" in *Social Theory and health* Vol. 9, No 4.

Borowitz, Michael, Atun, Rifat (2006). "The unfinished journey from Semashko to Bismarck: health reform in Central Asia from 1991 to 2006" in *Central Asian Survey* Vol. 25(4).

Cerami, Alfio (2009). "Mechanisms of Institutional Change in Central and Eastern European Welfare State Restructuring" in Cerami, Alfio and Vanhuysse, Pieter (eds.) *Post-Communist Welfare Pathways: Theorising Social Policy Transformation in Central and Eastern Europe* (Hampshire: Palgrave Macmillian).

Cholewka, Patricia A. (2001). "Challenges to institutionalizing sustainable total quality management programs in health care systems of post-Soviet countries" in *International Journal of Economic Development* Vol. 3, No. 3.

Cholewka, Patricia A. (2004) "Healthcare system restructuring and the effects of globalization on post-Soviet transitional economies" International Journal of Economic Development Vol. 6, No 3.

Cook, Linda J. (2007). *Postcommunist Welfare States: Reform Politics in Russia and Eastern Europe* (Ithaca and London: Cornell University Press).

Dingeldey, Irene and Rothgang, Heinz (2010). "Introduction: Governance and Comparative Welfare State Research" in Dingeldey, Irene and Rothgang, Heinz (eds.) *Governance of Welfare State Reform: A Cross National and Cross Sectional Comparison of Policy* Globalization and Welfare (Cheltenham: Edward Elgar).

Eckardt, Sebastian and Goldthau Andreas (2007). "Reforming into Growth or Growing into Reform? A Critical Note on the Post Washington Consensus" in Sanghera, Balihar, Amsler, Sarah and Yarkova, Tatiana (eds.) *Theorising Change in Post-Soviet Countries: Critical Approaches* (Bern: Peter Lang).

Ferge, Zsuzsa (1997). "Social Policy Challenges and Dilemmas in Ex-Socialist Systems" in Nelson, Joan M, Tilly, Charles and Walker, Lee (eds.) *Transforming post-Communist Political Economies* (Washington, D.C.: National Academy press).

Field, Mark G. (1973). "The concept of the 'health system' at the macrosociological level" in *Social Science and Medicine* Vol. 7.

Footman, Katharine and Richardson, Erica (2014). "Organization and governance" in Rechel, Bernd, Richardson, Erica and McKee, Martin (eds.) *Trends in health systems in the former Soviet countries* 35th ed.: Observatory Studies Series Vol 24.

Footman, Katharine, Richardson, Erica, Roberts, Bayard, Alimbekova, Gulzhan, Pachulia, Merab, Rotman, David et al. (2014). "Foregoing medicines in the former Soviet Union: Changes between 2001 and 2010" in *Health Policy* Vol. 118.

Freeman, Richard, Moran, Mochael, (2000). "Reforming healthcare in Europe" in *West European Politics* Vol.23 (2).

Gedik, Gulin, Oztek, Zafer, Lewis, Anthony (2002). "Modernizing primary health care" in McKee, Martin, Healy, Judith and Falkingham, Jane (eds.) *Health care in Central Asia* (Buckingham: Open University Press).

Gordeev, Vladimir S, Pavlova, Milena and Groot, Wim (2011). "Two decades of reforms. Appraisal of the financial reforms in the Russian public healthcare sector" in *Health Policy* Vol. 102 (2 – 3).

Haggard, Stephan and Kaufman, Robert R (2009). "The Eastern European Welfare State in Comparative Perspective" in Cerami, Alfio and Vanhuysse, Pieter (eds.) *Post-Communist Welfare Pathways: Theorising Social Policy Transformation in Central and Eastern Europe* (Hampshire: Palgrave Macmillian).

Health system reviews (HiTs) in *European Observatory on Health Systems and Policies* in <http://www.euro.who.int/en/about-us/partners/observatory/publications/health-system-reviews-hits/full-list-of-country-hits> accessed 30 April 2017.

Healy, Judith, Falkingham, Jane, McKee, Martin (2002). "Health care systems in transition" in McKee, Martin, Healy, Judith and Falkingham, Jane (eds.) *Health care in Central Asia* (Buckingham: Open University Press).

Horak, Slavomir, Sir, Jan (2009). "Dismantling Totalitarianism? Turkmenistan under Berdimuhamedow" in *Silk Road Paper* March 2009 <https://www.files.ethz.ch/isn/106328/js09turkmenistanunder.pdf> accessed 05 September 2017.

Hovhannisyan, Samvel (2004). "Health care in Armenia. Economic and sociopolitical problems mean the healthcare system is in transition" in *BMJ* 329 (7465): 522 – 523 in <https://www.ncbi.nlm.nih.gov/pmc/articles/PMC516090/> accessed 30 April 2017.

Immergut, Ellen M. (1992). *Health Politics: Interests and institutions in Western Europe* (Cambridge University Press).

Inglot, Tomasz (2009). "Czech Republic, Hungary, Poland and Slovakia: Adaptation and Reform of the Post-Communist 'Emergency Welfare States'" in Cerami, Alfio and Vanhuysse, Pieter (eds.) *Post-Communist Welfare Pathways: Theorising Social Policy Transformation in Central and Eastern Europe* (Hampshire: Palgrave Macmillian).

Isabekova, Gulnaz, (2016). "Wer bekommt wieviel? Entwicklungshilfe im Gesundheitswesen der zentralasiatischen Staaten" in *Zentralasien-Analysen* Vol. 108.

Klugman, Jeni, Schieber, George, Heleniak, Timothy, Hon, Vivian (2002). "Health Reform in Russia and Central Asia" in McKee, Martin, Healy, Judith and Falkingham, Jane (eds.) *Health care in Central Asia* (Buckingham: Open University Press).

Kornai, Janos (1997). "Reform of the Welfare Sector in the Post-Communist Countries: A Normative Approach" in Nelson, Joan M, Tilly, Charles and Walker, Lee (eds.) *Transforming post-Communist Political Economies* (Washington, D.C.: National Academy press).

Kuhlbrandt, Charlotte and Boerma, Wienke (2015). "Primary care reforms in countries of the former Soviet Union: success and challenges" in *Eurohealth* Vol. 21, No. 2.

Kukava, Mikheil, (2013). "State-sponsored universal healthcare program: problems and recommendations" in <http://www.transparency.ge/en/blog/state-sponsored-universal-healthcare-program-problems-and-recommendations>

Kutzin, Joseph, Cashin, Cheryl, Jakab, Melitta, Fidler, Armin and Menabde, Nata (2010). "Implementing health financing reform in CE / EECCA countries: synthesis and lessons learned" in Kutzin, Joseph, Cashin, Cheryl and Jakab, Melitta (eds.) *Implementing health financing reform. Lessons from countries in transition*. 21st ed. (United Kingdom: European Observatory Series).

Leive, Adam (2010). "Economic Transition and Health Care Reform. The Experience of Europe and Central Asia" in *IMF Working Paper* WP / 10 / 75 https://www.imf.org/external/pubs/ft/wp/2010/wp1075.pdf accessed 30 April 2017.

Lewis, Maureen (2007). "Informal Payments And The Financing Of Health Care In Developing And Transition Countries" *Health Affairs* Vol. 26(4).

MacArthur, Ian, Shevkun, Elena (2002). "Restructuring public health services" in McKee, Martin, Healy, Judith and Falkingham, Jane (eds.) *Health care in Central Asia* (Buckingham: Open University Press).

McKee, Martin, Figueras, Josep and Chenet, Laurent (1998) "Health reform in the former Soviet Republics of Central Asia" in *International journal of health planning and management* Vol. 13.

Ministry of Health Georgia, (2017). "Universal health care program (საყოველთაო ჯანდაცვის პროგრამა)" in <http://www.moh.gov.ge/ka/529>.

Mirzoev, Tolib, Green, Andrew, Newell, James (2010). "Health SWAps and external aid— a case study from Tajikistan" in International Journal of Health Planning an Management Vol. 25.

Morris, Jeremy, Kovacs, Borbala, Harboe, Ida (2016). "Informality and the welfare state" in Polese, Abel (eds) *Limits of a Post-Soviet State: How Informality Replaces, Renegotiates, and Reshapes Governance in Contemporary* Ukraine (Stuttgart: ibidem press).

Nelson, Joan M. (1997). "Social Costs, Social-Sector Reforms, and Politics in Post-Communist Transformations" in Nelson, Joan M, Tilly, Charles and Walker, Lee (eds.) *Transforming post-Communist Political Economies* (Washington, D.C.: National Academy press).

OECD, (1987). *Financing and Delivering Health Care: A Comparative Analysis of OECD Countries* (OECD Social Policy Studies).

OECD, (2006). "DAC Guidelines and Reference Series Harmonising Donor Practices for Effective Aid Delivery" in <https://www.oecd.org/dac/effectiveness/34583142.pdf>

OECD.stat (2017). "Health status" in <http://stats.oecd.org/index.aspx?DataSetCode=HEALTH_STAT#>.

Oka, Natsuko (2015). "Informal payments and connections in post-Soviet Kazakhstan" *Central Asian Survey* Vol. 34(3).

Orem, Juliet N., Marchal, Bruno, Mafigiri, DavidKaawa, Ssengooba, Freddie, Macq, Jean, Da Silveira, Valeria C., Criel, Bart (2013). "Perspectives on the role of stakeholders in knowledge translation in health policy development in Uganda" in *BMC Health Services Research* Vol. 13(324).

Orenstein, Mitchell A. (2009). "Transnational Actors in Central and East European Pension Reforms" in Cerami, Alfio and Vanhuysse, Pieter (eds.) *Post-Communist Welfare Pathways: Theorising Social Policy Transformation in Central and Eastern Europe* (Hampshire: Palgrave Macmillian).

Oxford Living Dictionaries (2017). "Interaction" in <https://en.oxforddictionaries.com/definition/interaction> accessed 10 August 2017.

Polovinka, Alexandra (2016). "Three Essays on Informal Payments in the Health Care Sector in Russia" PhD Dissertation Western Michigan University in <http://scholarworks.wmich.edu/cgi/viewcontent.cgi?article=2935&context=dissertations> accessed 05 September 2017.

Polubinskaya S.V. (2000). "Reform in psychiatry in post-Soviet countries" in Acta Psychiatrica Scandinavica Vol. 101.

Rajevska, Feliciana, Romanovska, Laura (2016). "Latvia: Both Sides of the Economic Recovery Success Story" in Schubert, Klaus, de Villota, Paloma, Kuhlmann, Johanna (eds.) *Challenges to European Welfare Systems* (Switzerland: Springer).

Rechel B. and Khodjamuradov, G. (2010). "International involvement and national health governance: The basic benefit package in Tajikistan" in *Social Science and Medicine* Vol. 70 (12).

Rechel, Bernd and McKee, Martin (2009). "Health reform in central and eastern Europe and the former Soviet Union" in *The Lancet* Vol. 374 (9696).

Rechel, Bernd, Ahmedov, Mohir, Akkazieva, Baktygul, Katsaga, Alexandr, Khodjamurodov, Ghafur and McKee, Martin (2012). "Lessons from two decades of health reform in Central Asia" in *Health policy and planning* Vol. 27, No. 4.

Reshetnikov, V.A., Nesvizhsky, Yu.V., Kasimovskaya, N.A., "N.A. Semashko—theorist and organizer of public health" in *History of medicine* Vol. 3(3).

Richardson, Erica (2014). "Health financing" in Rechel, Bernd, Richardson, Erica and McKee, Martin (eds.) *Trends in health systems in the former Soviet countries* 35th ed.: Observatory Studies Series Vol. 24.

Rivkin-Fish, Michele (2005). *Women's Health in Post-Soviet Russia: The Politics of Intervention* (Indiana University Press).

Rothgang, Heinz (2010). "Introduction" in Rothgang Heinz, Cacae, Mirella, Frisina, Loraine, Grimmeisen, Simone, Schmid, Achim and Wendt, Claus *The State and Healthcare: Comparing OECD Countries* Transformations of the State CRC 597 (Hampshire: Palgrave Macmillian).

Rothgang, Heinz (2010b). "Conceptual framework of the study" in Rothgang Heinz, Cacae, Mirella, Frisina, Loraine, Grimmeisen, Simone, Schmid, Achim and Wendt, Claus *The State and Healthcare: Comparing OECD Countries* Transformations of the State CRC 597 (Hampshire: Palgrave Macmillian).

Ruget, Vanessa (2007). 'Social Rights and Citizenship in Kyrgyzstan: A Communitarian Perspective" in Sanghera, Balihar, Amsler, Sarah and Yarkova, Tatiana (eds.) *Theorising Change in Post-Soviet Countries: Critical Approaches* (Bern: Peter Lang).

Savas, Serdar, Gedik, Gulin and Craig, Marian (2002). "The reform process" in McKee, Martin, Healy, Judith and Falkingham, Jane (eds.) *Health care in Central Asia* (Buckingham: Open University Press).

Schecter, Kate, (1997). "The Russian Compulsory Medical Insurance System" The National Council for Eurasian and East European Research in <https://www.ucis.pitt.edu/nceeer/pre1998/1997-812-17G-3-Schechter.pdf>.

Schmid, Achim and Wendt Claus (2010). "The Changing Role of the State in Healthcare Service Provision" in Rothgang Heinz, Cacae, Mirella, Frisina, Loraine, Grimmeisen, Simone, Schmid, Achim and Wendt, Claus *The State and Healthcare: Comparing OECD Countries* Transformations of the State CRC 597 (Hampshire: Palgrave Macmillian).

Schmid, Achim, Cacae, Mirella and Rothgang, Heinz (2010). "Health care financing" in Rothgang Heinz, Cacae, Mirella, Frisina, Loraine, Grimmeisen, Simone, Schmid, Achim and Wendt, Claus *The State and Healthcare: Comparing OECD Countries* Transformations of the State CRC 597 (Hampshire: Palgrave Macmillian).

Sehngelia Lela, Pavlova Milena and Groot, Wim (2016). "Impact of Healthcare Reform on Universal Coverage in Georgia: A Systematic Review" in *Diversity & Equality in Health and Care* <http://diversityhealthcare.imedpub.com/impact-of-healthcare-reform-on-universalcoverage-in-georgia-a-systematic-review.php?aid=17029> accessed 30 April 2017.

Stepurko, Tetiana, Pavlova, Milena, Gryga, Irena, Murauskiene, Liubove, Groot, Wim (2015). "Informal payments for health care services: The case of Lithuania, Poland and Ukraine" in *Journal of Eurasian Studies* Vol. 6.

Tonoyan, Tamara (2004). "Healthcare system in Armenia: past, present and prospects" in https://www.wm.tu-berlin.de/fileadmin/f8/wiwidok/diskussionspapiere_wi widok/dp11-2004.pdf accessed 30 April 2017.

Transparency International Georgia (2012). "The Georgian Hospital Sector" in <http://www.transparency.ge/sites/default/files/post_attachments/TIG%20Hospital%20report%20_5%20Jul_%20final.pdf> accessed 15 August 2017.

Ulikpan, Anar, Mirzoev, Tolib, Jimenez, Eliana, Malik, Asmat and Hill, Peter S. (2014). "Central Asian post-soviet health systems in transition: has different aid engagement produced different outcomes?" in *Global Health Action* Vol. 7.

Vang, Johannes, Haioff, Steve (2002). "Rationalizing hospital services" in McKee, Martin, Healy, Judith and Falkingham, Jane (eds.) *Health care in Central Asia* (Buckingham: Open University Press).

World Bank 2017 "World Development Indicators" in <http://databank.worldbank.org/data/reports.aspx?source=2&series=SH.XPD.PUBL&country=#>.

Wendt, Claus, Frisina, Lorraine, Rothgang, Heinz (2009). "Healthcare System Types: A Conceptual Framework for Comparison" in *Social Policy and Administration* Vol. 43(1).

WHO, (2017). "SWAP in Republic of Moldova" in <http://www.euro.who.int/en/health-topics/Health-systems/health-systems-governance/activities/donor-coordination-and-a-sector-wide-approach-to-health-swap/swap-in-republic-of-moldova> accessed 10 August 2017.

CHAPTER 12:
DIVERSIFIED CONVERGENCE: UNEVEN WELFARE TRAJECTORIES IN CENTRAL AND EASTERN EUROPE

Noémi Lendvai-Bainton

INTRODUCTION

While welfare regime theory has long argued that welfare states are distinctive socio-economic regimes with coherent and consistent patterns of delivering welfare, more and more contemporary research points not only to the internal inconsistencies of those regimes, but also to the regional diversification within regime types. In this chapter, I will argue that while the cluster of Central and Eastern European (CEE) welfare states as a particular sub-type within post-communist welfare regimes still points to many similarities and converging tendencies, there is also a fundamental divergence occurring within this cluster. These trends have in part been driven by the reoccurring crises and regimes of austerity capitalism post-2008, as some countries in CEE have opted for radical welfare state reforms reversing some of the reforms introduced in the 1990s. Neoliberal convergence is a strong pattern. While in some countries this is a gradual process, in other countries it is introduced abruptly and suddenly. Divergence on the other hand is important because while some of the welfare states in the region show stability and gradual recalibration, others show radical retrenchments and populist, nationalist and paternalist backlashes. I will also argue that transnational actors—such as the European Union and the International Monetary Fund (IMF)—continue to have a significant influence over welfare reforms across all the countries. A multi-scalar framework for analyzing welfare state reforms is therefore crucial if we are to trace the transformation of welfare regimes in the region.

WELFARE REGIMES: POST-COMMUNIST WELFARE IN THE VISEGRAD COUNTRIES

After the collapse of the communist regimes across the region, the Visegrad countries—that is Hungary, the Czech Republic, Slovakia and Poland[1]—have enjoyed a much better initial economic and social conditions than that of the Baltic States or Romania and Bulgaria (Gebel, 2008). The higher GDP *per capita* was coupled with fast pro-market reforms in all the four countries with strong IMF and World Bank influence particularly in Hungary and Poland. For Bohle and Greskovits (2012), the Visegrad countries have opted for a distinctive 'embedded neoliberal' regime in which market reforms and social cohesion and protective welfare have gone hand in hand. This embedded regime has been contrasted to the 'pure' or radical neoliberal regimes of the Baltic States and the neo-corporatist regime in Slovenia. The Visegrad countries have used welfare policies extensively to compensate for marketization and to negotiate between fast economic reforms and political legitimacy. Importantly, while all four countries have converged towards a Foreign Direct Investment (FDI)-led economic model, significant differences emerged in terms of privatization patterns, International Organizations' (IOs) influence, as well as underlying political discourses around economic development. In terms of welfare patterns, the historical legacies of Bismarckian influences (Inglot, 2008) continued to dominate throughout the 1990s and 2000s, even despite the scattered radical neoliberal reforms of pension and social benefit systems. Deacon (2000), in his seminal work, was spot on arguing that the internal tensions of post-communist welfare states arose from how to reconcile the legacies of the Bismarckian insurance-based system with the pressures arising from the integration into the global economy, associated pressures on budgets, the liberal agenda of IOs, and the pressure towards residual social policies.

---

1   The Visegrád Group, Visegrád Four, or V4, founded in 1991, is a cultural and political alliance of four Central European states—the Czech Republic, Hungary, Poland and Slovakia.

THE CONVERGENCE DEBATE: POST-ACCESSION DEVELOPMENTS

Ever since 1998, when CEE countries have started their accession negotiations resulting in the 2004 EU Accession, the main assumption of both EU policy-makers as well as many academic scholars has been the assumed socio-economic convergence and catch-up of New Member States (see Vojinovic, Oplotnik and Prochniak, 2010; Horridge and Rokicki, 2017). Convergence was anticipated economically as fast economic growth was predicted; social convergence was both expected to follow economic convergence and was assumed to be facilitated by EU soft governance and the Open Method of Coordination (OMC) processes (Borras and Jacobssson, 2004; Lendvai-Bainton, 2017). Europeanisation of social policy literature emerged emphasizing policy learning, best practices and mainstreaming and streamlining policies all contributing to the 'modernization of social protection systems' (Lendvai, 2007, 2011, 2017). By the time the New Member States had joined the EU in 2004, soft governance rapidly expanded as a main policy tool and covered key policy areas such as employment, education, social inclusion and social protection. The 2008 economic crisis has, however, fundamentally changed the social policy landscape both at supranational as well as national level. Soft governance has lost its significance and coercive, fiscal-based, governance tools started to dominate the EU framework (Rodrigues and Xiarchogiannopoulou, 2014). Austerity hit all CEE countries with different sequencing, wrapped in a variety of domestic discourses, resulting in varied social outcomes. Following largely declining social spending as a percentage of GDP between 2004 and 2007, social spending hiked rapidly from 2007 until 2009, after which social spending fell again in Hungary, Poland and the Czech Republic. Slovakia, as the lowest welfare spender in the region, has been an exception.

Figure 1   Social spending as a share of GDP between 2004 and 2016 in four Central Eastern European countries (OECD data).

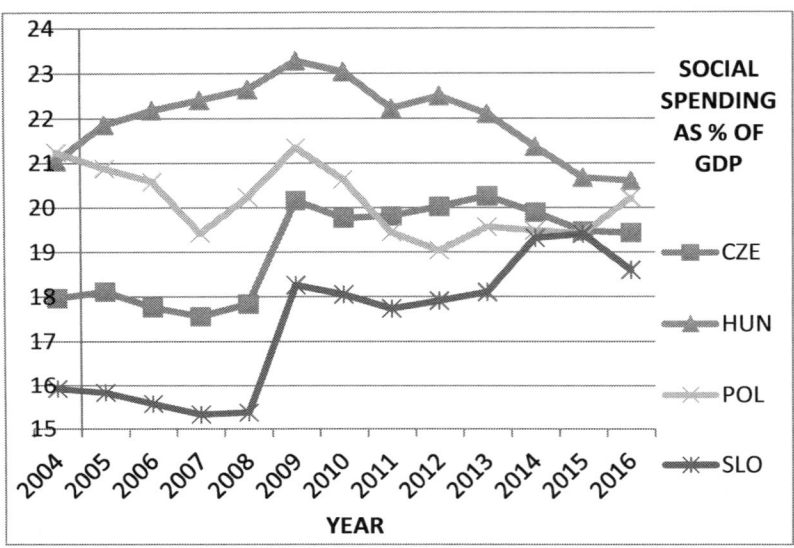

Source: OECD social spending database, accessed on the 31 September 2017.

What is noticeable from Figure 1 is that CEE counties have converged to a consistently low level of social spending as a percentage of GDP between 2004 and 2016, compared to Old Member States. Importantly, since 2010, there has been a significant drop in social spending both in terms of the percentage of GDP as well as *per capita* in three out of the four countries. In Hungary, social protection spending per capita has decreased by 11 percent between 2007 and 2013 (OECD, 2017). In 2014, based on EU calculations, the gap between social spending in CEE countries and the average of the EU-28 is around 10 percentage points. The same figure in 2006 was 8 percentage points, which suggest that the social spending gap has in fact widened (Eurostat data). This implies that the social gap between the 'west' and the 'east' has not diminished.

I argue in this chapter that the expected social convergence was preempted by two main factors: economic integration and political resistance. The first makes social convergence impossible while the second makes it undesirable. Economic and social convergence has been at the forefront of broader socio-economic expectations associated with EU Membership by a variety of actors such as the EU, Member State governments, and academics alike. EU integration was assumed to bring about rapid economic growth and a form of 'catch-up'. However, while indeed some economic growth has been impressive, economic convergence has produced a diverse set of outcomes. As Leitner and Romish (2015) argue, in terms of economic convergence measured as GDP *per capita* at Purchasing Power Parity (PPS) between 1995 and 2011, the Visegrad countries have done very well. Taking the EU-27 at 100 percent, the Czech Republic's GDP increased from 76.3 percent in 1995 to 81.9 percent by 2011. Hungary has similarly impressive trends of climbing from 50.3 percent to 65.4 percent of the EU-27. Slovakia has had the biggest hike from 46.8 percent to 73.6 percent, while Poland improved from 41.5 percent in 1995 to 63.6 percent in 2011. Importantly, as Leitner and Romish argue, the problem with aggregate GDP data is that it 'does not take into account changes in the distribution of income in an economy' (ibid, 5). Indeed, they show income convergence to have been much slower, with the Czech Republic showing a relative deterioration of Gross Disposable Income (GDI) between 1995 and 2011. A crucial explanation they argue to explain this trend is that corporate profits have converged much faster that household income.

Table 1   Corporate and Household Gross Disposable Income per capita at PPS, 1995 and 2011, EU-27=100.

	CR	HUN	POL	SLO	**CEE-10 average**
Corporate disposable income 1995	106.6	38.5	27.3	65.7	**40.5**
Corporate disposable income 2011	81.8	67.6	68.6	88.2	**74.2**
Difference between 1995 and 2011	−24.8	29.1	41.3	22.5	**33.7**
Households Disposable income 1995	65.4	51.0	45.7	40.5	**44.0**
Households Disposable income 2011	70.7	60.8	61.0	71.0	**58.5**
Difference between 1995 and 2011	5.3	9.8	15.3	30.5	**14.5**

Source: Leitner and Romish 2015; 8

These data point to the fact that the relationship between economic and social convergence is complex. Leitner and Romish argue that economic convergence has been faster than social. Social convergence has been considerably suppressed by poor labor market performance such as low activity rates, compressed wage levels, tax collection and tax competition, and by overall national debt. As Table 2 shows, the region still has low minimum wages (particularly in relation to minimum subsistence levels) and relatively high poverty rates, with Hungary suffering from extremely high severe material deprivation rate and Poland from high in-work poverty rates.

Table 2 Selected social indicators in Visegrad countries

Countries	Average net wage (2014)	Minimum wage	In-work poverty (2010)	At risk of poverty rate (2014)	Severe material deprivation (2015)	Gini (2015)
Czech R.	€837	€407	3%	15%	6%	25
Hungary	€615	€413	7%	32%	19%	28.2
Slovakia	€755	€435	5%	18%	9%	23.7
Poland	€775	€454	11%	25%	8%	30.6

Source: Eurostat data, accessed on 31 September 2017.

While economic growth has failed to contribute to a significant boost of disposable household incomes and to the reduction of poverty, political factors have also played an important role. On the one hand, the political elite across the region has been pressurized by the EU to keep national debt low and suppress or reduce public spending in order to foster economic growth and encourage FDI. On the other hand, many of the EU's regulatory as well as soft governance frameworks for social policy have either been very expensive (i.e. active labor market policies) or have been undesired by New Member States (i.e. gender equality and gender mainstreaming policies). While the EU assumed that western European-style welfare policies will quickly be 'learned' by New EU Member States (whether it be 'social investment' policies, 'activation', or 'social inclusion'), political contestation has had a considerable effect on issues such as active labor market policies (ALMP), gender mainstreaming and gender equality policies, pro-poor policies as well as anti-discrimination. The political contestation of these issues has had a notable effect on the 'Europeanisation' of post-communist social policies, one which was not necessarily resulting in adaptation, learning and convergence, but rather the first quiet, later louder, rejection or alteration of these policies. The traversing of ALMPs into punitive public work programs in Hungary, or the banning of the term gender in Poland points to the significance of those political contestations. Eurostat data on public spending patterns confirms that public spending on economic affairs, public order, defense and cultural and religious activities are higher in the region than in the

Old Member States. Social spending in the Visegrad countries also show not only high fragility, but also strong concentrations; so for example while most CEE spending is high on pensions (hence Rhodes' classification of CEE welfare as pension states), Slovakia shows a very high spending on health care. And while the Visegrad countries operate the largest and most comprehensive welfare states in the region (with the exception of Slovenia, which is the frontrunner in the region), particular forms of social polarizations (whether it be along ethnic, religious, or regional lines) remain strong in all four countries. Welfare developments have been highly fragile, both in terms of economic as well as in terms of political development (Greskovits and Bohle, 2012).

In the section below, I shall focus on a particular pattern of welfare development post-2008, most prominently emerging in Hungary and Poland, but with some potential ramifications for other countries in the region.

POPULISM, AUSTERITY AND WELFARE: THE RISE OF AUTHORTARIAN NEOLIBERALISM IN CENTRAL AND EASTERN EUROPE

While for many the 2000s has been marked as a decade of 'Europeanisation of welfare', where fast economic catch-up allows for 'modernization of social protection' in the New EU Member States, the 2008 economic crisis fundamentally changed the socio-economic and socio-political governance of the region. New forms of populist political mobilization have emerged most prominently in Hungary and in Poland with distinct patterns of austerity and anti-welfare populism.

Theoretically speaking, populism and nationalism both have important ramifications for the institutional and political architecture of the welfare state and for the techniques of governing more broadly. While there is very little European literature on authoritarianism and welfare, we know much more about the intersection of populism and welfare states. In the European context, Swank and Betz's (2003) analysis of radical right-wing populist (RRWP) parties in 16 Western European countries between 1981 and 1998 found that a universal welfare state with generous social protection provisions suppressed the electoral support for these parties. They define RRWP parties as ones that (a) advocate fundamental change to the existing socio-economic and political order; (b) foster or accentuate social inequalities; and (c) appeal to public sentiments of resentment, disillusionment and anxiety. They argued that 'RRWP parties typically embrace neoliberal economic programs, xenophobia and strident anti-establishment positions' (ibid.; 218). Here, strong welfare states suppress radical politics to emerge as mainstream governing political power. Mau and Veghte (2007) focus on the perception of welfare states of populist parties, arguing that right-wing populism has strong anti-welfare state sentiments for a number of reasons. Firstly, right-wing populism operates with a sentiment where equality is reduced to one's own people: 'through this idea, equality is defined in particularistic terms and is difficult to reconcile with the universalistic premises of welfare state ideology' (ibid.; 190). Secondly, anti-statism, anti-establishment, and the anti-institutional elements of populism will also foster hostility towards the welfare state. Nordensvard and Ketola (2015) demonstrate how exclusionist views of the welfare state are combined with deep-rooted nationalism, where the 'national' character of the welfare state is reclaimed. They have looked at the Finnish and Swedish radical right in their discursive position towards the welfare state and found that right-wing Scandinavian populist parties promote an exclusive and exclusionist welfare state that favors ethnic nationals. Within this exclusive and exclusionist approach, 'new rightist parties not only argue against welfare for foreigners but also criticize the way welfare is arranged and delivered in a manner that neglects the interests of the "common man"' (Nordensvard and Ketola, 2015; 358). In their analysis, they find that 'populist parties in Finland and Sweden move away from both a universal social democratic and a neo-liberal economic framing of the welfare state and thereby introduce a third framing of the welfare state: the welfare *nation* state' (ibid.; 372, emphasis in original). Similarly, Keskinen and his colleagues (2016) argue that the economic crisis is likely to accelerate welfare chauvinism, which they see as part of a broader process of neoliberal restructuring of the welfare state.

While, for many scholars, populism and nationalism are short-term political projects, the sustained electoral success of authoritarian neoliberal regimes in countries such as Hungary and Poland, calls for a more systematic consideration of these new regimes. Ekiert (2017) argues that both Poland and Hungary are rapidly becoming 'electoral authoritarian regimes' with ultra-nationalist leadership. Ekiert argues that these regimes 'have learned how to live with relatively clean elections and some trappings of political opposition and civil society. They tolerate even open borders and free flow of economic resources' (ibid.; 7). As a political project, Ekiert argues 'politics [in Poland] is no longer about the common good and cooperation in solving the country's problem but about enemies who need to be destroyed and friends who need to be supported, regardless of the moral or political cost' (8). Colin Crouch (2017), reflecting on the populist assault on contemporary democracy, similarly argues that populism has become a key ingredient accompanying neoliberalism in the construction of social democracy.

Both in Hungary and in Poland, populist and nationalist governance can be conceptualized as a distinct social-redistributive project, one which pursues welfare governmentality in radically new ways. These regimes represent a widespread assault on the welfare state in their anti-establishment discourse. The welfare state as an establishment institution comes under attack through a variety of claims on how public resources should be allocated, exploiting social, gender, racial, ethnic, or territorial divides. The politics of common good and cooperation is replaced by divisions, exclusions and new normative values based on nationalism, religious affiliation and the idea of 'good citizens'. In this context, the welfare state is constructed as an 'outmoded' institutional structure, that is 'inefficient' and one that conveys the 'wrong' values and moral imperatives. The 'liberal' foundations of welfare states are questioned and replaced by a moral economy that reifies 'new communitarianism' (Bathory, 2016). The reification of new nationalist, populist and religious values then gives rise to the institutionalization of new redistributive dynamics—one that is generous to certain groups, such as Hungarians living in neighboring countries, and meagre to others, such as the disabled, Roma and the poor. As such, in both Poland and Hungary, a kind of authoritarian nationalism emerges where political authoritarianism is accompanied by social authoritarianism. Political authoritarianism not only removes checks and balances and allows for radical constitutional changes (Ekiert, 2017), but as I will argue below in the case of Hungary, it is also accompanied by social authoritarianism.

I will analyze different aspects of social authoritarianism in this chapter. I draw upon the notion of Bruff (2016) for whom the 2008 economic crisis marks a significant new era of permanent austerity, which triggered a variety of authoritarian and coercive state practices, with the prominence of the 'brutal effects of austerity on the possibility for living'. For Bruff, austerity is state-directed coercion with a widespread attack on a range of social rights. For Giroux (2015; 5), the new neoliberal authoritarianism is defined as a 'new politics of normalization of culture of fear, war, surveillance and exploitation', and a 'politics of disposability with its expanding machineries of civic and social death, terminal exclusion, and zones of abandonment'. For both Bruff and Giroux, authoritarianism is a social project using both economic and political tools to produce targeted and systematic patterns of social divisions, marginalization and insecurities.

HUNGARY AS A MINI-CASE STUDY: THE POPULIST ATTACK ON THE WELFARE STATE

In 2010, the Hungarian political landscape has seen a significant and lasting shift in consolidating a distinctively new populist, nationalist right-wing regime led by Viktor Orban. While many scholars have argued that populism is a temporary and largely short-term political phenomenon, Orban's electoral success in 2014 consolidated authoritarian neoliberalism in Hungary and continues to deliver electoral support likely to be successful again in 2018. The 2008 economic crisis triggered a major socio-economic and socio-political crisis in Hungary. Once an economic front-runner and leading pioneer of the post-communist transformation in Eastern Europe, by 2008, the country had accumulated huge economic debts, was riddled by political corruption and had a stagnant labor market. The huge external and household debt of the country continued to build up throughout the 2000s, and made the country very vulnerable at the outbreak of the global economic crisis. To avoid insolvency, Hungary was the first to receive a 20 billion Euro emergency loan from the IMF and the EU (Greskovits and Bohle, 2012). Orban was elected in 2010 following radical austerity measures being introduced by the previous government, in the context of rising unemployment and poverty. Orban promised unorthodox economic policies such as withdrawing from the IMF loan, and imposing new taxes and levies on banks. In conjuncture with the economic crisis, the current refugee crisis allowed Orban to sustain a systematic political and religious discourse that has been deeply conservative, populist and nationalist.

Authoritarian neoliberalism in Hungary is assembled with seemingly very disparate elements. 'Illiberal democracy' is a flagship concept, which entails the

> abandonment of liberal methods and principles of organizing society, as well as the liberal way to look at the world, and parting ways with Western European dogmas, making ourselves independent from them ... This is about an ongoing reorganization of the Hungarian state. Contrary to the liberal state's organizational logic of the past twenty years, this is a state originating from national interests. (Orban's speech, 26th July 2014)

While clearly the notion of 'illiberal democracy' is an oxymoron, the term 'illiberal' signals a critique of western style 'individualism', 'rights-based approaches', and 'welfare-statism'. It has instigated widespread constitutional changes removing checks and balances, strong centralization of government structures, moving towards a much more presidential style of governing, challenging freedom of speech, and represents a strong grip on the media. Democratic institutions are systematically sidelined and the political community is only mobilized through 'national consultations', largely on issues such as migrant quotas and immigration. In a seemingly unlikely coupling, alongside illiberalism, a very strong 'competition state' (Drahokoupil, 2010) is being built with strong neoliberal elements: in 2017 corporation tax has been reduced to 9 percent, the lowest in the EU; in 2011 progressive taxation was replaced by a 16 percent flat income tax, while massive subsidies and tax exemptions are offered to multinational co-operations. However, in its radical reconfiguration of socio-economic governing, the regime also mobilizes strongly nationalist, often anti-market, elements. Widespread re-nationalization of public utilities, banks and other key strategic sectors have been undertaken. Neoliberalism is delivered in a nationalist framework in which the 'competition state' is selectively delivered by *both* the market and the state. As such, the 'illiberal' and the 'neoliberal' goes hand in hand in delivering a unique governance that offers a coherent discursive framework. This emerging Hungarian regime is very similar to the one envisaged by Cahill (2014), who foreshadowed the possibility of the emergence of what he calls 'authoritarian economic nationalism', which pursues nationalistic policies with 'widespread assault upon labor conditions and freedoms in order to both stifle sources of dissent and to impose a settlement of terms favorable to capital' (ibid.; 152). This regime is built in the post-crisis landscape, enabled by the emergence of a robust state; this is a state which manages austerity and imposes new regulations, all the while promoting strong nationalization. The relationship between 'authoritarian neoliberalism' and 'authoritarian nationalism' is complex; at times it is mobilizing illiberal, anti-market, anti-FDI policies while at other times it is very much pro-market, neoliberal in its essence in terms of cutting corporate taxation, introducing generous subsidies for FDI and building the competition state.

Importantly, the illiberal state is also the one that signals the 'end of the welfare state'. As Orban argued 'it is better to acknowledge, even if it is difficult, that the concept of welfare state is over. Instead of that, we should try to build up workfare states and replace entitlements with a merit-based society.' (Orbán, speech, 26th July 2014, translated by Mihaly Koltai). Ever since 2010, there has been a significant reconfiguration of the welfare state. Overall social spending has been cut drastically; social assistance schemes have been terminated, and compulsory and punitive public works programs have been rolled out (Bako et al., 2014; Szikra, 2014). At the same time, generous mortgage subsidies have been introduced to the middle class, and a tax credit system was expanded to support hard working families (Bohle and Greskovits, 2012). The illiberal state as such presents a fundamental change to the previous social contract, one which replaces a welfarist social contract (with higher social spending) with a nationalist one based on identity politics, along with lower social spending and attacks on certain social groups.

Crucially, illiberal neoliberalism in Hungary is a deeply redistributive project, one that entails the restructuring of the economy and public spending, the state and society with distinctly new techniques of illiberal governmentalities. Batory (2016) emphasizes the authoritarian element of the regime that holds a strong vision of the new society, which is based on self-responsibility as well as 'a system of national cooperation', conveying communitarian values in direct opposition to liberalism. This self-responsibilizing has been a particularly strong feature of the illiberal government policies in the field of employment. The new labor code has introduced a wide range of deregulations and increased labor market flexibility. The elimination of unemployment benefit and the introduction of compulsory public works has also removed the universal and collective protection, and replaced it with an individualistic, and often punitive, scheme that offers bare survival.

Juhasz (2012) highlights the massive backlash in gender issues, with gender mainstreaming being replaced by 'family mainstreaming' underpinned by a Christian ideology focusing on demographic growth and deep paternalism. Gender as a term has been erased from government documents and strategies and replaced by 'family'. A UN (2016) report expressed alarming trends in terms of 'pervasive and flagrant stereotyping of women, including by some political leaders, as unsuited to political power and the insistence on a woman's role as primarily wife and mother' which undermines women's political, economic and social rights. Gero and Kopper (2013) assert that illiberal governmentalities feature the active and sustained effort to close down, marginalize and silence civil society organizations. Civil society organizations get selectively supported providing they promote religious or conservative values; otherwise they are closed down, accused of carrying out political activities critical of the government.

Illiberal governmentalities promote a deep social polarization along ethnic, religious, social, territorial and gender lines. The latest Eurostat data shows that, in 2015, 28 percent of the population were at risk of poverty and social exclusion, and 19.4 percent of the population are severely materially deprived. The poverty rate for children is even higher: in 2014, 38 percent of children were at risk of poverty (Eurostat, 2016). Other studies suggest that 45 percent of the population has no wealth nor savings, and can only barely survive and go on with their everyday life (Kolosi and Fabian, 2016). Social deprivation has also become much more territorially concentrated, with pockets of poverty in regions described as 'third-world poverty'. Educational segregation of the Roma communities has been rolled out. The rise of homelessness, extreme poverty, and high suicide rates all point to increasing precariousness, growing insecurity and increasing commodification of life. Authoritarian neoliberalism delivers a range of insecurities, in which steps to remove support are actively rolled out for the 'other' (whether it be the poor, the Roma, the unemployed, the immigrants, the welfare dependent, disabled, etc.) and only mitigated for a select few. Securities and protections are rolled back, and spending on social protection and education has decreased significantly (Lendvai-Bainton, 2017). Mass out-migration created severe shortages in the health care system and skills shortages are becoming more acute across the economy.

Ironically, while the EU's discursive frame is very much around 'social investment', the Hungarian regime has shifted much more towards a 'social divestment' model since 2010. Core public funding to social assistance, active labor market measures, health, education, and housing have been significantly contracting. The EU's 2016 Country Report for Hungary highlights significant social challenges Hungary faces with regards to:

- Social indicators improved less significantly than the overall economic and labor market situation;
- Poverty rates are high in regional comparison;
- The adequacy and coverage of social assistance remains a challenge and recent reforms could further restrict access conditions for a number of benefits;
- Poor health outcomes continue to be a major challenge (in terms of life expectancy);
- Educational segregation has increased rapidly and dramatically.

Three distinctive elements dominate the new vision of the 'end of the welfare state'. First, a workfare state that is illiberal in character. Second, although austerity as a notion never entered the public domain as a discourse in Hungary, radical austerity measures have been introduced since 2010. Third, the 'end of the welfare state' involves the radical reconfiguration of both the language of 'welfare' and the 'social'.

Illiberal workfare has been founded on the assumption that the chronic problems of the Hungarian labor market lie on the supply side in that overly generous benefits create disincentives for people to enter the labor market (Bako et al., 2014). As such, in 2011, the Orbán government rolled out compulsory public employment schemes, the so-called 'National Public Work Program' and radically reduced employment-related and social benefits. In 2012, the government cut unemployment benefit from nine months to three months (Szikra, 2014). They also reduced the amount of long-term unemployment benefit from 95 to 70 Euros per month, as well as radically restricting eligibility. Despite the European Commission expressing concerns of 'a risk that the drastic cut in unemployment benefit, together with the reduced capacities of the

Public Employment Service, will result in channeling and locking people into public works' (European Commission, 2012: 20), public work programs have been rolled out. In these programs, the unemployed are forced to accept work paying at 50 percent of minimum wage, at a large scale managed by the Ministry for the Interior (Szikra, 2014), and implemented in a rather militaristic style. While between 2011 and 2014 public works became the largest employment-related program in the country—tripling the public expenditures on the scheme—several researchers highlighted its inefficiency (Bako et al., 2014; Koltai, 2012). For example, Bako at al found that only 10 percent of participants were able to find a job on the primary labor market six months after the scheme (2014; 4). Public work has also crowded out other active labor market measures. Considering the program's complex dynamics, it is questionable whether we could consider it as an 'active labor market measure' at all. The rolling out of the program continued even after 2014, the latest announcement being that public work schemes will allow people to join the Armed forces and become volunteer soldiers as part of their public work. Importantly, public work schemes continue to be fundamentally punitive, ethnically selective (targeting Roma and other ethnic minorities) and essentially decoupled from the competitive labor market. Should anybody refuse to participate, this would mean losing all their eligible benefits altogether. Finally, as Bako and his colleagues argue, while public work as a policy tool has been around for a long time, 'the idea that it can and should replace the entire social benefit system is a brand-new ambition' (2014; 4).

The second formative characteristic of the end of the welfare state is the radical retrenchment of social benefits without a public discourse of austerity. In contrast with a British governmental discourse in which austerity is seen as a disciplined response to managing debt, the Hungarian post-crisis discourse does not reference austerity at all, and instead is built on a moral discourse of work and merit within a 'new national contract' based on 'national co-operation'. The comprehensive reconfiguration of the Hungarian welfare state within the new contract started soon after 2010. In 2011 a flat tax system was introduced at 16 percent, which meant a substantial tax increase for low income earners who lost their previous tax exemptions. A complete freeze on all benefits and public sector wages were introduced for four years. Not only was the duration of unemployment benefit cut dramatically to the shortest in Europe, but so also was the monthly amount of long-term unemployment benefit. New, much more flexible labor laws have been introduced to make it easier for employers to fire and hire. In order to compensate for a shortfall in public revenues, VAT was increased to 27 percent, the highest in Europe. Public expenditure on education has been cut and higher education spending has seen a 30 percent cut between 2010 and 2014. Between 2008 and 2016, social spending on benefits has been scaled back dramatically. Unemployment related benefits have fallen from 0.4 percent of GDP in 2008 to 0.1 percent in 2016; sickness payments and disability benefits were reduced from 1.8 percent GDP to 1.3 percent, child benefits have fallen from 2.0 percent to 1.5 percent of GDP. Total social protection spending as a share of GDP has fallen from 15.9 percent in 2008 to 14.3 percent in 2016 (Policy Agenda 2015). In 2015 a new law on social benefits was introduced which discontinued the state social assistance system and replaced it with a decentralized one. As part of the new system, some forms of social assistance were stopped altogether, such as housing benefit and discretional carers' benefit, while the remaining forms of social assistance were delegated to local municipalities, most often without any funding resources and on a discretionary basis. As Bako et al. (2014) argue, uniquely amongst OECD countries, Hungary has reduced the net value of all employment-related and social benefit payments by 6 percent between 2011 and 2014.

The 'new social contract' also comes with a new language. While we have seen above that 'illiberal' is viewed as positive and authoritative, and 'the end of the welfare state' is declared, the change to the linguistic landscape is even broader than those grand declarations; it aims to reconfigure and rebuild forms and practices of social solidarity, social bonds and relations in the widest possible terms. As noted earlier, an example of this changing linguistic landscape is the replacement of 'gender mainstreaming' with the term 'family mainstreaming' (Juhasz, 2012). 'Social assistance' has been renamed as 'parish assistance', with deliberate paternalistic and feudal connotations dating back to the 13th century. Abolished by the Communist Party in 1983, this administrative unit has been reinstated, with parish assistance being discretionary and subject to the financial resources available to the parish. Child benefit becomes 'pedagogical and educational support' with an explicit reference to the duty of parenting as well as its conditionality upon compulsory education—educational support is suspended after 50 hours of unauthorized absence from school. Many of the former social benefits were renamed in a way that the 'social' becomes eradicated and replaced either with employment or parish-related terminologies. The reorganization of social and child care services around these new parish territorial units, also means that, often, these services become unavailable within rural and remote areas, where accessing services such as legal support or counselling is 50 – 60 km away.

Table 3   New Social Policy Dictionary in Hungary

Old terminology	New terminology
Ministry of Social Affairs	Ministry of Human Resources
Child benefit	Pedagogical and educational support
Unemployment benefit	Jobseeker support
Regular social support	Employment-replacing support
Social assistance	Parish assistance
Gender mainstreaming	Family mainstreaming

CONCLUSION

The triple transformation of post-communist Europe posed very demanding pressures in terms of how to negotiate the contradictory demands for establishing a market economy, democracy and nation-states (Offe, 2001). Within this context, Bohle and Greskovits (2012) argue that nationalism, identity politics and / or welfarism have emerged as key pacifying mechanisms in Central and Eastern Europe through which economic losses and insecurities were mitigated and managed. Their stark warning becomes very relevant when they argue that:

> we sense a trade-off between welfarist and identity politics. Once embedding neoliberalism in socially protective arrangements becomes untenable, democratic politics is likely to lose balance, and stabilization may occur via larger doses of identity politics leading in the worst case, to sacrifices of democratic quality. (2012; 265)

In both the case of Hungary and Poland, a marked shift from welfarist politics to identify politics can be identified, which has brought about new nationalist and populist discourses in the realm of economic, politics and the social.

The populist turn in Visegrad countries suggests that in Hungary and Poland the welfarist strategy has been replaced by identity politics and nationalism with a radical contraction of the welfare state. This shift points to downwards welfare convergence in the region which will sustain very low social spending and a widening social gap between the 'west' and the 'east' in Europe. It will also promote wider social and regional inequalities within the countries.

Authoritarian neoliberalism marks a new paradigm for the welfare state, one which not only calls for the end of the welfare state, but also one that celebrates social disinvestment, so similarly rooted in the neoliberal project. In this new 21st century paradigm, the economic rationalities that underpin the European social investment model are replaced by, and then go beyond, political rationalities. Now the welfare state is no longer necessary—not even for political purposes. In this radical and troubling scenario, it is the welfare state itself that has been made discursively redundant. Crucially, this new discursive claim does not prevent the state from expanding, reconfiguring, and reallocating public spending, as well as redistributing public resources.

The rise of authoritarian neoliberalism in Hungary is one of the by-products of EU integration. The de-politicization of economic integration during the Accession process, as well as the intensification of austerity and fiscal discipline in the EU's crisis management has opened up spaces for a 'break away from the resurgent orthodoxy' (Bohle and Greskovits, 2012; 267). As much as the case cannot be anything other than a historically and culturally unique domestic construction, it is also a transnational product of the EU's consolidation state. As such, if one considers the British 2016 referendum and Brexit to be a symptom of disintegration and dissent, the Hungarian regime is also a dissent: a dissent from the EU's economic and political integration, a dissent from open borders, a dissent from fiscal governance. The 'illiberal democracy' is then an attack on the EU integration project and on the European Social Model itself.

REFERENCES

Appel, Hilary and Orenstein, Mitchell (2013). Ideas Versus Resources. Explaining the Flat Tax and Pension Privatization Revolutions in Eastern Europe and the Former Soviet Union, *Comparative Political Studies* vol. 46 no. 2: 123 – 152.

Bako, Tamas, Cseres, Gergely. Kalman, Judit, Molnar Gyorgy and Szabo Tibor (2014). A munkaeropiac peremen levok es a koltsegvetes [The budget and people on the edge of the labor market]. MTA Kozigazgatasi Intezet.

Batory, A. (2016). Populists in government? Hungary's "system of national cooperation", *Democratization* 23(2): 283 – 303.

Bohle, Dorothee and Greskovits, Bela (2012). *Capitalist Diversity on Europe's Periphery*, Cornell University Press: Ithaca.

Böröcz, József. (2001). "The Fox and the Raven: the European Union and Hungary renegotiate the margins of 'Europe'." In *The Empire's New Clothes: unveiling EU enlargement*, József Böröcz and Melinda Kovács, eds., 51 – 100. Telford: Central Europe Review.

Bozoki, A. (2011). Occupy the State: The Orbán Regime in Hungary, *Debate* 19(3): 649 – 663.

Bloom, P. (2016). *Authoritarian Capitalism in the Age of Globalization*. Edward Elgar: Cheltenham.

Brown, W. (2015). *Undoing the Demos. Neoliberal Stealth Revolution*. Zone Books: New York.

Bruff, I. (2014). The Rise of Authoritarian Neoliberalism, *Rethinking Marxism: A Journal of Economics, Culture & Society*, 26(1): 113 – 129.

Cahill, D. (2014). *The End of Laissez-Faire?* Edward Elgar: Cheltenham

Cook, L., Orenstein, M. and Rueschmeyer, M. (eds.) (1999). *Left Parties and Social Policy in Postcommunist Europe*. Westview Press: Boulder.

Country Report Hungary (2016). Commission Staff Working Document, Brussels 26.2.2016, SWD (2016) 85 Final.

Deacon, B. (2000). Eastern European welfare states: the impact of the politics of globalisation. *Journal of European Social Policy* 10(2): 146 – 161.

De Koster, Willen, Achterberg, Peter and Van der Waal, Jeroen, (2012). The new right and the welfare state: the electoral relevance of welfare chauvinism and welfare populism in the Netherlands. *International Political Science Review* (34) 1:3 – 20.

Drahokoupil, J. (2010). *Globalization and the State in Central and Eastern Europe*. Routledge: London.

Fowler, B. (2006). Concentrated Orange: Fidesz and the Remaking of the Hungarian Centre-Right 1994 – 2002, in: Szczerbiak, A. and Hanley, S. eds. *Centre-Right Parties in Post-Communist East-Central Europe*. Routledge: London. pp. 80 – 115.

Gebel, M. (2008). Labour markets in Central and Eastern Europe, in: Kogan, I., Gebel, M. and Noelke, C. eds. *Europe Enlarged*, Policy Press: Cheltenham, pp. 35 – 62.

Gero, Marton and Kopper, Akos (2013). Fake and Dishonest: Pathologies of Differentiation of the Civil and the Political Sphere in Hungary, *Journal of Civil Society* 9(4): 361 – 374.

Györffy, Dora (2015). Austerity and growth in Central and Eastern Europe: Understanding the link through contrasting crisis management in Hungary and Latvia, *Post-Communist Economies* 27(2): 129 – 152.

Halmai, Gábor (2015). *Viktor Orbán's rampage to attract more far right voters*, VerfBlog, 2015 / 5 / 07, http://verfassungsblog.de/viktor-orbans-rampage-to-attract-more-far-right-voters/.

Horridge, M. Rokicki, B. (2017). The impact of EU accession on regional income convergence within the Visegrad countries. *Regional Studies*, published online 3 July 2017.

Jensen, C. (2014). *The Right and the Welfare State*. Oxford University Press: Oxford.

Johnson, Juliet and Barnes, Andrew (2015). Finacial nationalism and its international enablers: the Hungarian experience, *Review of International Polictical Economy*, 22(3): 535 – 569.

Keskinen, Suvi, Norocel, Christian and Jorgensen Martin (2016). The politics and policies of welfare chauvinism under the economic crisis. *Critical Social Policy* 36(3): 321 – 329.

Kitchelt, Herbert and Maggan, Anthony (1995). *The Radical Right in Western Europe: a Comparative Analysis*, University of Michigan Press, Ann Arbor.

Leitner, S. and Romisch, R. (2015). Economic and Social Convergence in the EU: A Policy Note. Working Paper Series, GRINCOH, Paper N. 1.13.

Lendvai, Noémi. and Stubbs, Paul. (2015). Europeanization, Welfare and Variegated Austerity Capitalisms—Hungary and Croatia, *Social Policy & Administration* 49(4): 445 – 465.

Majone, G. (2014). *Rethinking the Union of Europe Post-Crisis. Has Integration Gone Too Far?* Cambridge University Press: Cambridge.

Mau, Steffen and Veghte, B. (eds.) (2007). *Social Justice, Legitimacy and the Welfare State*, Routledge: London.

Nordensvard, Johan and Ketola, Markus (2015). Nationalist Reframing of the Finnish and Swedish Welfare States—The Nexus of Nationalism and Social Policy in Far-right Populist Parties, *Social Policy & Administration* 49(3): 356 – 375.

Parker, Camilla and Bulic, Ines (2013). Befektetes a multba? A totalis intezetek bezarasa es a Strukturalis Alapok politikaja Kozep_kelet-Europaban. [Investment into the Past? The closing down of totalitarian institutions and the politics of Structural Funds in Central and Eastern Europe.], European Coalition for Community Living, Report published by Open Society Foundations.

Peck, J. (2010). *Construction of Neoliberal Reason*. Oxford University Press: Oxford.

Roudgries, M. and Xiarchogiannopoulou, E. (eds.) (2014). *The Eurozone crisis and EU governance*. Routledge: London.

Sissenich, B. (2007). *Building States Without Society*. Rowman and Littlefield: Lanham.

Streeck, W. (2014). *Buying Time. The Delayed Crisis of Democratic Capitalism*. Verso: London.

Swank, Duane and Betz, Hans-Georg (2003) Globalization, the welfare state and right-wing populism in Western Europe, *Socio-Economic Review* 1(2): 215 – 245.

Szikra, Dorottya (2014). Democracy and welfare in hard times: The social policy of the Orbán Government in Hungary between 2010 and 2014, *Journal of European Social Policy*, (11). pp. 1 – 15.

Vanhuysse, Pieter (2006). *Divide and Pacify: Strategic Social Policies and Political Protests in Post-Communist Democracies*, Budapest-New York: Central European University Press.

Vojinovic, M, Oplotnik, M. and Prochniak, A. (2010). EU enlargement and real economic convergence, *Post-communist Economies* 22(3): 303 – 322.

CHAPTER 13:
REFORMING WELFARE ASSEMBLAGES IN SEMI-PERIPHERAL SPACES: UNDERSTANDING 'DRIVERS OF INERTIA' IN BOSNIA-HERZEGOVINA, CROATIA AND SERBIA

Paul Stubbs and Siniša Zrinščak

INTRODUCTION

Studying the post-Yugoslav space offers an ideal opportunity to understand the impacts on social policy of the confluence of post-socialist transition, new nation state building, post-conflict reconstruction, the large-scale presence of diverse international actors, and variegated Europeanisation. Nevertheless, large parts of what was once socialist Yugoslavia are almost entirely absent from the comparative social policy literature. Work on social policy in the region occupies a marginal position with little or no influence on discussions regarding welfare trajectories in wider Europe, and is largely absent from the literature on social policy in post-socialist Central and Eastern Europe and the former Soviet Union.

This may be a result of the fact that the wars of the Yugoslav succession throughout much of the 1990s meant that in-depth research was difficult to undertake, and statistics were hard to obtain. The region may simply look too complicated for the outside observer to grasp, with a wide range of fluctuating political and institutional relationships, contested sovereignties and unstable citizenship claims. A mainstream social policy literature finds it hard to address welfare paths which are complicated and hard to classify. It may also be that the preoccupations of social and political scientists remain firmly fixed on questions of war and peace, ethnicized nationalisms, and regional stability with little interest in exploring other questions of public policy.

Attempts to 'bring the region back in' are few and far between, and not always adequate. Bohle and Greskovits' (2012) understanding of Croatia, alongside Bulgaria and Romania, as a weak, neocorporatist, state, relies on a few texts on political economy with no direct engagement with the social policy literature. Stambolieva's (2016) extensive study of welfare state transformations in the Yugoslav successor states dealing, in turn, with Slovenia, Croatia, Serbia and Macedonia, whilst a useful point of reference, is overly influenced by historical institutionalism and welfare regime theory. The welfare outcomes described, a heady mix of liberal, conservative, social democratic, neo-liberal, neocorporatist and more, merely show the necessity of going beyond what Abrahamson (1999) termed 'the welfare modelling business', and of jettisoning the idea of coherent, path-dependent, welfare regimes, in favor of the concept of complex, unstable, welfare assemblages, or welfare 'patchworks' (Stubbs and Zrinščak, 2007).

The concept of 'welfare assemblages' directs us to 'complex becoming and multiple determinations' (Venn, 2006; 107). Radically unfinished, fluid, 'welfare settlements' are a contingent product of complex interactions between agency, structure, institutions and discourses: the ASID framework (cf. Moulaert and Jessop, 2006; Deacon and Stubbs, 2013). Following Moulaert and Jessop, 'agency' refers to individual or collective behavior that 'makes a significant difference'; 'structure' refers to social realities which are resistant to agency-driven change; 'institutions' are interconnected sets of governing routines, an 'enduring ensemble of structural constraints and opportunities'; and 'discourses' are 'meanings produced inter-subjectively' (Moulaert and Jessop, 2006; 2 – 3).

The ASID framework fits with the need to define welfare, or social policy, very broadly, and not to over-commit to a crude notion of the 'core' of social policy as composed of a number of 'sectors' such as 'pensions', 'social protection' (usually including cash and care services), and 'health and long-term care'. This is because, over time, there is evidence of both 're-domaining', that is, shifting understandings of the nature and limits of formal welfare, and the creation of new 'domains', through processes of Europeanization, for example (Lendvai, 2007). With the rise of a 'new right' conservatism, the social policy arenas of 'family policy' and 'demographic renewal' also become important, if contested (Dobrotić, Matković and Zrinščak, 2013). In much of the post-Yugoslav space, 'veterans' policies' are also important, not least as they have a distorting effect on other social policy domains (Stubbs and Zrinščak, 2015).

In this chapter, focusing on the three most populous post-Yugoslav states—Bosnia and Herzegovina, Croatia and Serbia—we turn our earlier concern with 'drivers of change' (Stubbs and Zrinščak, 2006) on its head, since what is in need of explanation in the social policy arena is the relative lack of change, framed here in terms of understanding 'drivers of inertia'. The cases are illustrative of the 'paradoxical' nature of reforms in 'semi-peripheries', whereby exhortations to 'modernize' social protection systems are met with 'simultaneous opposition and acceptance, imitation and rejection' (Blagojević, 2009; 99). This is not, of course, to blame the semi-periphery, rather to address the complex and contradictory nature of relations between diverse visions of reform. There is much experimentation, the 'performance of reform' (Stubbs, 2015), which rarely impacts on institutional structures and rarely leads to systemic change. Reform mantras become translated as 'fictions' (Lendvai, 2015; 145), hyperactive spaces where everything appears up for grabs but nothing substantially changes. If we understand 'path dependency' in terms of the 'lock-in effects' of 'socialist legacies' not as a pre-given certainty, but as a contingent empirical reality, then, socialist legacies may have a role to play, although always reworked, reconstructed and reconnected with other forces and currents.

What follows is, then, an attempt to explore post-Yugoslav welfare trajectories and, crucially, analyze the paradox of large-scale experimentation, limited explicit reform, *de facto* erosion and complex 'layering' of social rights in three post-Yugoslav states. In other words, inertia can still be produced as an unexpected outcome of agentic hyperactivity, institutional experimentation, novel discursive forms, and profound structural change. Whilst not an in-depth ethnographic analysis, it is an attempt to construct a 'critical cultural story' (Spry, 2009) of welfare reforms. In the process, it challenges an orthodox tradition of social policy research, usually 'from above or from nowhere' (Marcus, 1995), which appears to be based on the maxim that 'nothing can be analyzed until everything has been described'. Its methodology is close to a 'bending and blending approach' (Lendvai and Stubbs, 2007) creating and ordering research material through a reflexive lens based on multiple roles as researchers, policy advocates and consultants. It is complemented by material gathered in spring 2017, when we interviewed around a dozen key actors involved in, or knowledgeable about, reform processes in Serbia and Bosnia and Herzegovina, complementing our more direct in-depth knowledge of the Croatian reform process. The empirical material presented is, necessarily, uneven and patchy. The same domains are not addressed to the same extent in each country case, not least because their significance varies across the cases described.

SERBIA: CHAOS, MODERATED NEO-LIBERALISM AND STEALTH AUSTERITY

Throughout the 1990s, until the overthrow of the Milošević regime in October 2000, social welfare in Serbia was marked by what one respondent described as 'total chaos'. A militaristic, nationalist and authoritarian populist state had presided for a decade or more over rampant hyperinflation, deindustrialization and the *de facto* collapse of a social security system which, *de jure*, had remained unchanged. This had resulted in massive arrears in terms of insurance-based benefits such as pensions, and a concomitant rise in informality, corruption, organized crime, and clientelism. The new Government, led by Prime Minister Zoran Đinđić from January 2001 until his assassination in March 2003, was composed of a mixture of young technocrats, radical reformers, and former dissidents, tasked simultaneously with restoring a degree of normality to a collapsed system and engaging in transition and change in adverse economic conditions; this all took place amidst a 'crowded playground' (Arandarenko and Golicin, 2007; 167) of diverse international actors.

Leading reformers, including the 'technocratic' G17 Plus party, economists from the Institute of Economics and the Hayek-inspired think tank The Centre for Liberal Democratic Studies (CLDS), immediately started work with the International Monetary Fund (IMF) on a loan agreement and with the World Bank on a Poverty Reduction Strategy Programme (PRSP). It is an overstatement, however, to suggest that 'consistent with its liberal orientation and commitments taken towards the international organizations, the government had initiated a welfare state withdrawal, considering it a remnant of socialism' (Stambolieva; 2016; 164). Rather, as Stambolieva herself suggests, the newly appointed Minister of Social Affairs, economist Gordana Matković, 'shaped social policies as corrective measures to the adverse effects of initiated economic liberalization' (ibid; 169). This was a moderate and moderated approach (Arandarenko and Golicin, 2007; 174), combining elements of neo-liberalism with 'a stronger emphasis on social justice' (ibid; 169).

Matković's tenure at the Ministry was unusual, not least because she brought her own ideas and strategic vision to the reform process. Gathering a strong team of advisors drawn from the region but with experience of working internationally, she largely succeeded in establishing a degree of 'local ownership' of welfare reforms. Crucially, Matković resisted the imposition of the World Bank's model three pillar pension reform, preferring to restore a system largely based on the pay-as-you-go (PAYG) system. Although taking control of the PRSP away from World Bank experts, the broad thrust of reforms was still based on 'targeting' benefits towards the most vulnerable, in line with the dominant World Bank mantra. At the same time, maintaining a less restrictive means-test for the receipt of child benefits was an important counter to the Bank.

It is in terms of the development of community-based services, based on partnerships with Non-Governmental Organizations (NGOs), in the service of what became known as 'deinstitutionalization', the reduction in the number of children, and persons with disabilities, in residential care, where Matković's reforms perhaps had the greatest impact. The Ministry countered accusations that the reforms were 'top down' by establishing a number of working groups and, crucially, engaging in a large number of regional consultations. Supported by the Government of Norway, by UNDP, and others, a Social Innovation Fund (SIF) was established, in operation from 2003 – 2010, envisaged as 'a transitory mechanism providing competitive funding and management support to reform-oriented social services projects at the local level … implemented through partnerships between a plurality of service providers' (Bošnjak and Stubbs, 2007; 158). Judged as more successful in introducing new services than in institutionalizing them (Golicin and Ognjanov, 2010; 28), SIF was, at least, a home-grown institutional innovation, albeit contributing towards 'a project-culture rather than needs-based provision' (Arandarenko and Golicin, 2007; 175), and ushering in a new mantra of 'partnership'.

Apart from SIF, the other main institutional innovation in social policy in Serbia was the establishment, in 2002, of the Poverty Reduction Unit, later called the Social Inclusion and Poverty Reduction Unit (SIPRU). Although situated within the Office of the Deputy Prime Minister, SIPRU was described by one respondent as, to all intents and purposes, 'an advocacy NGO within the Government.' Largely funded by the Government of Switzerland, SIPRU provides a space for reformist thinking, as part of an interlocking network of researchers and activists, including the Centre for Social Policy, a 'spin-off' of the CLDS, where

Matković is now based. In the face of successive governments which have little or no interest in pursuing actively welfare reforms, SIPRU maintains an illusion of reform activity, through strategic documents which are little more than discursive 'fictions' (Lendvai, 2015), offering a channel for a range of projects, and having some leverage through convincing politicians of the importance of social policy reform as a key part of accession to the European Union.

The Koštunica government from 2004 to 2008 did not only opt 'for a strategy of postponed transformation in order to … preserve social peace' (Stambolieva, 2016; 165) but was responsive to particular interest groups, notably war veterans, whose additional benefits, whilst significantly less than their counterparts in Croatia (cf. Dokić, 2017), were not questioned. In addition, 'old style' disability associations resisted plans to merge a Fund for Disability with the Social Innovation Fund. Subsequently, SIF itself was abolished, in part because those who designed it were concerned that once international donors withdrew it was in danger of becoming a non-transparent instrumentalized tool in the hands of local and national politicians.

The onset of the economic crisis in 2008 produced cuts in a number of social benefits, including pensions, but no real push for substantive reforms. A notable exception was a new Law on Social Welfare, finally implemented in 2011, in part a legacy of Matković's period in office when it was decided that legal change should only be attempted after reforms on the ground, and in part a result of the efforts of a strong Working Group. One effect of the new Law, albeit also linked to impoverishment produced by the crisis, was that the number of households receiving social assistance increased by about 55 percent, supporting the argument that the 'neoliberal penetration of the welfare system' (Stambolieva, 2016; 170) was limited or postponed.

In short, then, with some notable exceptions, a key driver of inertia regarding social welfare in Serbia from 2004 until the present day has been the lack of political will, combined with a lack of technical competence. A kind of 'neo-liberalism by stealth' has been ushered in by diverse parties and coalitions, including reformed versions of what might have become 'dinosaur parties of the old regime' (Arandarenko and Golicin, 2007; 171), notably the Serbian Radical Party (SRS) and the Socialist Party of Serbia (SPS). Thus, after Matković, successive Ministers of Social Policy showed little interest in reforms and, indeed, tended to be marginal political figures, sometimes drawn from minorities, largely conceding power to Ministries of Finance, as well as to the IMF and World Bank.

The absence of the European Union as an important factor in social welfare reform in Serbia was stressed by those who look to the EU as a potential corrective to the lack of domestic political interest in social welfare (cf Šunderić, 2015). Serbia's ambivalent relationship to European integration was, perhaps, most positive at the height of the economic crisis when the EU itself was as much focused on austerity and debt reduction as the IMF. A renewed interest in social welfare from within the EU seems unlikely to have any significant impact, however, beyond a new wave of 'projectized' interventions. A focus on 'vulnerable groups', their 'activation' in the labor market, and measures such as the 'youth guarantee' scheme, translated in Serbia into a 'packet for youth' because of lack of resources, have a discursive rather than a practical meaning. Issues such as non-take-up of benefits, the need for in-work benefits, and benefits as rights seem unlikely to be placed on the political agenda in the near future.

BOSNIA-HERZEGOVINA: DIVISION, PROJECTIZATION AND INSTRUMENTALIZATION

If the war which raged in Bosnia and Herzegovina (B-H) from April 1992 to December 1995 did not completely obliterate any prospects for a developed and equitable social welfare system, then the Dayton Peace Agreement (DPA) which ended the war effectively completed the process. Although only one part of the larger wars of the Yugoslav succession, Bosnia and Herzegovina was by far the hardest hit, with war raging across the whole of the territory, resulting in the deaths of over 150,000 people, brutal acts of systematic ethnic cleansing and genocide, and millions becoming refugees or displaced persons (Maglajlić and Stubbs, 2017). The DPA essentially froze the conflict, creating a cumbersome administrative structure and a weak central state, with power resting within ethnically defined entities, *Republika Srpska* (RS) and the Federation of Bosnia-Herzegovina (FB-H), itself further divided along ethnic lines across ten Cantons, between ethnic Muslims (Bošnjaks) and ethnic Croats. When District Brčko is added into the mix, B-H effectively has thirteen separate social systems, each one, with the possible exception of the tiny Brčko district, 'ethnically based, founded on clientelism and networks and discriminatory' (Keil, 2011; 47).

Never a full protectorate, Bosnia-Herzegovina still resembles more of an improvised state (Jeffrey, 2013) marked by a 'mobile sovereignty' (Pandolfi, 2003) of multi-scalar agencies constituting an unfinished and competing set of governance apparatuses. Annex 4 of the DPA, the (externally-written) constitution of Bosnia and Herzegovina, established 'the worst possible' structure for the development of social policy post-conflict (Stubbs, 2001; 100), with responsibilities for social policy at the entity, Cantonal (in FB-H) and municipal level. Creating the conditions for separate, divergent, 'ethnicized' welfare assemblages, with no social policy functions at the central state level, the DPA created what one respondent called 'the most decentralized social policy framework in the world', with social rights set at entity and cantonal levels but responsibility for financing these rights set at the level of municipalities.

Not only are 'fundamental inequities in the realization of rights and entitlements ... built into the system' (Stubbs, 2001; 101) but the effect of this is that 'the services one receives still largely depend on where one lives' (Maglajlić Holiček and Rašidagič, 2007; 163). Although pressure from the World Bank and the IMF led to the merging of two separate pension funds in FB-H on 1 January 2002, rights based on health insurance in the Federation still remain Canton-based, with the Croatian state also investing in health care in those areas dominated by Bosnian Croats. The deep and intransigent nature of Bosnia and Herzegovina's social problems, including poverty, unemployment, emigration and de-population is, of course, compounded by a lack of timely and accurate statistical data, with no census between 1991 and 2013 (cf. Maglajlić and Rašidagić, 2011).

Whether channeling humanitarian aid through Centers for Social Work (CSWs) during and after the war, developing 'pilot' projects with 'vulnerable groups and communities' in the war's immediate aftermath, or seeking to support the establishment of local NGOs as part of an 'exit strategy' in the early 2000s, social welfare practice on the ground in B-H has been thoroughly 'projectized', dominated by an endless stream of diverse, uncoordinated, time-limited, largely unsustainable, and sometimes 'outright disastrous' (Maglajlić and Rašidagić, 2011; 37) initiatives led by international actors. Generally, these projects had little or no connection with state structures at any level, beyond encouraging an instrumentalization of local actors, as when CSWs would form their own NGOs to receive grants or when Assistant Ministers received honoraria for sitting on project advisory boards in a 'private' capacity (Maglajlić Holiček and Rašidagić, 2007; 161). A subsequent shift from 'projects' to 'strategic support' did little more than 'projectize' the very strategies themselves, with the mantra of 'local ownership' contradicted by the absence of counterparts able or willing to implement them. One consequence of this was what might be termed the 'sub-contracting' of welfare governance to hybrid, flexible, and largely unaccountable, intermediaries. All manner of analytical, strategic, and capacity building initiatives, including the creation of a Directorate of Economic Planning (DEP) to supposedly steer B-H's largely fictional Medium-term Development Strategy (MTDS), were donor-driven and although, for a short period, had a degree of political 'buy in' from some actors judged by sections of the international community as more 'technocratic' than 'nationalist', they soon became 'empty shell' institutions, staffed by incompetent political appointees (Stubbs, 2015; 89).

In part because governance within the entity is rather centralized, social protection has been somewhat more coherent in *Republika Srpska* compared to the Federation of B-H, not least in terms of children's rights with an entity-based Children's Fund setting criteria for child benefits, compared to the Federation where only a small number of Cantons have any child benefit system or even maternity rights for women outside of the public sector. Respondents in *RS* suggested that there was a 'window for reform' in the late 2000s, marked by a period of stability and growth and the tenure, from 2006 to 2015, of a more progressively minded Assistant Minister for Social Welfare, Ljubo Lepir, given a degree of autonomy for much of that time, by the then Minister for Health and Social Welfare. Credited with pushing through a Law on Social Protection in 2012 which, as he suggested, established 'the grounds for reform', political changes subsequently meant that the reform momentum was again lost, however.

In the context of the economic and financial crisis, both entities faced intense scrutiny of their social policies from the IMF and the World Bank, combining the mantra of targeting social benefits with an insistence on tightening the criteria for benefits for war veterans, disabled veterans and civil victims of war. The situation was particularly dramatic in the Federation where increased benefits for precisely these groups was an important pre-election measure aimed to shore up political support for nationalist parties (Obradović, 2016). When the IMF insisted on benefit cuts in return for a significant loan, a series of protests led by war disabled groups led to a stand-off. In the end, benefits were reduced for all except those with the most severe disabilities, with formally stricter criteria and more frequent monitoring leading to a situation which meant, in the words of one respondent, that only those with 'connections' were able to realize their rights in practice (cf. Brković, 2017).

A constant refrain, echoed by social workers in Bihać studied by Hromadžić (2017), was of reforms as 'dead letters on paper', with rights enshrined in laws never realized in practice. Perhaps not dissimilar from their colleagues across the region, social workers in B-H were generally described as disempowered, demotivated and demoralized, with a phase of un-coordinated 'capacity building', endless training courses on 'casework', 'supervision' and the like, followed by complete disinvestment, the absence of 'managerial' approaches, and increasing distrust between workers in CSWs and local NGOs (Ćuk, 2016). 'Progressive' directors of CSWs only kept their positions through political connections and were often removed once the political make-up of the Government changed. In the last few years, even cursory attempts at reform have stalled, with the views of professionals and welfare users, systematically ignored.

Not unlike in Serbia, the European Union was described as very much a 'shadow' actor, disengaged except through IPA (Instrument of Pre-Accession Assistance)-funded 'projects'. As Hromadžić points out, international discourses, including those promulgated by the EU, combine a 'neoliberal discourse of loan conditionality, fiscal deficit, and credit-oriented policy' with a 'discourse of human rights and social inclusion' (Hromadžić, 2017; 3), although both are largely silent on the deep politicization of social welfare in B-H, with rights' discourses 'perpetually fragmented, hijacked and ethnicized, and where politicians use the cannibalistic "thick structures" of the state to satisfy their and their parties' 'private' agendas' (ibid.; 4).

CROATIA: CLIENTELISM, CONSERVATISM AND WELFARE PLURALISM

Croatia's nationalist state building project, steered by President Tuđman throughout the 1990s, consisted of semi-authoritarian rule within a formally democratic frame (cf. Dolenec, 2013). War and ethnicized conflict, directly affecting large parts of the territory, strengthened nationalist sentiment with a political elite presiding over what has been termed re-traditionalization, de-secularization and re-patriarchalization (Županov, 2001); this occurred at the same time as systematic de-industrialization and a process of privatization described by one economist as 'organized robbery' (Baletić, 2003). A highly centralized Government structure, albeit with over a third of Croatia's territory outside of its control until military actions in 1995 and the peaceful reintegration of Eastern Slavonia in 1998, faced a massive influx of refugees and internally displaced persons and tasked underfunded Centers for Social Work, the Catholic charity Caritas and the Croatian Red Cross to respond, with large numbers of international actors effectively working in parallel to state structures (Stubbs and Zrinščak, 2006). Hence, throughout the 1990s, social policy issues were largely focused on refugees and displaced persons, the re-establishment of social infrastructure in the territories returned to Croatian control, and 'firefighting' social problems in the face of rising poverty and unemployment (Stubbs and Zrinščak 2009).

Although not incompatible with the mix of 'crony' and 'predatory' capitalism prevalent in newly independent Croatia, the successful implementation of a radical pension reform in the second half of the 1990s, eventually completed under a Social Democratic-led coalition government in 2001, is in need of explanation. With the ratio of insured to pensioners changing from 3:1 in 1990 to 1.8:1 in 1995 (Stubbs and Zrinščak, 2006), largely because the Government pushed early retirement as a supposed solution to unemployment, a crisis-like situation was created. This opened a space to be filled by the World Bank whose Chilean-inspired model, articulated in 'Averting the Old Age Crisis' (World Bank, 1994), appealed to the political elite, keen to show that it could work with international actors, allowing the transnational pension fund business to gain a foothold in Croatia as an 'emerging economy' and regional center.

Although, in the end, the system was reformed along the lines of the more modest Argentinian model, maintaining a revised PAYG first pillar with the introduction of two private pension pillars, one compulsory and one voluntary, this was still a radical change, underpinned by a neo-liberal faith in free market solutions, and pushed by a coalition of experts, as a driver of future economic growth. In retrospect, the three-pillar framework, neither solved problems of pension sustainability nor of adequacy. Pro-reform voices including the entire Government, the World Bank and the IMF, transnational and domestic financial institutions and a coalition of neo-liberal and technocratic economists, completely drowned out the few oppositional voices, notably some Trades Unions and some social policy experts. The absence of the ILO and the European Union, who might have cautioned against radical reform, is also notable.

Symbolically at least, the death of Tuđman and the election of a center-left coalition Government in January 2000, marked a sea change in terms of democratization, greater openness towards international organizations in general and membership of the European Union and NATO in particular. Collaborations between Government and 'civil society' were institutionalized and, by implication at least, the possibility of social welfare reform was created. The Ministry of Labour and Social Welfare agreed to a World Bank-led social welfare reform project. The Social Democratic Party Minister Davorko Vidović was keen to define the reform as 'technical' or, at least, 'consensual', rather than 'political' and 'ideological', a 'reform to last a generation' as he described it. As such he explicitly drew on the momentum of pension reform, bringing together foreign and domestic consultants under the leadership of Nino Žganec, brought from teaching in the School of Social Work in the University of Zagreb to be Assistant Minister.

Although generating a new set of discursive frames to guide the reforms, the so-called '3 Ds' of decentralization, deinstitutionalization and de-statization (reducing the role of the state and promoting a new welfare mix), within a more 'active social policy' (Puljiz, 2001), the project, was spectacularly unsuccessful in reforming anything. This set a pattern of reforms on paper not translated into practice. Over time, the World Bank retreated from a broad concern with social welfare to a focus on the familiar mantras of targeting and cost containment, including the rationalization of diverse social benefits emanating from different levels of Government. A pattern emerged of World Bank experts allied with Croatian economists outlining the case for reforms the evidence base for which was, frequently, contested by Croatian social policy experts, sometimes with the support of agencies such as UNDP (cf. Šućur et al., 2016).

The European Union did have some influence on social welfare reforms in Croatia in the period leading up to accession, through the process of preparing, implementing and monitoring the Joint Memorandum on Social Inclusion (JIM), signed in March 2007. Stung by criticisms of the ineffectiveness of the JIM process in the earlier new Member States, the European Commission, through its Directorate General for Employment, took the process more seriously. Party because both the JIM Working Group and those evaluating progress for the Commission included social policy scholars, a set of priorities emerged which, whilst never implemented in full, did set an agenda for change, some of which, notably commitments related to deinstitutionalization, resulted in progress on the ground. These were steered by the State Secretary of the Croatian Liberal Party (HSLS), a minority party in the Croatian Democratic Union (HDZ)-led Government. Perhaps even more importantly, annual EU progress reports forced the Government to improve its monitoring and evaluation procedures and drew attention to the difficulties of any meaningful linkages between social welfare, health, and education.

In the face of a prolonged economic crisis, the European Union has tended to be more relevant in its focus on fiscal discipline and debt reduction than social policy prescriptions. At the same time, both the Bank and the Commission have noted the relative lack of spending on social assistance of last resort. The SDP-led coalition which came to power in December 2011, creating a new Ministry of Social Policy and Youth, lacked a clear reform vision. The HDZ-led Government formed in January 2016, returned to power under new leadership in October 2016, appears likely to resist a World Bank conditionality which would shift the administration of social assistance payments form Centers for Social Welfare to country administration offices. However, outside of reforms to promote 'demographic renewal', the Government also lacks a clear vision for social welfare.

Beyond the role of international actors and, notwithstanding the lack of political will for reform, two broad forces are dominant in shaping social welfare in Croatia. The first is war veterans' associations keen to maintain and even extend significant benefits in return for continued support for HDZ, a quasi-institutionalized form of 'social clientelism' (Stubbs and Zrinščak, 2015). These benefits represent the most significant 'layering' of social welfare in Croatia today, with veterans able to mobilize quickly and effectively whenever there is any perceived threat to these benefits. Interestingly, the World Bank has made only very vague references to the distortions produced by these benefits, arguing that this is a political choice which should not be challenged. The European Commission's Staff Working Document for 2017 noted that 1.8 percent of GDP is spent on war veterans and noted the lack of assessment 'in the context of other social expenditure items ... [and] labour market effects' (European Commission, 2017; 37). Although the Country Specific Proposals within the European Semester was silent on the issue, the preparation of a new Law extending veterans' rights may come under more scrutiny in the future, not least because it fits uneasily with commitments to 'fiscal responsibility'.

The second potential force for change is a newly empowered radical right, promulgating a conservative Catholic agenda of a return to 'traditional' family values, opposing abortion rights and gay rights. Not unlike similar movements in Poland, Slovakia and Hungary, the movement can be read as part of a backlash to the concessions supposedly forced on the Government to obtain membership of the European Union. Although victory in a referendum held on 1 December 2013 to define marriage in the Croatian constitution as 'a union of a man and a woman' can be seen as symbolic, and was countered by the SDP-led Government introducing a law on civil partnerships, the influence of the movement may be amplified given the renewed concerns, both real and ideological, with 'demographic renewal'. The creation of a new Ministry of Demographics, Family, Youth and Social Policy shows, discursively at least, the new Government's prioritizing of this issue, in the context of low birth rates and significant emigration of people of working age, including skilled workers and some professionals. Plans to introduce universal child benefits and to increase maternity benefits are a challenge both to pleas to reduce social spending and to increase the participation of women in the labor market. In many ways, the balance of forces within Croatian society, and the exhortations of diverse international actors, constitutes a specific, and new, driver of inertia, somewhat different from the drivers of inertia in the past.

CONCLUSIONS: REVISITING THE ASID FRAMEWORK

Analyzing the case studies through the ASID framework discussed in the Introduction, suggests that there are many similarities in the nature of social welfare development across the region. A focus on 'agency' does not lead us to concur with Arandarenko and Golicin (2007; 182) on the 'randomness' of outcomes, however; whilst specific 'choices' at particular conjunctural 'moments' may have been 'accidental or arbitrary' (Deacon, Lendvai and Stubbs, 2007; 223), it is the complex and pervasive reproduction of inertia which is most in need of explanation. Clearly, across the region, the relative indifference of political parties to the issue of social welfare has been pronounced, with periods of intense commitment to reform rather short-lived, very much identified with particular personalities, and often undone by their successors in Government. Social welfare reforms have tended to be more implicit than explicit and influenced by the prescriptions of the World Bank, the IMF and, later, in conditions of economic and financial crisis, by the fiscal consolidation orthodoxies of The Economics and Finance Directorate General (DG ECFIN) within the European Commission, that is to say driven by neo-liberal economic reform frameworks. The impact of the region's *troika* has, itself, been blunted, however, since political elites' survival appears to rest less on commitment to these economic reforms and more to the maintenance of nationalist ideas, allied with the maintenance of clientelistic networks, leading to a form of 'capture' in terms of governance, social and citizenship rights and the distribution and redistribution of services and resources (Stubbs and Zrinščak, 2015). Although most pronounced in Bosnia and Herzegovina, the sub-contracting of welfare reforms to flexible intermediaries has occurred across the case studies, almost as if the pervasive and highly lucrative rent seeking opportunities afforded to elites in the region have been mirrored within a somewhat less lucrative, but no less significant, semi-public reform sphere filled by think tanks, NGOs, consultancy companies, and the like. The influence of international actors, whilst not negligible, must be seen, then, as a complex, contested and contradictory translation process with outcomes which are uncertain and variegated (Lendvai and Stubbs, 2015; 448), and overdetermined by the actions of political elites. In this sense, at least, agentic power has thrived in new institutional forms, prioritizing instrumental rewards over real change.

In many ways, a nuanced understanding of the complex political economy of being positioned at the (European) periphery or (global) semi-periphery allows us to address the structural constraints on welfare settlements and outcomes more clearly. A full understanding of the region's 'modes of insertion in the global economy' (Cerami and Stubbs, 2011; 23) is, of course, beyond the scope of this chapter although the changing nature of class power, and its intersectional relations to structures of oppression based on gender, age, disability, sexuality, and locality is a theme which needs to be foregrounded more in the future. How, *inter alia*, processes of marketization, commodification, and financialization work in the countries of the region, in the context of 'predatory' foreign capital and 'impatient' International Financial Institutions (IFIs), both setting limits to and creating new possibilities for managing variegated 'debt-states' and 'crisis-states' within a global economic order, is crucial for understanding welfare settlements in the European semi-periphery. Tracing how the 'dynamics of welfare layering, welfare clientelism and ethno-nationalist politics conjoin with ongoing pressures from the "debt-state" to create welfare that can be mobilized, scaled back, scaled up or ethnicized' (Lendvai and Stubbs, 2015; 461) is an urgent task theoretically, politically and empirically, then.

Taking 'institutions' in their narrow sense, we can see that there has been very little institutional innovation in social welfare in Croatia, outside of early pension reform and, to an extent, the JIM process; there has been some innovation in Serbia, through SIPRU and the transitional Social Innovation Fund. Large-scale innovation in Bosnia and Herzegovina has occurred, a complex product of separate entity-based state building programs alongside international actor-driven improvised 'agencification' at the central state level. The uneven institutionalization of NGOs is also worthy of note, with Serbia perhaps the clearest example of a degree of formal integration of NGOs within partnerships for delivering social services. Although central and local state funded NGOs are important actors in Croatia, too, this has tended to reinforce a kind of 'welfare parallelism' between statutory actors on the one side and non-state actors on the other. NGO involvement in social welfare in Bosnia and Herzegovina tends still to be largely donor-driven, albeit in the context of donor fatigue, often marshalled through privatized and sub-contracted funding mechanisms and intermediaries, and is, perhaps, the closest to a neo-liberal frame in which NGO services become a poor and uneven substitute for state provision.

The differences between these countries and the broad post-Soviet space was not the main focus of this chapter. Nevertheless, the impacts of the wars of the Yugoslav succession, not least in interrupting economic and social development, have led to rather different welfare settlements, and weakened social protection systems, compared to those in the first wave of post-communist EU Member States. At the same time, the 'comparative advantage' of the rather well-developed welfare system during Yugoslav socialism, although eroded in the economic crisis of the 1980s and, certainly, in the wars of the 1990s, has led to more positive welfare outcomes compared to those countries of the former Soviet Union, including the Russian Federation, which are neither EU Member States nor candidates for accession (cf. Cerami and Stubbs, 2011; Cook, 2007). One important part of the exceptional nature of Yugoslav socialism, making it very different from those parts of Eastern Europe within the Soviet bloc, was the establishment of statutory Centers for Social Work in the early 1960s. These are multi-disciplinary institutions with a central role for social workers trained, originally in high schools, and later in universities, across SFRY, and which have proved resilient even in the face of wars and radically re-arranged governance structures. Although the Yugoslav socialist welfare settlement, combining socialist self-management with Bismarckian insurance-based systems, was very uneven, decentralized and primarily oriented to the social protection of new urban industrial workers, it has proved resistant to radical reforms and, in the popular imagination at least, has appeared robust enough to be worth defending. Hence, we would argue that, although in Bosnia-Herzegovina, it has been eroded and replaced by a highly residualized system, this is not the case in Serbia and, perhaps even less the case in Croatia where, in some ways, a driver of inertia may be a sense that the system is 'good enough'.

The study has also shown both the multiplication and divergence of welfare discourses across the region and over time. The 'social' EU has, perhaps, had a significant role in, to an extent, disrupting World Bank-informed discourses of 'poverty reduction', marshalling its influence through the lens of 'social inclusion'. At the same time, it has joined with the IFIs in promoting discourses of 'activation', 'responsibilization', and 'competition', in ways which have, albeit in complex ways, 'socialized' dominant market discourses of 'innovation', 'enterprise' and 'investment'. The marginalization of 'rights-based approaches'—articulated still by service users and by the UN social agencies, notably UNICEF, UNDP and the ILO, and enshrined within a legalistic institutional environment marked by a significant gap between 'rights on paper' and the possibility of realizing those rights in practice—is significant, and suggests that there are also discursive limits to the kinds of radical welfare settlements which may be envisaged in the future (cf. Matković, 2017). Welfare has been 'layered' with clear divisions between those 'deserving' of support and those 'underserving' in each of the countries and, in the case of B-H, entities, although this is more complicated than the usual division between those capable and incapable of work, refracted through lenses of ethnicity, regions, and war service.

Finally, our use of the ASID framework has contributed to a kind of middle-range comparative study of drivers of inertia which impact on welfare reforms, open to both 'the play of contingency' and to the continued relevance of structural factors including levels of development and forms of political economy. In the future, it may act as a bridge between macro-level analyses of welfare regimes and more recent ethnographic approaches to lived encounters of welfare.

REFERENCES

Abrahamson, Peter (1999). 'The Welfare Modelling Business', *Social Policy and Administration* 33(4); 394 – 415.

Arandarenko, Mihail and Pavle Golicin (2007). 'Serbia', in Bob Deacon and Paul Stubbs (eds.) *Social Policy and International Interventions in South East Europe*, Cheltenham: Edward Elgar; 167 – 186.

Baletić, Zvonimir (2003). 'A Wrong Conception of Stabilisation', in M. Meštrović (ed.) *Globalization and its Reflections On (in) Croatia*, New York: Global Scholarly Publications; 275 – 299.

Blagojević, Marina (2009). *Knowledge Production at the Semi-Periphery: a gender perspective*, Belgrade: Institute for Criminological and Sociological Research.

Bohle, Dorothee and Béla Greskovits (2012). *Capitalist Diversity on Europe's Periphery*, Ithaca: Cornell University Press.

Bošnjak, Vesna and Paul Stubbs (2007). 'Towards a New Welfare Mix for the Most Vulnerable: reforming social services in Bosnia-Herzegovina, Croatia and Serbia', in Z. Lovrinčević et al. (eds.) *Social Policy and Regional Development: proceedings*, Zagreb: The Institute of Economics and Friedrich Ebert Stiftung; 139 – 165.

Brković, Čarna (2017). *Managing Ambiguity: how clientelism, citizenship and power shape personhood in Bosnia and Herzegovina*, Oxford: Berghahn.

Cerami, Alfio and Paul Stubbs (2011). 'Post-communist Welfare Capitalisms: bringing institutions and political agency back in', *EIZG Working Papers* EIZ-WP-1103, Zagreb: EIZG, web: http://hrcak.srce.hr/75324 (accessed 4 August 2017).

Cook, Linda (2007). *Postcommunist Welfare States: reform politics in Russia and Eastern Europe*, Ithaca: Cornell University Press.

Ćuk, Mira (2016). *Reforme socijalne zaštite u Bosni i Hercegovini* (Reforms of social protection in B-H), Istočno Sarajevo: Zavod za udžbenike i nastavna sredstva.

Deacon, Bob and Paul Stubbs (2013). 'Global Social Policy Studies: conceptual and analytical reflections', *Global Social Policy* 13(1); 5 – 23.

Dobrotić, Ivana, Teo Matković and Siniša Zrinščak (2013). 'Gender Equality Policies and Practices in Croatia—the interplay of transition and late Europeanization', *Social Policy & Administration* 47(2); 218 – 240.

Dokić, Goran (2017). 'Veterans' Policy in the Semi-Periphery: a comparison of Croatia and Serbia', Paper presented to workshop 'Translating Policies in the Semi-Periphery', Regensburg, Germany, May.

Dolenec, Danijela (2013). *Democratic Institutions and Authoritarian Rule in Southeast Europe*, Colchester: ECPR Press.

European Commission (2017). Commission Staff Working Document, Country Report Croatia, SWD (2017) 76 final, Brussels: European Commission, web: https://ec.europa.eu/info/sites/info/files/2017-european-semester-country-report-croatia-en.pdf (accessed 3 August 2017).

Golicin, Pavle and Galjina Ognjanov (2010). *Assessment of Results of the Social Innovation Fund*, Belgrade: FREN.

Hromadžić, Azra (2017). 'Seeing Like a Social Worker: social policies, social services and the state in Bosnia and Herzegovina', Paper presented to workshop 'Translating Policies in the Semi-Periphery', Regensburg, Germany, May.

Jeffrey, Alex (2013). *The Improvised State: sovereignty, performance and agency in Dayton Bosnia*, Chichester: Wily-Blackwell.

Keil, Soeren (2011). 'Social Policy in Bosnia and Herzegovina Between State-Building, Democratization and Europeanization', in Marija Stambolieva and Stefan Dehnert (eds.) *Welfare States in Transition: twenty years after the Yugoslav welfare model*, Sofia: Friedrich Ebert Stiftung, Office Bulgaria; 41 – 57, web: http://library.fes.de/pdf-files/bueros/sofia/08711.pdf (accessed 1 August 2017).

Lendvai, Noémi (2007). 'Europeanization of Social Policy? Prospects and challenges for South East Europe', in Bob Deacon and Paul Stubbs (eds.) *Social Policy and International Interventions in South East Europe*, Cheltenham: Edward Elgar; 22 – 44.

Lendvai, Noémi (2015). 'Soft Governance, Policy Fictions and Translation Zones: European policy spaces and their making', in John Clarke et al. *Making Policy Move: towards a politics of translation and assemblage*, Bristol: Policy Press; 131 – 156.

Lendvai, Noémi and Paul Stubbs (2007) 'Policies as Translation: situating transnational social policies', in Sue Hodgson and Zoe Irving (eds.) *Policy Reconsidered: meanings, politics and practices*, Bristol: Policy Press; 173 – 190.

Lendvai, Noémi and Paul Stubbs (2015). 'Europeanization, Welfare and Variegated Austerity Capitalisms: Hungary and Croatia', *Social Policy and Administration* 49(4); 445 – 465.

Maglajlić, Reima Ana and Paul Stubbs (2017). 'Occupying Liminal Spaces in Post-Conflict Welfare Reform? Local professionals and international organizations in Bosnia and Herzegovina', British Journal of Social Work, https://doi.org/10.1093/bjsw/bcx031 (accessed 1 August 2017).

Maglajlić Holiček, Reima Ana and Ešref Kenan Rašidagić (2007) 'Bosnia-Herzegovina', in Bob Deacon and Paul Stubbs (eds.) Social Policy and International Interventions in South East Europe, Cheltenham: Edward Elgar; 149 – 166.

Maglajlić, Reima Ana and Ešref Kenan Rašidagić (2011). 'Socio-Economic Transformation in Bosnia and Herzegovina', in Marija Stambolieva and Stefan Dehnert (eds.) Welfare States in Transition: twenty years after the Yugoslav welfare model, Sofia: Friedrich Ebert Stiftung, Office Bulgaria; 16 – 40, web: http://library.fes.de/pdf-files/bueros/sofia/08711.pdf (accessed 1 August 2017).

Marcus, Goerge (1995) 'Ethnography in / of the World System: the emergence of multi-sited ethnography', *Annual Review of Anthropology* 24; 95 – 117.

Matković, Gordana (2017). The Welfare State in Western Balkan Countires—challenges and options Belgrade: Center for Social Policy, web: http://csp.org.rs/en/assets/publications/files/The_Welfare_State_in_Western_Balkan_Countries_Position_Paper.pdf (accessed 25 January 2018).

Moulaert, Frank and Bob Jessop (2006). 'Discussion Paper', Paper prepared as part of the project Demologos: development of models and logistics of socio-economic organization in space, web: http://demologos.ncl.ac.uk/wp/wp2/disc.php (accessed 21 July 2017).

Obradović, Nina (2016) '*Reforme socijalne zaštite u Bosnia I Nercegovini*' ('Social Protection Reform in Bosnia and Herzegovina During the Crisis'), *Revija za socijalnu politiku* (Croatian J. of Social Policy) 23(1); 121 – 136, web: http://www.rsp.hr/ojs2/index.php/rsp/article/viewFile/1282/1323 (accessed 2 August 2017).

Pandolfi, Mariella (2003). 'Contract of mutual (in)difference: government and the humanitarian apparatus in contemporary Albania and Kosovo', *Indiana Journal of Global Legal Studies* 10 (1); 369 – 381.

Puljiz, Vlado (2001). 'Hrvatska: od pasivne prema aktivnoj socijalnoj državi' ('Croatia: from a passive to an active welfare state'), *Revija za socijalnu politiku* (Croatian J. of Social Policy) 8(1); 1 – 18, web: http://hrcak.srce.hr/index.php?show=clanak&id_clanak_jezik=47381&lang=en (accessed 3 August 2017).

Spry, Tami (2009). 'Bodies of / as Evidence in Autoethnography?', *International Journal of Qualitative Research* 1(4); 603 – 610.

Stambolieva, Marija (2016). *Welfare State Transformation in the Yugoslav Successor States: from social to unequal*, Abingdon: Routledge.

Stubbs, Paul (2001). 'New Times?: towards a political economy of 'civil society' in contemporary Croatia', *Narodna umjetnost (Croatia J. of Ethnology and Folklore Research)*, 38(1); 89 – 103.

Stubbs, Paul (2015). 'Performing Reform in South East Europe: consultancy, translation and flexible agency', in John Clarke et al. *Making Policy Move: towards a politics of translation and assemblage*, Bristol: Policy Press; 65 – 94.

Stubbs, Paul and Siniša Zrinščak (2006). 'International Actors, 'Drivers of Change', and the Reform of Social Protection in Croatia', Paper presented to ISA World Congress, Durban, July, web: http://paulstubbs.pbworks.com/f/Stubbs%20Zrinscak%20Durban%20Final.pdf (accessed 21 July 2017).

Stubbs, Paul and Siniša Zrinščak (2007). 'Croatia', in Bob Deacon and Paul Stubbs (eds.) *Social Policy and International Interventions in South East Europe*, Cheltenham: Edward Elgar; 85 – 102.

Stubbs, Paul and Siniša Zrinščak (2009). 'Croatian Social Policy: the legacies of war, state-building and late Europeanization', *Social Policy and Administration* 43(2); 121 – 135.

Stubbs, Paul and Siniša Zrinščak (2015). 'Citizenship and Social Welfare in Croatia: clientelism and the limits of 'Europeanisation'', *European Politics and Society* 16(3); 395 – 410.

Šućur, Zoran et al. (2016). *Struktura naknada, izdaci i korisnici programa socijalne zaštite u Republici Hrvatskoj* (Structure of benefits, grants and users of social protection programmes in Croatia), Zagreb: Ministry of Social Policy and Youth, European Commission and UNDP.

Šunderić, Žarko (2015). *Uloga institucija u stvaranju socijalne kohezije* (The role of insttituions in establishing social cohesion), Belgrade: CLDS.

Venn, Couze (2006). 'A Note on Assemblage', *Theory, Culture and Society* 23(2?3); 107 – 108.

World Bank (1994). *Averting the Old Age Crisis: policies to protect the old and promote growth*, New York: Oxford University Press.

Županov, Josip (2001). 'Theses on Social Crisis: the case of Croatia', *South East Europe Review* 1; 39 – 49.

CONTRIBUTOR BIOGRAPHIES

Sofiya An is an Assistant Professor of Sociology at the School of Humanities and Social Sciences at Nazarbayev University, Astana, Kazakhstan. She earned her Master's degree in Social Work from Columbia University in New York City (2002) and her PhD from the University of Toronto (2014). Her research interests lie at the intersection of post-Soviet social policy and global and transnational social policy. In her current research, she examines post-Soviet changes in welfare institutions, Soviet legacies, and the agency of state and non-state domestic and global policy actors. She is a member of the European Social Work Research Association and co-convener of the Special Interest Group on Post-Soviet and Post-Socialist Social Work.

Natalija Atas is a Lecturer in Social Policy at Liverpool Hope University, UK. Her research interests incorporate key areas of social policy enquiry related to welfare, poverty, social problems and stratification. She is currently researching Social Care, Health and Wellbeing. Dr. Atas has international research and teaching experience as she has spent her academic life between universities in Lithuania and the United Kingdom. She obtained a PhD from the University of Sheffield, Department of Sociological studies in 2016. Her recent publications include 'The cost of becoming a neo-liberal welfare state: A cautionary case of Lithuania' *Critical Social Policy* (2018), and 'The immediate impact of the global financial crisis and neo-liberal austerity policies on the in-work poverty dynamics in Lithuania' *Journal of Baltic Studies* (2018).

Tatiana Chubarova holds a PhD (Social Policy, LSE) and Doctor of Sciences (Economy, Russian Academy of Sciences) degree and is a Senior Research Fellow, Institute of Economy, Russian Academy of Sciences, Moscow. Her professional interests include health and social policy in Russia in a comparative perspective; organization and financing of health care; and gender issues. She has contributed to a number of books such as *Health Reforms in Central and Eastern Europe: options, obstacles, limited outcomes* (Nemec and Bjorkman (eds) Eleven Publishing, The Hague, 2014), *Implementation of New Public Management Tools: Experience from Transition and Emerging Countries* Ed. (Nemec and de Vries (eds) Bruylant-Bruxelles, 2015) and *Comparative Health Care Federalism*

(Fierlbeck and Palley (eds) Ashgate, 2015). She is a member of the New Economics Association (Russia) and the International Public Policy Association.

Bob Deacon (28 May 1944 – 1 October 2017) was Honorary Professor in Global Social Policy at the University of York, UK and Emeritus Professor of International Social Policy, University of Sheffield, UK. Over a fifty-year academic career, Bob was a key figure in radical social policy, the social policy of socialism and post-socialism and, latterly, in global and regional social policy. In addition to his three key books on the topic: *Global Social Policy* (with Michelle Hulse and Paul Stubbs, Sage, 1997), *Global Social Policy and Governance* (Sage, 2007), and *Global Social Policy in the Making* (Policy Press, 2013), Bob maintained a commitment to advancing progressive social policy through establishing links between academic, advocacy and policy-making fields.

Esuna Dugarova is a policy specialist at the United Nations Development Programme in New York where she conducts research and analysis on social policy, gender equality and sustainable development. Prior to joining UNDP, she worked as a research analyst at the United Nations Research Institute for Social Development in Geneva. In addition to her work at the UN, she has been doing research and published several articles on social protection, family policies, gender and childcare in post-Soviet states. Originally, Esuna is from the Republic of Buryatia in Russia and holds a PhD in Asian Studies from Cambridge University.

Maja Gerovska Mitev is a Full Professor at the Faculty of Philosophy, Ss. Cyril and Methodius University in Skopje. Her main research interests are: poverty, social exclusion and comparative / European dimension of social protection systems. Her recent publications include: chapter on 'Social Policy during a Decade of Centre-Right Governance in Macedonia' (Springer, 2019); chapter 'Social Policy Challenges and Strategic Priorities in the EU Candidate Countries' (European Perspectives, 2016); chapter 'Welfare State Realities in Macedonia: Trends and Perspectives' (Springer, 2016). She is Editor in Chief of the Journal of Social Policy, published by the Faculty of Philosophy, University of St Cyril and Metodius, Skopje. She is a member of the European Social Policy Network, and a member of the Scientific Advisory Committee of UNESCO's Management of Social Transformations Programme.

Natalia Grigorieva is Professor of Sociology, Faculty of Public Administration, Lomonosov Moscow State University (Moscow, Russia). She holds a Doctor of Science Degree in Political Science (MSU). Her professional interests include comparative social policy, with a special interest in health care policy and gender studies. She is the author or co-author of nine books and more 100 journal articles and reviews. Her recent publications include 'From Tradition to Innovation: Modern Health Care Reforms' (with Viktor Sadovnichi and Tatiana Chubarova), Publishing House 'Economica'), Comparative Health Care Federalism (with Tatiana Chubarova, Ed. by Katherine Fierlbek and Howard Palley, Routledge Taylor & Francis Group), 'Policy and Management of Social Sector' (edited with Alexander Solovyov, Agramak-Media). She is Editor in Chief of the Health Management Journal.

Igor Guardiancich is a Slovenian political economist who is currently a Research Fellow at the Sant'Anna School of Advanced Studies in Pisa, Italy. His main research interests are on European social policy, welfare states in Central and Eastern Europe, political economy of transition and integration. He has published in international peer-reviewed journals, such as *Europe-Asia Studies, European Union Politics, Journal of Common Market Studies, Regulation & Governance, West European Politics* and others. He recently co-edited with Oscar Molina the volume 'Talking through the Crisis: Social Dialogue and Industrial Relations Trends in Selected EU Countries' (International Labor Organization, 2017).

Gulnaz Isabekova works at the Research Centre for East European Studies at the University of Bremen, Germany where she is a member of Collaborative Research Centre 1342 "Global Dynamics of Social Policy", which is funded by the Deutsche Forschungsgemeinschaft (DFG, German Research Foundation). Her main research interests are related to welfare policy and healthcare, development aid, sustainability and inequality.

Saltanat Janenova is a Kazakhstan-born public policy researcher who is currently an Assistant Professor in the Graduate School of Public Policy, Nazarbayev University, Astana, Kazakhstan. Saltanat has a master's degree in Sociology from the University of Durham, UK (2000) and a PhD in Social Policy, University of Edinburgh (2010). Her main research interests focus on public sector reforms in the post-Soviet countries including public service innovations, open government, and public participation. Her recent journal articles include 'Civil Service Reform in

Kazakhstan' (with Colin Knox, in *International Review of Administrative Sciences*), 'One Stop Shops' (with Colin Knox, in *Oxford Research Encyclopedia of Politics*) and a book chapter 'Trajectories of Civil Service Development in the Former Soviet Union Countries' (with Alikhan Baimenov, Palgrave Macmillan).

Noémi Lendvai-Bainton is a Senior Lecturer in Comparative Public Policy at the School for Policy Studies, University of Bristol. Her research interests cover post-communist welfare states, EU integration, EU social policy, global social policy and the impact of International Organizations, East-West migration, comparative research methods and critical policy studies. Her 2015 book co-authored with John Clarke, David Bainton and Paul Stubbs '*Making Policy Move: Politics of Translation and Reassemblage*' (Policy Press: Bristol) explores 'translation' as a possible new theoretical lens for critical policy studies. She has also widely published on the transformation and Europeanisation of post-communist welfare states in journals such as the *Journal of European Social Policy*, *Social Policy & Administration*, and *European Societies*.

Elena Maltseva is an Assistant Professor of Political Science at the University of Windsor in Windsor, Canada. Elena has a master's degree in East European and Russian Studies from Carleton University, Ottawa, Canada (2004) and a PhD in Political Science from the University of Toronto (2012). Her current research focuses on left-wing politics in post-Soviet states, and social security reforms, labor issues and regime stability in post-communist countries. Her recent publications include an article 'Framing a Welfare Reform: The Social Benefits Reform in Russia and Kazakhstan' (in *Canadian Slavonic Papers / Revue Canadienne des Slavists*), and two book chapters 'Cracks in the System: What the Zhanaozen Incident Says about Regime Performance in Kazakhstan' (University of Pittsburgh Press) and 'Lost and Forgotten: The Conflict Through the Eyes of the Donbass People' (Routledge).

Ann-Mari Sätre holds a PhD and is Associate Professor of Economics and Senior Lecturer in Eurasian studies, IRES Institute for Russian and Eurasian Studies at Uppsala University, Sweden. She specializes in the structure and performance of the Soviet / Russian economy. She is also an international partner at the Centre of Excellence in Russian studies at Aleksanteri Institute, University of Helsinki, Finland. Her current research focuses on poverty, local development and women's work in Russia. She is the author or co-author of five books and nearly fifty articles and book chapters on the Soviet / Russian political economy. Her most recent books are *Attitudes, Poverty and Agency in Russia and Ukraine* (2016, edited with Asztalos Morell, Routledge), *The Other Russia: Local experience and societal change* (2017, Routledge, together with Leo Granberg) and *The Politics of Poverty in Contemporary Russia* (2019, Routledge).

Paul Stubbs is a UK-born sociologist who is currently a Senior Research Fellow in the Institute of Economics, Zagreb, Croatia. His main research interests focus on civil society and social movements, social policy, and policy translation. He is currently undertaking research on historical aspects of Yugoslav socialism and the Non-Aligned Movement. His recent publications include 'Making Policy Move' (with John Clarke, Dave Bainton and Noémi Lendvai, Policy Press), 'Transformations in Global and Regional Social Policies' (edited with Alexandra Kaasch, Palgrave Macmillan) and 'Social Inequalities and Discontent in Yugoslav Socialism' (co-edited with Rory Archer and Igor Duda, Routledge). He is a member of the Editorial Board of Critical Policy Studies and the Croatian Journal of Social Policy.

Siniša Zrinščak is Professor and Chair of Sociology at the Faculty of Law, University of Zagreb, Croatia. His main scientific interests include religious changes in post-communism, Church-State relations, European and comparative social policy, and gender. He is a member of the Scientific Committee of the European Union Agency for Fundamental Rights (FRA), and Associate Editor of the European Journal of Social Work. His recent publications include: Giordan, G., Zrinščak, S. (2018) 'One pope, two churches: Refugees, human rights and religion in Croatia and Italy', *Social Compass*, 65(1), and Zrinščak, S. (2017) 'Religion, welfare and gender: the post-communist experience', in Molokotos-Liederman et. al. (eds) *Religion and welfare in Europe: Gendered and minority perspectives* (Bristol, Policy Press).

ibidem.eu